Journal of Consciousness Studies
controversies in science & the humanities

Vol. 10, No. 6–7, June/July 2003

SPECIAL ISSUE: PARAPSYCHOLOGY

Edited by James Alcock, Jean Burns & Anthony Freeman

Continued overleaf

ISSN: 1355 8250

Cover Art: stevek@conceptstudio.co.uk

JCS is indexed and abstracted in: *Social Sciences Citation Index*[®], *ISI Alerting Services* (includes *Research Alert*[®]), *Current Contents*[®]*: Social and Behavioral Sciences, Arts and Humanities Citation Index*[®]*, Current Contents*[®]*: Arts & Humanities Citation Index*[®]*, Social Scisearch*[®]*, PsycINFO*[®] and *The Philosopher's Index.*

Table of contents continued

ABOUT AUTHORS

James E. Alcock is professor of psychology at York University in Toronto, Canada, where his areas of specialization are Social Psychology and Clinical Psychology. His research interests lie in the area of belief systems, with a particular focus on formation of belief in extraordinary phenomena He has lectured and written extensively on the subject of psychological explanations for paranormal experience, and on methodological problems in parapsychological research. He is a Fellow of the Committee for the Scientific Investigation of Claims of the Paranormal, as well as a member of its Executive Council, a Fellow of the Canadian Psychological As-sociation, and a long-time member of the International Brotherhood of Magicians. He is author of *Parapsychology: Science or Magic?* (Pergamon, 1981), and *Science and Supernature* (Prometheus, 1990), and co-author of *A Textbook of Social Psychology* (Pearson, 2001).

Peter Brugger was born in 1957 in Zurich, Switzerland, and received his PhD in Zoology in 1992 from the University of Zurich. He is currently head of the neuropsychology unit of the University Hospital, Zurich. His main research interests are the representation of body and space, and neuropsychiatry.

Jean E. Burns is a physicist who is interested in the relationship between consciousness and physical laws and has published various papers and reviews on the subject. She is a founder Associate Editor of the *Journal of Consciousness Studies*.

Geoffrey Dean received his PhD from the University of London. Since 1974 he has conducted large-scale studies of astrology and has authored or co-authored many critical articles, debates, surveys, and prize competitions for research into astrology. He once practised as an astrologer and is a Fellow of the United States-based Committee for the Scientific Investigation of Claims of the Paranormal. He is a British freelance technical writer and editor living in Perth, Western Australia.

Anthony Freeman holds degrees in chemistry and theology from Oxford University. He has been managing editor of the *Journal of Consciousness Studies* since 1994 and lectures and writes on theology and consciousness matters. His books include *God In Us: A Case for Christian Humanism* (1993/2001) and *Consciousness: A Guide to the Debates* (2003).

Christopher French is professor and Head of the Anomalistic Psychology Research Unit (http://www.gold.ac.uk/apru) in the Department of Psychology, Goldsmith's College, University of London. He received his BA from Manchester University in 1977 and PhD from Leicester University in 1983. He has worked at Goldsmith's since 1985 and was Head of Department 1997–2000. One of his main interests is in the psychology of paranormal belief and ostensibly paranormal experiences. He is currently co-editor of *The Skeptic*, the UK's longest-running sceptical publication. He often appears on radio and television and in the national and international press, providing a sceptical perspective on paranormal and related claims.

Stanley Jeffers obtained his PhD in applied physics from Imperial College in 1968. After a post-doctoral fellowship in the Department of Astronomy, University of Toronto, he joined the Department of Physics at York University. He has worked in the areas of opto-electronics, observational astronomy, theoretical physics and in the investigation of claims for anomolous phenomena associated with consciousness. He has published in *Nature, The Astronomical Journal, The Astrophysical Journal, Astronomy & Astrophysics, Foundations of Physics* etc. He enjoys skiing, cooking, motorcycling, gardening and the martial arts. He is a second degree Black Belt in Aikido and a first degree Black Belt in Iaido and Jodo.

Ivan W. Kelly received his PhD from the University of Calgary. Since 1979 he has been Professor of Educational Psychology at the University of Saskatchewan, Saskatoon, Canada. He is chairman of the Astrology Subcommittee of the United States-based Committee for the Scientific Investigation of Claims of the Paranormal, and author or co-author of over one hundred scientific or philosophical articles including many critical works on astrology, human judgement, and alleged lunar effects on behaviour.

Fotini Pallikari, a condensed matter physicist at the Athens University, has been involved for about thirty years in the study of physical properties of complex molecular systems and the modelling of their dynamics. During the last twelve years she also ventured experimental and theoretical research into the question of the mind and its possible coupling with the rest of physical reality.

John Palmer is Director of Research at the Rhine Research Center in Durham, NC. He received his PhD in psychology from the University of Texas at Austin and after two years on the psychology faculty at McGill University, he entered parapsychology on a full-time basis. He has worked at John F. Kennedy University and held research positions at the University of Virginia, UC Davis, and the University of Utrecht in The Netherlands. He has served as President of the Parapsychological Association and he edits the *Journal of Parapsychology*. Dr. Palmer has published numerous scientific articles and book chapters, and he is co-author of the book *Foundations of Parapsychology: Exploring the Boundaries of Human Capability*.

Adrian Parker is a senior lecturer (associate professor) in psychology at the University of Gothenburg, Sweden. He qualified as a clinical psychologist at the Tavistock Clinic in 1994, having received his PhD in psychology from the University of Edinburgh in 1977. Part of the doctoral work was published in the form of a course book *States of Mind* (1976) which summarizes research on consciousness and psi-phenomena. His doctoral research initiated the use of the ganzfeld technique in parapsychology. Dr Parker is a member of the Swedish Psychological Association, the British Psychological Society, the Society for Psychical Research. He has been for the last three years been Editor of the *European Journal of Parapsychology*.

Christopher Roe is a senior lecturer in psychology at University College, Northampton. He is currently a Perrott-Warrick researcher and the Parapsychology Foundation's International Affiliate for England. He is editor of the *Journal of the Society of Psychical Research*. In 1996 he obtained his PhD from the University of Edinburgh for work on the psychology of psychic reading. He was awarded the 1999 D. Scott Rogo Award for Parapsychological Literature. He has conducted research into the nature and origin of paranormal beliefs and experiences, and also has conducted experimental tests of PK and ESP effects, particularly looking for psychological correlates. With Simon Sherwood he teaches a module on 'Parapsychology and Anomalous Experiences' and they are currently engaged in Ganzfeld ESP research.

Simon Sherwood is currently working as a lecturer in psychology and as a Perrott-Warrick researcher at University College, Northampton. He obtained his PhD in psychology from the Koestler Parapsychology Unit, University of Edinburgh. He was the recipient of the Parapsychological Association's Gertrude Schmeidler Student Award for 2000 and the Parapsychology Foundation's Frances P. Bolton Fellowship for 2003. He has conducted research into hypnogogic/hypnopompic experiences, the psychology of anomalous beliefs, and dream ESP. With Christopher Roe he teaches a module on 'Parapsychology and Anomalous Experiences' and they are currently engaged in Ganzfeld ESP research.

Matthew D. Smith is a lecturer at Liverpool Hope University and was awarded his PhD on the psychology of luck by the University of Hertfordshire. His research interests span the areas of parapsychology, the psychology of superstition and paranormal belief, and the psychology of deception. He is an active member of the Society for Psychical Research (SPR) and an Associate member of the Parapsychological Association.

Kirsten I. Taylor was born in 1970 in California. She received her PhD in psychology in 2002 from the University of Zurich, and is currently engaged in postdoctoral research in the UK at the University of Cambridge on the behavioural neurology and neuropsychiatry of the semantic system.

Anthony Freeman

A Long Time Coming

A Personal Reflection

The history of this collection goes back to 1994 and the very first issue of the *Journal of Consciousness Studies*. That number included a short paper by John Beloff on the subject of conscious machines, and it evoked some controversy for *JCS* because he quoted Alan Turing as saying that the evidence for psi is overwhelming. Beloff drew attention to a seldom noted aspect of Alan Turing's paper that introduced his famous Turing test for machine intelligence (Turing, 1950). Turing had suggested that extrasensory perception (ESP) might provide the one means to smoke out even the most sophisticated computer trying to imitate a human being:

> Thus, given that you had a human being gifted with ESP in one room and a computer in another, the player in his imitation game could ask the two candidates to guess a given sequence of cards. Since the computer, using a random number generator, would be able to guess only at chance levels it would soon become clear which of the two was the human being and which the computer. 'Unfortunately', writes Turing, 'the statistical evidence, at least for telepathy, is overwhelming'. (Beloff, 1994, p. 35.)

Beloff claimed that materialist scientists and philosophers refuse to accept the reality of the paranormal, not for lack of evidence (evidence that Turing found 'overwhelming'), but because it 'upsets the physicalist applecart' (p. 36). In particular, according to Beloff, the proven existence of parapsychological (psi) phenomena would show the mind is able to interact causally with matter, and thus remove at a stroke the chief objection to the 'radical dualism', which he himself espouses.

Reading Beloff today, I find it is hard to see this as more than an eye-twinkling bit of fun, teasingly invoking 'the father of artificial intelligence' in support of a crusade against physicalism. The article contained nothing new or threatening. But at the time it undoubtedly exposed a fear that the new journal might be 'flakey' (to borrow the adjective applied at the time by Thomas Metzinger). The implication was that no mainstream scientist or philosopher would want to have

Correspondence: Anthony Freeman, Imprint Academic, PO Box 200, Exeter EX5 5YX, UK.

Journal of Consciousness Studies, **10**, No. 6–7, 2003, pp. 1–5

anything to do with *JCS*. Nine years on, with reputable scholars from all branches of consciousness studies contributing to the journal, such fears might appear fanciful, but they were real enough at the time. The editors, some of whom shared in the concerns about Beloff's paper, were properly cautious in their response to criticisms of the article.

Our main concern has always been to achieve dialogue about the many controversies in the field of consciousness studies, in line with the journal's subtitle, and to achieve balance in what we publish. Since a journal can only host a dialogue if it has the confidence of all parties, it was essential that *JCS* should quickly establish its reputation on the mainstream scientific and philosophical side of the consciousness community. The stature of many of the early contributors helped to achieve this. For instance, the second and third numbers of the journal carried a heavyweight two-part paper titled 'Consciousness as an Engineering Issue' (Michie, 1994/1995). Its author was Donald Michie, professor emeritus of machine intelligence at Edinburgh University, editor-in-chief of the Machine Intelligence series, and coincidentally a former colleague of Turing in the code-breaking group at Bletchley Park in World War II. On the philosophy side, the second year of publication saw contributions from senior figures such as Pat Churchland, Daniel Dennett, John Searle and Colin McGinn, among others. Despite the confidence this engendered, there was a continuing degree of editorial unease where psi-related submissions were concerned, and they were handled differently from other papers for the remainder of the 1990s. The result was a protracted review process and consequent delays that were felt to be unsatisfactory by some of those whose submissions were affected.

The underlying problem was to find a way of including psi papers in the journal without appearing to accept uncritically the claims for paranormal or anomalous phenomena that such submissions regularly contained. The obvious solution was to publish a balance of sceptical and parapsychological papers, but that was easier said than done. The sceptics seemed to regard the war as won. For them to take the issue seriously and set out again the arguments against psi would, in their view, simply lend the alleged phenomena a spurious legitimacy. Parapsychologists on the other hand were eager to publish their results in a mainstream journal and not just preach to the converted in the *Journal of Parapsychology*. The result was a steady stream of pro-psi submissions to *JCS* and rarely a flicker of anything from the other side. The only way to remedy this seemed to be for the journal's editors to take a proactive stance and invite contributions to what it was hoped would be an even-handed special issue with all views fairly represented.

As early as mid-1995 the publication of such a collection was seen as the best way to establish *JCS* as a level playing field. Once its neutrality was affirmed, the editors believed, individual contributions from either side could be published from time to time without appearing to commit the journal to any particular viewpoint. There was a complication due to the fact that some people, including some of the editors, felt that Beloff's article, and possibly one or two other published contributions, had already tilted us in a pro-psi direction, and that a sceptical emphasis would therefore be needed in future to restore the balance.

Others were more inclined to draw a line under the past and aim for an internally balanced collection. But either way the principle of the special issue was agreed.

None of the core editorial team at *JCS* is even a psychologist, let alone a parapsychologist, so having agreed in principle to run a special issue on the subject it was essential to find some suitably qualified scholar to act as guest editor. No easy task. The person to whom we first offered the editorship was a scholar with appropriate knowledge of both the pro-psi and sceptic points of view, who after provisionally accepting later dropped out, pleading poor health and other commitments. Some continuing indecision on the part of the regular *JCS* editors as to exactly what they wanted in the issue may also have been a factor in the withdrawal. It subsequently proved impossible to find any one person willing to undertake the task who was acceptable to both the psi and sceptical communities as a neutral umpire, so the editors decided to try making up a team from both sides.

This led in 1997 to a team of two parapsychologists and two sceptics undertaking jointly the task of commissioning and refereeing a balanced collection of papers, in liaison with myself as the journal's representative editor. There was a meeting in Brighton when by good fortune most of us were able to get together, followed by intermittent correspondence and much good will — and even quite a few promises of contributions — but by the end of 2000 there was still no sign even of an agreed set of abstracts. I allowed things to drift for a little longer, but in March 2001, to save everybody from embarrassment and with a feeling that it was kill-or-cure time, I thanked the 'gang of four' for their efforts and took control of the project back into my own hands.

Meanwhile frustration with the journal had been building up among some parapsychologists. I had at that time about ten psi-related submissions that had come in unsolicited and had been put on the shelf pending some movement on the special issue. I was under considerable pressure to get on and do something about them. One option was to try to build a focused parapsychology number of *JCS* around those existing submissions, but need for perceived balance rendered that impossible. I wrote to one complaining author about that time as follows:

> I can assure you that your own frustration in this matter is more than matched by my own. I joined *JCS* as managing editor at the time of its launch in November 1994 and my correspondence relating to the projected special issue on parapsychology goes back to June 1995. There is so much suspicion and mistrust between the protagonists of anomalous effects and the sceptics that after five and a half years we have still not succeeded in putting together a package of papers that is recognized on all sides as being fair and balanced. Coming to the journal after 25 years full-time involvement with the Church, nothing in the theological world had prepared me for the degree of antagonism generated by the psi question.

I should say that as well as getting pressure, I was also in receipt of quiet support from a number of academics sympathetic to parapsychology. They understood the problems I faced and helped to explain my difficulties to their colleagues.

Another possible way forward was to commission a single hard-hitting and partisan paper and then invite open peer-commentary on it. Or perhaps a pair of opposing targets. It was by then well over a decade since the *Behavioral and*

Brain Sciences had published their very high-quality symposium with a pro-psi target paper by Ramakrishna Rao and John Palmer (1987) and a sceptical one by James Alcock (1987). I thought that the time might be ripe to try a similar exercise.

In the event I went back to the original idea of a balanced collection of papers, none more important than another, and with some trepidation I asked James Alcock if he would be prepared to assist me either as an adviser or as co-editor. To my relief he agreed to give the venture his support as a full editor, and together with Jean Burns, an associate editor of *JCS* since its inception and the member of our inner team closest to the psi community, we set about getting the long-delayed parapsychology issue into the hands of our readers. Having reviewed the psi papers already on my shelf, we decided that whatever their individual merits it would be better for the special issue to begin with a clean slate. Somehow the year slipped by and it was January 2002 when the following carefully drafted call for papers was published on specially selected websites used by the psi and sceptical communities. It was a matter of principle to us that identical wording should be used in all notices.

> This announcement is to invite submissions for a special issue on parapsychology to be published by the *Journal of Consciousness Studies* (*JCS*) in spring of 2003. The editors of the issue will be Jim Alcock, Jean Burns, and Anthony Freeman. We ask for abstracts to be submitted by March 1, 2002. Invitations for articles will be chosen from these abstracts by the editors and sent no later than March 28. We will need completed articles by August 1, 2002. We are also looking for people who will volunteer to review articles. (All articles will be reviewed by both a parapsychologist and a skeptic.)
>
> *JCS* is a multidisciplinary journal, with readers in neurobiology, physics, psychology, philosophy, and other fields, and this special issue is meant to give our readers more familiarity with both the findings of parapsychology and skeptical arguments about them. We especially would like articles which review experimental findings (e.g., ganzfeld, remote viewing, PK, DMILS, global consciousness). If there is a controversy within the parapsychology field about the phenomena (e.g., PK v. DAT), that should be mentioned in the article, with references that direct the reader to further literature about it. Articles on interpretation of data (e.g., PK vs. precognition) and on the history of parapsychology (or some aspect of it) are also welcome. Please mention in your article the relevance of consciousness (the topic of our journal) to your subject.
>
> On the other hand, we do not want for this issue articles which describe one set of experimental runs only, or articles which describe a new finding, not previously published and therefore not yet thrashed through in the parapsychology literature.
>
> This issue will have a peculiarity which potential contributors should know about. In earlier years *JCS* has published several articles which are favorable to psi, but not so far any skeptical articles. The journal's senior editors feel that this imbalance should be remedied, and we anticipate that the special issue will reflect this by having the page count and/or number of articles skewed toward the skeptic side. However, please be assured that we intend to have scholarly articles on both sides of the parapsychology/skeptic debate which properly reflect all facts and findings referred to.
>
> I hope you will give serious consideration to sending us an abstract and/or volunteering to review articles. I am hopeful that this special issue will help inform the

academic/research community about the findings of parapsychology and the ongoing skeptical/parapsychology debate.

Please send correspondence to any of the following: [names and contact details followed].

I give the text in full because it may help to explain something of the make-up of the present volume, and the constraints that the contributors were under. It is also a clear reflection of the mind of the three editors at that stage in the process.

As submissions began to come in, it was clear that a policy decision had to be made with regard to the parapsychology papers. If we held them to the same standards that apply in mainstream science, then we should end up insisting they all be re-written, and in a way that parapsychologists would most likely find unacceptable. That followed from the nature of the discussion about parapsychology, which largely turns upon questions of what counts as acceptable evidence. If, as it seems to some, there has never been any reasonable evidence to support the notion that psi actually exists, nor any good theoretical reason for suggesting that it does, then there would be nothing substantive to publish in this volume, but only conjecture. So the question for the editors became this: How could we have a special issue of the journal, treating both sides of the discussion openly and without prejudice, unless we let parapsychologists express what is arguably the 'standard view' of parapsychology? Consequently we agreed to allow certain assumptions and claims to stand in this collection of essays that most in the scientific community, and some of the editorial team, would not personally accept. We operated on the assumption that the purpose of the exercise was to expose readers equally to parapsychologists' and sceptics' views of the field, and let them make their own judgment on the merits of each side. So as long as parapsychologists were representing the mainstream of their community reasonably well, their papers should be accepted. The review process involved critiques by other parapsychologists and that, we felt, was the appropriate form of quality control, and enough to ensure that parapsychology was not being mis-represented.

From thereon the frustrations and dead-ends of the previous six years gave way to a mercifully smooth process more like the normal running of a special issue of the journal. We have had our disappointments and further slight delays, and none of us would claim that the result is perfect in every respect. But the basic goal is now achieved and I wish to express my thanks to the two guest editors and to all who have helped to bring about this outcome, whether by active participation or by their patience and forbearance. It's been a long time coming.

References

Alcock, J.E. (1987), 'Parapsychology: science of the anomalous or search for the soul?', *Behavioral and Brain Sciences*, **10** (4), pp. 553–65.

Beloff, J. (1994), 'Minds and machines: a radical dualist perspective', *Journal of Consciousness Studies*, **1** (1), pp. 32–7.

Michie, D. (1994/1995), 'Consciousness as an engineering issue, Parts 1 & 2', *Journal of Consciousness Studies*, **1** (2), pp. 182–95, and **2** (1), pp. 52–66.

Rao, K.R. and Palmer, J. (1987), 'The anomaly called psi: recent research and criticism', *Behavioral and Brain Sciences*, **10** (4), pp. 539–51.

Turing, A. (1950), 'Computing machinery and intelligence', *Mind*, **59**, pp. 433–60.

Jean E. Burns

What is Beyond the Edge of the Known World?

Abstract: Experiments show that psi differs from known physical processes in a variety of ways, and these differences are described herein. Because of these, psi cannot be accounted for in terms of presently known physical laws. A number of theories, of which we review a sampling, suggest ways in which known physical laws might be expanded in order to account for psi. However, there is no agreement on which of these theories, if any, will ultimately provide a general explanation. A further problem in studying psi is that it is elusive, i.e., methods are not presently known by which it can be reliably produced. However, if psi is real, its study can open the door to a new frontier of knowledge and contribute to our understanding of consciousness.

In the early fifteenth century it was not thought possible to sail past Cape Bojador on the northwest coast of Africa. Maps of the time showed Jerusalem at the centre of the world, with the continents of Europe, Africa and Asia arranged symmetrically around it. Surrounding them was an ocean called the 'Great Outer Sea of Boundless Extent'.

However, in previous years there had been improvements in both ship-building and navigation, with the compass coming into common use. So Prince Henry of Portugal became determined to send an expedition around Cape Bojador. Many expeditions failed, each time for a different reason, but finally one succeeded. Soon thereafter Portuguese sailors travelled around the southern tip of Africa and then to India. A few years after that Columbus set sail across the Atlantic. The attempts to travel past the edge of the known world were successful (Spar, 2001).

The present search by parapsychologists to understand psi in many ways resembles the search for a way to travel past Cape Bojador. As then, there are no maps to provide guidance. Present-day technology and experimental methodologies can help make the search. But is there only boundless ocean (no psi phenomena) beyond present knowledge? Is there any land (phenomena) at all? If psi

Correspondence:
Jean Burns, 1525 – 153rd Street, San Leandro, CA 94578, USA. *Email: jeanbur@earthlink.net*

Journal of Consciousness Studies, **10**, No. 6–7, 2003, pp. 7–28

exists and we can come to understand it, the rewards of new knowledge could be great. So far parapsychology has had some encouraging views of what may be land, and indications of what that land is like (if it's there), as we will see below. But, in this analogy, parapsychologists have yet to round Cape Bojador.

More specifically, and as we will see in further detail in the following sections, present knowledge of psi (or what appears to be psi) is as follows. Experiments show that it differs from known physical processes in a variety of ways. On the other hand, correlations of psi with some physical variables are known (e.g. local sidereal time), although the reasons for these correlations are not known. There are a number of theoretical models for psi (we will review a sampling), but there is no generally accepted theory of it. Finally, psi is elusive, in that the psychological conditions which produce it are not well understood and it cannot reliably be produced at any given time. Indeed, some major efforts to replicate experiments have failed to produce a detectable amount of psi, as we will see. In order to be considered an established phenomenon, it would seem that either a theory should be known which explains the differences between psi and presently known physics and gives testable predictions, or at least it should be possible to reliably produce it. But neither is the case at present.

We should note that there are two types of psi usually studied in parapsychology experiments: extrasensory perception (ESP) and psychokinesis (PK). ESP refers to the transfer of information without using any known physical mechanism, and PK refers to the action of mental intention on matter without using any known physical mechanism.

Ways in Which Psi Differs from Presently Known Physical Principles

Psi appears to follow principles which are very different from the presently known laws governing the physical world. For one thing, a variety of experiments have shown that the distance between source/sender and effect/receiver makes no difference to results (Jahn and Dunne, 1987; Rao, 2001). In presently known physics nearly all influences decrease inversely as the square of the distance involved. The only exception, quantum non-locality, can only influence correlations between random sequences — it cannot transfer any information (Eberhard, 1978) and so cannot account for psi effects. (We will examine this point in more detail in the section on Theories of Psi. For now we need only note that unless conventional physics is modified in some way, quantum non-locality cannot explain the transfer of information by psi.)

Another difference is that in presently known physics all transfer of information involves a signal (which can travel no faster than the velocity of light). The transmission of information by psi is presumably not instantaneous, because that possibility is contrary to special relativity.[1] However, no physical signal has ever been found. Electromagnetic signals, which would be the obvious thing to look for, have been ruled out because numerous experiments have shown that psi

---

[1] An instantaneous signal can define an absolute time, the same in all inertial frames, and special relativity does not permit this.

results can be obtained even when the receiver is shielded by a Faraday cage (Stokes, 1997).[2]

Another distinction between psi and physical effects is the way they depend on surrounding conditions. A physical result depends on various conditions, at varying distances and locations, as specified by physical laws. But a person who responds via psi to some distant event does not respond to the totality of conditions which could produce a physical effect, but only to some particular event which has meaning to him or her. No explanation is known of how this selective response can be produced.

Classical and quantum randomness

In order to understand the relationship of psi to randomness, we should first understand the way randomness appears in presently known physics. First we should make a distinction between (a) events that merely follow a random pattern because they are determined by a large number of independent causes and (b) events that are quantum random. The first type of events can be described in terms of classical (deterministic) physics, and we will refer to these as 'classically random'. An example would be the flipping of a coin, because the results of each coin flip depends on random air currents, the way it is thrown, etc. On the other hand, quantum random events are inherently unpredictable, i.e., it is not possible to completely describe them in terms of specific causes. An example of a quantum random event is the location where a photon arrives on photographic film in the double slit experiment (a well-known experiment in physics). The pattern the photons make when many have arrived can be predicted — it is a series of bright lines. Furthermore, any individual photon must arrive at a place where a bright line, not a dark one, will be when the full pattern is made. However, aside from that, the location where any individual photon arrives is quantum random — inherently unpredictable. The process is like assembling a jigsaw puzzle, with the pieces being added in random order. You always get the same picture at the end, and the randomness only has to do with which piece is added next.

Quantum randomness is associated with a phenomenon called collapse of the wave function. However, the phenomenon of collapse is not well understood. The problem is that although the equations of quantum mechanics can be used to make detailed predictions about physics experiments, collapse is not described by these equations, but is separate from them.[3] So physicists do not agree on what collapse is and when or whether it occurs. A minority of physicists say there is no such thing as collapse (e.g. Bohm and Hiley, 1993; Etter and Noyes, 1999). However, most physicists consider collapse to be an objective physical event. Some say it occurs regardless of whether an observer is present, but others say it can

---

[2] The possibility that psi is carried by extremely low frequency (ELF) electromagnetic waves has been explored, as these could penetrate some Faraday cages. However, such waves can be ruled out because their capacity for carrying information is very low (Puthoff and Targ, 1979).

[3] This distinction is explained in detail by Penrose (1989).

only occur in the presence of a conscious observer. (For examples of interpretations of collapse, see Freeman (2003) and Herbert (1985).)

Does quantum randomness affect our daily lives? Most physicists agree that
collapse occurs when measuring instruments are used which are designed to
detect quantum events, although the latter group would require a conscious
observer also. For instance, in the double slit experiment, most physicists who
say that no conscious observer is needed would say that collapse occurs when
each photon reaches the film. But the group who says an observer is needed
would say that collapse occurs when a conscious observer views the film. However, events in people's lives do not usually depend on the results of such experiments. Most physicists would probably also agree that collapse takes place in
nature even without the presence of scientific measuring instruments, although
why, when or how it takes place is not understood. Many physicists in the first
group (no conscious observer needed) would probably agree that collapse takes
place at the molecular level. But events in people's lives do not ordinarily depend
on events at the molecular level and so would not depend on quantum randomness. Most physicists in the second group (conscious observer needed) would
probably feel that collapse takes place at the macroscopic level. Even so, probably
most events in people's lives would be viewed as determined by classical physics, but some events might depend on quantum randomness. So we can answer
the above question by saying that in some interpretations of quantum mechanics
quantum randomness might sometimes affect our daily lives. We will leave the
possibility open.

We should note, however, that experiments in parapsychology laboratories
make use of microscopic events involving quantum randomness, such as radioactive decay or quantum tunnelling. So the random sequences produced in these
experiments can depend on quantum randomness. Let us now go on to see how
randomness is involved with precognition and psychokinesis, and the issues each
raises with respect to presently known physics.

Precognition

The way random processes play a part in precognition experiments is that targets
are usually chosen randomly after the subject's guesses have been recorded.
Sometimes this process uses mechanical shufflers or the like and is obviously
classically random. Sometimes a quantum random process is used. For instance,
a subject might try to predict the time when an electron from radioactive decay is
detected by a Geiger counter (Schmidt, 1969). The reader is probably asking at
this point, given that quantum processes are inherently unpredictable, does precognition work for these? No formal study has been done which compares precognition results for targets selected in a classical random process with those for
targets selected in a quantum random process. However, no obvious differences
in the two types of experiment have been noted, and it appears that precognition
works about as well for quantum randomness as it does for classical randomness.
No explanation is known for how this can be.

One way to learn how precognition works is to model various possibilities and see which model(s) the data fit best. One possibility is that a person learns about present conditions through clairvoyance (ESP in present time) and then makes a rough extrapolation into the future. In this way the future could be known roughly, but not accurately. In another possibility we can assume that the macroscopic events of the future are entirely pre-specified and can be displayed in a Great Cosmic Record in the Sky. In order to know a future event a person would simply have to find the relevant place in the Record, presumably an easier task than in the former case. But we should also allow for the possibility of a future that changes. We will allow for the possibility that quantum randomness can affect the course of some daily events. Also, views differ on whether we have free will, but if we do, this also would affect the future. We can describe the third model as the Great Cosmic Website in the Sky, connected to everything and constantly updated.[4]

According to the first model, precognition involves not only knowledge of present conditions, but also extrapolation of these conditions into the future. Not all of the conditions which affect the future might be taken into account, or the projections might be inaccurate, so this method would presumably be less successful than clairvoyance. In the second model, precognition and clairvoyance would be equally successful. In the third model, precognition would be about as successful in some circumstances, but not in others, depending on the possibilities for change. A meta-analysis which compared the results of precognition and clairvoyance experiments done up to that time shows that these were approximately equally successful (Steinkamp *et al.*, 1998). This study would seem to support Models 2 or 3, but not Model 1.

Further light can be shed on comparisons of the models by some recent experiments which have determined the precognitive target in more complex ways. Specifically, the precognitive target was determined from the closing price of a specific stock, together with the temperature of a world city, on a certain date (Steinkamp, 2000). Because weather is sensitive to a large number of conditions and stock prices involve many individual decisions, the target would depend on a complex array of factors. One experiment showed significant results for the clairvoyance target, but chance results for the precognition target (Steinkamp, 2000). This finding would support Model 1 and Model 3 (the latter because of the dependence on volition and perhaps quantum randomness), but not Model 2. However, follow-up studies have not shown significant results in either category,

---

[4] This model could work in the following way. The Cosmic Website could track all present physical conditions and project the future according to the mathematical laws of physics. The specific outcome of a quantum random event is inherently non-computable, as we have seen, but each time one occurs the Website updates. Because all physical conditions are tracked, the patterns in people's brains which describe their present intentions are also tracked and the effects of these intentions are included in the display of the future. If free will exists, then by its nature it cannot be described by a mathematical formula (otherwise it would not be free). (For an analysis of the physics involved, see Mohrhoff (1999).) However, each time a free-will decision is made which produces physical action or simply affects intentions in the brain, the Website updates. For the most part freei-will decisions are conditioned by the brain, and any changes to the future are small, but sometimes a more substantial change is made.

although with near significance for precognition in some cases (Steinkamp, 2001), so results are inconclusive.

We can distinguish between the models in another way. According to Model 1 there would be a decrease in accuracy as the period between prediction and the actual event increases because of the increased difficulty in making an estimate. In Model 2 the time period probably would not matter, and in Model 3 it might matter somewhat, depending on conditions. Time intervals described in anecdotal accounts range from minutes or hours to years. (Anecdotal cases in which the time period is a year or more are usually dreams (Stokes, 1997).) Analyses of several collections of anecdotal accounts show that the number of accounts reported decreases with increasing time interval, but the accuracy and number of details stays about the same (Stokes, 1997). However, anecdotal accounts can be subject to selective reporting, so these results are inconclusive. Time intervals involved in laboratory experiments on precognition vary from seconds to several days or longer. A meta-analysis of precognition experiments which explored whether success depends on the period between prediction and actual event was also inconclusive (Honorton and Ferrari, 1989),[5] so this question remains open.

Probably our best conclusion as regards the models is that not enough is known to decide which ones fit the data better, and further experimental work is needed. However, given that precognition is (by definition) the ability of a person to predict a future event which is determined by factors not known to that person by any presently known physical means, we can conclude that precognition is not explained by presently known physical laws.

Psychokinesis

Experiments on PK can be generally described as follows. Because it is a small effect, experiments to investigate it are usually designed to produce a random sequence of events, with the goal of influencing this sequence to be non-random. Statistical analysis can then be made to detect PK. Tumbling cubes (dice) and devices called random event generators (REGs), which produce binary bit sequences (0's and 1's) from a random source such as electronic noise, are often used in experiments (Radin, 1997).

A random sequence has on average an equal number of 0's and 1's, and an operator (person attempting to use PK) tries to produce more 0's in half her target sequences and more 1's in the other half. Meta-analysis shows that operators can successfully produce these desired shifts (Radin, 1997). The distribution of bits in a random sequence has the shape of a Gaussian curve with a mid-point at zero. The distribution of bits in a set of PK trials will have the same shape, but the mid-point will be slightly shifted towards more 1's when the goal is 1's and

---

[5] The data of the meta-analysis shows a decrease in results with increasing time periods. However, this result is not consistent among different subgroups of subjects, and Honorton and Ferrari (1989) suggest that the difference in results between subgroups might be accounted for by differences in motivational factors. Therefore, as Stokes (1997) points out, the overall results may depend on these factors rather than precognitive attrition. Stokes (1997) also reviews other experimental findings, but does not find conclusive evidence for precognitive attrition.

slightly shifted towards more 0's when the goal is 0's (Jahn and Dunne, 1987). In each case the curve as a whole is shifted, and this can be interpreted to mean that the effect of the intention of the operator is to alter the probability of each event from 50/50 to a slight bias favouring the desired result (Jahn and Dunne, 1987). In this respect PK seems able to produce an ordering of random physical processes, with the direction of ordering associated with the intention of the operator. It is not known how this can occur.

In addition to trials in which the operator holds an intention, two other types of trials can be made. First, all experiments include control runs (also called calibration runs), which simply ensure that the random sequences being produced continue to be random when no operator is present. Also, some laboratories include runs, called baseline runs, in which the operator is present but is instructed to hold no intention. Baseline runs typically show no shift in the Gaussian curve, as would be expected. But curiously, a very large number of trials shows the consistent result that in this case the width of the curve (a measure of a statistical quantity called the variance) is narrower than in the control runs (Jahn and Dunne, 1987). It is as if the operator, in an effort to have no intention, decreases the variation normally present in a random sequence in some sort of unconscious process.

It has recently been found, in separate investigations by Pallikari (2003; Pallikari and Boller, 1999) and Schmidt (2000a, 2000b), that in the PK datasets they analysed, sequences of bits cluster more than they would in a random sequence. In other words, in a random sequence there will be two consecutive 1's or two consecutive 0's a certain proportion of the time, three consecutive 1's or three consecutive 0's a smaller proportion of the time, and so forth. But in the above datasets, analysis using a statistical measure of correlations within a sequence showed that the same bit appeared consecutively, or nearby, more often than random.[6] This is called the 'gluing effect' by Pallikari (2003) and 'bunching' by Schmidt (2000a, 2000b). Pallikari (2003) did not find the gluing effect in a baseline run she analysed. However, aside from that, little is presently known about this effect, e.g. whether it occurs consistently in PK runs or is sporadic,[7] whether an anti-correlation effect is sometimes produced, and similar questions.

PK results (shifting of the mean) appear to be independent of physical parameters involved in producing a random sequence when comparisons are made between parameters which are not markedly different. For instance, in experiments using tumbling cubes results do not seem to depend on whether only a few or up to ninety-six cubes are used at a time (Stanford, 1977). In a similar vein, when operators were presented with interspersed trials from two REGs, with results from one depending on one binary bit and results from the other depending on one hundred binary bits, results from the two machines were not

---

[6] Pallikari and Boller (1999) used a Hurst exponent for their analysis, and Schmidt (2000a) used a new measure which he developed.

[7] Stanford (1977) summarizes several early experiments which looked for clustering (which he also called 'stringing') of PK hits and misses. These experiments did not find such an effect, which implies that it does not always occur.

significantly different (Schmidt, 1974).[8] However, in a scaled-up version of the latter experiment, with results depending on two hundred and two million bits, respectively, results were significantly better for the machine which presented the *larger* number of bits (Ibison, 1998). Further experiments would need to be done in order to confirm this result. However, assuming it is confirmed, no explanation is known of why PK results would be better when a larger number of bits must be acted on.

It has also been found that if two unrelated people both hold the intention to influence an REG, the result is somewhat better than if only one does it (Dunne, 1993). If the two people have a close relationship, results are about four times better than those of a single operator (Dunne, 1993). Experiments also show that if a large number of people hold a common focus of interest, REGs can be affected during the time this focus is held. For instance, during an Academy Award ceremony, which had a worldwide television audience of about one billion people, REGs showed non-random results during times of high interest, such as opening an envelope to give an award, but normal random behaviour at other times. Similarly, during the Opening Ceremonies of the 1996 Olympic Games, watched by about three billion people, REGs became non-random, but operated normally before and after (Radin, 1997).

Time-displaced PK, the experimenter-psi effect, and the complexity of psi targets

Experiments show that if a random sequence is entirely specified — for instance, by a mathematical algorithm — no PK results can be produced on that sequence (Jahn and Dunne, 1987), a finding which is not at all surprising. (The latter type of sequence is called pseudorandom.) But then what are we to make of the following experiment (Schmidt, 1976), which has shown the same basic result in many replications over the past twenty-five years? The experimenter records a series of random sequences, which are physically random (e.g. from radioactive decay), not pseudorandom. He does not look at the results, but makes a copy (by automated means) to present to the operator, and places the master copy in a safe place. The operator then plays the recorded copy and attempts to influence the sequences, just as though he were experiencing them in real time. Common sense would say that the operator cannot possibly affect them because they have already been recorded. However, when the data is examined, it shows PK results in accordance with the intention the operator was instructed to hold. (The copy of the data the operator acted on is identical to the master copy, so the data itself was presumably not changed.) This effect is called 'time-displaced PK'. (The name derives from some of the proposed explanations for the effect.)

Three explanations for this phenomenon have been considered in parapsychology. The first is called the 'experimenter-psi effect'. This explanation notes

[8] In an earlier experiment Schmidt (1973) found that if binary trials were presented at two different rates, operators did better at the lower rate. However, because of the rate difference the operators had conscious knowledge of which machine they were using in each trial, and this could have predisposed them towards a preference for the lower rate.

that more than one person can affect the outcome of a PK experiment, and the persons who affect it are not necessarily aware of their effect. So PK results can be produced by the experimenter and/or any other persons involved in the experiment, not only the so-called operator. In early versions of the above experiment (Schmidt, 1976) the operator was instructed by the experimenter as to what intention (target) to hold, so the experimenter could have produced the PK. In later experiments, sometimes a third person specified the targets after the data had been recorded (Schmidt, 1993). In that case the experimenter might foresee by precognition the targets the third person will choose and produce these by PK. Alternatively, the third person could use ESP at an unconscious level (with this faculty perhaps augmented by linkage to the experimenter and others involved in the experiment). By this means he or she could learn the pattern present in the recorded sequence and then choose targets that best fit this pattern.

Another explanation, proposed by Helmut Schmidt, the originator of these experiments, is that PK can only occur when a conscious observer collapses the quantum mechanical wave function (Schmidt, 1982). Because nobody has observed the data until the operator acts on it, the operator in that case would be able to produce PK results. (Presumably the master copy and the operator's copy would collapse simultaneously.) Schmidt tested this hypothesis by giving a group of operators sequences of randomly interspersed pre-observed and non-pre-observed data. However, the results were inconclusive (Schmidt and Stapp, 1993), and the question of whether pre-observation has any effect is unresolved.

A third, rather exotic, possibility is that psi signals can travel backwards in time (theories reviewed by Stokes, 1987; 1997; see also Shoup, 2002). In that case the operator would hold the intention to affect the data, and the psi signal would then travel backwards in time to affect what had happened earlier.

Although the experimenter-psi effect would seem to provide a simple explanation for the above experiments, a possible problem for this explanation is that in later experiments the specification of the PK targets has become more complex. For instance, in a set of experiments done by Helmut Schmidt with various third parties, the pre-recorded data was divided into consecutive blocks. (No one saw the data before target assignment; it was simply identified by blocks.) The third party assigned the targets by obtaining a copy of a pre-specified newspaper and then deriving a 6-digit seed number from the last digits in a pre-specified weather column. This number was used to determine an entry point into a random number table, and the random sequence generated by that entry point then determined the targets for the consecutive blocks of data (Schmidt, 1993; Schmidt and Stapp, 1993). Obviously, all the targets were determined by the seed number obtained from the weather readings.

The experiments using the above procedure cumulatively showed a significant deviation from the mean (Schmidt, 1993). This result can be explained by experimenter-psi if the experimenter (with his efforts perhaps augmented by unconscious linkage to others involved in each experiment) knew the 6-digit seed numbers by precognition, accessed the random number table by ESP, and then produced data by PK which conformed to the targets.[9] However, this process is obviously very complex.

Can psi use a process that is this complex? We saw earlier that PK results appear to be improved when they depend on a larger number of bits. On the other hand, it is inconclusive as to whether precognition results can be obtained in a process as complex as this. Whether time-displaced PK can be explained in terms of the experimenter-psi effect depends on the limitations, presently unknown, as to what psi can do.

Although PK itself is not explained by presently-known physics, the time-displaced aspect of the above experiments is not actually that far from it. If the explanation is experimenter-psi, there is no time displacement. Although the explanation for collapse of the wave function is not considered established in contemporary physics, collapse by a conscious observer is among the hypotheses considered. Because the dynamical equations of physics fulfil a condition called 'time reversibility', the possibility of a signal travelling backwards in time is allowed by these equations (Shoup, 2002).

Correlations of Psi with Physical Effects

When information reaches a person via psi, in whatever way this may occur, this information evidently has to be processed by the brain before the person can use it. One reason for this conclusion is that event-related potentials (negative slow wave at 150–500 msec) are associated with the presentation of psi targets (McDonough *et al.*, 2002).

Another reason for this conclusion comes from comparison with the way the brain processes sensory data — it is sensitive to differences in physical quantities, such as light intensity or sound intensity, and processes these differences, rather than absolute levels. In a similar vein, although there is some scatter in the data, several parapsychology experiments suggest that pictures which have a greater change in the variation of light intensity when different parts of the picture are compared (indicating a more complex picture at the sensory level) produce better psi results than those which have less change in the variation of light intensity (May *et al.*, 1994; 2000).[10] This suggests that the brain processes incoming psi information at a basic sensory level.

Additionally, Millay (1999) has shown that colours and shapes transmit better than the conceptual understanding of what these represent, which also suggests that incoming psi data enters the brain at a basic sensory level.

Incoming psi data can also produce physiological effects. For instance, experiments have shown that if one person attempts to influence another by psi, the recipient shows physiological effects such as changes in skin conductivity (Braud and

---

[9]   An alternative, more exotic, possibility is that the experimenter, linked with others in the experiment, affected the weather readings by PK to produce targets which fit fluctuations in the data sequences.

[10] A picture having a greater variation of light intensity across it is more technically described as having a greater Shannon entropy. The pictures which produce better psi results have a greater change (gradient) in Shannon entropy when each part of the picture is compared to adjacent parts and these changes are averaged.

Schlitz, 1991; Radin, 1997; Schlitz and LaBerge, 1997). Physiological effects can also occur precognitively. When emotionally provocative pictures are shown, skin conductance, heart rate and blood volume are affected not only during the presentation, but also two seconds before. Pictures with a calming or neutral theme, randomly interspersed with the others, do not show this effect (Radin, 1997).

Correlations of psi with several physical conditions are also known. Analysis of a large number of ESP experiments has shown that fluctuations in the earth's magnetic field[11] have a negative correlation with psi results (Spottiswoode, 1997a). A possible interpretation of this result is that the magnetic field fluctuations produce some sort of low-level interference with brain processing, so that processing of a weak effect such as psi is interfered with.

It has also been shown that ESP results are correlated with local sidereal time (LST). (The latter describes the relative position of the stars for a given observer.) More specifically, at 13:30 LST, plus or minus about an hour, ESP scores increase three-fold over their average value (May, 2001; Spottiswoode, 1997b). Nearly all the ESP data was collected at northern latitudes, and for these latitudes the central part of the galaxy is below the horizon at 13:30 LST (May, 2001). A possible interpretation is that some sort of radiation, or perhaps fluctuations in radiation, comes from the central part of the galaxy and interferes with brain processing of weak effects. When the central part of the galaxy is below the horizon at 13:30 LST, its effect is shielded by the earth, and brain processing of weak effects would be thereby improved. It is unknown what sort of radiation might produce such an effect, however.

Theories of Psi

As we have seen in the preceding section, it does not appear that psi is governed by laws which are similar to presently known physical principles. On the other hand, assuming it does follow laws, these must necessarily be *compatible* with known physical principles because these are experimentally verified. So it seems likely that there would be points of commonality between the laws of psi, whatever these may be, and known physical principles, and most theories of psi start from an assumed commonality.

Herein we will simply consider a sampling of theories that show the sort of ideas being considered in the field. Before doing that we will examine quantum non-locality, to see why conventional physics must be modified if this phenomenon is to be invoked to explain the distance independence of psi. We will then examine some general theories of psi which include explanations for its independence of distance.[12] Finally we will consider a few of the more detailed models of PK. For an extensive bibliography of theories, see Stokes (1987; 1997).

---

[11] The correlation is with the ap geomagnetic index.

[12] Experiments have shown that when an operator is at a distance from the PK apparatus, comparable results are obtained to when the operator is nearby (Jahn *et al.*, 1997). This finding suggests that PK is independent of distance although the possibility that these results can be accounted for by experimenter-psi has not been ruled out.

Quantum non-locality

The reason the concept of quantum non-locality must be modified from conventional physics when used in a theory of psi is that psi effects involve the transfer of information, whereas quantum non-locality permits correlations, but does not permit transfer of information. It is important to understand this distinction, and we will take it up in some detail. But first, let's see what the phenomenon is. Quantum non-locality permits a correlation between two sequences of measurements, one sequence at location A and one sequence at location B, with this correlation independent of distance. We saw earlier (in the section on Randomness) that if a sequence of measurements has a range of possible results, then the overall results must fulfil some pattern (the probability distribution), which is determined by the laws of quantum mechanics. However, if the two sequences are linked by quantum non-locality, they are constrained in a further way — in that case each measurement at A has a correspondence, to the extent of the correlation, with a measurement at B. For instance, suppose both measurements can be represented by binary sequences. Let's suppose the correlation links 0s with 0s and 1s with 1s, with a correlation of 75%. Then 75% of the time, when there is a 0 at A, a 0 occurs at B and similarly, when there is a 1 at A, a 1 occurs at B. This correlation occurs independently of the distance between A and B.

If the sequence at A could be controlled, it would be possible to send a message to B. (If the correlation is less than 100%, the message would have some inaccuracies, but nevertheless a message could be sent.) But the order in which each result appears is random, i.e., it is inherently unpredictable and uncontrollable. For instance, in the above example there is no way to control the order of 0s and 1s. There is no way to impose a message on the sequence, so no message can be sent in this way.

There is more to know about non-locality which at first glance appears to be a promising way to send a message, so let's go on. The pre-determined overall patterns at A and B can vary according to different knob settings (parameters) on the measurement apparatus. The degree of correlation is also specified by the laws of quantum mechanics and depends on the knob settings. So we ask, couldn't we use the knob settings at A as a code? For instance, if there are three knob settings, A1, A2 and A3, these could be used for a three-element code. Measurements at A could be made for a while using knob A1. The person at B could choose some knob setting, say B2, produce the corresponding sequence, and check it with the known probability distributions and correlations which correspond to each combination of B2 with the knobs at A. It would seem that he could determine by this means which knob was used at A. Unfortunately, the laws of quantum mechanics and special relativity, taken together, imply that the probability distributions and correlations combine in a way which prohibits the person at B from learning which knob A used. In fact, these laws taken together prohibit the transfer of information via non-locality by any method at all (Eberhard, 1978).[13] (This

[13] Eberhard (1978) points out that signals could be sent via non-locality if an alternate to special relativity could be used in which the order of all events was determined in an absolute way in some preferred frame of reference.

finding is known as Eberhard's Theorem.) So even though a correlation exists between the sequences at A and B, it is not possible for a person at A to transfer any information to B.

Theories involving quantum non-locality

For the above reason theories of psi which invoke quantum non-locality propose a modification, in one way or another, to presently known physics. For instance, Josephson and Pallikari-Viras (1991) propose that living organisms can detect patterns in sequences that by scientific standards would be considered random. They point out that randomness is determined scientifically by taking an average over many sequences, and they suggest that living organisms may be able to discriminate information in individual sequences even though the overall pattern of many sequences appears random. In that case the information in the sequences could be transmitted non-locally.

Von Lucadou (1995) takes a different approach. Physical laws involve both abstract principles and properties, such as mass and distance, which the principles apply to. Von Lucadou proposes that the principles involved in quantum mechanics can apply unchanged to systems which can be described in terms of properties that are analogous to mass, distance and the other quantities used in conventional physics. He further proposes that psychological variables can be used in such an analogous system, which could thereby describe the action of psi. Because this proposed system would use the same laws as conventional physics, there would be no way to transfer information non-locally — there would only be correlations between random sequences. However, von Lucadou proposes that ESP and PK both occur via correlations only.

Atmanspacher, Römer and Walach (2002) make a different proposal regarding non-locality. They list the mathematical conditions which underlie the structure of quantum mechanics, and ask how these might be varied or weakened in order to be applied to other fields. They suggest that a weakened version of quantum theory could be applied to a model in which persons are linked by a collective unconscious, with non-local transfer of mental states possible between those who are linked.

Theories involving hyperspace

Alternatively, it has been proposed that ESP is independent of ordinary three-dimensional space because of connections in additional dimensions. For instance, Rauscher and colleagues have proposed extending Minkowski space (the four-dimensional space used in special relativity) to the complex plane and have shown that events separated by space or time in ordinary space can coincide in this extended space (Rauscher, 1993; Rauscher and Targ, 2001).

In another hyperspace theory Sirag (1993a,b; 1996) considers the ten-dimensional space which forms the basis of string theory (and thereby forms the basis of all physical laws). He points out that a generalization of this space can be shown mathematically to intersect with another space, with different properties.

Because the first space incorporates all the principles of the physical world, the second space must be something different, and Sirag proposes that this other space describes the properties of universal mind.[14] The intersection of these spaces would describe the way consciousness and the physical world interact, and therefore would account for the properties of psi. In particular, the properties of the intersection include time, but not physical space (Sirag, 1993a), so the lack of dependence of psi on space could be explained in this way.

Theories of psychokinesis

Now let's examine some theories of PK. As we have seen in the examples of time-delayed PK, in many experiments it is difficult to know whether psi results should be ascribed to psychokinesis or precognition, and May and co-workers have explored the possibility that results that appear to be due to PK could actually be due to precognition (May, Utts, *et al.*, 1995). They point out in their theory, called Decision Augmentation Theory or DAT, that in many experimental situations the process which produces binary bits is ongoing, and the beginning of a sequence to be affected is decided by the initiative of an operator, by a button push or some similar action. Therefore, if an operator knows by precognition what sequence is about to be produced by random noise or radioactive decay, it is not really necessary for her to affect this process by PK. Instead, she can simply push the button when a favourable sequence is coming up. They show that the z-score (a statistical measure) has a different dependence on the number of bits affected, depending on whether PK or precognitive selection is operating, and in this way the two processes can be distinguished experimentally. This test has been applied to sets of experimental data that included sequences with different numbers of bits. However, conclusions on whether PK or DAT was operating depend on details of the analysis, and there has not been agreement about this (Dobyns and Nelson, 1998; May *et al.*, 1995). Additional experimental considerations to distinguish DAT from PK have been proposed by Ibison (2000).

Several PK theories — Schmidt (1982) and Walker (1975; 1979) — have proposed that PK occurs via collapse of the wave function by a conscious observer. These theories have also proposed modifications to the equations of quantum mechanics which would allow for PK (non-random transitions) to occur. In these theories a system can be affected by PK until it is viewed by a conscious observer. Therefore, according to these theories, PK results can be found in sequences which are *not* pre-observed, but not in sequences which are. As discussed above (in the section on time-displaced PK), Schmidt compared results for the two kinds of sequences in an experiment, but results were inconclusive (Schmidt and Stapp, 1993).

Walker (1975) has also proposed that PK can only produce changes within the limits of the uncertainty principle. Such changes would be extremely small. However, Walker (1975) has shown that for cases in which an effect of such a

---

[14] The first space is based on a finite subgroup of SU_2 and the second space is a Lie algebra. The mathematical properties of the first space have a known correspondence to properties of the physical world. However, it is not known what properties of mind correspond to the properties of the Lie algebra.

change can be magnified exponentially, the final change can be macroscopic. Specifically, he showed that if a travelling cube (used in many early PK experiments) undergoes a small change in orientation at the beginning of the trajectory, then after the cube travels a certain minimum distance, it undergoes a macroscopic change in endpoint which increases as the cube travels forward.[15] According to this theory the wave function would reflect this possible change in endpoint, and wave function collapse at the end of the trajectory would make the PK deviation manifest.

Burns (2002a) also proposes that PK can only make changes within the limits of the uncertainty principle, but in a different context. The action of vacuum radiation produces constant fluctuations in matter particles within the limits of the uncertainty principle. The effect of these fluctuations is magnified as molecules interact with each other, with the result that the direction of travel of molecules is randomized after only a few interactions (Burns, 1998). As a result the action of vacuum radiation can account for entropy increase at the microscopic level (Burns, 1998; 2002d). Burns (2002a) proposes that PK occurs through the ordering of these random motions in particles. She shows that the impact of about 10^5 ordered air molecules could change the initial position of a travelling cube sufficiently to produce a sideways deviation of several centimetres after 50 cm of forward travel (Burns, 2002b,c).

Pallikari (2003) makes a different sort of proposal. As we saw earlier, experimental data shows that the action of PK on a random binary sequence not only produces a shifting of the mean, but also a bunching or gluing effect, in that both 0's and 1's tend to be adjacent to or near each other more often than would be found in a random sequence. Pallikari proposes that this gluing is the only physical effect PK produces. In that case, a shift in the mean can occur in relatively short sequences because the gluing would leave an imbalance in the number of 0's and 1's, but no shift in the mean would be found in long sequences. She points out that if gluing is the only effect of PK, any effect of mean-shifting would be sufficiently small that its lack of observation in scientific experiments could be explained.

Psychological Factors Associated with the Production of Psi

Having considered physical aspects of psi, both experimental and theoretical, let us now turn to psychological variables which may influence the production and reception of psi.

A few personality traits have consistently been associated with increased reception of ESP. For instance, those who believe that ESP will occur in a testing session score better on the average than those who do not; this result is called the 'sheep–goat effect' (Palmer, 1971; 1972; 1978).[16] Extraverts obtain higher ESP

---

[15] A more detailed analysis of the dynamics of the cube has recently been done (Burns, 2002b, 2002c). The results differ from Walker's in some particulars, but confirm the above conclusions.

[16] This correlation has been found for a belief that ESP will take place in the testing session, and is not found as strongly for simply a belief in ESP in the abstract (Palmer, 1978; Rao, 2001). In a similar vein persons who report having previous psi experiences are found to score better in ganzfeld experiments (Dalton, 1997).

scores on the average than introverts (Honorton *et al.*, 1998; Palmer and Carpenter, 1998). Less defensive subjects (as measured on the Defense Mechanism Test) tend to score better on ESP tests (Haraldsson and Houtkooper, 1995). Also, those with creative ability tend to score better (Dalton, 1997). Little is known about the most favourable traits for senders of ESP, however (Bem and Honorton, 1994).

Some findings seem related to the comfort and relaxation of the subject. For instance, experimental studies have shown that relaxation of the subject increases ESP scores (Rao, 2001). Also, it is generally thought that psi results are better when the laboratory personnel the subject interacts with are supportive of obtaining those results (Dalton, 1997; Delanoy, 1997). This view is supported by a study in which two parallel sets of experiments were run, with conditions the same except that in one the subjects were informed of experimental procedures by a psi proponent and in the other by a sceptic. The experiment with the psi proponent showed statistically significant results, but the one with the sceptic did not (Wiseman and Schlitz, 1997). Additionally, if there is a sender, results are better if the sender and receiver are emotionally or biologically close (Dalton, 1997).

Sometimes instead of matching a target, a subject will produce psi results which miss the target to a statistically significant amount. This phenomenon is called 'psi missing'. This phenomenon seems to occur more often when the subject is uncomfortable with the experiment or some conditions in it, or is sceptical that psi exists (Rao, 2001). In a probably related phenomenon if a subject is asked to switch back and forth between contrasting targets during an experiment, he may have a positive score on one and a negative score (psi missing) on the other (Rao, 2001). The latter is called the 'differential effect'.

It seems likely that ESP scores are better when interest in the target and/or the experiment is heightened, and this is often considered to be the explanation for the 'decline effect' which has been found in a broad array of ESP and PK experiments. In this effect psi scores are better in the first test unit, decrease in the second, revert to random or near random at about the third, and then gradually return to the previous scores. This effect occurs at all levels, e.g. at the trial level (the third trial of a run reverts to near random) and run level (the third run of a series reverts to near random), and even occurs across sets of experiments done by the same laboratory (Dunne *et al.*, 1994). The effect of series position on results is also known in conventional psychology (Dunne *et al.*, 1994), which supports the idea that the decline is caused by flagging interest at the mid-point of a series. However, the actual cause is unknown.[17]

The characteristics of ESP targets presumably contribute to the participants' interest. Some experiments have shown better results for dynamic ESP targets, such as film clips, than for static targets, such as photos, although this has not

---

[17] We should note that although there is considerable scatter in the magnitude of results from different laboratories for any given type of psi experiment, a polynomial regression plot shows a decline to near random and subsequent recovery across laboratories and across decades for various types of experiments (Bierman, 2001, Figures 4, 7, 8). (A few categories are fit by a steadily declining line.) Bierman (2001) proposes that these effects are due to the relationship of psi to the physical/ontological nature of reality, rather than being a psychological effect.

been a consistent finding (Rao, 2001). A review of ESP experiments suggests that multisensory targets (e.g. music with pictures, sound with videos) are preferable to targets that are solely visual (Delanoy, 1988).

In order to help the subject become aware of the target, it is generally thought that an environment of uniform low-level visual and audio fields, as is provided in ganzfeld experiments (see description by Palmer in this issue), is helpful, because psi appears to be processed in the brain like a weak sensory signal (Broughton, 1991; Rao, 2001). However, whether sensory reduction actually does help scores has apparently not been specifically tested.

Besides all the above considerations, it appears to be helpful in producing psi if the subject has a heightened focus and holds certain attitudes. With respect to heightened focus, several psi experimenters suggest that a subject should only do one session per day, which should be the highlight of the day (Delanoy, 1997; Targ and Katra, 1997). Stanford (1977), in reviewing descriptions in the literature of attitudes which may help produce PK, cited 'intention without effort to make things happen' and 'release of effort'. In the first attitude the goal can be treated as a game and approached in a playful way. In the second the intention to make something happen is first held and then let go. In a phenomenological study Heath (2000) described components common to the experiences of eight people who had produced PK events. These components included a sense of connection to the target and/or other people, a feeling of dissociation from the usual ego identity, the presence of playfulness and/or peak levels of emotion, and release of effort.

Replicability of Psi Effects

A large number of experiments have now been done on phenomena which appear to be psi, those described in this article and others, such as those on psi in the dream state (Sherwood and Roe, 2003) and remote viewing (Hyman, 1996; Radin, 1997; Utts, 1996). We will not review the statistical analysis of these experiments here (see Radin, 1997). However, this analysis strongly supports the view that some sort of anomalous process is affecting data which would otherwise be random. But is this process psi? Let us remind ourselves that by psi we mean information transfer (ESP) and/or physical change (PK) involving the presence of consciousness, using no presently known physical mechanism, which occurs independently of distance and to some extent across time. Given the various effects on the data (such as described herein), the process appears to be psi. But alternative hypotheses are always possible. The most that can be said is that an anomaly is demonstrably present, but it conceivably could be a garden-variety anomaly of unknown nature.

Nevertheless, although the existence of psi is not proved, there is sufficient evidence for it that if psi were any ordinary phenomenon, it would probably be provisionally accepted and non-controversial. That this is not the case appears to be due to (1) its elusive nature (as we will discuss next), (2) its major differences from known physical principles (as we have seen herein), and (3) the lack of any generally accepted theory which can account for those differences.

Even though some factors important to producing psi are known, methods to produce it reliably in the laboratory remain unknown, as all parapsychologists are aware. It is the practice in parapsychology to publish all studies intended to study psi, whether it appears or not (this is done because the inclusion of null results is needed for a proper statistical analysis).[18] And it is commonplace to see papers which say in essence, 'This experiment was intended to study X attribute of psi. Unfortunately, we didn't detect any psi.' It may be possible to learn specifically what psychological states are needed to produce psi, such that one can reliably produce it. But without such knowledge psi is elusive.

One of the most frustrating aspects of this elusiveness is the failure to replicate large studies which in cumulative effect had given highly significant statistical evidence for psi. The ganzfeld experiments give one example. A meta-analysis of experiments in 1985 showed a p-value of 2.2×10^{-11} (where the smaller the p-value is compared to 1, the less likely it is that results were obtained by chance) (Honorton, 1985; p-value from Milton, 1999). In other words the analysis strongly suggested that an anomalous phenomenon was present. At this point parapsychologist Charles Honorton and sceptic Ray Hyman jointly published guidelines for replication of the experiments (Hyman and Honorton, 1986). Eleven further studies, which met these guidelines, were then done by Honorton's laboratory, and these were also statistically significant (p-value of 3.3×10^{-4}) (Bem and Honorton, 1994; p-value from Milton, 1999). By 1997 thirty additional experiments had been published from other laboratories. If this effect is to be considered replicable, it is reasonable to expect that a sufficient number of these experiments would produce significant effects that the cumulative total of this data would also reach statistical significance. However, although some of these experiments showed statistical significance (i.e., evidence that psi was produced), not all did, and a meta-analysis did not show statistical significance (Milton, 1999; Milton and Wiseman, 1999). As Palmer (2003) has discussed, after ten more studies were published and added, results went back into significance (p-value of 4.8×10^{-3}). However, meta-analyses which go in and out of significance as more studies are added cannot be said to give robust evidence for a phenomenon. If by 'replicable' phenomenon we mean that researchers can be given a list of instructions on how to produce it, and most (not necessarily all) will then be able to produce it, then a more definitive specification of how to produce results is needed.

A similar problem is seen in the attempt to replicate the results of the extensive PK database of the PEAR (Princeton Engineering Anomalies Research) laboratory. Results for the first set of experiments were compiled over a period of twelve years. The shift in the mean value of the data was small (about 10^{-4} bits deviation for every bit processed), but the database was so huge that the resulting p-value was 3.5×10^{-13} (Jahn et al., 1997). In 1996 a consortium of three laboratories (at Freiberg and Giessen in Germany, plus the original PEAR lab) was formed in order to replicate these results. Physically random sequences were

---

[18] The omission of null results is called the 'file drawer' problem.

generated using the same type of equipment as in the first project. Experimental protocols and data analysis procedures were essentially the same. But no shift in the mean was found, not even in the portion of the data generated by the PEAR laboratory. Although the experimenters raised various possibilities that might be involved in this difference in result, they were unable to specify any definite reason for it (Jahn *et al.*, 2000).

Conclusion

In spite of this elusiveness, if there were some theoretical structure which could make predictions about the dependence of psi on physical parameters, such that when psi does appear it would follow these predictions, probably psi would be accepted, at least as a subject of study. But, as we have seen, there is no generally accepted theory of psi — only some competing proposals. It would seem that psi needs either a recipe for reliably producing it or an experimentally verifiable theory of its relationship to known physics before it will be considered an established phenomenon.

On the other hand, psi should not be written off as having negligible chance of existing simply because it is not consonant with presently known physical laws. Or at least, something else should first be taken into account. Not everyone believes that free will exists. However, as we have seen, presently known physical laws encompass only determinism and randomness. So if free will exists, and if by this concept we mean something free and intended, not determined or random, then free will is not described by these laws (Burns, 1999). Furthermore, the only difference between free will and PK is that free will initiates action by affecting neural processes within the brain, whereas PK can act outside the body. So if PK is written off because it is not consonant with contemporary physical laws, then free will must be written off also.

For that matter the concept of consciousness does not appear in any presently known physical laws. Furthermore, the description of consciousness is very different from that of physical matter, in that consciousness does not appear to occupy physical space and characteristics such as qualia appear to be different from known physical quantities. So regardless of the ontological status of consciousness — emergent physicalism, dualism or anything else — it seems likely that the principles which govern it will differ from known physical laws. Psi phenomena may be giving us an advance view of some of these principles.

In summary, we have likened the signs that psi exists to the signs of land past Cape Bojador seen in the fifteenth century. Are these signs only akin to a tangled mass of seaweed, drifting aimlessly in the current, which merely appears to be land? Or is there a huge continent of further findings, with all that this implies? Time will tell. In the meantime, although you — the reader — may not want to join a voyage to the edge of what may be boundless ocean, you may want to be informed of the reports from people who do voyage there. It is the purpose of this Special Issue to inform you of the present state of these explorations.

Acknowledgments

My thanks for helpful comments on the draft manuscript to James Alcock, Geoffrey Dean, Anthony Freeman, Fotini Pallikari, Adrian Parker, Helmut Schmidt, Stefan Schmidt and Harald Walach.

References

Atmanspacher, H., Römer, H. and Walach, H. (2002), 'Weak quantum theory: complementarity and entanglement in physics and beyond', *Foundations of Physics*, **32**, pp. 379–406.

Bem, D.J. and Honorton, C. (1994), 'Does psi exist? Replicable evidence for an anomalous process of information transfer', *Psychological Bulletin*, **115**, pp. 4–18.

Bierman, D.J. (2001), 'On the nature of anomalous phenomena', in *The Physical Nature of Consciousness*, ed. P. van Loocke (New York: Benjamins), pp. 269–92.

Bohm, D. and Hiley, B.J. (1993), *The Undivided Universe* (New York: Routledge).

Braud, W.G. and Schlitz, M.J. (1991), 'Consciousness interactions with remote biological systems: anomalous intentionality effects', *Subtle Energies*, **2** (1), pp. 1–46.

Broughton, R.S. (1991), *Parapsychology: The Controversial Science* (New York: Ballantine).

Burns, J.E. (1998), 'Entropy and vacuum radiation', *Foundations of Physics*, **28**, pp. 1191–207.

Burns, J.E. (1999), 'Volition and physical laws', *Journal of Consciousness Studies*, **6** (10), pp. 27–47.

Burns, J.E. (2002a), 'Quantum fluctuations and the action of the mind', *Noetic Journal*, **3** (4), pp. 312–17.

Burns, J.E. (2002b), 'The tumbling cube and the action of the mind', *Noetic Journal*, **3** (4), pp. 318–29.

Burns, J.E. (2002c), 'The effect of ordered air molecules on a tumbling cube', *Noetic Journal*, **3** (4), pp. 330–9.

Burns, J.E. (2002d), 'Vacuum radiation, entropy and the arrow of time', in *Gravitation and Cosmology: From the Hubble Radius to the Planck Scale*, ed. R.L. Amoroso, G. Hunter, M. Kafatos and J.-P. Vigier (Dordrecht: Kluwer), pp. 491–8.

Dalton, K. (1997), 'Is there a formula to success in the ganzfeld? Observations on predictors of psi-ganzfeld performance', *European Journal of Parapsychology*, **13**, pp. 71–82.

Delanoy, D.L. (1988), 'Characteristics of successful free-response targets: experimental findings and observations', *Proceedings of the 31st Parapsychological Association Annual Convention*, pp. 230–46.

Delanoy, D.L. (1997), 'Important psi-conducive practices and issues: Impressions from six parapsychological laboratories', *European Journal of Parapsychology*, **13**, pp. 63–70.

Dobyns, Y.H. and Nelson, R.D. (1998), 'Empirical evidence against Decision Augmentation Theory', *Journal of Scientific Exploration*, **12** (2), pp. 231–57.

Dunne, B.J. (1993), 'Co-operator experiments with an REG device', in *Cultivating Consciousness*, ed. K.R. Rao (Westport, CT: Praeger), pp. 149–63.

Dunne, B.J., Dobyns, Y.H., Jahn, R.G. and Nelson, R.D. (1994), 'Series position effects in random event generator experiments, with appendix by Angela Thompson', *Journal of Scientific Exploration*, **8** (2), pp. 197–215.

Eberhard, P. (1978), 'Bell's theorem and the different concepts of locality', *Nuovo Cimento*, **46B**, pp. 392–419.

Etter, T. and Noyes, H.P. (1999), 'Process, system, causality, and quantum mechanics: a psychoanalysis of animal faith', *Physics Essays*, **12** (4).

Freeman, A. (2003), *Consciousness: A Guide to the Debates* (Santa Barbara, CA: ABC-CLIO).

Haraldsson, E. and Houtkooper, J.M. (1995), 'Meta-analyses of 10 experiments on perceptual defensiveness and ESP', *Journal of Parapsychology*, **59** (3), pp. 251–71.

Heath, P.R. (2000), 'The PK zone: a phenomenological study', *Journal of Parapsychology*, **64** (1), pp. 53–71.

Herbert, N. (1985), *Quantum Reality* (New York: Doubleday).

Honorton, C. (1985), 'Meta-analysis of psi ganzfeld research: a response to Hyman', *Journal of Parapsychology*, **49**, pp. 51–91.

Honorton, C. and Ferrari, D.C. (1989), 'Meta-analysis of forced-choice precognition experiments', *Journal of Parapsychology*, **53**, pp. 281–308.

Honorton, C., Ferrari, D.C. and Bem, D.J. (1998), 'Extraversion and ESP performance: a meta-analysis and new confirmation', *Journal of Parapsychology*, **62** (3), pp. 255–76.

Hyman, R. (1996), 'Evaluation of a program on anomalous mental phenomena', *Journal of Scientific Exploration*, **10** (1), pp. 31–58.

Hyman, R. and Honorton, C. (1986), 'A joint communique: the psi ganzfeld controversy', *Journal of Parapsychology*, **50**, pp. 350–64.

Ibison, M. (1998), 'Evidence that anomalous statistical influence depends on the details of the random process', *Journal of Scientific Exploration*, **12** (3), pp. 407–23.

Ibison, M. (2000), 'An acceptance–rejection theory of statistical psychokinesis', *Journal of Parapsychology*, **64** (2), pp. 165–79.

Jahn, R.G. and Dunne, B.J. (1987), *Margins of Reality* (New York: Harcourt Brace Jovanich).

Jahn, R.G., Dunne, B.J., Nelson, R.D., Dobyns, Y.H. and Bradish, G.J. (1997), 'Correlations of random binary sequences with pre-stated operator intention: a review of a 12-year program', *Journal of Scientific Exploration*, **11** (3), pp. 345–67.

Jahn, R., Mischo, J., Vaitl, D., *et al.* (2000), 'Mind/machine interaction consortium: PortREG replication experiments', *Journal of Scientific Exploration*, **14** (4), pp. 499–555.

Josephson, B.D. and Pallikari-Viras, F. (1991), 'Biological utilization of quantum nonlocality', *Foundations of Physics*, **21**, pp. 197–207.

May, E.C. (2001), 'Towards the physics of psi: correlation with physical variables', *European Journal of Parapsychology*, **16**, pp. 42–52.

May, E.C., Spottiswoode, S.J.P. and Faith, L.V. (2000), 'The correlation of the gradient of Shannon entropy and anomalous cognition', *Journal of Scientific Exploration*, **14** (1), pp. 53–72.

May, E.C., Spottiswoode, S.J.P. and James, C.L. (1994), 'Shannon entropy: a possible intrinsic target property', *Journal of Parapsychology*, **58** (4), pp. 384–401.

May, E.C., Spottiswoode, S.J.P., Utts, J.M. and James, C.L. (1995), 'Applications of Decision Augmentation Theory', *Journal of Parapsychology*, **59** (3), pp. 221–50.

May, E.C., Utts, J.M. and Spottiswoode, S.J.P. (1995), 'Decision augmentation theory', *Journal of Parapsychology*, **59** (3), pp. 195–220.

McDonough, B.E., Don, N.S. and Warren, C.A. (2002), 'Differential event-related potentials to targets and decoys in a guessing task', *Journal of Scientific Exploration*, **16** (2), pp. 187–206.

Millay, J. (1999), *Multidimensional Mind: Remote Viewing in Hyperspace* (Berkeley, CA: North Atlantic Books).

Milton, J. (1999), 'Should ganzfeld research continue to be crucial in the search for a replicable psi effect? Part I', *Journal of Parapsychology*, **63** (4), pp. 309–33.

Milton, J. and Wiseman, R. (1999), 'Does psi exist? Lack of replication of an anomalous process of information transfer', *Psychological Bulletin*, **125**, pp. 387–91.

Mohrhoff, U. (1999), 'The physics of interactionism', *Journal of Consciousness Studies*, **6** (8–9), pp. 165–84.

Pallikari, F. (2003), 'Must the magic of psychokinesis hinder precise scientific measurement?', *Journal of Consciousness Studies*, **10** (6–7), pp. 199–219.

Pallikari, F. and Boller, E. (1999), 'A rescaled range analysis of random events', *Journal of Scientific Exploration*, **13** (1), pp. 25–40.

Palmer, J. (1971), 'Scoring in ESP tests as a function of belief in ESP: Part I: The sheep–goat effect', *Journal of the American Society for Psychical Research*, **65**, pp. 363–408.

Palmer, J. (1972), 'Scoring in ESP tests as a function of belief in ESP: Part II: Beyond the sheep–goat effect', *Journal of the American Society for Psychical Research*, **66**, pp. 1–25.

Palmer, J. (1978), 'Extrasensory perception: research findings', in *Advances in Parapsychological Research II: Extrasensory Perception*, ed. S. Krippner (New York: Plenum).

Palmer, J. (2003), 'ESP in the ganzfeld: analysis of a debate', *Journal of Consciousness Studies*, **10** (6–7), pp. 51–68.

Palmer, J. and Carpenter, J.C. (1998), 'Comments on the extraversion-ESP meta-analysis by Honorton, Ferrari and Bem', *Journal of Parapsychology*, **62** (3), pp. 277–82.

Penrose, R. (1989), *The Emperor's New Mind* (New York: Oxford).

Puthoff, H.E. and Targ, R. (1979), 'A perceptual channel for information transfer over kilometer distances', in *Mind at Large*, ed. C.T. Tart, H.E. Puthoff and R. Targ (New York: Praeger), pp. 13–76.

Radin, D. (1997), *The Conscious Universe* (New York: HarperCollins).

Rao, K.R. (2001), *Basic Research in Parapsychology*, 2nd edition (Jefferson, NC: McFarland).

Rauscher, E.A. (1993), 'A theoretical model of the remote-perception phenomenon', in *Silver Threads: 25 Years of Parapsychology Research*, ed. B. Kane, J. Millay and D. Brown (Westport, CT: Praeger), pp. 141–55.

Rauscher, E.A. and Targ, R. (2001), 'The speed of thought: investigation of a complex space-time metric to describe psychic phenomena', *Journal of Scientific Exploration*, **15** (3), pp. 331–54.

Schlitz, M.J. and LaBerge, S. (1997), 'Covert observation increases skin conductance in subjects unaware of when they are being observed: a replication', *Journal of Parapsychology*, **61** (3), pp. 185–96.

Schmidt, H. (1969), 'Precognition of a quantum process', *Journal of Parapsychology*, **33**, pp. 99–108.

Schmidt, H. (1973), 'PK tests with a high-speed random number generator', *Journal of Parapsychology*, **37**, p. 105.

Schmidt, H. (1974), 'Comparison of PK action on two different random number generators', *Journal of Parapsychology*, **38**, p. 47.

Schmidt, H. (1976), 'PK effect on pre-recorded targets', *Journal of the American Society for Psychical Research*, **70**, pp. 267–92.

Schmidt, H. (1982), 'Collapse of the state vector and psychokinetic effect', *Foundations of Physics*, **12**, pp. 565–81.

Schmidt, H. (1993), 'Observation of a psychokinetic effect under highly controlled conditions', *Journal of Parapsychology*, **57** (4), pp. 351–72.

Schmidt, H. (2000a), 'A proposed measure for psi-induced bunching of randomly spaced events', *Journal of Parapsychology*, **64** (3), pp. 301–16.

Schmidt, H. (2000b), 'PK tests in a pre-sleep state', *Journal of Parapsychology*, **64** (3), pp. 317–31.

Schmidt, H. and Stapp, H. (1993), 'PK with prerecorded random events and the effects of pre-observation', *Journal of Parapsychology*, **57** (4), pp. 331–49.

Sherwood, S.J. and Roe, C.A. (2003), 'A review of dream ESP studies conducted since the Maimonides dream ESP studies', *Journal of Consciousness Studies*, **10** (6–7), pp. 85–109.

Shoup, R. (2002), 'Anomalies and constraints: can clairvoyance, precognition, and psychokinesis be accommodated within known physics?', *Journal of Scientific Exploration*, **16** (1), pp. 3–18.

Sirag, S.-P. (1993a), 'Consciousness: a hyperspace view', appendix to J. Mishlove, *Roots of Consciousness*, 2nd edition (Tulsa, OK: Council Oak Books), pp. 327–65.

Sirag, S.-P. (1993b), 'Hyperspace reflections', in *Silver Threads: 25 Years of Parapsychology Research*, ed. B. Kane, J. Millay and D. Brown (Westport, CT: Praeger), pp. 156–65.

Sirag, S.-P. (1996), 'A mathematical strategy for a theory of consciousness', in *Toward a Science of Consciousness*, ed. S.R. Hameroff, A.W. Kaszniak and A.C. Scott (Cambridge, MA: MIT Press), pp. 579–88.

Spar, D.L. (2001), *Ruling the Waves* (New York: Harcourt).

Spottiswoode, S.J.P. (1997a), 'Geomagnetic fluctuations and free-response anomalous cognition', *Journal of Parapsychology*, **61** (1), pp. 3–12.

Spottiswoode, S.J.P. (1997b), 'Apparent association between effect size in free-response anomalous cognition and local sidereal time', *Journal of Scientific Exploration*, **11**, pp. 109–22.

Stanford, R.G. (1977), 'Experimental psychokinesis: a review from diverse perspectives', in *Handbook of Parapsychology*, ed. B. Wolman (New York: Van Nostrand), pp. 324–81.

Steinkamp, F. (2000), 'Does precognition foresee the future? A postal experiment to assess the possibility of true precognition', *Journal of Parapsychology*, **64** (1), pp. 3–18.

Steinkamp, F. (2001), 'Does precognition foresee the future? Series 2, a laboratory replication and Series 3, a world wide web replication', *Journal of Parapsychology*, **65** (1), pp. 17–40.

Steinkamp, F., Milton, J. and Morris, R.L. (1998), 'A meta-analysis of forced-choice experiments comparing clairvoyance and precognition', *Journal of Parapsychology*, **62** (3), pp. 193–218.

Stokes, D.M. (1987), 'Theoretical parapsychology', in *Advances in Parapsychological Research 5*, ed. S. Krippner (Jefferson, NC: McFarland), pp. 77–189.

Stokes, D.M. (1997), *The Nature of Mind: Parapsychology and the Role of Consciousness in the Physical World* (Jefferson, NC: McFarland).

Targ, R. and Katra, J. (1997), 'Psi-conducive protocols', *European Journal of Parapsychology*, **13**, pp. 95–95.

Utts, J. (1996), 'An assessment of the evidence for psychic functioning', *Journal of Scientific Exploration*, **10** (1), pp. 3–30.

von Lucadou, W. (1995), 'The model of pragmatic information (MPI)', *European Journal of Parapsychology*, **11**, pp. 58–75.

Walker, E.H. (1975), 'Foundations of paraphysical and parapsychological phenomena', in *Quantum Physics and Parapsychology*, ed. L. Oteri (New York: Parapsychology Foundation).

Walker, E.H. (1979), 'The quantum theory of psi phenomena', *Psychoenergetic Systems*, **3**, pp. 259–99.

Wiseman, R. and Schlitz, M. (1997), 'Experimenter effects and the remote detection of staring', *Journal of Parapsychology*, **61** (3), pp. 197–207.

James E. Alcock

Give the Null Hypothesis a Chance
Reasons to Remain Doubtful about the Existence of Psi

Is there a world beyond the senses? Can we perceive future events before they occur? Is it possible to communicate with others without need of our complex sensory-perceptual apparatus that has evolved over hundreds of millions of years? Can our minds/souls/personalities leave our bodies and operate with all the knowledge and information-processing ability that is normally dependent upon the physical brain? Do our personalities survive physical death?

Experience suggests to many people that the answer to such questions is 'Yes'. Indeed, year after year, surveys show that the majority of people believe that such paranormal phenomena exist, and personal experience is one of the primary reasons for their belief. Many such experiences are emotionally powerful and bring with them meaning and existential comfort.

What accounts for these reported experiences? Do they really, some of them at least, reflect a reality beyond the materialistic world as it is now understood by science — that is, are they really 'paranormal'? Or are they the product of normal but misunderstood brain function? That is, do our brains sometimes produce or interpret experiences in such a way that they seem to be paranormal even though they are not? Parapsychologists are motivated by and large by the former interpretation, and seek scientific evidence to support that view. Mainstream science, on the other hand, takes the latter stand, usually rejecting out of hand any paranormal claims.

Whatever the explanation, given that these experiences appear to be relatively common and are often very striking, they merit study in their own right. Unfortunately, such study is rather rare. Most psychologists, eschewing paranormal and supernatural claims, have by and large ignored such experiences, while parapsychologists, on the other hand, give scant attention to normal explanations and focus instead on the paranormal possibilities. Thus, what should be of common interest to both psychologists and parapsychologists instead falls through the cracks, with one camp persuaded that the paranormal is real and the explanation

Correspondence: James E. Alcock, Dept. of Psychology, Glendon College, York University, Toronto, Canada. *Email: jalcock@yorku.ca*

Journal of Consciousness Studies, **10**, No. 6–7, 2003, pp. 29–50

for many such experiences, and the other camp rejecting the paranormal while also ignoring the experience.

As a result, parapsychologists and sceptical scientists most often speak to each other in a *dialogue aux sourds*, a dialogue of the deaf. Yet, it is always a good thing to try to build bridges in the hope of bringing intellectual protagonists together, and this special issue of the *Journal of Consciousness Studies*, which includes articles by some of the leading proponents and critics of parapsychology, may help build such a bridge. As much as they may differ in terms of their views on the paranormal, it is important to note that the contributors are 'all on the same side' in at least one important way: all share a deep respect for science and are committed to the scientific method as the appropriate approach to exploring reality. They are all seeking truth, not delusion; fact, not fiction. Arguably, the only significant differences that distinguish the proponents from the sceptics in this collection of articles are in terms of their *a priori* subjective weighings of the likelihood that psychic phenomena exist, which in turn may influence their evaluations of the adequacy of the research protocols that have been employed in parapsychological research and the quality of the data thus obtained.

Those in the scientific community who have little familiarity with parapsychology are often unaware of the wide spectrum of opinion, expertise and degree of respect for science, that exists amongst those who call themselves parapsychologists. At one end are those described in the last paragraph, of whom some have contributed to this volume. At the other are numerous writers and researchers who view science as an inadequate tool for grappling with the mysteries of the paranormal, and who base their beliefs in the paranormal solely on the kinds of experiences served up by trance mediums, putative apparitions, and so forth. Their writings are not to be found in this Special Issue, nor are the writings of those who believe that the verdict is already in, that parapsychology has long since established a sound scientific footing for paranormal phenomena and no controversy remains. (Indeed, this touches on a demarcation problem, in that scholarly, research-oriented parapsychologists reserve the label of 'parapsychologist' for themselves, and do not consider members of the general public who use this title to be parapsychologists. This important distinction is often difficult to make for those outside parapsychology.)

There is also a spectrum of opinion, expertise, and yes, of the degree of respect for science, amongst sceptics too, and again, those at the far end who only sneer dismissively at any mention of the paranormal, or those whose dogmatism shows an inability or unwillingness to be objective, are not to be found in this Special Issue.

Thus, to the sceptical reader, I stress that these parapsychological writers are in our camp, the scientific camp. They believe in science and strive to apply it. To the reader who leans towards belief in the paranormal, the sceptical writers you will find here are not motivated by any desire to drive parapsychology into the desert, but only by the desire to truly understand human experience.

That being said, I have myself long been a critic of parapsychological research, and it is only fair that I state my views 'up front'. I have yet to find any empirical evidence that persuades me that it is likely that paranormal phenomena actually exist. Moreover, I am well aware of just how often our brains can mislead us, and can lead us to believe that we have had a paranormal experience even when no such thing has happened. Indeed, even if there is no such thing as a paranormal phenomenon, human information processing works in such a way that we are all likely from time to time to have experiences that *seem* for all the world to be paranormal. For me as a psychologist, these experiences themselves — the reports of extrasensory perception and the like — are fascinating in their own right, even if, as I presume, they are not paranormal, for they can tell us a great deal about how our brains work and about our beliefs and needs and expectations, if we are willing to listen.

I approached my own reading of the articles in this Special Issue in part with the personal desire to find out if there is any new and compelling evidence that might nudge me away from my strong scepticism about the existence of paranormal phenomena. There are for me a number of reasons to be doubtful about the existence of paranormal phenomena (I shall adumbrate some of the more important ones below), and thus, I perused each article against the backdrop of those concerns, and considered whether its conclusions supported the Psi hypothesis (that psychic, or 'psi', phenomena exist), or were they more in line with the Null hypothesis (that is, that the observed results came about naturally, and had nothing to do with psi). I advocate that the reader take a similar approach, keeping in mind not just the Psi-hypothesis, but the Null hypothesis as well.

Reasons to Remain Doubtful about the Existence of Psi

1. Lack of definition of subject matter

One of parapsychology's most vexing problems has to do with the very definition of its subject matter. What is it that is being studied, and how are the phenomena under study themselves defined? Are ghosts, levitation and trance channellers part of the accepted range of subject matter? Or is the subject matter at this time restricted to subtle mind-induced influences at the micro level? If mainstream science is challenged to consider seriously the claims of parapsychology, just what claims are we talking about — ghost sightings, or small but statistically significant changes in a distribution of outcomes of a random event generator in a laboratory experiment? Parapsychological opinion as to its proper subject matter varies widely. Consider, for example, the views of the following organizations:

The Parapsychological Association (PA) defines itself as 'the international professional organization of scientists and scholars engaged in the study of "psi" (or "psychic") experiences, such as telepathy, clairvoyance, remote viewing, psychokinesis, psychic healing, and precognition . . .', and its webpage states:

> The diversity found within PA membership also leads to many different 'schools of thought' regarding the phenomena studied — ranging from those who suspect that psi will eventually turn out to be an artifact of no major significance, to those who

believe it will be accounted for through new developments in physics or biology, to those who argue that psi phenomena suggest a basis for spiritual beliefs.

(*www.parapsych.org*)

In Britain, the venerable Society for Psychical Research states that:

> The principal areas of study of psychical research concern exchanges between minds, or between minds and the environment, which are not dealt with by current orthodox science. This is a large area, incorporating such topics as extrasensory perception (telepathy, clairvoyance, precognition and retrocognition), psychokinesis (paranormal effects on physical objects, including poltergeist phenomena), near-death and out-of-the-body experiences, apparitions, hauntings, hypnotic regression and paranormal healing. One of the Society's aims has been to examine the question of whether we survive bodily death, by evaluating the evidence provided by mediumship, apparitions of the dead and reincarnation studies.

(*www.spr.ac.uk/about.html*)

The American Society for Psychical Research (*www.aspr.com/topics.htm*), which describes itself as the oldest psychical research institute in the United States, lists as its subject matter an extensive range of topics, from extrasensory perception to psychic healing to trance channellers and survival after death to dowsing and poltergeists.

The point is that there is a great variety of opinion as to what constitutes the essential and appropriate subject matter of parapsychology. Some parapsychologists want to adhere to the rules of evidence as they exist in modern science, while others rely on anecdotal accounts of wondrous events — such as the supposed levitation of the medium Daniel Douglas Home during a seance in 1852 — as the best evidence that psi phenomena are real. Recently, some prominent members of the Society for Psychical Research have become very interested in the study of spirit mediums once again, based on sittings in Scole, England, and view this evidence as strongly suggestive of communication with a spirit world (Keen, Ellison and Fontana, 1999). Yet, such research would probably be considered quaint and unscientific by more laboratory-oriented parapsychologists such as those whose articles appear herein, and such research, despite the importance it is given in some parapsychological circles, is not even mentioned by the parapsychologists who have contributed to this Special Issue.

This all reflects the fact that to the extent that parapsychology constitutes a 'field' of research, it is a field without a core knowledge base, a core set of constructs, a core set of methodologies, and a core set of accepted and demonstrable phenomena that all parapsychologists accept. Moreover, I consider it doubtful that parapsychologists could agree amongst themselves as to just what experiments or demonstrations in the literature constitute the best case for psi. This immediately distinguishes parapsychology from any other scientific research field, where there is always a common core of knowledge as well as key demonstrations that can reliably be produced and taught, even while there may be controversy about various concepts and research findings at the frontiers of the field.

2. Definition of constructs

Quite apart from differences of viewpoint in what constitutes the range of appropriate subject matter, a much more important definitional problem arises in terms of defining and measuring specific psi phenomena. The problem arises primarily because psi phenomena are defined, not in terms of what they are, but only in terms of what they are not. Telepathy is the simultaneous sharing or transfer of information between two brains *in the absence of any 'normal' mechanism that could account for it*; precognition involves seeing future events *in a manner that cannot be accounted for by any means understood by contemporary science*, and so on. Telepathy is not telepathy if sender and receiver communicate by 'silent' dog whistles that one of them is able to hear, or if they have some sort of secret code that allows them to communicate without the knowledge of the researcher. Psychokinesis is not psychokinesis if the psychic causes an object to move by hidden, although normal, means. Indeed, parapsychology is the only realm of objective inquiry in which the phenomena are all *negatively* defined, defined in terms of ruling out normal explanations. Of course, ruling out all normal explanations is not an easy task. We may not be aware of all possible normal explanations, or we may be deceived by our subjects, or we may deceive ourselves.

If all normal explanations actually could be ruled out, just what is it that is at play? What is *psi*? Unfortunately, it is just a label. It has no substantive definition that goes beyond saying that all normal explanations have apparently been eliminated. Of course, parapsychologists generally presume that it has something to do with some ability of the mind to transcend the laws of nature as we know them, but all that is so vague as to be unhelpful in any scientific exploration. Some parapsychologists, recognizing the problem of trying to provide a positive rather than a negative definition of psi, choose to sidestep the issue and instead focus on 'anomalies'. Psi effects are thus thought of as anomalous findings that apparently should not occur if the current scientific worldview is accurate. These are not just any such anomalies, of course. They are anomalies that involve, in one way or another, the mind.

Anomalistic observations that do not fit with accepted theory are vital to scientific progress, for they force us to modify our theories and to gather additional data until they can be understood and accommodated into a revised theory. For example, to AIDS researchers it is quite anomalous that some Nairobi prostitutes show an inherent resistance to HIV infection, but only as long as they continue to have exposure to multiple partners. This is an important anomaly — it does not make immediate sense in terms of what is known about this illness, but coming to understand it will undoubtedly lead to a much better understanding of HIV in general. Elsewhere in science, anomalies sometimes lead to such fundamental changes in theory that philosophers of science speak in terms of a paradigm shift. The precession of Mercury in its orbit behind the sun was anomalous; for it did not fit with Newton's theory of gravity and the derivative understanding of the movement of planets. Scientists a century ago went so far as to speculate that Mercury's orbit behind the sun was actually disrupted by the gravitational field of an unseen planet (they called it Vulcan) on the far side of the sun. However,

Einstein's general theory of relativity was able to account for the perihelion shift of Mercury, resolving the anomaly and thereby helping to usher in a new scientific worldview.

Yet, when parapsychologists seek to establish their subject matter in terms of anomalies, there is something quite different going on compared to either of the examples above. In mainstream science, one does not deliberately seek anomalies; they present themselves. They are unexpected and unpredicted by current theory, that is why, after all, they are called anomalies. However, no psi anomaly has ever presented itself in the course of research in mainstream science. Consider the particularly delicate experiments in subatomic physics, which might be ideal for the manifestation of putative psi forces, given that they involve very tiny amounts of matter and energy, highly precise measurements and very highly motivated researchers with, at least at times, varying expectations. We do not read research reports that suggest that the outcomes of such experiments seem to depend on who was operating the linear accelerator at the time, and that a particular effect is found only when certain researchers are present and not otherwise, reflecting perhaps a researcher's 'psychic' influence. In the course of doing normal science, anomalies suggestive of psi just do not pop up. Rather, parapsychologists, in their work, deliberately try to generate them; they are the goal of much parapsychological research and are only labelled as anomalous by the rather circular route of deeming them to be impossible if current science is accurate and complete.

Parapsychologists need to be able to provide a positive definition of psi, to tell us how to identify psi 'anomalies' in ways other than exclusion, and to tell us how to rule out psi, how to know when it is absent. This problem is as great now as it has ever been, and no progress has been made in overcoming it across more than a century of empirical parapsychological research. Because of its negative definition, we are left with no idea as to when psi might occur, and more importantly to the scientist, as to when it will *not* occur. There is no way, we are told, that psi can be blocked or attenuated by the researcher, and thus we cannot compare conditions where psi could not occur to those where, were it to exist, it could be observed. Moreover, because it is claimed that psi influences can occur without any attenuation as a function of distance, and can occur backwards and forwards in time, it becomes impossible ever to truly 'control' the conditions of an experiment.

3. Failure to achieve replication

If parapsychologists cannot provide a positive definition of psi, then at least one would hope that they could provide a reliable, replicable, demonstration of the subject of their study, be it an 'anomaly' or whatever. Mainstream science accords a high value to replicability, for it is perhaps the best safeguard against being taken in by results produced by error, self-delusion or fraud. Yet replicability itself is a somewhat complex concept. Simply repeating an experiment and getting the same results is not by itself enough, for whatever errors or self-delusions may have occurred in the first instance might also be part of subsequent repetitions of the experiment (Hyman, 1977). That was precisely the case when, at the beginning of the twentieth century, the French physicist, Professor Blondlot, 'discovered' N-rays, an apparently new form of energy. He replicated his experiments many times, and indeed, a score or more of other scientists reported that they had confirmed the existence of N-rays in their own laboratories. Yet sceptical scientists were unable to replicate these results, and ultimately Blondlot's findings were shown to be a product of self-delusion (Alcock, 1981). The concept of replicability, to be useful, implies that researchers in general, provided that they have the expertise and equipment, should be able to reproduce the reported results, and not just those who are believers and enthusiasts.

Because parapsychologists have *never* been able to produce a successful experiment that neutral scientists, with the appropriate skill, knowledge and equipment, can replicate, some parapsychologists have gone so far as to argue that the criterion of replicability should not be applied to psi research because the phenomena are so different from the usual subject matter of science (Pratt, 1974). Yet, what a risky adventure it would be to yield to special pleading and relax the very rules of scientific methodology that help to weed out error, self-delusion and fraud in order to admit claims that violate the basic tenets of science as we know it!

Several of the papers in this Special Issue address the problem of replicability in psi research:

(1)   My good and respected friend Adrian Parker acknowledges the highly problematic inconsistencies in parapsychology that reflect both failures to replicate and situations where some experimenters, but not others, can replicate a set of findings. Yet he does not take this to suggest that the Psi hypothesis might be wrong and the Null hypothesis correct, but instead views these irregularities as reflecting possible *properties* of the ostensible phenomenon, such as the *psi-experimenter effect* (discussed below). This is begging the question. When there has been a failure to replicate, it is not appropriate to engage in the circularity of assigning to this failure a label (psi-experimenter effect), and then implicitly suggesting the label as its explanation. Since there is no other way of defining or identifying the psi-experimenter effect, it has no *explanatory* value. Using it as a possible explanation only leads to a tautology: by substituting the definition of the psi-experimenter effect, one gets 'The failure to replicate may be a manifestation of "one researcher failing to replicate a finding that another researcher had made".' This circular reasoning excludes from the debate a possibly fruitful aspect of research, in terms of coming to understand the reasons, other than psi, that might account for the fact that different experimenters have obtained different results.

(2)   With regard to ESP in the ganzfeld, Palmer concludes that, while he finds statistically significant departures from the Null hypothesis across the aggregate data bases that he has examined, 'the marked heterogeneity of results across experiments leaves doubt about the future replicability of the phenomenon outside parapsychology'.

(3)   In their article, Sherwood and Roe examine attempts to replicate the well-known Maimonides dream studies that began in the 1960s. They provide a good review of these studies of dream telepathy and clairvoyance, but if one thing emerges for me from their review, it is the extreme messiness of the data adduced. Lack of replication is rampant. While one would normally expect that continuing scientific scrutiny of a phenomenon should lead to stronger effect sizes as one learns more about the subject matter and refines the methodology, this is apparently not the case with this research. They conclude: 'Overall, the Maimonides studies were more successful than the post-Maimonides studies but this may be due to procedural differences.' Indeed, this leads the authors to indicate that 'more recent work has concentrated on the question of whether consensus methods are superior to individual performance. With consensus judgement procedures, the responses from a number of individuals are combined to give a single judgement.' To the sceptic, this is a strange turn of events. The phenomenon of interest is the alleged ability of some individuals to paranormally receive information while they are asleep. Because research cannot demonstrate this clearly, the researchers choose to complicate the situation immensely by combining information from a number of subjects.

(4)   Jeffers' article also bears directly on the question of replicability. Jeffers stands in lonely company as one of the very few neutral scientists who have empirically investigated the existence of psi phenomena. My first interaction with Jeffers is memorable to me. Jeffers, a physics professor at my university, was inspired by the work of Robert Jahn (e.g. Jahn, 1982), that purported to demonstrate the influence of the human mind on the output of a random event generator, and he decided to carry out his own psi experiments. His methodology was different from Jahn's (or indeed from other psi experiments) in that it investigated the possible effect of psi on the interference of light. He reasoned, and Jahn had agreed, that if Jahn's results were due to subjects' mental influence on quantum processes, then that same influence might be expected to affect the interference patterns produced when two beams of light are sent through narrow slits. In Jahn's work, a series of numbers appeared on a computer screen, the ultimate result of a quantum process, and subjects strove to affect the magnitude of those numbers. In Jeffers' work, a bar appeared on a computer screen, its length determined by a quantum process (fringe contrast in the interference pattern) and subjects attempted to influence the height of the bar. Thus, Jahn and Jeffers were both attempting to measure subjects' ability to influence quantum processes by mentation alone and, given that different methodology was used, were Jeffers' research to have produced significant results this would have added even more weight to Jahn's conclusions than would a straight replication. This is because Jeffers studied the same construct, or concept, from a slightly different angle, thereby making his research capable of producing convergent evidence, whereas a straight replication using exactly the same methodology might also reproduce any undetected errors and biases in the original.

Back to our initial meeting: Jeffers came to me at least a tad defiantly, requesting that I review his experimental design and offer any suggestions and criticisms before he began his research. He stressed that I should not after the fact, were he to obtain data supporting the parapsychological interpretation, then argue that the experiment was not to be taken seriously because it had fallen methodologically short in some fashion. Thus began our relationship, which was to grow into the very positive one that it is today. I reviewed his experimental design, and I raised some reservations — the same reservations that I had written about (Alcock, 1990) with regard to Jahn's work. While so far as I am aware, Jahn's group never paid any heed to my comments, Jeffers incorporated changes that satisfied all my concerns. As Jeffers reports in his paper, his research findings give no support to the Psi hypothesis.

Jeffers' research makes a very important contribution to the study of putative psi phenomena, in my opinion, for the following reasons:

1. It was carried out by a neutral scientist who approached the subject with great interest and motivated by the possibility that Jahn may really have discovered something very important — the influence of human mentation on random physical processes. This should be an ideal condition for producing the desired results: Jeffers was very much open to the possibility of psi and was motivated to find it.

2. The research began with the full approbation of both proponent and sceptic. Jeffers' had the full-fledged support of Jahn himself and, as noted above, I fully supported the appropriateness of the revised methodology that he employed. Had he produced positive results, Jahn no doubt would have viewed this as a significant conceptual replication of his own work by a neutral scientist, and I in turn would have had to admit that the research was done carefully and correctly, and that I had no basis for rejecting it on methodological grounds.

However, when Jeffers' research did not produce results supportive of the Psi hypothesis, other researchers in the area dismissed it, and now it receives virtually no attention from parapsychology at all. (To be precise, his article discusses two kinds of experiments, one single-slit and one double-slit. The results of the single-slit experiment, carried out at York University, were null. There were two sets of double-slit experiments, one conducted at York University and one carried out in Jahn's laboratory at Princeton. The York experiment produced a null outcome, while that at Princeton produced 'marginal' significance ($p = 0.05$), which Jeffers views, as do I, as unconvincing). This neglect of Jeffers' research is most unfortunate. Although his data, as reviewed in his current paper, is in line with the Null hypothesis, the fact that it is now ignored within parapsychology is another instance of not giving the Null hypothesis a fair chance.

Incidentally, Jahn's laboratory more recently collaborated with researchers at two German universities to attempt a carefully controlled replication of the basic claims of Jahn's research group. The result? Neither the researchers at Jahn's lab nor those in the two German universities found anything of significance with regard to the hypotheses under test (Jahn et al., 2000). They did, however, on a *post-hoc* basis — as is so often the case in parapsychology —

find some 'anomalies' in the patterning of the data which they argue call for more sophisticated experiments and theoretical models in order to understand 'the basic phenomena involved'. Again, failure to confirm predictions does not, in their view, give strength to the Null hypothesis. By post-hoc data snooping, a success of sorts can always be wrestled away from the jaws of the Null.

In sum, parapsychologists have never been able to produce a demonstration that can be reliably replicated by researchers in general, and failures to replicate are either ignored, explained away or interpreted as evidence for the existence of arbitrary properties of psi, as is discussed below.

4. Multiplication of entities

Despite William of Ockham's exhortation that one should not increase the number of entities required to explain a phenomenon beyond what is necessary ('Ockham's Razor'), parapsychology has unabashedly invented a number of such entities by way of explaining away failures to produce consistent and replicable data. For example:

1. As touched on earlier, if only some researchers can obtain an effect — and then only some of the time — while other researchers using identical methods cannot, this is taken, not as lending support to the Null hypothesis, but as a manifestation of a property of psi — the *psi-experimenter effect*. This 'effect' supposedly occurs because some experimenters, perhaps because of their own psi abilities, are conducive to the production of psi in experiments, while others are not.

    Smith's article in this Special Issue provides a good overview of the enduring problem of the experimenter effect in parapsychology, but his analysis also indirectly serves to demonstrate the problem that I am addressing. While acknowledging the issue of replication in parapsychology, Smith argues that 'replication difficulties in parapsychology may be due, at least in part, to psi-related experimenter influences'. He recognizes that this view is difficult from the point of view of science because it suggests that 'it is only those researchers who believe that psi exists that are likely to be able to replicate positive results'. Nonetheless, as he reflects upon this problem, Smith's optimism is not diminished and he argues: 'the scientific approach adopted by psi research has so far achieved some limited success in identifying factors associated with obtaining positive results in psi experiments, and it is my view that it is such an approach that is likely to reveal more of these factors in future research. Only when we have a much more detailed recipe for success can more consistent levels of replication be expected.' Thus, while aware of the problem he sidesteps it.

    Parker also addresses this subject, and states that 'experimenter effects and psi-conduciveness are every bit as integral part of the phenomena being studied as, say, placebo effects are in psychological treatment'. The problem is that the 'experimenter effect' is really only a lack of consistency, a lack of general replicability, which itself is more in line with the Null hypothesis than anything else. There is no reason, no justification, to engage in further multiplication of explanatory entities, to use Ockham's language. What we have here is a failure to replicate. Period. The psi-experimenter effect provides the ultimate Catch-22: if you find the psi effect you are looking for, well and good. If you do not find it, this might be because of the experimenter effect, and so this too could be a manifestation of psi!

2. The *sheep–goat effect* refers to the observation that believers in psi are more likely than non-believers to demonstrate evidence of psi in an experiment.

3. If subjects fail to obtain the above-chance scores predicted in a psi experiment, that is not taken as lending weight to the Null hypothesis. Instead — so long as they fail miserably enough that their data deviate statistically significantly in the non-predicted direction, then this is taken as support for the Psi hypothesis, and another 'effect' — the *psi-missing effect* is invoked, allowing the interpretation that the miserable failure was indeed a success.

4. If a 'gifted' subject scores well in early trials but then, as is so often the case, scores only at a chance level later, this is not taken as support for the Null hypothesis. Instead, it is taken as evidence for another 'property' of psi — the *decline effect*. Thus, failure is often interpreted as a kind of success, as an indication of the weird properties that this elusive psi possesses.

I note that one such 'effect', at one time well-known within parapsychology, appears to have quietly disappeared. I am referring to the *quartile-decline effect*, much discussed by the pre-eminent parapsychologist Joseph Banks Rhine, and so-named because it was noted that when subjects' scores were recorded in two columns to a page, there was often a significant decline in subjects' success if one compared the scores in the upper left-hand quadrant of the page to those in the lower right-hand quadrant. While such an 'effect' always struck sceptical observers as somewhat convenient and arbitrary, it was touted as again suggesting some strange property of psi.

Indeed, the very fact that it has proven so difficult to produce a reliable demonstration of a psi phenomenon has led some researchers to think of this general elusiveness not as something in line with the Null hypothesis, but rather as another property of psi. Parker's paper speaks to this: 'For whatever reason the phenomena appear to have an elusiveness as a defining characteristic that makes them intrinsically difficult to capture in the laboratory in a stable, predictable and controllable fashion.'

Note that none of these so-called effects are anything other than arbitrary, post-hoc labels attached to unexpected negative outcomes. The employment of arbitrary *post hoc* constructs to explain away failures and inconsistencies in the data is a serious problem when one considers the scientific status of parapsychology. The Null hypothesis is not given a fair chance when data that are consistent with it are explained away in this manner.

5. Unfalsifiability

Obviously, the use of such 'effects' as those just discussed serves to make claims about psi essentially unfalsifiable, for any failure to produce the predicted effect, or any inconsistency in the data, can be explained away in terms of one or another of them. Failure to produce data consistent with psi has never been taken as providing weight to the null hypothesis.

Falsifiability is an important concept in science, especially when highly unusual claims are made. Science did not ignore Roentgen's rays just because they did not fit in with what was known at the time. On the other hand, science did not ignore Blondlot's rays (N-rays) either. The former turned out to be a highly replicable phenomenon that demanded changes in physical theory to account for it. The latter, despite numerous independent 'replications' initially, turned out to be a figment of the imagination. This is why falsifiability is so important.

6. Unpredictability

This problem is also related to the replication difficulty. Parapsychologists cannot in general make predictions before running experiments and then confirm them. Yet, as discussed earlier, even if predictions are not confirmed, researchers often point to some apparent irregularity in the data that suggests, *post-hoc*, that some other psi event occurred.

Yet, if psi is real, one might expect that psi manifestations would be predictable, as least to some extent. With the vast amounts of data that parapsychologists typically collect, it would be straightforward enough to calculate the number of datapoints needed to obtain an effect size of an arbitrary magnitude, and then rerun the study with that number of data points, and find the predicted effect if it is there. It never works out that way. This has led Palmer to admit to 'what appears to be an intractable problem in parapsychology. Until we can predict such outcomes ahead of time, the establishment of lawful relationships still evades us.' This unpredictability, I must point out, is what one would expect to find if the Null hypothesis, rather than the Psi hypothesis, obtains. If the Null hypothesis is true, if there is no such thing as psi, then 'significant results' occur from time to time because of a concatenation of chance factors, flaws in the experimental design, and so on. In such a case, one would not expect any lawfulness in the data, and one would not be able to predict what should occur in the next experiment based on what has happened in the last.

7. Lack of progress

Not only is there a problem of general inconsistency in the data, as discussed above, there has not been any real improvement in this situation over time. Despite the use of modern random event generators and sophisticated statistical analyses, parapsychologists are no closer to making a convincing scientific case for psi than was Joseph Banks Rhine back in the 1930s. There has been no growth in understanding. Psychic phenomena, if they exist, remain as mysterious as ever. No consistent patterns have emerged. Effect sizes do not grow over time as a result of refinements in methodology. No well-articulated theory supported by data has been developed. Indeed, rather than producing a gradual accumulation of knowledge and an evolution of better and better methodology, every decade seems to spawn some new methodology or paradigm or research programme that offers promise of the long-awaited breakthrough, but that gradually loses its glitter. The famous Rhine experiments (e.g. see Rhine *et al.*, 1966/1940) are no longer held up as strong evidence for the Psi-hypothesis. Soal's research (e.g. Soal and Bateman, 1954), once trumpeted, is now forgotten, and for good reason. Targ and Puthoff's remote-viewing experiments (e.g. Targ and Puthoff, 1974) , which showed early promise, now are virtually ignored, again for good reason. The Maimonides research has been difficult to replicate, as Sherman and Roe point out. Jahn's research group at Princeton continues its efforts (e.g. Jahn *et al.*, 2000), but its impact is minimal within modern parapsychology, partly due to methodological problems identified by other parapsychologists and critics alike. There has been no real growth in understanding or in the ability to isolate the putative phenomena over time. New research strategies seem to 'fret and strut their hour upon the stage' and then are heard little more.

8. Methodological weaknesses

Given that psi is defined negatively, and can only assumed to have been present if all possible normal explanations can be ruled out, critics of parapsychology are naturally inclined to look for flaws in the experimental design and execution of research that would account for whatever positive effects parapsychologists have adduced. Of course, this quest is hampered by the fact that experimental reports will only rarely capture sources of error of which the experimenter was oblivious, and so it is not always possible in the first instance to find normal sources of putative psi effects based on the write-ups alone. The nub of the debate between sceptic and proponent is most typically the adequacy of the methodology. I think it fair to say, and I suspect that both Parker and Palmer would agree with me on this, for they have been strong methodological critics of much parapsychological research themselves, methodological weaknesses have, in a large number of studies, vitiated the claim to have demonstrated something paranormal. However, some parapsychologists have argued that even when errors and weaknesses are found, the onus is on the critic to show that the error could have produced the observed effects. That argument is not persuasive however, for the onus is always on the researcher to demonstrate that he or she has done the experiment well, and flaws in design or procedure show that it was not done well, and that perhaps other less obvious methodological problems have also been a factor. The answer is simply to run the experiment again, doing it right this time. That is what is expected in mainstream science. The problem for parapsychology, however, is that the difficulty in replication means that it may not be possible to get the same results a second time, whether the methodology is cleaned up or not.

However, are sceptics too intent on finding methodological flaws and in so doing failing to see the phenomenon of interest? One must, of course, be careful not to throw the baby out with the bathwater when one approaches data that do not fit in with the contemporary scientific worldview. There are many examples were the baby was thrown out, only to be rediscovered years later, crying out for attention. Mesmer argued that he was 'curing' hysterics by means of animal magnetism. Mainstream scientists of the day who were charged with the evaluation of his claims demonstrated that his explanation was wrong, that when the metal rods that he used in his procedure were secretly removed, this made no difference to the outcome, and his patients still responded positively to the procedure. Mesmer would not back down; he stood by his theory of animal magnetism, and the necessity of the metal rods. The scientists would not back down; they stood by their findings that magnetism had nothing to do with it. As a result, Mesmer's clinic was shut down, and both sides in the dispute missed a wonderful opportunity to discover and explore what we now call 'hypnosis'.

I agree with parapsychologists when they declare that if a single instance is known in which 'action at a distance' occurred, we at least know that contemporary science does not encompass the whole story about nature. Yet, if the observed action at a distance is not replicable, then it is questionable whether it has really been demonstrated to occur. Indeed, it is important to remember that hypnosis was ultimately 'discovered', though its true nature remains subject to some debate even today. While not everyone appears to be susceptible to hypnosis, just about anyone can quickly learn to produce hypnosis in susceptible subjects simply by following a standard script. In comparison, over a century of parapsychological inquiry has as yet failed to produce a publicly replicable demonstration of psi, and that despite its long history, parapsychology still lacks the evidence it needs to be placed before the scientific community for judgment. (Hyman, 1977; 1985; 1989). At some point, it seems justifiable to presume that there may not be a baby in the bathwater, and that the Null hypothesis is correct!

9. Reliance on statistical decision-making

Because of the failure to be able to produce a straightforward demonstration of psi ability, such as might be the case if a psychic could reliably predict winning lottery numbers, or if, as Gardner (1957) suggested many years ago, a psychic could cause a fine needle, which is carefully balanced on another needle and housed under a Bell jar from which the air had been evacuated, to rotate, parapsychologists at the more scientific end of the spectrum came to depend more and more upon statistical analyses to demonstrate their putative phenomena. With such an approach, subjects make guesses or make mental attempts to influence random event generators, and then their success or failure is judged by a statistical comparison with what would be expected by chance alone.

Statistical analysis was applied first in psychological research as a means of protecting the researcher against error. It allowed the researcher to evaluate the likelihood that his or her results, no matter how strong the data appeared to the naked eye, could have occurred by chance alone. In recent years, such analysis has been employed to do much more than simply provide guidance about the likelihood that particular data may well have arrived by chance alone. Powerful statistical techniques now exist for finding patterns in data that elude the naked eye, and this provides an important tool for researchers in many domains. Thus, statistical analysis originally helped cool our ardour about what appeared to be meaningful effects in the data, whereas now, those statistical tools are used to find significant effects that we would not otherwise detect. Now, in modern parapsychology (and, alas, in mainstream psychology as well to some extent), statistical analyses are being used to define and defend the importance of differences so small that they would have carried no interest to researchers of a century ago. If subjects score at a rate of 51% when the chance rate is 50%, it is unlikely that anyone would have taken any notice a century ago. Now, provided the sample size is large, such a small difference may well be 'statistically significant'.

There is no reason in principle that such analysis should not also be used in parapsychology, but there is an important difference in the way that it is used in that field. In regular science, statistics are used either to look for covariation amongst well-defined variables, or to evaluate whether a given measurement is affected by the presence or absence of an 'independent' variable. However, in parapsychology, there are no well-defined variables, and there is no way of controlling whether psi (if it exists) is present or absent, and so the statistical process is used, not to evaluate the effect of one or more variables on other measurable variables, but as a basis for inferring the presence of psi itself. One begins with the assumption that a particular mathematical distribution describes the probability distribution of outcomes of a randomly generated event. A subject in some way tries mentally to influence the distribution of outcomes (even if he or she knows nothing about the nature of that distribution, or about the generator that produces it, or even where the generator is physically located). If the outcomes depart from the theoretical distribution to a significant extent, this is taken as evidence that a psi influence caused the departure.

Any such statistically significant departure is viewed as an 'anomaly' relating to psi, and thus is viewed as support for the Psi hypothesis. However, statistical significance tells us nothing about causality. If a person tries to guess or 'intuit' what number will come next in a randomly generated sequence, and succeeds better than one would expect by chance, that tells us absolutely nothing at all with regard to why such results were obtained. The departure from chance expectation could be due to any number of influences — a non-random 'random generator', various methodological flaws, or . . . Zeus. (I could posit that Zeus exists and likes to torment parapsychologists, and thereby gives them significant outcomes from time to time, but does not allow replication outside parapsychology. The significant outcome would provide as much support for my hypothesis that Zeus exists as it does for the Psi hypothesis that the human subject's volition caused the results.)

Joseph Banks Rhine, whose psi research was motivated in part by the desire to find scientific evidence for post-mortem survival, passionately believed in the scientific method, and consequently he shepherded parapsychology into the laboratory and into the research paradigms favoured by experimental psychologists — studies with specific targets, controlled conditions and statistical analysis of data. It was at that juncture that, despite the admirable effort to harness emerging social science technology, formal parapsychology began to lose touch with the very experiences that originally motivated its pursuit. Rather than focusing on conditions that seem to be conducive to paranormal experiences such as telepathy in everyday life, and then seeking at first to understand the experience in terms of normal psychology, these laboratory studies focused only on one explanation of such experiences — the notion that somehow there is a transfer of information that does not involve any known sensory apparatus or energy. Thus, the laboratory approach involved trying to 'send' information from one brain to another, or trying to 'read' objects hidden from view, or trying to predict the outcome of the roll of dice before they are thrown. Note that such activities have virtually nothing to do with human experiences that seem to many to be paranormal. Worse, verification of the supposed success of the psi task became a statistical one. No longer was it a question of whether a person had dreamed of his father's funeral in detail, not knowing that miles away his father had died, but rather, what is the series of cards that will next be turned up?

10. Problem of theory

That quintessential investigator Sherlock Holmes once opined: 'It is a capital mistake to theorize before one has data. Insensibly one begins to twist facts to suit theories, instead of theories to suit facts.' This is also good advice when it comes to theorizing in parapsychology. The database does not at this time justify the development of explanatory theory, for, as I have discussed above, it is far from clear that there is anything to explain. Notwithstanding the absence of good evidence, there have been many attempts to develop theories to explain putative psi phenomena, among them the Conformance Behaviour model (Stanford, 1990); Decision Augmentation Theory (May, Utts and Spottiswoode, 1995); a teleological (goal-seeking) theory (Schmidt, 1975); a quantum mechanical theory (Walker, 1984); the Thermal Fluctuation Model (Mattuck, 1982) that proposes that the 'mind' somehow alters the outcome of an event by manipulating the thermal energy of molecules; and, as described in this Issue, Pallikari's statistical balancing theory (discussed below). Such theorizing in the absence of reliable data, especially when it attempts to interpret quantum mechanical theory in such a way as to accommodate psi, lends an unjustified patina of scientific respectability to parapsychology, especially in the eyes of those who are outside the world of physics.

Jeffers' paper critically discusses the argument often heard within parapsychology that quantum physics in some way or another can accommodate/explain psi. Pallikari, on the other hand, begins with the assumption that psychokinesis occurs, and her analysis concludes that it only operates at a micro-level, and therefore does not show up at the macro level. She proposes a theoretical approach to understanding such micro-PK, and inherent in this notion is the idea of statistical balancing in the long run, so that macro-PK will not be observed. While I admire Pallikari's efforts, they are premature, for the problem remains that to date there are no substantive empirical data to justify such theorizing. Of course, her conclusion that psychokinesis does not show up except at the micro level is at variance with what many other parapsychologists have claimed to have observed at the macro level.

11. Failure to jibe with other areas of science

A major criticism of parapsychology is that it fails to jibe with other areas of science. The late neuropsychologist Donald Hebb (1978) once commented that if parapsychology is right, then physics and biology and neuroscience are horribly wrong in some fundamental respects. He went on to say that science has been wrong before, but that parapsychology would need very strong evidence if it was going to be able to challenge successfully the current state of knowledge in mainstream science. For example, psi influences, unlike any known energy, are invariant over distance. Time produces no barrier either, apparently, for such influences are said to be able to operate backwards and forwards in time. If the 'out-of-body experience' is a psi effect, then it would apparently demonstrate that the complex mechanisms of the brain, while extremely vulnerable to disruption or total destruction as a result of disease or injury, are apparently unnecessary for perception or cognition in the out-of-body individual. To be fair, some parapsychologists have argued that their data tends to support the idea that the brain does indeed process incoming psi. Yet such processing is not a simple matter, for as Beyerstein (1987) noted, in pointing to the profound implications that psi would have for the neurosciences. He pointed out that perception, memory and emotion involve extremely complex neurochemical configurations that are the result of the spatiotemporal integration of activity in millions of widely-distributed neurons and their internal components. *Extrasensory* perception would by definition bypass the activity of peripheral receptors and nerves that normally determine these central electrochemical configurations. To experience the emotion or the percept, then, any hypothetical 'psi signal' would have to produce the corresponding central electrochemical configurations directly, which would involve influencing the internal chemical processes of millions of neurons in the correct sequences and in the appropriate anatomical pathways. This, in the view of neuroscientists in general, is highly unlikely. Yet while there are attempts to interpret physical theory in such as way as to accommodate psi (e.g. Pallikari in this Issue), parapsychologists appear disinterested in the contradictions between parapsychology and neuroscience (Kirkland, 2000).

On the other hand, failure to jibe with other areas of science is in a very real sense the *sine qua non* of parapsychology. As discussed earlier, something is only considered paranormal if it defies current scientific models of reality.

12. Disinterest in competing hypotheses

Unfortunately, the focus in parapsychology seems to be more on finding the anomaly than on explaining the experience. The retreat into the laboratory has led to a focus on statistical deviations that thoroughly distracts researchers from seeking other, more prosaic, 'normal' explanations, for psychic experiences. That is too bad, for as I have indicated earlier, such experiences warrant study in their own right, regardless of whether there is any need to appeal to paranormal explanations. I have many times argued (e.g. Alcock, 1981) that even if psi does not exist, we should still expect that most people will have experiences in their lifetimes that *seem* to yield to no other explanation than a psychic one, and I have explained just why that should be so and have offered explanations as to how various paranormal experiences can be the result of normal (and sometimes abnormal) brain function. Many other psychologists (e.g. Beyerstein, 1987–8; 1988; Blackmore, 1982; Marks, 2000; Neher, 1990) have also provided substantial and detailed explanations with regard to how normal and abnormal psychological processes are capable of producing all the elements of paranormal experiences. This information should be of great interest, one might think, to parapsychologists, but the question of normal causality seems usually to be dismissed out-of-hand as being unimportant to the study of the paranormal.

Several of the articles in this Special Issue address some of the factors that might explain why some people believe that they have witnessed or experienced paranormal phenomena even if they have not.

1. Ultimately, 'real-life' accounts of paranormal experiences, the very sort of accounts that led to parapsychological research in the first place, rely on processes of perception, interpretation and memory. French provides a good discussion of how such factors as hallucinations, imagery, suggestibility, dissociative tendencies and unreliable memory may be the well-spring of many such accounts.

2. Dean and Kelly are the preeminent critics of astrology and its claims, and they note that astrology actually seems to 'work' for many people — perhaps many millions of people — around the globe. Thus, there is widespread belief in astrology just as there is in parapsychology, and there is a similarity between the two, in that both essentially involve correlations between two events, and the imputation of causality. In parapsychology, one 'wishes' or 'guesses' — either in real life or in the laboratory, and then any significant correlation between wish/guess and outcome is taken as evidence of causality. For example, in a psychokinesis study, a subject wishes to produce high numbers in the output of a random number generator, while in a telepathy study, the subject essentially guesses at what the sender is sending. Similarly in astrology, the astrologer produces a description of one's future, and to the extent that it seems to correspond with what happens later, it is taken to support the notion that the position of the stars at birth is related causally to later events in one's life. Dean and Kelly show that astrology seems 'to work' because of the cognitive errors that individuals make in reacting to their

horoscopes — the fallacy of personal validation. A similar explanation can be applied to the readings offered by psychics. What is particularly important to the discussion of parapsychology in their article is the pervasive extent to which people can come to strongly believe in a demonstrably false system of causality.

3. Brugger and Taylor adduce evidence that supports their contention that believers in paranormal phenomena more readily perceive meaningful associations in random stimuli than do disbelievers, and argue that believers develop an 'illusion of control', perceiving a causal relationship between their actions and environmental events that produces a strong belief in a paranormal causation of the event. They further argue that believers tend not to test alternative hypotheses. To me, their paper is a particularly important one, for it shows the way towards understanding how the exigencies of both everyday life and the parapsychology laboratory can be expected to generate strong impressions that something 'psychic' has occurred.

These are some of the reasons that I would urge caution in one's approach to parapsychological claims. However, no doubt parapsychologists would argue that I am being unfair and overly negative.

This leads me to another question: *Has mainstream science been unfair?* Parker contends that mainstream science has not given parapsychology a fair hearing. I respectfully disagree. I have detailed elsewhere (Alcock, 1987; 1990) how conventional science and mainstream psychology have actually provided numerous opportunities over the years for parapsychologists to bring their work to a larger scientific audience. Indeed, when the American Society for Psychical Research was founded in 1885, its membership included several prominent psychologists of the day, most of whom eventually left the organization when they failed to find any evidence of psychic phenomena. Again, in the early part of the twentieth century, other prominent scientists and psychologists were open to the study of parapsychology, and some undertook studies of their own but gave up when their efforts failed to produce results. In the 1930s, not only did the American Psychological Association sponsor a round-table discussion of parapsychology, but a 1938 poll found that 89% of psychologists at that time felt that the study of ESP was a legitimate scientific enterprise (Moore, 1977). Various scientific publications over the years, including prestigious psychological journals such as *Psychological Bulletin*, have brought parapsychological research and views to the non-parapsychological scientific community. Indeed, between 1950 and 1982, more than fifteen-hundred parapsychological papers were abstracted in the American Psychological Association's *Psychological Abstracts* (McConnell, 1977). Nonetheless, mainstream science continues to reject parapsychology's claims. In my mind, this is not because of some unfair bias, but simply because parapsychologists have not been able to produce data that persuade the larger scientific community that they have a genuine subject matter to study.

This lack of acceptance by science no doubt creates cognitive dissonance on the part of those parapsychologists who are convinced that they do have real phenomena. This dissonance can be resolved either by assuming that the exclusion from the halls of mainstream science is unfair and unjustified, or that there is some reason other than lack of persuasive data that underlies the rejection. As an instance of the latter, the prominent parapsychologist Charles Tart once wrote that sceptical scientists may be unconsciously so afraid of their own psychic abilities that they have to attack any evidence that might provoke knowledge of their own ability (Tart, 1982; 1984). Parker, in this Issue, argues that perhaps sceptical psychologists do not really want to resolve the issue about the reality of psi for fear of the 'unwanted implications' for psychology if it were shown that psi really does exist. He may be correct, but I doubt it. In my many years in the field of psychology, I have never detected anything other than simple disinterest in parapsychology from the vast majority of psychologists. They simply assume that psi phenomena have never been shown to exist. On the other hand, I am certain that were there suddenly to be produced compelling evidence for the reality of psi, parapsychologists would be knocked over in the stampede by experimental psychologists to explore an exciting new area of research.

Can the psi question be resolved? Parker argues that the technology now exists that would allow a resolution of the question of whether psi exists, and that it would be relatively straightforward to resolve the question, were it not for a lack of funding from mainstream science. He also states that parapsychology might turn out to present genuine phenomena — or, it could turn out to be based on a mixture of fraud, artefact and subjective validation.

I would certainly applaud any effort and investment directed at resolving the psi issue, but I do not think that it is really possible to resolve it, unless of course compelling and replicable demonstrations of the existence of psi are forthcoming. I do not believe that parapsychologists give the Null hypothesis a proper chance, and I cannot conceive of any research that could serve to persuade parapsychologists that psi does not exist. It would be far easier, were good and reliable data available, to persuade sceptics of the reality of psi than to dissuade parapsychologists. What evidence can one produce with regard to 'disproving' the psi hypothesis? Certainly not carefully executed studies that fail to replicate, that fail to produce any evidence of a psi anomaly. Those are too easily explained away in terms of the 'experimenter effect' or simply ignored, as is the case with Jeffers' research. Finding prosaic explanations for a given data set may persuade parapsychologists that, in that particular instance, there was no evidence for psi, but what about all the other data sets yet to come? Parapsychologists can neither tell us under what circumstances psi, if it is real, does not occur, nor can they tell us how it would be possible to disprove its existence.

While some parapsychologists, as noted earlier, ascribe hidden motivations to the continued resistance of mainstream scientists to bring parapsychology into the scientific fold, I judge it unlikely that parapsychologists would under any circumstances abandon their belief in and pursuit of the paranormal. In fact, while Brugger and Taylor propose the joint collaboration of traditional parapsychology and neuroscience in the hope that findings from prospective research conducted by representatives of two apparently conflicting views will most likely be taken seriously by both sides, they also foresee what many parapsychologists would consider to be an unacceptable downside: 'We thus anticipate that, although psi would vanish from the scene as a process of information transfer, it would live on as a phenomenon of subjective probability worthy of scientific investigation.'

Finally, even if one were to produce a set of circumstances that would lead some parapsychologists to abandon the psi hypothesis, parapsychology as a whole would carry on much as it always has, and the conclusions of those who left the field would be downplayed or ignored, just as were Blackmore's conclusions when she pronounced that she had become sceptical with regard to psi and was leaving the field, or Wiseman's as he had become more and more identified with the sceptical position (Wiseman, 1997). Of course, for those who appropriate for themselves the label 'parapsychologist', but do not really subscribe to the appropriateness of a scientific examination of psi in any case, any agreement by science-oriented parapsychologists that resolves the psi question in a negative direction would carry no weight at all.

Thus, the search for psi will go on for a long time to come, for I can think of nothing that would ever persuade those who pursue it that the Null hypothesis is probably true. Yet, as this search goes on, those of us who are sceptics should applaud and support the approach taken by parapsychologists who have contributed to this Special Issue — not because we agree with their conclusions, for we shall continue to scrutinize and, when appropriate, find fault with their methodology and challenge their interpretations — but because they share our belief in the power of the scientific method to reveal truth in nature. I do marvel at their tenacity, however, for they labour in search of psi despite a lack of the evidentiary and other rewards that are earned by mainstream scientists in their research. Yet, that being said, and as I have stated before (Alcock, 1985; 1987), I continue to believe that parapsychology is, at bottom, motivated by belief in search of data, rather than data in search of explanation. It is the belief in a larger view of human personality and existence than is accorded to human beings by modern science that keeps parapsychology engaged in their search. Because of this belief, parapsychologists never really give the Null hypothesis a chance.

Acknowledgements
I wish to thank Jean Burns and Anthony Freeman for their very helpful comments with regard to the draft version of this manuscript.

References

Alcock, J.E. (1981), *Parapsychology: Science or Magic?* (London: Pergamon).
Alcock, J.E. (1985), 'Parapsychology as a "spiritual science" ', in *A Skeptic's Handbook of Parapsychology*, ed. P. Kurtz (Buffalo, NY: Prometheus Books), pp. 537–69.
Alcock, J.E. (1987), 'Parapsychology: science of the anomalous or search for the soul?', *Behavior and Brain Sciences*, **10** (4), pp. 553–65.
Alcock, J.E. (1990), *Science and Supernature: A Critical Appraisal of Parapsychology* (Buffalo, NY: Prometheus Books).
Beyerstein, B.L. (1987), 'Neuroscience and psi-ence', *Behavioral and Brain Sciences*, **10** (4), pp. 571–2.

Beyerstein, B.L. (1987–8), 'The brain and consciousness: implications for psi phenomena', *The Skeptical Inquirer*, **12** (2), pp. 163–73.

Beyerstein, B.L. (1988), 'The neuropathology of spiritual possession', *The Skeptical Inquirer*, **12** (3), pp. 248–62.

Blackmore, S.J. (1982), *Beyond the Body: An Investigation of Out-of-Body Experiences* (London: Heinemann).

Gardner, M. (1957), *Fads and Fallacies in the Name of Science* (New York: Dover).

Hebb, D.O. (1978), Personal Communication, cited in Alcock, J.E. (1981), *Parapsychology: Science or Magic?* (New York: Pergamon).

Hyman, R. (1977), 'The case against parapsychology', *The Humanist*, **37**, pp. 37–49.

Hyman, R. (1985), 'A critical overview of parapsychology', in *A Skeptic's Handbook of Parapsychology*, ed. P. Kurtz (Buffalo, NY: Prometheus Books), pp. 3–96.

Hyman, R. (1989), *The Elusive Quarry: A Scientific Appraisal of Psychical Research* (Buffalo, NY: Prometheus Books).

Jahn, R.G. (1982), 'The persistent paradox of psychic phenomena — an engineering perspective', *Proceedings of the IEEE*, **70**, pp. 136–70.

Jahn, R., Dunne, B., Bradish, G., Dobyns, Y., Lettieri, A., Nelson, R., Mischo, J., Boller, E., Böösch, H., Vaitl, D., Houtkooper, J. and Walter, B. (2000), 'Mind/Machine Interaction Consortium: PortREG Replication Experiments', *Journal of Scientific Exploration*, **14** (4), pp. 499–555.

Keen, M., Ellison, A. and Fontana, D. (1999), 'The Scole Report', *Proceedings of the SPR*, **58**, pp. 150–392.

Kirkland, K. (2000), 'Paraneuroscience?', *The Skeptical Inquirer*, **24** (3), pp. 40–3.

Marks, D. (2000), *The Psychology of the Psychic* (Buffalo, NY: Prometheus Books).

Mattuck, R.D. (1982), 'Some possible thermal quantum fluctuation models for psychokinetic influence on light', *Psychoenergetics*, **4**, pp. 211–25.

May, E.C, Utts, J.M. and Spottiswoode, S.J.P. (1995), 'Decision Augmentation Theory: towards a model of anomalous phenomena', *Journal of Parapsychology*, **59** (3), pp. 195–220.

McConnell, R.A. (1977), 'The resolution of conflicting beliefs about the ESP evidence', *Journal of Parapsychology*, **41**, pp. 198–214.

Moore, L. (1977), *In Search of White Crows* (Oxford: Oxford University Press).

Neher, A. (1990), *The Psychology of Transcendence* (New York: Dover).

Pratt, J.G. (1974), 'In search of a consistent scorer', in *New Directions in Parapsychology*, ed. J. Beloff (London: Elek Science).

Rhine, J. B., Pratt, J.G., Stuart, C.E., Smith, B.M. and Greenwood, J.A. (1966), *Extra-Sensory Perception after Sixty Years* (Boston: Bruce Humphries). (Original work published 1940.)

Schmidt, H. (1975), 'Towards a mathematical theory of psi', *Journal of the American Society for Psychical Research*, **69** (4), pp. 301–20.

Soal, S.G. and Bateman, F. (1954), *Modern Experiments in Telepathy* (New Haven, CT: Yale University Press).

Stanford, R.G. (1990), 'An experimentally testable model for spontaneous psi events', in *Advances in Parapsychological Research*, **6**, ed. S. Krippner (Jefferson, NC: McFarland and Co), pp. 54–167.

Targ, R. and Puthoff, H.E. (1974), 'Information transfer under conditions of sensory shielding', *Nature*, **252**, p. 602.

Tart, C. (1982), 'The controversy about psi: two psychological theories', *Journal of Parapsychology*, **46**, pp. 313–20.

Tart, C. (1984), 'Acknowledging and dealing with the fear of psi', *Journal of the American Society for Psychical Research*, **78**, pp. 133–43.

Walker, E.H. (1984), 'A review of criticisms of the quantum mechanical theory of psi phenomena', *Journal of Parapsychology*, **48**, pp. 277–332.

Wiseman, R. (1997), *Deception and Self-Deception: Investigating Psychics* (Buffalo, NY: Prometheus Books).

John Palmer

ESP in the Ganzfeld

Analysis of a Debate

Abstract: *This paper reviews the debate over the evidence for ESP provided by experiments using the ganzfeld technique, a simple method used to induce a mild altered state of consciousness. The quantitative literature review technique called meta-analysis has played a prominent role in this controversy. The first question addressed by the reviewer is whether the data establish that ESP in the ganzfeld is replicable. Issues discussed include the effect of multiple analyses, the 'file-drawer' problem and statistical errors. The second question asks, if the effect is real, can it be explained by methodological artifacts? Potential flaws discussed include sensory leakage, problems of randomization and participant fraud. The reviewer's first conclusion is that the aggregate database does provide evidence for a genuine psi effect. However, heterogeneity of results across experimenters indicates that the phenomenon is not easily replicable. The second conclusion is that conventional alternative explanations offered for the observed results tend to be conceivable, but even critics sometimes agree that they are implausible.*

One of the more pressing questions in the debate about the reality of psychic phenomena is whether psi effects in the laboratory are repeatable, or replicable. Some critics of psi research have insisted that results be replicable on demand, but this requirement is usually not realistic for research involving psychological processes such as psi. Most commentators are willing to accept statistical replication, which essentially means that replication is successful more frequently than expected by chance. In recent years, a technique called meta-analysis has been widely used in psychology and other sciences to address this question in a relatively objective fashion. Because of the important role that meta-analysis has played in the ESP-ganzfeld debate, a brief tutorial seems appropriate at this point for readers who might not be conversant with the technique.

Correspondence:
John Palmer, Rhine Research Center, 2741 Campus Walk Aveune, Building 500, Durham, NC 27705, USA. *Email: john@rhine.org*

Journal of Consciousness Studies, **10**, No. 6–7, 2003, pp. 51–68

The Basics of Meta-Analysis

Meta-analysts begin with studies gleaned from all reputable published sources they can find that address a common hypothesis or effect. The core procedure is to convert the outcomes to a *p*-value, convert the *p*-value to a *z*-score, and then sum the *z*-scores and divide the sum by the square root of the number of studies. This provides a statistic called a Stouffer *Z*, and the *p*-value associated with the Stouffer *Z* is then consulted to determine if the group of experiments considered as a whole is statistically significant. Meta-analysts also pay great attention to the effect size, a standardized measure of the strength of the relationship. The simplest and most widely applicable way to compute the effect size for a single study is to take the *z* derived from the *p*-value and divide it by the square root of the number of scores. The effect size for the sample as a whole is then simply the mean of the effect sizes for the individual studies. A study is sometimes considered to have been successfully replicated if the effect size of the second study falls within the 95% confidence intervals of the effect size of the first study. Meta-analysts also sometimes consider the dispersion, or heterogeneity, of the individual study outcomes. Significant heterogeneity is sometimes taken as evidence for a lack of replicability. Finally, meta-analysts often try to assess if a sample produces confirmation of a given hypothesis because of methodological artifacts. The most common approach to this issue is to code the individual studies for methodological quality and correlate these quality codes with the effect sizes or *z*-scores of the studies. A significant positive correlation means that methodological artifacts played an important role and inferences that the hypothesis is really true are suspect.

Although meta-analysis is often touted as an 'objective' way to tackle the issues it addresses, and it is indeed an improvement over previous, seat-of-the-pants, methods, there are a number of subjective decisions that meta-analysts routinely must make to implement the procedure. For example, when is a study similar enough, conceptually or methodologically, to what might be called the population norm to be included in the sample? Meta-analysts call this the 'apples and oranges' problem, and there is no recipe that can guarantee consensus when borderline examples are confronted. Another area of possible disagreement is how to derive quality codes. Milton (1996) attempted to develop a set of uniform standards for coding psi studies by polling psi researchers, but there was, as one would expect, a lack of complete agreement about the necessity of eliminating many of the flaws. Some meta-analysts believe that studies should be removed from the sample entirely if they fail to meet some threshold of methodological purity, whereas others maintain that all the studies should be included in the correlations. Finally, and most importantly, what outcome is necessary or sufficient to support the claim of replicability? Is a significant Stouffer *Z* enough? Is a significant Stouffer *Z* unnecessary if the mean effect size from the second sample falls within the 95% confidence intervals of the mean effect size of the first sample? Does significant heterogeneity mean replicability has failed, whatever the other outcomes? Whether or not one finds the ESP-ganzfeld results to be replicable will depend in part on how one answers these questions.

Meta-analysis requires at least a moderately large group of studies testing the same hypothesis with comparable methodology. Ideally, they should be conceptual if not direct replications. Parapsychologists take the replication issue very seriously, in part because it is demanded by their critics, and so they are very conscientious about replicating both their own studies and related studies of others. This has led to a large number of meta-analyses of various experimental paradigms, including attempts to influence by psychokinesis (PK) mechanical dice throwing, the output of electronic random number generators (RNGs), and biological processes. On the ESP side, there have been meta-analyses of forced-choice precognition studies such as card-guessing, free-response ESP studies not involving the induction of an altered state of consciousness, and the relations between ESP and extraversion and the belief in ESP. For a summary, see Radin (1997). However, the paradigm to which meta-analysis has been applied most extensively involves the application of an altered state induction technique called the ganzfeld to facilitate ESP performance. The debate about this body of research will occupy the remainder of this paper.

The Ganzfeld Procedure

The ganzfeld is a mild form of sensory deprivation or isolation developed originally by psychologists (Bertini, Lewis and Witkin, 1964). The credit for first applying the technique to parapsychology is jointly shared by Charles Honorton, William Braud and Adrian Parker, although it has been most closely identified with Honorton. For Honorton (1978), the technique had the potential to facilitate ESP because it created what he called an 'internal attention state'; in the absence of competing external stimulation, participants are encouraged to focus their attention inward, thereby increasing the likelihood that they will identify subtle mental impressions. In a similar vein it can be argued that the ganzfeld facilitates mental imagery, because the brain is otherwise starved of information. However, Rex Stanford conducted a series of experiments that collectively suggested that ganzfeld success is more probably attributable to its tendency to increase the spontaneity of participants' thought processes than to the creation of an internal attention state (e.g. Stanford et al., 1989).

The ganzfeld is designed to minimize *patterned* sensory stimulation from the environment. In the visual mode, this is accomplished by the low-tech procedure of affixing halves of ping-pong balls over the receiver's eyes and having them look into a red light. This creates a homogenous pinkish-red visual field. In the auditory mode, it is accomplished by having the receiver listen to pink noise through headphones. Pink noise is white noise with the high-frequency components filtered out. This adjustment makes the sound more pleasant, and it resembles the sound of a waterfall. The reason for maintaining unpatterned stimulation, rather than, for example, just having receivers close their eyes, is to maintain a sufficient level of arousal and discourage the receiver from falling asleep. It is also common in ganzfeld experiments to precede the test period with progressive relaxation suggestions played through headphones. This has the effect of minimizing kinesthetic stimulation, which is also facilitated by having the receiver seated in a comfortable recliner. The relaxation suggestions are customarily followed by hypnotic-like suggestions for success in the ensuing ESP task.

The receiver stays in the ganzfeld environment for from 30 to 45 minutes following cessation of the relaxation suggestions. Receivers are instructed that during this time they should report out loud any mental images or impressions that come to them. These utterances are tape recorded and written down by the experimenter, who is located in another room.

The targets consist of pictorial material, which can be 'static' (e.g. photographs, art prints) or 'dynamic' (e.g. movie clips). It is generally considered desirable that the targets also be emotionally evocative. The target for a given session is randomly selected from a large pool of potential targets. In most ganzfeld experiments a sender in a third room periodically observes the target during the time the receiver is attempting to gain impressions, trying to 'send' the information to the receiver.

Following the reception period, the experimenter, who is blind to the target, reads back to the receiver the notes taken of their utterances, to refresh the receiver's memory. Then the experimenter removes the headphones and ping-pong balls and commences the judging task. The receiver is shown four possible targets, one of which is a duplicate of the real target, and asked to rank them based on their correspondence to his or her impressions. By chance the correct target will be ranked first 25% of the time. This is called a 'direct hit'. If the target is ranked first or second, it is called a 'binary hit', with a chance probability of 50%. Because a ganzfeld session comprises only one trial, success cannot be demonstrated statistically for a single session, although sometimes the correspondence of the mentation to the target is so close in detail that success is obvious. Success is claimed statistically if the mean hit rate or effect size over a group of sessions is significantly greater than chance.

The Ganzfeld Databases

Over one hundred formal ganzfeld experiments have been published over a twenty five year period from 1974 to 1999. I will compartmentalize them into three separate databases, defined in relation to a pivotal set of ten or eleven experiments conducted under the supervision of Charles Honorton at the Psychophysical Research Laboratories in the 1980s. Thus, for this article the databases will be labelled as the 'Pre-PRL', 'PRL' and 'Post-PRL' databases.

The first formal analysis of ganzfeld studies was conducted by critic Ray Hyman. Until Hyman arrived on the scene, criticism of this research focused on attempts to demonstrate that isolated 'crucial' experiments, usually conducted with so-called 'gifted' participants, could conceivably have been caused by trickery by the participant, the experimenter, or both. The main proponent of this approach was C.E.M. Hansel (1989). Hyman (1981) criticized Hansel's approach as, among other things, unfalsifiable, and advocated a type of criticism more in line with what one finds in mainstream psychology. The ganzfeld debate reflects this new approach, as illustrated by the prominent role played by meta-analysis.

Is the Ganzfeld Replicable?

The meta-analyses address two separate issues, and it is important to keep them separate. The first is the replicability issue and the second is whether, assuming the effect is indeed replicable (in effect, real), can the success be adequately accounted for by methodological artifacts. We will begin with the replicability issue. Is there an effect at all?

The Pre-PRL Database

Hyman (1985) chose the ganzfeld paradigm as representing the best research parapsychologists had to offer and asked Honorton to send him published reports of all the ganzfeld studies published up to that time (1981). The forty two studies Honorton provided constitute the Pre-PRL database. According to Hyman (1985), Honorton had originally claimed that 55% of these studies provided significant positive results. This figure became the jumping-off point for his critique, which sought to demonstrate that the true figure is not significantly greater than the 25% expected by chance.

Multiple Analyses. The most important of Hyman's criticisms concerns multiple analyses. This problem arises when a researcher conducts multiple statistical tests of the same hypothesis and considers the hypothesis confirmed if any one of them is significant. Assuming the tests are all independent of one another, the criterion level of significance, or alpha level, is not the customary 0.05, but 0.05 divided by the number of analyses. Although such analyses are rarely even close to being independent, a modestly significant result still can quickly lose its significance when multiple analyses are taken into account. A good way around the problem is to specify in advance which analysis one considers to be crucial, but that was rarely done in the ganzfeld reports. Multiple analyses could have occurred in a variety of ways. For example, success could be based on direct hits, binary hits, average rank, or some other method. Sometimes the judging was done both by the participants themselves and by outsiders working with transcripts of the participants' mentation reports. Sometimes the mean of the experimental group was compared both to the theoretical mean score and the score obtained by a control group.

Honorton (1985) conceded that multiple analysis was a problem. His solution was to conduct a meta-analysis restricted to the twenty eight studies (from ten laboratories) that reported direct hits, the most common scoring scheme employed in the database. These twenty eight studies yielded a Stouffer Z of 6.60 ($p < 10^{-9}$).[1] Twenty three of the twenty eight studies were in the positive direction, and twelve of the twenty three were statistically significant. It is noteworthy

---

[1] All p-values are one-tailed unless noted otherwise.

that the twenty eight direct-hit (DH) studies were also the ones that got the best results. According to Palmer and Broughton (2000), the mean effect size for the twenty eight direct hits studies was 0.263, compared to 0.055 for the remaining eleven studies for which effect sizes could be calculated. The hit rate for the DH studies, based on an adjustment that rendered each study as having a 25% chance of success (four target alternatives) was subsequently calculated to be 35%, with the 95% confidence interval from 28% to 43% (Bem and Honorton, 1994).

The File-Drawer. Another of Hyman's criticisms concerned a point well known to meta-analysts, referred to as the 'file-drawer' problem. The assumption is made that unsuccessful studies tend not to get published, so that the published studies represent a positively biased sample of all those conducted. Hyman speculated that in the present case many of the studies in the file drawer were aborted before completion because the results did not look as though they would be significant. In support of his speculation, Hyman found, contrary to what one would ordinarily expect, that the studies with the smallest sample sizes got the best results. One explanation for such a result is that low-N studies with poor results were back in the file drawer.

The flip side of failing to report low-N studies with poor results is to report low-N studies with good results, studies one would not have reported had the results been poor. Hyman cited two apparent examples of such 'retrospective studies' in the database: one was a composite of sessions conducted for visiting film crews (Honorton, 1976) and the other from a classroom demonstration (Child and Levi, 1979). The latter study, incidentally, yielded significant psi-missing and removing it would have helped support the positive psi hypothesis.

While noting that a survey of ganzfeld researchers by Blackmore (1980) had failed to find much evidence for unpublished ganzfeld studies, as well as the policy of the Parapsychological Association that its affiliated journals not discriminate against publication of negative results, Honorton's most effective rebuttal was to employ a statistical technique developed by meta-analyst Robert Rosenthal (1979) to estimate the number of studies that would need to be in the file-drawer for the overall result of the DH studies to be reduced to non-significance. The number he came up with was 423, or more than 12,000 sessions. Although 12,000 is probably an overestimate because Hyman's aborted studies would have low Ns, the idea that even half that number of sessions were conducted and not reported seems unlikely, particularly since a typical ganzfeld experiment takes about two hours to conduct and the number of parapsychologists is quite small. As for the negative correlation between success and sample size, Honorton noted that it could also be caused by a loss of experimenter enthusiasm as a long study drags on. He cited evidence from two large-N studies that scores declined when the number of sessions per day was increased so the study could be completed within the specified time frame.

Statistical Errors. Although Hyman (1985) included statistical errors among his methodological flaws, these more properly belong under replicability, because they impact whether there is an effect, independently of whether or not that effect is paranormal. Hyman found twelve of the forty two studies to have statistical errors, the most common of which (four cases) was failing to add probabilities more extreme than the designated one when computing Fisher's exact probability test. Honorton (1985) agreed that six of the suspect twelve studies had statistical errors but made no comment about the other six.

A Meeting of the Minds. Following the publication of the debate described above, Hyman and Honorton (1986) published a 'joint communiqué' summing up their impressions at that time. In this paper, Hyman joins in the following quote:

> Although we probably still differ on the magnitude of the biases contributed by multiple testing, retrospective experiments, and the file-drawer problem, we agree that the overall significance observed in these studies cannot be reasonably explained by these selective factors. Something beyond selective reporting or inflated significance levels seems to be producing the nonchance outcomes. (p. 352)

However, the authors continued to disagree on our second question, whether the results could be attributed to methodological flaws, a topic to be addressed later in this paper.

The PRL Database

The PRL studies were designed by Honorton to remedy the methodological criticisms raised by Hyman (1985; Hyman and Honorton, 1986). This database is by far the most homogenous of the three, as all the experiments were conducted at the same laboratory using the same basic procedure (Bem and Honorton, 1994; Honorton *et al.*, 1990). It consists of eleven studies, one of which was removed from some analyses for methodological reasons. The remaining ten comprised 329 trials completed by 240 different receivers. The hit rate was 32%, $z = 2.89$, $p = 0.002$; Stouffer $Z = 2.55$, $p = 0.005$, with a 95% confidence interval ranging from 30% to 35%. Nine of the ten results were in the positive direction, but only one was independently significant.

It is worth mentioning that a significant negative correlation of -0.64, $p < 0.05$, two-tailed, was found between the sample sizes and effect sizes of the ten studies. This mimics the trend found by Hyman (1985) for the Pre-PRL database, but it clearly cannot be attributed to unreported low-N studies, as all trials contributing to the database were reported.

The legitimacy of the statistical significance as such of the PRL database has not been challenged.

The Post-PRL Databases

At the end of their report on the PRL studies (which, incidentally, was published in a prestigious mainstream psychology journal, *Psychological Bulletin*), Bem and Honorton (1994) noted that a final conclusion about the evidentiality of the ganzfeld paradigm would depend upon the success of subsequent investigators in replicating the PRL studies. This call inspired a number of other parapsychologists to attempt their own ganzfeld experiments, conforming to varying degrees with the PRL procedure. Milton and Wiseman (1999) published a meta-analysis of thirty post-PRL ganzfeld studies that collectively were quite close to chance, with a Stouffer Z of 0.70, $p = 0.24$, and an effect size of 0.013. It thus appeared that the PRL studies had not been successfully replicated.

A Meta-Meta-Analysis. The Milton and Wiseman analysis was criticized by Storm and Ertel (2001), primarily for ignoring the pre-PRL data in their calculations. The authors also came up with a set of eleven ganzfeld studies published between 1982 and 1986 that reported direct hits but had not been considered by any of the previous analysts. (If they had been, they would have been included in the pre-PRL database.) These studies were independently significant with a Stouffer Z of 3.46, but when the studies were weighted for quality of the methodology, the Z dropped dramatically to 1.06.

Storm and Ertel reasoned that the best measure of overall success in the ganzfeld would be a figure based on all the databases combined, provided that they did not differ significantly among themselves. Although the extended pre-PRL ('old') database was found to have produced significantly higher scores than the PRL and post-PRL ('new') databases by an ω^2 method suggested by Hays (1963), they did not differ significantly by another method suggested more recently by Cohen (1988, p.179), and the authors decided this latter criterion was preferable. Combining the twenty eight pre-PRL direct hit studies identified by Honorton, their own eleven pre-PRL studies, the ten PRL studies, and the thirty post-PRL studies, they arrived at a sample of seventy nine studies. The Stouffer Z was 5.66, $p = 7.8 \times 10^{-9}$, with an effect size of 0.138.

Storm and Ertel also pointed out that the possibility of below-chance scores (so-called psi-missing) needs to be taken into account. Although such results are uncommon in ganzfeld experiments, they do occur occasionally. The authors cited statistical evidence that both the pre-PRL and post-PRL databases were significantly heterogeneous, a point I will return to later in this paper.

In response, Milton and Wiseman (2001) argued that it was illegitimate to include the pre-PRL database because of the methodological weaknesses pointed out by Hyman (1985), and if it was to be incorporated, the non-DH studies should have been included as well, as such studies were included in the post-PRL sample. They also complained that Storm and Ertel applied quality codes only to the eleven new pre-PRL studies and the codes themselves were inadequate. They pointed out further that the heterogeneity statistic did not say anything directly about psi-missing. Finally, they complained that z-scores for individual studies were based on the normal approximation to the binomial, even in cases where the sample sizes were too small to justify this procedure.

Updating the Post-PRL Database. Milton (1999) published a new meta-analysis updating the one she published in the *Psychological Bulletin* (Milton and Wiseman, 1999). She included eight new studies, but she excluded a highly significant study by Dalton (1997) because she considered it to be an outlier that unduly weighted the final outcome. This updated post-PRL database of thirty eight studies yielded a marginally significant Stouffer Z of 1.45, $p = 0.074$, which Milton still considered inadequate for claiming that the ganzfeld is replicable.

Yet another updated post-PRL meta-analysis, conducted independently of Milton's, appeared in the literature shortly thereafter (Palmer and Broughton, 2000; Bem, Palmer and Broughton, 2001). This analysis added ten new studies, compared to Milton's eight. One of these was the Dalton (1997) study mentioned above, and another one was a successful study published after Milton's update was completed (Alexander and Broughton, 1999). (There appears to be one other minor difference in the samples but it is not clear what it is, because Milton did not state precisely what studies were included in her analysis.) The Bem, Palmer and Broughton (BPB) meta-analysis yielded a clearly significant Stouffer Z of 2.59, $p = 0.0048$, with an effect size of 0.051 and a hit rate of 30%.

Methodological Standardness. Milton's (1999) updated meta-analysis was followed in the *Journal of Parapsychology* by the publication of an email debate among numerous parapsychologists concerning the status of ESP ganzfeld research (Schmeidler and Edge, 1999). Space limitations prohibit a full review of this debate, but one major point does need to be raised. Several commentators complained that one important reason that the Milton and Wiseman (1999) meta-analysis yielded such poor results is that they included studies that employed non-standard ganzfeld methodology. Recall that this issue also came up in the debate about the pre-PRL database (Honorton, 1985; Hyman, 1985). The present critics cited in particular three studies that yielded below chance results, two in which musical pieces were used as targets (Willin, 1996a, 1996b), and one in which the sender was periodically presented with the target slide sub-liminally, interrupting a PK test (Kanthamani and Palmer, 1993). However, these judgments of standardness were subjective and made with knowledge of the experimental results.

BPB sought to remedy this latter problem experimentally (Palmer and Broughton, 2000; Bem, Palmer and Broughton, 2001). Three of Bem's graduate psychology students were given the method sections only of the forty studies in the updated (by the authors) post-PRL database and asked to rate them for standardness. As a criterion for standardness they were given a section describing 'The Ganzfeld Procedure' from Bem and Honorton's (1994) *Psychological Bulletin* article covering the pre-PRL and PRL databases, and a more detailed description of the method used in the PRL studies (Honorton *et al.*, 1990). As the debate concerned the ganzfeld *procedure*, they were not told to consider how participants were selected. The judges were told to base their ratings on how much they thought the departure from standardness might affect the results, based on the rationale of the ganzfeld. Thus, inconsequential departures from standardness were given little if any weight in the ratings.

The mean standardness rating of the forty studies, averaged over the three judges, on the 1–7 scale (with 7 being maximum standardness) was 5.33. These standardness ratings were positively correlated with ESP effect size, $r_s(38) = 0.31, p = 0.024$. The twenty nine 'standard' studies that fell above the midpoint of the scale (4) yielded a Stouffer Z of 3.49, $p = 0.0002$, an effect size of 0.096 and a hit rate of 31%. Nine 'nonstandard' studies falling below the midpoint yielded a negative Stouffer Z of -1.30, *ns*, and a hit rate of only 24%. The two samples differed significantly ($p = 0.02$).[2] These data clearly show that including the non-standard studies did indeed adversely affect the results of the Milton and Wiseman (1999) meta-analysis.

Only one of the twenty nine standard studies did not report direct hits. Eliminating this study raises the Stouffer Z slightly to 3.78 (Palmer and Broughton, 2000), with the hit rate maintaining itself at 31%. This hit rate falls inside the 95% confidence intervals reported by Bem and Honorton (1994) for both the post-PRL (28%–43%) and the PRL (30%–35%) databases. Note, however, that standardness ratings have never been computed for the pre-PRL database and this database doubtless included a number of studies that would have been rated as non-standard by Bem's judges. As non-standard methodology and failure to report direct hits closely mirrored each other in the post-PRL database, it is likely that the use of non-standard methods in the non-DH studies in the pre-PRL database helps explain why these studies yielded such poor results compared to the DH studies in that database. Thus, it does seem prudent to say that claims of replicability of the ganzfeld should have the caveat 'provided standard methods were employed, as defined by BPB'.

Conclusions

Honorton (1985), Milton and Wiseman (1999), and BPB (Bem, Palmer and Broughton, 2001; Palmer and Broughton, 2000) all used highly conservative methods to obtain the p-values for individual studies. The later two used the exact binomial, which actually yields a negative z when the number of hits is exactly at chance, and according to Donald Burdick, Professor of Statistics at Duke University, 'will overestimate ["the probability that random guesses would produce at least as many hits as were obtained . . ."] by a substantial margin' (personal communication, 9 October 2001). For example, even the thirty studies in the Milton and Wiseman meta-analysis produce a significant positive result when a simple z-test is applied using individual trials as the unit of analysis.[3] Part of the success of this latter method is that it effectively weights the z for each study by the number of trials in the study. All the meta-analyses used unweighted z's. The unweighted method decreased significance for the post-PRL database but increased it for the other databases.

However, the most important factor distinguishing the nonsignificant Milton and Wiseman (1999; Milton, 1999) and the significant BPB (Bem, Palmer and Broughton, 2001; Palmer and Broughton, 2000) meta-analyses of the post-PRL database is the decision to include or not include the highly successful Dalton (1997) study. As I wrote in the email debate (Schmeidler and Edge, 1999), I strongly disapprove of removing outliers from databases, even though it is advocated or at least tolerated by some meta-analysts. My primary reason for this

---

[2] The Willin (1996a, 1996b) studies with musical targets received the lowest average standardness score in the database. However, the Kanthamani and Palmer (1993) study with subliminal sending scored above the midpoint on standardness and thus was included in the standard group.

[3] I thank Dean Radin for bringing this fact to my attention.

view is that removing outliers misrepresents the data, which is the cardinal sin in any data analysis. (In the debate, I made this point in response to someone who was an advocate of the ganzfeld's evidentiality, not to Milton.)

On the other hand, the Dalton data contribute to a statistic that does deserve to be taken seriously, namely heterogeneity. It turns out that all the various pre- and post-PRL databases are significantly heterogeneous (Palmer and Broughton, 2000). For example, the p-values for heterogeneity for both the DH studies in the pre-PRL database and the twenty eight standard DH studies in the post-PRL database are 10^{-5}. This implies that unaccounted for factors that vary from study to study influence ganzfeld success. It is clear that we do not have a very good idea what these factors are. Elements of the debate that I have not covered in this paper concern the consistency with which various personality and target-type variables influence ganzfeld success. However, even if some of these variables turn out to be reliable predictors they will not account for enough of the variance to put a major dent in this huge heterogeneity.

In my opinion, the strongest predictor of ESP results generally is the identity of the experimenter (Kennedy and Taddonio, 1976). Whether or not this is demonstrated in the ganzfeld depends on how the effect is analysed. For example, Honorton (1985) noted that six of the ten laboratories in the pre-PRL database reported significant overall positive results, but Rosenthal (1986) found that 'these 10 investigators differed significantly and importantly in the average magnitude of the effects they obtained' (p. 327).

In conclusion, it seems to me that all three databases have provided overall significant evidence of ESP and fit reasonably well within each other's confidence intervals. This is an impressive rate of stability that clearly cannot be attributed to just a handful of investigators, but at the same time, investigator differences do seem to play some role. Furthermore, the successful investigators all come from a fairly narrowly defined population of experimental parapsychologists who may not be very representative of scientific researchers generally. The huge heterogeneity suggests that we still have a lot to learn about the factors that determine ganzfeld success, a theme that has been stressed by the critic Milton (1999). Until we find out what these factors are, it is anyone's guess how widely replicable the ganzfeld will be outside the parapsychological community. It would be immensely valuable for such 'outside' researchers, particularly benevolent neutrals on the subject, to give ganzfeld research a try and help us learn what the crucial variables are.

Is it all Methodological Artifacts?

The collective statistical significance or the replicability of ESP in the ganzfeld mean nothing so far as providing evidence for a paranormal process if the success can be attributed to flaws in the way the studies were conducted. Such methodological artifacts have been a major component of the ganzfeld debate, and it is now time to examine the arguments of the two sides.

The Pre-PRL Database

At the beginning of the paper I mentioned that one aspect of meta-analysis that is vulnerable to subjective bias is the assignment of quality ratings or codes by the meta-analyst. This is particularly true when the analysts are aware of the outcomes of the studies in question and have strong theoretical predispositions. This problem is illustrated dramatically in the debate between Hyman (1985) and Honorton (1985) on the pre-PRL database. Both employed the standard technique described earlier of correlating the quality codes with measures of ESP scoring. As one might expect from the preceding discussion, Hyman found that methodological artifacts did account for the ganzfeld success and Honorton found that they did not.

In addition to the statistical flaws addressed earlier, Hyman (1985) designated five categories of methodological flaws in the pre-PRL database. The first, called *single target*, occurred in the earlier ganzfeld studies when a paper target such as an art print was included in the judging packet after being handled by the sender. It is possible that the receiver could be tipped off to the identity of the target by noting which of the four art prints displayed handling cues, such as fingerprints. I previously conducted a study demonstrating that Dutch college students were able to successfully identify such handling cues when told to look for them (Palmer, 1983). The solution, adopted in later ganzfeld studies, is to use a duplicate judging set. The problem is eliminated in the auto-ganzfeld by presenting the target and judging materials by videotape.

The next two flaws seem for the most part to assume cheating on the part of the sender. A *security* flaw was assigned when an experimenter also served as the sender, rather than having separate experimenters monitor the sender and receiver. A *documentation* flaw was assigned when the report did not make it clear how many senders were friends of the receiver or whether this made a difference in the results. Perhaps, for example, the sender at the time of judging could somehow substitute the picture which best coincided with the receiver's impressions for the actual target. Security and documentation flaws were assigned for a few other isolated problems, many of which were not specified. One that was specified, rolling a clay ball over the target picture, would be better placed in the single-target category, because it involved the mechanism of sensory cues on the target in the judging pack.[4]

The final two flaws involved problems with randomization. This could become a factor if, say, due to inadequate randomization a picture that in general receives high ratings from receivers whether or not it is the target appears more frequently as a target than do other pictures. A *randomization* flaw was assigned if the targets were selected by a suboptimal procedure, such as shuffling a deck of cards, or the method of randomization was not reported. Modern parapsychologists generally use either random number tables (RNTs) or electronic RNGs for target selection. A *feedback* flaw was assigned when the location of the target

---

[4] This happened to be a study I conducted (Palmer and Aued, 1975), and I was careful to roll the clay ball *lightly* over the target picture and checked to be sure it left no visible mark. The clay was hard and never stuck to the picture.

picture within the judging packet was not randomized. Hyman only assigned this flaw if a single judging set was used, but it would appear that the same problem would occur even if a duplicate set was used for judging. It presumably would occur if, say, receivers are biased to choose the first picture they see in the judging packet as the target, and due to poor randomization the target picture actually appears first in the packet more frequently than in other locations.

Hyman submitted his flaws to a factor and a cluster analysis. Each revealed the same three factors or clusters, one of which correlated significantly with the ESP measures. This factor included three flaws as predictors: randomization, feedback and documentation, and each of these three correlated significantly with ESP by themselves. He then computed regression equations to show that one would expect chance results from studies in which the three crucial flaws were eliminated.

Honorton (1985) gave a number of specific examples of what he considered to be erroneous coding by Hyman, especially inconsistencies in applying his criteria. For randomization he claimed misclassification of at least five studies; for example, in one case the author (York, 1977) states: 'individual targets . . . selected using a random number generator from each mini-target pool by an otherwise uninvolved assistant' (pp. 48–9). He asserts that seven of the ten studies to which Hyman assigned the feedback flaw 'describe procedures for ordering targets at judging' (Honorton, 1985, p. 75). It is possible that in these cases of disagreement Hyman recognized that an RNG was used or an ordering procedure was applied, but that the specific ways these procedures were carried out were somehow inadequate. Such, however, was not mentioned in his report.

As stated above, when Honorton assigned his own quality codes he found no significant correlations between Hyman's flaw categories and ESP. Although this difference in results is due partly to differences in coding of particular studies, in the case of randomization it is evident that differences in the coding criteria themselves played a role. Both Honorton and Hyman coded the randomization flaw on a three-point scale. Both gave the highest score to studies using RNTs or RNGs. However, whereas Hyman gave the lowest rating to studies that used suboptimal methods such as card shuffling, and intermediate ratings to studies where the method was not reported, Honorton did the reverse. In my opinion, Hyman's method makes more sense.

Honorton (1985) recruited a specialist on factor analysis named David Saunders to write an appendix discussing the validity of Hyman's factor and regression analyses. His most important point was that Hyman was guilty of not properly correcting for multiple analyses. Ironically, this is the same generic criticism Hyman made of a number of studies included in the pre-PRL database.

The differences in coding between the protagonists resulted in Hyman assigning many more flaws than Honorton. By my count Hyman listed ninety nine separate flaws, ranging from ten for security and feedback to thirty one for randomization. I think it is fair to infer that Hyman considers the sheer volume of alleged flaws to be sufficient to discredit the database, regardless of what the correlations show. Honorton did not list specific flaws in his report, but it is safe to assume that it was much less than ninety nine. He builds his case on examples which appear to show that either Hyman did not follow his own coding criteria or that proper control was achieved, even though not by the specific method Hyman coded for. The latter is particularly an issue for the security and documentation flaws. For instance, Honorton discusses in some detail an experiment by Braud, Wood and Braud (1975) in which precautions were taken to prevent sender cheating even though the experimenter served as the sender. The scenario of the sender substituting a bogus target for the real one presumes that he has access to the judging packet after learning the receiver's mentation, so that he or she knows which picture to substitute. That was not the case in Braud's experiment, and may not have been the case in other studies Hyman cited for this flaw.

Experimenter Fraud? A major contributor to the pre-PRL database, whose results were consistently positive, was Carl Sargent. A critic, Susan Blackmore (1987), was able to observe some of Sargent's ganzfeld sessions and noted protocol violations in the procedure. Sargent used a stack of envelopes from which the target was to be randomly selected. Although the stack was supposed to contain an equal number of each target, Blackmore uncovered some slight departures from this equality. She cited one specific instance in which the discrepancy could have indicated that Sargent as experimenter knew the identity of the target when he attempted to guide the participant to choose that target as his response during judging. Sargent (1987) and his associates (Harley and Matthews, 1987) gave what I consider to be plausible reasons for the discrepancies, and Blackmore did not reply to their replies. In my opinion, the discrepancies represent random errors rather than systematic bias or fraud. In any case, Honorton (1985) reported that the pre-PRL database remains significant when Sargent's data are removed.

The PRL Database

Randomization. The first round of methodological criticisms of the PRL database occurred in a debate by Hyman (1994) and Bem (1994) immediately following the report of the PRL studies in the *Psychological Bulletin* (Bem and Honorton, 1994). Hyman praised the PRL studies as being a significant improvement methodologically over the pre-PRL studies but still had some complaints. The most important involved randomization. Although Honorton used the RNG-based method that received the highest quality codes in the pre-PRL debate and agreed upon in the 'joint communiqué' (Hyman and Honorton, 1986), Hyman took the argument a step further in the PRL debate. He argued in effect that even an adequate randomization procedure could (and indeed almost certainly would) result in pictures or movie clips in the target pool appearing as targets different numbers of times. If it happened that *by chance* the pictures selected most frequently as targets were the same as those tending to receive relative high ratings from receivers, whether they were targets or not, then a spurious excess of hits could result. Hyman said that the number of times each target appeared should have been equalized in advance, with only their order randomized.

Bem (1994) responded by doing a reanalysis of the data. For each trial he computed an adjusted chance probability influenced by receiver response biases. Thus, if the target for a trial happened to be a popular one with all the receivers in the study, the adjusted chance probability would be greater than the original 25%. The adjusted hit rate was 30.7%, only trivially different from the original 31.5% hit rate.

Hyman's criticism is a potentially serious one because it could apply not just to the PRL studies but to all the other ganzfeld studies and, in fact, to most studies in parapsychology that use a procedure where the frequency of each target is free to vary. Parapsychologists almost never perform the kind of control analyses reported by Bem (1994). Has Hyman unwittingly undermined a huge amount of the psi literature? The answer is no, and the reason is that the bias at issue is not systematic. In other words, it could just as easily lead to a deficiency of hits as to an excess of hits, depending upon whether the most frequent targets contradict or match participant response biases. As Hyman himself notes, this effect cancels itself out over a large number of studies. That is one reason we do replications; successes based on such 'lucky' matches of targets and response biases will not replicate very well.

Hyman applied essentially the same criticism to the order of the targets in the judging pack. Recall that a similar issue defined the feedback flaw in Hyman's (1985) critique of the pre-PRL database. The locations of the targets within each judging pack were fixed in the PRL studies, so these locations depended upon which pictures or movie clips were randomly selected as targets. When Bem (1994) examined the distribution of target locations he did find a slight bias ($p < 0.05$), but it was the opposite of the receiver's biases: the receivers preferred the first and fourth locations, whereas the most frequent location of the actual targets was third.

Finally, Hyman found a complex internal effect in the data that he found suspicious, although he did not indicate how it might have produced a spurious conclusion. He noted that hitting was concentrated on trials in which the target picture or movie clip had been a target in previous sessions *and*, as sometimes happened in these studies, the experimenter (who was blind to the target) assisted the receiver in the judging task. Bem noted that Hyman's conditions were most likely to apply to the later studies in the database, in which other methodological refinements were introduced that were responsible for the success. For example, the highly successful 'Julliard' study (Schlitz and Honorton, 1992) restricted to artistic participants was the eighth of the ten experiments.

Sensory Leakage. Wiseman, Smith and Kornbrot (1996) proposed a method by which sensory leakage could have accounted for the successful PRL results. Although the receivers were located in an acoustically isolated chamber, the senders were not. This arrangement allowed for possible auditory stimuli travelling from the sender to the experimenter, rendering the latter non-blind. If the experimenters were honest and they were aware of such cues, they would have aborted the session. As the authors did not want to postulate experimenter fraud, they assumed that the auditory stimuli were subliminal, which also allowed for the stimuli to be quite weak in amplitude. Unfortunately, the PRL lab had been torn down by the time Wiseman *et al.* devised their scenario, so the actual degree of sound isolation between the sender and experimenter could not be determined. The authors were thus relegated to making estimates. They concluded that in the worst of cases 'sender-to-experimenter leakage *could* . . . have taken place' (Wiseman, Smith and Kornbrot, 1996, p. 119, italics in original). This would have required the sender to be making loud noises (preferably at times when the receiver said something that matched the target — in the autoganzfeld, the sender could hear the receiver's ongoing mentation report through headphones), but senders had been instructed not to make such sounds.

Wiseman *et al.* bolstered their case by noting that sessions in which the experimenter helped the receiver with the judging yielded higher ESP scores than those without experimenter assistance ($p = 0.026$), although the authors note this also would be predicted by an ESP hypothesis. Although the unassisted trials were independently significant, the authors point out that the experimenter reading back to the receiver the notes of their preceding mentation might allow a basis for a contaminated experimenter to unwittingly bias receivers in their judging.

As Wiseman *et al.* point out, a way to settle this matter is to have the transcripts of the suspect sessions re-judged by an outsider. Bem has conducted just such an analysis and says that the results remained significant, although not strongly so (personal communication to Palmer, 15 June 2001). However, too much weight should not be placed on this finding until the report is subjected to peer review and published.

Honorton himself reported another potential sensory leakage problem that potentially contaminated 80% of the trials (Honorton *et al.*, 1990). At this point in the process of data collection, the researchers discovered that when an external amplifier was placed between the VCR and the receiver's headphones and the pink noise turned totally off, the soundtrack accompanying the dynamic targets (which were responsible for all the significance) could faintly be detected. Of course, under the conditions pertaining in the actual study (i.e. pink noise and no amplifier) the sound track could not be detected (supraliminally), although perhaps subliminal detection was possible. The results did not decline over the last 20% of the trials, which contradicts what one would expect if this leakage actually took place.

Finally, a weakness of these subliminal perception critiques is that auditory subliminal perception itself has not been well established scientifically — far less so than visual subliminal perception, on which much more research has been conducted.

The Post-PRL Database

This section is easy to write because there have been as yet no published methodological criticisms of the post-PRL studies. The good news for ganzfeld proponents is that the most successful studies are generally the ones that most closely followed the 'standard' PRL protocol, which has come through the wars relatively unscathed, certainly much better than did the pre-PRL studies.

Conclusions

My impression over many years is that critics of parapsychology are very good at providing *conceivable* normal explanations for psi effects but rather poor at providing *plausible* normal explanations for them. This principal is abundantly illustrated in the ganzfeld debate. Even Hyman (1994) acknowledges that his alternative explanations are unlikely to account for the data. He sees them instead as symptoms, presumably of some unidentified, more serious problems. I find this argument to be a *non sequitur*; it doesn't follow that overlooking relatively trivial problems implies overlooking more serious ones. Of course, psi is implausible to many people as well, so in the final analysis readers must decide for themselves whether a unified psi process is more implausible than a plethora of arcane alternatives. Someday psi effects may become so strong and so repeatable that the opposition will simply be overwhelmed, but that day has yet to arrive.

References

Alexander, C.H. and Broughton, R.S. (1999, 'CL1-Ganzfeld study: A look at brain hemisphere differences and scoring in the autoganzfeld', *Proceedings of Presented Papers*: The Parapsychological Association 42nd Annual Convention, pp. 3–18.

Bem, D.J. (1994), 'Response to Hyman', *Psychological Bulletin*, **115**, pp. 25–7.

Bem, D.J. and Honorton, C. (1994), 'Does psi exist? Replicable evidence for an anomalous process of information transfer', *Psychological Bulletin*, **115**, pp. 4–18.

Bem, D.J., Palmer, J. and Broughton, R.S. (2001), 'Updating the ganzfeld database: a victim of its own success?', *Journal of Parapsychology*, **65**, pp. 207–18.

Bertini, M., Lewis, H. and Witkin, H. (1964), 'Some preliminary observations with an experimental procedure for the study of hypnagogic and related phenomena', *Archivo di Psicologia Neurologia e Psychiatra*, **6**, pp. 493–534.

Blackmore, S. (1980), 'The extent of selective reporting of ESP ganzfeld studies', *European Journal of Parapsychology*, **3**, pp. 213–19.

Blackmore, S. (1987), 'A report of a visit to Carl Sargent's laboratory', *Journal of the Society for Psychical Research*, **54**, pp. 186–98.

Braud, W.G., Wood, R. and Braud, L.W. (1975), 'Free-response GESP performance during an experimental hypnagogic state induced by visual and acoustic ganzfeld techniques: a replication and extension', *Journal of the American Society for Psychical Research*, **69**, pp. 105–13.

Child, I.L. and Levi, A. (1979), 'Psi-missing in free-response settings', *Journal of the American Society for Psychical Research*, **73**, pp. 273–89.

Cohen, J. (1988), *Statistical Power Analysis for the Behavioral Sciences* (Hillsdale, NJ: Erlbaum).

Dalton, K. (1997), 'Exploring the links: creativity and psi in the ganzfeld', *Proceedings of Presented Papers: The Parapsychological Association 40th Annual Convention*, pp. 119–34.

Hansel, C.E.M. (1989), *The Search for Psychic Power: ESP and Parapsychology Revisited* (Buffalo: Prometheus).

Harley, T. and Matthews, G. (1987), 'Cheating, psi, and the appliance of science: a reply to Blackmore', *Journal of the Society for Psychical Research*, **54**, pp. 199–207.

Hays, W.L. (1963), *Statistics for Psychologists* (New York: Holt, Rinehart & Winston).

Honorton, C. (1976), 'Length of isolation and degree of arousal as probable factors influencing information retrieval in the ganzfeld [Abstract]', in *Research in Parapsychology 1975*, ed. Joanna D. Morris, William G. Roll and Robert L. Morris (Metuchen, NJ: Scarecrow Press).

Honorton, C. (1978), 'Psi and internal attention states: information retrieval in the ganzfeld', in *Psi and States of Awareness*, ed. Betty Shapin and Lisette Coly (New York: Parapsychology Foundation).

Honorton, C. (1985), 'Meta-analysis of ganzfeld research: a response to Hyman', *Journal of Parapsychology*, **49**, pp. 51–9.

Honorton, C., Berger, R.E., Varvoglis, M.P., Quant, M., Derr, P., Schechter, E.I. and Ferrari, D.C. (1990), 'Psi communication in the ganzfeld: experiments with an automated testing system and a comparison with a meta-analysis of earlier studies', *Journal of Parapsychology*, **54**, pp. 99–139.

Hyman, R. (1981), 'Further comments on Schmidt's PK experiments', *Skeptical Inquirer*, **5** (3), pp. 34–40.

Hyman, R. (1985), 'The ganzfeld psi experiment: a critical appraisal', *Journal of Parapsychology*, **49**, pp. 3–49.

Hyman, R. (1994), 'Anomaly or artifact? Comments on Bem and Honorton', *Psychological Bulletin*, **115**, pp. 19–24.

Hyman, R. and Honorton, C. (1986), 'A joint communiqué: the psi ganzfeld controversy', *Journal of Parapsychology*, **50**, pp. 350–64.

Kanthamani, H. and Palmer, J. (1993), 'A ganzfeld experiment with "subliminal sending" ', *Journal of Parapsychology*, **57**, pp. 241–57.

Kennedy, J.E. and Taddonio, J.L. (1976), 'Experimenter effects in parapsychological research', *Journal of Parapsychology*, **40**, pp. 1–33.

Milton, J. (1996), 'Establishing methodological guidelines for ESP studies: a questionnaire survey of experimenters' and critics' consensus', *Journal of Parapsychology*, **60**, pp. 289–334.

Milton, J. (1999), 'Should ganzfeld research continue to be crucial in the search for a replicable psi effect? Part I. Discussion paper and an introduction to an electronic mail discussion', *Journal of Parapsychology*, **63**, pp. 309–33.

Milton, J. and Wiseman, R. (1999), 'Does psi exist? Lack of replication of an anomalous process of information transfer', *Psychological Bulletin*, **125**, pp. 387–91.

Milton, J. and Wiseman, R. (2001), 'Does psi exist? Reply to Storm and Ertel (2001)', *Psychological Bulletin*, **127**, pp. 434–8.

Palmer, J. (1983), 'Sensory contamination of free-response ESP targets: the greasy fingers hypothesis', *Journal of the American Society for Psychical Research*, **77**, pp. 101–13.

Palmer, J. and Aued, I. (1975), 'An ESP test with psychometric objects and the ganzfeld: negative findings [Abstract]', in *Research in Parapsychology 1974*, ed. Joanna D. Morris, William G. Roll and Robert L. Morris (Metuchen, NJ: Scarecrow Press).

Palmer, J. and Broughton, R.S. (2000), 'An updated meta-analysis of post-PRL ESP ganzfeld experiments', *Proceedings of Presented Papers: The Parapsychological Association 43rd Annual Convention*, pp. 224–40.

Radin, D. (1997), *The Conscious Universe: The Scientific Truth of Psychic Phenomena* (San Francisco: HarperEdge).

Rosenthal, R. (1979), 'The "file drawer" problem and tolerance for null results', *Psychological Bulletin*, **86**, pp. 638–41.

Rosenthal, R. (1986), 'Meta-analytic procedures and the nature of replication: the ganzfeld debate', *Journal of Parapsychology*, **50**, pp. 315–36.

Sargent, C. (1987), 'Sceptical fairytales from Bristol', *Journal of the Society for Psychical Research*, **54**, pp. 208–18.

Schlitz, M.J. and Honorton, C. (1992), 'Ganzfeld psi performance within an artistically gifted population', *Journal of the American Society for Psychical Research*, **86**, pp. 83–98.

Schmeidler, G.R. and Edge, H. (1999), 'Should ganzfeld research continue to be crucial in the search for a replicable psi effect? Part II. Edited ganzfeld debate', *Journal of Parapsychology*, **63**, pp. 335–88.

Stanford, R.G., Frank, S., Kass, G. and Skoll, S. (1989), 'Ganzfeld as an ESP-favorable setting: Part II. Prediction of ESP-task performance through verbal-transcript measures of spontaneity, suboptimal arousal, and internal attention state', *Journal of Parapsychology*, **53**, pp. 95–124.

Storm L. and Ertel S. (2001), 'Does psi exist? Milton and Wiseman's (1999) meta-analysis of ganzfeld research', *Psychological Bulletin*, **127**, pp. 424–33.

Willin, M.J. (1996a), 'A ganzfeld experiment using musical targets', *Journal of the Society for Psychical Research*, **61**, pp. 1–17.

Willin, M.J. (1996b), 'A ganzfeld experiment using musical targets with previous high scorers from the general population', *Journal of the Society for Psychical Research*, **61**, pp. 103–6.

Wiseman, R., Smith, M. and Kornbrot, D. (1996), 'Exploring possible sender-to-experimenter acoustic leakage in the PRL autoganzfeld experiments', *Journal of Parapsychology*, **60**, pp. 97–128.

York, M. (1977), 'The Defense Mechanism Test (DMT) as an indicator of psychic performance as measured by a free-response clairvoyance test using a ganzfeld technique [Abstract]', in *Research in Parapsychology 1976*, ed. William G. Roll and Robert L. Morris (Metuchen, NJ: Scarecrow Press).

Matthew D. Smith

The Role of the Experimenter in Parapsychological Research

Abstract: *A major challenge facing modern parapsychology continues to be the replicability of psi. Whilst some researchers appear to consistently obtain positive evidence for psi, others, equally consistently, appear to be less successful. Previous research has attempted to explain this so-called 'experimenter effect' in terms of both psychological variables (in terms of how the experimenter treats his or her participants) and parapsychological variables (the experimenter may use his or her own psi to affect the data). In this paper, both of these interpretations are considered, as are other possible interpretations (such as experimenter error and experimenter fraud). Research in this area emphasises the important role of the experimenter in parapsychology. The paper concludes with a discussion of possible implications for the study of consciousness.*

Introduction

Parapsychology has for many years been considered a controversial area of study. Indeed, the majority of researchers and theorists in those fields that would be most likely to inform parapsychological research, such as psychology, philosophy and physics, are typically amongst those most sceptical of parapsychological claims (e.g., McClenon, 1982; McConnell & Clark, 1991; Wagner & Monnet, 1979). However, the study of psi[1] experiences may be regarded as an important aspect of all these endeavours as such experiences have the potential to extend our understanding of how people interact with their environment. Most notably, the study of such experiences from a psychological perspective is likely to be most fruitful. This is because psychological understanding will be extended whether or not such experiences can be shown to have a paranormal basis. Philosophers and physicists are likely to be most interested if such experiences do turn out to reflect a hitherto unexplained form of human–environment interaction.

Correspondence: Matthew D. Smith, Psychology Dept, Liverpool Hope University College, Hope Park, Liverpool L16 9JD, UK. Email: *smithm3@hope.ac.uk*

[1] The term 'psi' is used in this paper to refer to apparently anomalous processes of information transfer, and so subsumes terms such as extra-sensory perception (ESP) and psychokinesis (PK).

Journal of Consciousness Studies, **10**, No. 6–7, 2003, pp. 69–84

One of the reasons that controversy continues to surround parapsychological research is that experimental studies of psi phenomena are still unable to produce the level of replicability that would satisfy critics of parapsychology. If parapsychologists were able to demonstrate a psi effect as easily as psychologists might demonstrate a Stroop effect, then the scientific community at large would probably take a little more notice. However, the 'experimenter effect' in parapsychology is one obstacle that has hindered replication attempts of psi effects, thus preventing widespread acceptance of the field within mainstream science.

For many years, psi proponents and their critics have noticed that some experimenters tend to be consistently more successful than others at obtaining evidence in favour of psi (e.g., MacFarland, 1938; Nicol & Humphrey, 1953; Pratt & Price, 1938; West & Fisk, 1953; Wiseman & Schlitz, 1997; 1999). This observation, labelled the 'experimenter effect', has led researchers to consider why this might be the case. Why do some investigators seem to be consistently unable to obtain evidence for psi, whilst others continue to obtain psi effects in their experiments? What is it about these apparently 'successful' experimenters that distinguish them from 'unsuccessful' experimenters? As these questions lie at the heart of the issue of replication in parapsychology, the experimenter effect has been described as 'the most important challenge facing modern experimental parapsychology' (Palmer, 1986, p. 220).

It comes as little surprise to learn that 'successful' psi experimenters tend to have more positive attitudes towards psi phenomena than 'unsuccessful' experimenters. For example, successful experimenters tend to be more likely to think that psi exists, that they have some psi ability, and that it is possible to demonstrate psi in an experimental study (Smith, in press). This relationship between attitudes towards psi phenomena and success as an experimenter may be explained in two ways. First, obtaining positive findings in one's psi experiments is likely to have a positive impact upon one's own attitudes towards psi. Likewise, an experimenter who consistently does not obtain evidence for psi is likely to become less convinced of the reality of psi. Second, and more importantly for the present discussion, it may be that more positive attitudes to psi result in being more successful in obtaining evidence in favour of psi. If this is the case, then a number of mechanisms present themselves as possible mediators of this relationship, and as possible explanations for the 'experimenter effect'.

If experimenters with more positive attitudes towards psi make more successful experimenters, this might, for example, be explained in terms of experimenter error. That is, such experimenters may be more motivated to produce results that are consistent with their prior beliefs about psi (e.g., that psi exists, and can be demonstrated in an experimental study) and so make biased, though not deliberate, errors in the design, running, analysis or reporting of their experiments. It is also possible that these motivated errors are deliberately intended by experimenters wishing to 'validate' their own beliefs about psi. Critics of parapsychology tend to favour these interpretations of the experimenter effect in psi research.

Psi proponents, however, tend to point to other possible explanations of the experimenter effect. For example, one might explain the relationship between attitudes towards psi and success as an experimenter in terms of experimenter–participant interactions. According to this interpretation, the experimenter communicates his or her attitudes towards psi to the participants so affecting participants' motivation, beliefs or expectations of success, which in turn affect the participants' performance on the psi task. Another interpretation highlights the possible role of the experimenter as a source of psi. That is, it is possible that (if one is willing to entertain the psi hypothesis) successful experimenters use their own psi ability, either consciously or unconsciously, to influence the outcome of their experiments.

In this paper, all of the above four interpretations of the experimenter effect in parapsychology (experimenter error; experimenter fraud; experimenter–participant interaction; experimenter psi) will be considered before focusing on the potential implications of the experimenter effect for research on consciousness.

The Experimenter Effect as Experimenter Error

As noted above, one possible interpretation of the experimenter effect in parapsychology is that apparently 'successful' experimenters make motivated (although unconscious) errors somewhere during the experimental process. According to this interpretation, these errors (whether they be at the design stage, the data collection stage or the analysis stage) are motivated by the experimenter's wish to obtain evidence in support of psi. Critics who have adopted this approach have typically done so on *a priori* grounds, arguing that it is more reasonable to believe that significant experimental results are best explained in terms of experimental error than to believe psi exists. However, the general argument is supported by a large body of literature that suggests that researchers in a wide range of scientific disciplines are susceptible to making systematic errors in support of the hypothesis they are testing (for a review, see Rosenthal, 1976).

Parapsychologists have also long been aware of such potential biasing factors. In an apparent test of extrasensory perception (ESP), Kennedy and Uphoff (1939) had participants attempt to psychically 'send' symbols on ESP cards (either a circle, cross, wavy lines, square or star) to the experimenter. Participants were also required to record the experimenter's guess for each trial. As the experimenter's guesses had been predetermined, it was possible to calculate the number of recording errors made by participants. It was found that just over 1% of the guesses were mis-recorded. More importantly, it was found that participants who had positive attitudes towards psi were more likely to make errors that artificially inflated the psi scores, whilst participants who had negative attitudes towards psi tended to make errors that deflated psi scores. A conceptually similar experiment using a psychokinesis (PK) task, in which participants attempted to both influence the fall of dice and record their scores, showed a comparable pattern of findings (Sheffield et al., 1952).

Whilst these studies reveal the extent to which an individual's attitudes towards psi may influence the types of recording errors in a psi experiment, it is unclear how much this tells us about the possible role of experimenter error in the experimenter effect in modern parapsychology. It seems possible that these kinds of motivated errors may have contributed to some of the findings of early experimental research. However, parapsychological research has for many years been characterized by the increasingly widespread use of automated methods for collecting, tabulating and analysing data. In addition, double-blind procedures often mean that persons responsible for collating data do not know the full meaning of the scores with which they are dealing. This is not to say that potential routes for experimenter bias do not still exist in more contemporary research studies. It is possible that experimenters who are favourable to the psi hypothesis tend to be more prone to designing studies that do not pay sufficient attention to ruling out non-psi methods of information transfer (e.g., sensory cueing) than are experimenters who are less favourable to psi. Similarly, although analytic procedures are now typically performed using standard computer-based statistical software packages and formal analyses of data should be pre-planned, it may still be up to the investigator to make a variety of decisions about exactly how to prepare the data for analysis (e.g., which outcome measure to use, excluding data, transferring data from one format to another, etc.). Future research would do well to empirically assess these possibilities.

The Experimenter Effect as Experimenter Fraud

Taking the arguments outlined above a stage further, a critic of parapsychology might even suggest that some of these kinds of experimental 'error' are, in fact, deliberate attempts by the experimenter to obtain findings that are in accord with his or her *a priori* beliefs about psi. Thus, according to this argument, researchers who appear to consistently obtain significant findings in support of psi may simply be engaging in fraud.

It has been suggested that scientific fraud may be more widespread than we often acknowledge. Broad and Wade (1982) discuss a number of cases of fraud in various scientific disciplines ranging from astronomy and physics to biology and medicine. They argue that the potential motives to engage in scientific fraud are high, with recognition going to the first to make a groundbreaking discovery (not to mention the possibility of lucrative research contracts). It is therefore not surprising, they argue, that deceit and dishonesty are no less common in science than they are in other endeavours. Within this context, documented instances of experimenter fraud appear to be no more common in parapsychology than in other disciplines. However, the few allegations of fraud in parapsychology have received widespread attention from its critics. There are two cases that have received the most attention both within and beyond parapsychology. The first of these relates to the work of S.G. Soal. Soal initially attempted, unsuccessfully, to replicate the card-guessing experiments conducted by J.B. Rhine and his team at Duke University. However, on re-examining his data he found two participants who showed highly significant between-trial displacement effects. This meant that, rather than scoring hits on the target intended for each trial, their calls showed significant hitting on either the target intended for the previous trial

(–1 displacement) or the subsequent trial (+1 displacement). (Note that trial-by-trial feedback was not given.) One of these participants was a photographer called Basil Shackleton. Soal decided to conduct a series of tests with Shackleton in order to confirm these effects and continued to find highly significant displacement effects, reporting odds against chance that were astronomically high (Soal & Goldney, 1943).

The first criticism of these experiments received much attention as they appeared in a leading scientific journal, *Science* (Price, 1955). Price speculated that if Soal had colluded with at least one of the other people involved in the experiments it would have been relatively easy for the data to be faked. Further criticism elaborated on these possible fraud scenarios (Hansel, 1960; 1966). Later criticisms, however, focused on allegations (initially made by one of the individuals involved in the experiments) that Soal had been seen altering the record sheets, and subsequent analyses provided empirical support for these claims (Markwick, 1978; Medhurst, 1971; Scott *et al.*, 1974). Consequently, Soal's data became disregarded as evidence for psi and his name a byword for fraud in parapsychology.

The second case is that of Walter J. Levy, whom J.B. Rhine hoped would take over as the director of the Institute for Parapsychology (the successor to the Duke University Parapsychology Laboratory) when Rhine retired. Levy had developed a procedure for demonstrating apparent PK effects in rodents. In his experiments, the rodents could seemingly influence an electric generator to activate electrodes that would stimulate their brains. After consistently obtaining positive findings with this procedure, results eventually returned to within chance expectation. Around this time, Levy's colleagues at the Institute became suspicious of the increased attention he seemed to be paying to the experimental equipment, and so secretly observed him during a testing session. They caught him tampering with the equipment so that it would produce what would appear to be positive results. The researchers-turned-sleuths reported what they had seen to Rhine. Although Rhine was clearly surprised by these revelations about his protégé, he responded quickly by going public with the case (Rhine, 1974b). An added irony with this case was that it occurred only a matter of months after Rhine had publicly commented on the rarity of cases of experimenter fraud in parapsychology at that time (Rhine, 1974a).

Of course, these are the only two cases of fraud in parapsychology that have been well documented. It is extremely difficult, if not impossible, to estimate the extent to which fraud takes place but goes undetected in parapsychological research. However, there is no data to suggest that fraud in parapsychology is any higher than in other scientific disciplines. Those critics who may take this view must do so on *a priori* grounds, which perhaps tells us more about the worldview of such critics than the state of the evidence in parapsychology. In short, it seems that experimenter fraud cannot, on its own, explain the experimenter effect in parapsychology.

The Experimenter Effect as Experimenter–Participant Interaction

Parapsychologists generally take a very different view regarding how the experiment effect might be interpreted. It has long been suggested that certain types of experimenter and, in particular, certain types of experimenter–participant interactions are more conducive to the elicitation of psi effects. For example, in their review of the state of the field in the 1950s, Rhine and Pratt (1957) argued that the experimenter must be able to provide 'the psychological conditions under which psi can operate' (Rhine & Pratt, 1957, p. 131). Others have even suggested that the relationship between the experimenter and his or her participants may well be the most important factor in determining the success of a psi experiment (e.g., White, 1976).

This argument implies that not only does psi exist but that the likelihood of observing psi phenomena in a laboratory setting is largely dependent upon who is conducting the study. More specifically, it suggests that the chances of obtaining evidence in favour of psi are greater if the experimenter who comes into contact with the participants is skilled in creating the appropriate psychological conditions. So what might these conditions be?

One condition that became apparent from some of the early experimental research was that successful experimenters were typically highly motivated to obtain support for the psi hypothesis and were, perhaps, able to convey this motivation to their participants (Murphy, 1949; Rhine, 1948). Although this observation was not directly tested, Rhine suggested that difficulties in replicating psi effects might be explicable in terms of a drop in researchers' motivation. The difficulties in recapturing this same level of motivation once that researcher had obtained initial support was proposed to be partly responsible for subsequent declines in scoring and the inability to replicate earlier findings (Rhine, 1948).

As noted earlier, there is also evidence that the most 'successful' psi experimenters are generally more likely to believe that psi is possible than do less successful experimenters (Smith, in press). Perhaps these attitudes towards psi are communicated to research participants, which influences the participants' levels of motivation or expectations of success on the experimental task. There is some evidence that an experimenter's attitudes towards psi and expectations of success in a psi experiment do influence participants' performance on a psi task.

Two recent studies on the experimenter's role in studies of 'remote staring' experiments perhaps illustrate this best (Wiseman & Schlitz, 1997; 1999). In these studies, designed to test the apparent role of psi in people's ability to sense when they are being watched, participants' galvanic skin response (GSR) is measured whilst the experimenter observes from a separate room linked by closed-circuit television. At randomly determined periods (to which the participant is blind) the experimenter either stares at the participant's image on the CCTV monitor, or looks away so that the image cannot be seen. In earlier research conducted by Schlitz (e.g., Schlitz & Laberge, 1997), it had been found that participants' GSR was significantly different during the 'stare' periods compared to the 'no-stare' periods. In Wiseman's research (Wiseman & Smith, 1994;

Wiseman *et al.*, 1995), however, no evidence for a remote-staring effect had been found. An important difference between these two researchers, which may go some way to explaining these contrasting findings, was their *a priori* beliefs about psi phenomena and their expectations about the likely success of their experimental trials. Wiseman is described as a 'sceptic regarding the claims of parapsychology' whilst Schlitz is described as a 'psi proponent' (Wiseman & Schlitz, 1997, p. 198). These researchers, therefore, collaborated to conduct a remote-staring experiment in which Wiseman acted as experimenter on half the trials whilst Schlitz acted as experimenter on the remaining trials. As hypothesised, they found a significant effect in the data from the trials conducted by Schlitz, with participants being more activated during the 'stare' periods than in the 'no-stare' periods, but not in Wiseman's data (Wiseman & Schlitz, 1997). A similar result was found in a replication attempt, although in this study Schlitz's data showed that participants were significantly calmer during the 'stare' periods than in the 'no-stare' periods (Wiseman & Schlitz, 1999).

One possible explanation for Wiseman and Schlitz's findings is that the experimenters' attitudes towards psi are communicated to their participants during the briefing stage of the experiment. Thus, experimenter's overtly expressed attitudes towards psi may influence participants' motivation or expectations of success in the experiment, which in turn impacts upon participants' psi scores. Note that when participants were asked to record their personal attitudes towards psi, after the briefing period, Schlitz's participants reported a stronger belief in psi compared to Wiseman's participants, although this difference did not reach significance. Also, recently published interviews with Wiseman and Schlitz revealed how Schlitz clearly put more effort into creating a rapport with participants than did Wiseman (Watt *et al.*, 2002).

Other research has measured the effect of directly manipulating experimenters' expectations of success upon participants' psi scores. Parker (1975, pp. 42–4) gave student experimenters either a positive or negative expectancy about the outcome of a psi experiment. Experimenters were given a brief lecture about extrasensory perception (ESP) research, and were either informed that previous research using the experimental procedure they were about to use had demonstrated the reality of ESP (for those experimenters in the positive expectancy group) or were told there was no reliable evidence to support the existence of ESP (for those experimenters in the negative expectancy group). In addition, experimenters in the positive expectancy condition were led to expect that participants would score between seven and ten hits per run, whilst the experimenters given the negative expectancy were to expect scores close to the mean chance expectation of five hits per run. As predicted, the total scores of participants when tested by experimenters with the positive expectancy were significantly higher than when they were tested by experimenters with the negative expectancy. In a similar study, Taddonio (1976) told student experimenters that the ESP test they were to use was a recently developed technique developed by Taddonio's colleagues and that the students were being asked to conduct a replication of their findings. Taddonio manipulated the expectancy of experimenters by telling those in one group that participants in previous studies using this new technique had consistently obtained above chance scores. These experimenters were assured that the test could not fail and that the results of the student's repli- cation would give the same high scores. Experimenters in the second group were told that Taddonio's colleagues who had developed the test were worried about it because participants were all scoring well below chance. They were led to believe that the test seemed to elicit psi-missing rather than psi-hitting and that there was no doubt that the student's replication would show the same level of low scoring. In both a pilot study and a confirmatory study, participants tested by the experimenters given the positive expectancy about the test scored signifi- cantly higher than participants tested by the experimenters given the negative expectancy. Taddonio suggested that these differences in scoring 'probably reflect differences in the psychological impact of the two experimenter groups upon their subjects' (p. 113). If this is the case, it is likely that such 'cueing' was conveyed through non-verbal behaviour and paralinguistic cues (such as tone of voice) given that all experimenters read from identical instructions sheets.

Some research has begun to explore more explicitly how the experi- menter–participant interaction in parapsychology experiments might impact upon the outcome of such experiments. For example, in some of the earliest research on the experimenter effect in parapsychology, Pratt and Price (1938) attempted to manipulate the way in which participants were handled when they took part in an ESP experiment. Price, who had consistently obtained significant results in earlier research, acted as the experimenter who interacted with the par- ticipants, whilst Pratt attended to the experimental controls. Price attempted to treat half her participants 'unfavourably', by not engaging in conversation with them, while she treated the other half 'favourably', by engaging in conversation both before and during the experiment. Participants were tested in pairs, with one member of each pair being treated favourably and the other being treated unfa- vourably. This experiment did not reveal any difference in ESP performance between the two groups. However, one problem with this study was that Price complained of the difficulty of trying to artificially induce the favourable and unfa- vourable conditions and that these constraints made it difficult to establish prop- erly favourable conditions for any of the participants. When Price was allowed to test participants without such restrictions, by simply aiming to obtain the best scores possible, significant results returned. In their review of their findings they noted that Price's natural method of handling her participants encouraged 'a free social atmosphere in which general conversation flourishes' (p. 92). It is possible that even in the 'favourable' conditions Price attempted to engender in the first part of their study, such a 'free and social atmosphere' was not present given the restric- tions of being required to present herself unfavourably to the second participant.

A clearer set of findings was found in a study in which experimenters were instructed to interact with their participants either in a 'casual', 'friendly' and 'supportive' manner or in a 'formal', 'unfriendly' and 'abrupt' manner. As antic- ipated, participants in the 'friendly' condition scored significantly above chance on a subsequent ESP task, whilst participants in the 'unfriendly' condition scored significantly below chance on this task (Honorton *et al.*, 1975). More recent attempts to manipulate the nature of the experimenter–participant interaction have yielded mixed results. In one study, participants were either tested in a 'personal' condition in which experimenters attempted to create a 'friendly, welcoming and lively' atmosphere or were tested in a 'neutral' condition in which they were simply presented with experimental instructions on a computer screen in order to keep experimenter–participant interaction to a minimum. No overall significant psi effect was found, nor were there any significant differences between the two conditions (Schneider *et al.*, 2000). In another study, the experimenter gave either 'supportive' or 'unsupportive' suggestions to participants. Although psi scores (on a remote attention-focusing task) did not differ between these two conditions, participants in the 'supportive' condition perceived the experimenter as warmer and more professional than participants tested in the 'unsupportive' condition (Watt & Baker, 2002).

A different approach was taken by researchers wishing to examine possible differences between those researchers who consistently obtained evidence in favour of psi (termed 'psi-conducive' experimenters) and those researchers who consistently did not obtain evidence for psi (termed 'psi-inhibitory'). Potential participants' perceptions of the warmth of 'psi-conducive' and 'psi-inhibitory' experimenters were investigated in a study in which students were asked to rate a number of parapsychologists against a list of descriptive adjectives after watching video-recorded conference presentations by each one (Schmeidler & Maher, 1981). Twenty-seven researchers were video-recorded giving presentations at the Annual Convention of the Parapsychological Association. Five 'psi-conducive' and five 'psi-inhibitory' researchers were selected who were matched in terms of age, sex, overt physical characteristics and whether they grew up in the USA. Students were shown the tapes in random order and asked to make judgements about each researcher's behaviour using a checklist of 30 descriptive adjectives. Responses to 14 of the 30 adjectives showed significant differences for the two types of investigator. Supposedly 'psi-conducive' experimenters tended to be rated as more flexible, friendly, free, likeable, warm, enthusiastic and playful whilst 'psi-inhibitory' experimenters were rated as more rigid, cold, overconfident, tense, irritable, egoistic and unfriendly. An attempted replication found 'psi-conducive' experimenters to be perceived as more active, nervous and enthusiastic with 'psi-inhibitory' experimenters being perceived as more poised, egoistic, cold and confident (Edge & Farkash, 1992, pp. 171–2). Thus, although in both studies there was a good deal of variance between judge's ratings, there would appear to be some agreement among potential participants that 'successful' psi experimenters come across as more enthusiastic, warmer and less egoistic than do their less successful counterparts. These findings were echoed in the comments of Bem and Honorton (1994) when they claimed that psi experiments conducted in a 'warm and sociable' atmosphere are more likely to be successful than those conducted in a formal atmosphere.

Thus, as we have seen, some parapsychological research has attempted to assess the extent to which certain types of experimenter–participant interaction may influence participants' performance on a psi task and has identified some possible determinants of successful experimental interactions (such as positive attitudes towards psi and an expectation of success in the experiment). However, parapsychologists have been slow to examine the details of the experimenter–participant interaction to find out exactly the ways in which experimenter's attitudes and expectancies might be communicated to participants.

Fortunately, social psychological research has accumulated considerable evidence of how experimenter's expectancy regarding the outcome of his or her experiment can be communicated through such subtle visual cues as how often the experimenter smiles and glances at the participant, and the length of time the experimenter devotes to different parts of the experiment (e.g., Friedman, 1967; Page, 1970; Rosenthal, 1976). Auditory cues such as the experimenter's tone of voice have also been shown to communicate experimenter expectancies in studies in which experimenters given different expectancies recorded instructions on to audio-tape (e.g., Adair & Epstein, 1967; Troffer & Tart, 1964). Several models have been put forward to explain exactly how these unintentional cues influence participants' responses (Rosenthal, 1969). For example, it has been suggested that these cues may serve to act as reinforcers when participants give responses on the psychological task which are consistent with the experimenter's hypothesis. However, Rosenthal has argued that if this were the case, then one would expect to find that the first of a series of responses given by a particular participant would not be affected by the experimenter's expectancy, and later responses would generally show more bias than earlier responses. Evidence from four experiments presented by Rosenthal (1976) does not support this notion. Instead, it was found that expectancy effects were in fact most notable for participants' first response than for later responses. Such data suggest that experimenter expectancy is more likely to be communicated during the initial 'meeting-and-greeting' stage of data collection. There is also evidence, although far from conclusive, to suggest that experimenters can learn to become more effective at unintentionally biasing participants in the direction of their hypothesis. That is, some studies have shown that expectancy effects are greater for participants tested later in an experimental series than for those tested earlier in the series (Rosenthal, 1969).

In short, research into experimenter effects in psychological experiments has revealed a number of interesting patterns that go some way to explaining how an experimenter's expectancy may be communicated to his or her participants. However, much of this research, conducted some years ago, focused on how experimenter effects are mediated in research on verbal learning tasks and person-perception tasks. It is yet to be confirmed whether experimenter expectancy effects in parapsychological research are communicated in the same way, although the research linking experimenter 'warmth' with performance on psi tasks may be regarded as a useful starting point for such research.

The Experimenter Effect as Experimenter Psi

The final interpretation of the experimenter effect in parapsychology to be considered here relates to the possible sources of psi in parapsychology experiments. If psi is real, then it is plausible, indeed likely, that the experimental participants are not the only source of psi in a successful parapsychology experiment. The experimenter may also exert a psi influence over the data. Given that apparently 'psi-conducive' experimenters typically tend to believe that psi exists, and are highly motivated to obtain findings in support of psi (often more so than their research participants) then one might argue that the experimenters are potentially a more significant source of psi than the participants.

Kennedy and Taddonio (1976) were among the first to elucidate the possible role of experimenter psi in parapsychology experiments.[2] Whilst acknowledging the likely importance of the experimenter–participant interaction in such experiments, Kennedy and Taddonio suggested that this was only part of the story. They introduced the term 'psi experimenter effect' to refer to 'unintentional psi which affects an experimental outcome in ways that are directly related to the experimenter's needs, wishes, expectancies, moods, etc.' (p. 5). They point to a wide range of studies that appear to suggest that psi experimenter effects are both possible and likely. For example, they note that procedures used in laboratory psychokinesis (PK) studies cannot rule out the influence of individuals other than the supposed 'subject' upon the target (including the experimenter). They cite several studies showing apparent statistical effects demonstrating psychokinesis even when PK targets are kept blind (e.g., Osis, 1953; Thouless, 1949–1952), suggesting that keeping the experimenter blind to the targets does not rule out possible psi influence by the experimenter. In a similar vein, they point to studies demonstrating apparent non-intentional PK effects (e.g., Schmidt, 1975; Stanford et al., 1975). These studies show that apparent PK effects may occur even when they are not being intentionally strived for. As it is assumed that experimenters do not necessarily intentionally strive to influence the outcomes of experiments, such studies provide support for the possibility of psi experimenter effects, as they suggest that intentional striving for a certain outcome is not required for a PK effect to occur.

A particularly interesting study in this context was that conducted by Stanford (1970). Participants were asked to listen to a dream report before being given a multiple-choice questionnaire to ostensibly assess their memory of the report. Although they were not aware of it, participants were actually taking part in an unusual ESP test. The multiple-choice test consisted of three types of question. A third of the questions had one correct answer, a third had two possible answers, and a third had no correct answer. This was because Stanford wanted to find out whether participants' performance on this 'memory' test could somehow be influenced through psi in accordance with the experimenter's aims. For each item on the test, one of the alternative responses was randomly designated as the

---

[2] Around the same time, White (1976) also discussed the possibility of experimenter's psi influencing the outcomes of parapsychological experiments.

target. Thus, in some cases the 'target' answer agreed with the story from the dream report, whilst in others it did not. This meant that it was possible to examine the extent to which participants might have been 'pushed' by psi to choose a target response that was counter to the dream report. The number of counter-report responses when the target response agreed with the report was just one out of 51 responses (2%). The number of counter-report responses when the target response did not agree with the correct response was 31 out of 189 responses (16%). One interpretation of this significant difference is that, even on an ostensibly non-psi task (in this case a memory test), psi may disrupt performance in accordance with the experimenter's aims. Kennedy and Taddonio (1976) took such findings to indicate that psi experimenter effects may even be strong enough to influence performance on well-structured psychological tasks.

Studies in which participants show differential psi performance for different experimenters, even though there is no experimenter–participant contact, also point to the experimenter as a potential source of psi. One of the seminal studies examining this issue was conducted by West and Fisk (1953). In this study, Fisk sent 32 sealed packets of 'clock card' targets through the post to each of twenty participants. The sequence of these targets had been generated using a table of random numbers. Without opening the packets, participants were required to make their responses by guessing the 'time' shown on each card. They did this for each trial by drawing a clock hand on a clock face pointing to one of the twelve hours. Once they had completed the task, they returned the unopened packets and their response sheets to Fisk. An important part of the design, however, was kept hidden from the participants. Fisk, who had consistently obtained significant results in previous parapsychology experiments, generated targets for, and checked, only half the data. The other half were generated and checked by West, who had a history of being generally unsuccessful in obtaining significant psi data. Whilst the overall data gave significant results, with participants making correct guesses more than would be predicted by chance, this significance rested solely on Fisk's data. West's data were at chance. Similar results were found in an experiment that extended this idea by examining the possible psi influence of the person who checks the data (Weiner & Zingrone, 1986).

Studies such as these, themselves in need of replication, do suggest that replication difficulties in parapsychology may be due, at least in part, to psi-related experimenter influences. One set of questions raised by these data relates to likely variables that moderate psi experimenter effects. As with studies examining how the experimenter–participant interaction can impact upon psi scores, an experimenter's attitude towards psi is likely to be important. For example, in one recent study reminiscent of those conducted by Parker (1975) and Taddonio (1976), fourteen students were trained to act as experimenters in a remote attention-focusing task. Nine of these student experimenters were classified as 'psi-believers' and five were classified as 'psi-disbelievers' on the basis of their responses on a 12-item belief in psi questionnaire. Over 36 trials, in which each experimenter conducted at least two trials, not only was an overall significant deviation from chance observed but, more importantly, this significance was entirely due to the data obtained by the psi-believer experimenters (Watt, 2002). Whilst this effect may be explained in terms of different experimenter–participant interactions in the two conditions, additional data reported by Watt do not lend support to this interpretation. Participants were asked to rate their experimenter in terms of 'warmth', 'professionalism', and their ability to 'instil confidence'. Those tested by the psi-believers did not rate their experimenters any more positively than those tested by the psi-disbelievers. This suggests that the apparent difference in psi performance was not due to psi-believers treating their participants in a manner that was noticeably different from the psi-disbelievers.

It has been suggested that an experimenter's motivation for obtaining evidence in support of psi is likely to be the over-riding moderator variable. Such motivation may be based upon a desire to have one's *a priori* beliefs in psi confirmed, or it may be how one's underlying expectations of success in the experiment manifest themselves. Either way, studies examining the putative role of experimenter psi in parapsychology (and psychology) experiments seem to suggest that an experimenter may have a direct, psi-based influence over the outcome of his or her studies in addition to any effect that may be mediated by how he or she interacts with participants.

Implications of the Experimenter Effect for the Study of Consciousness

It seems to me that the most wide-reaching implications of the research discussed in this paper for research on consciousness arise if, and only if, psi represents a genuine communication anomaly. If the experimenter effect in parapsychology can be satisfactorily explained by either experimenter error or experimenter fraud (or a combination of the two), then I see no reason why consciousness researchers should show any real interest, other than as a remarkable case study of unconscious and conscious self-deception. However, although more research is needed on the potential role of experimenter bias in contemporary parapsychological research, the experimenter error and fraud interpretations of the experimenter effect do not, in my view, appear to explain the existing data sufficiently.

The latter two sections of this paper suggest that the experimenter effect in parapsychology is likely to be of interest to researchers and theorists seeking to explore and explain the nature of consciousness. The research reviewed in these sections shows how an experimenter may unintentionally affect the data he or she is collecting. The research on the nature of the experimenter–participant interaction suggests that an experimenter's wishes, intentions and expectations may be communicated in ways that are familiar to social psychologists. The research on non-intentional psi suggests that these may even have a more direct impact upon the data, through experimenter psi. It should be noted that these two ostensible ways in which an experimenter's desires and expectations seem to impact upon data in psi experiments are not mutually exclusive, and they may well be mediated by both social psychological factors and psi-based factors.

From a methodological perspective, whatever the purported mechanism(s) of this effect of the experimenter upon the data, it does raise potential problems for sceptical researchers who wish to attempt to replicate psi experiments. This is because it suggests that such researchers, especially if they act as the experimenter who comes into contact with research participants, are less likely to obtain positive findings even if the psi effect is real. Rather than view this implication as a 'get-out clause' for pre-empting unsuccessful replication attempts, sceptical researchers should accommodate this possibility by, say, recruiting experimenters who have favourable attitudes towards psi, positive expectations of success, and are able to build a rapport with participants.

The suggestion that the outcomes of parapsychology experiments may be related, at least in part, to some kind of psi influence on behalf of the experimenter is probably the concept that many readers will find most uncomfortable.

For example, one might argue that the possibility of experimenter psi, and its impact upon the replicability of psi effects, raises an important challenge regarding the status of parapsychology as a science. This is because replication is a central tenet of the scientific method, and psi experimenter effects suggest it is only those researchers who believe that psi exists that are likely to be able to replicate positive results. According to this view, if sceptical researchers wishing to attempt replication cannot be expected to be successful due to their *a priori* beliefs about psi (no matter who they recruit in the role of experimenter), then parapsychology cannot be treated as a truly scientific discipline. However, the scientific approach adopted by psi research has so far achieved some limited success in identifying factors associated with obtaining positive results in psi experiments, and it is my view that it is such an approach that is likely to reveal more of these factors in future research. It is only when we have a much more detailed recipe for success can more consistent levels of replication be expected.

If psi experimenter effects are real, they have implications far beyond parapsychology. For example, more conventional experimental psychological research becomes difficult to interpret, as it would not be clear whether participants are the primary source of experimental findings (as is typically assumed) or whether the findings are simply an expression of the experimenter's own desires and expectations. Consciousness researchers would have to contend with the possibility that one's wishes and intentions could have a direct impact upon the wished for event; something which no currently accepted models of consciousness could accommodate. Palmer (1997) has recently argued that even parapsychologists themselves have not sufficiently considered the implications of experimenter psi, and pay insufficient attention to it when they design and conduct their experiments.

However, in the final analysis, it is left to the reader to decide whether research on the experimenter effect in parapsychology requires models of consciousness to be expanded. At the very least, it is hoped that this paper not only brings the literature surrounding this crucial issue that is central to parapsychology to a wider audience, but also encourages at least some to explore it further.

Acknowledgements

The preparation of this paper was supported by a grant from the Perrott–Warrick Fund.

References

Adair, J.G. & Epstein, J. (1967), 'Verbal cues in the mediation of experimenter bias', paper presented at the meeting of the Midwestern Psychological Association, Chicago, May 1967. Cited in Rosenthal, R. (1969), 'Interpersonal expectations: Effects of the experimenter's hypothesis', in *Artifact in Behavioral Research*, ed. R. Rosenthal, R.L. Rosnow. (New York: Academic Press).

Bem, D.J., Honorton, C. (1994), 'Does psi exist? Replicable evidence for an anomalous process of information transfer', *Psychological Bulletin*, **115**, pp. 4–18.

Broad, W., Wade, N. (1982), *Betrayers of the Truth: Fraud and Deceit in the Halls of Science* (London: Century).

Edge, H., Farkash, M. (1982), 'Further support for the psi-distributed hypothesis', in *Research in Parapsychology 1981*, ed. W.G. Roll, R.L. Morris, R.A. White (Metuchen, NJ: Scarecrow Press).

Friedman, N. (1967), *The Social Nature of Psychological Research* (New York: Basic Books).

Hansel, C.E.M. (1960) 'A critical review of experiments with Mr Basil Shackleton and Mrs Gloria Stewart as sensitives', *Proceedings of the Society for Psychical Research*, **53**, pp. 1–42.

Hansel, C.E.M. (1966), *ESP: A Scientific Evaluation* (New York: Scribners).

Honorton, C. Ramsey, M., Cabbibo, C. (1975), 'Experimenter effects in extrasensory perception', *Journal of the American Society for Psychical Research*, **69**, pp. 135–49.

Kennedy, J.E., Taddonio, J. (1976), 'Experimenter effects in parapsychological research', *Journal of Parapsychology*, **40**, pp. 1–33.

Kennedy, J.L., Uphoff, H.F. (1939), 'Experiments on the nature of extra-sensory perception: III. The recording error criticism of extra-chance scores', *Journal of Parapsychology*, **3**, pp. 226–45.

McClenon, J. (1982), 'A survey of elite scientists: Their attitudes toward ESP and parapsychology', *Journal of Parapsychology*, **46**, pp. 127–52.

McConnell, R.A., Clark, T.K. (1991), '"National Academy of Science" opinion on parapsychology', *Journal of the American Society for Psychical Research*, **85**, pp. 333–66.

MacFarland, J.D. (1938), 'Discrimination shown between experimenters by subjects', *Journal of Parapsychology*, **2**, pp. 160–70.

Markwick, B. (1978), 'The Soal–Goldney experiments with Basil Shackleton', *Proceedings of the Society for Psychical Research*, **56**, pp. 250–77.

Medhurst, R.G. (1971), 'The origin of the "prepared random numbers" used in the Shackleton experiments', *Journal of the Society for Psychical Research*, **46**, pp. 39–55.

Murphy, G. (1949), 'Psychical research in human personality', *Proceedings of the Society for Psychical Research*, **48**, pp. 1–15.

Nicol, J.F., Humphrey, B.M. (1953), 'The exploration of ESP and human personality', *Journal of the American Society for Psychical Research*, **47**, pp. 133–78.

Osis, K. (1953), 'A test of the relationship between ESP and PK', *Journal of Parapsychology*, **17**, pp. 298–309.

Page, S. (1970), 'Social interaction and experimenter effects in the verbal conditioning experiment', *Canadian Journal of Psychology*, **25**, pp. 463–75.

Palmer, J. (1986), 'ESP research findings: the process approach', in *Foundations of Parapsychology: Exploring the Boundaries of Human Capability*, ed. H.L. Edge, R.L. Morris, J. Palmer, J.H. Rush. (London: Routledge and Kegan Paul).

Palmer, J. (1997), 'The challenge of experimenter psi', *European Journal of Parapsychology*, **13**, pp. 110–25.

Parker, A. (1975), 'A pilot study of the influence of experimenter expectancy on ESP scores', in *Research in Parapsychology 1974*, ed. J.D. Morris, W.G. Roll, R.L. Morris (Metuchen, NJ: Scarecrow Press).

Pratt, J.G., Price, M.M. (1938), 'The experimenter–subject relationship in tests for ESP', *Journal of Parapsychology*, **2**, pp. 84–94.

Price, G.R. (1955), 'Science and the supernatural', *Science*, **122**, pp. 359–67.

Rhine, J.B. (1948), 'Conditions favoring success in psi tests', *Journal of Parapsychology*, **12**, pp. 58–75.

Rhine, J.B. (1974a), 'Security versus deception in parapsychology', *Journal of Parapsychology*, **38**, pp. 99–121.

Rhine, J.B. (1974b), 'Comments: a new case of experimenter reliability', *Journal of Parapsychology*, **38**, pp. 215–25.

Rhine, J.B., Pratt, J.G. (1957), *Parapsychology: Frontier Science of the Mind* (Springfield: C.C. Thomas).

Rosenthal, R. (1976), *Experimenter Effects in Behavioral Research*. Enlarged Edition. (New York: Irvington).

Rosenthal, R. (1969), 'Interpersonal expectations: Effects of the experimenter's hypothesis', in *Artifact in Behavioral Research*, ed. R. Rosenthal, R.L. Rosnow. (New York: Academic Press).

Schlitz, M.J., Laberge, S. (1997), 'Covert observation increases skin conductance in subjects unaware of when they are being observed: A replication', *Journal of Parapsychology*, **61**, pp. 185–96.

Schmeidler, G.R., Maher, M. (1981), 'Judges' responses to the nonverbal behavior of psi-conducive and psi-inhibitory experimenters', *Journal of the American Society for Psychical Research*, **75**, pp. 241–57.

Schmidt, H.S. (1975), 'Observation of subconscious PK effects with and without time displacement', in *Research in Parapsychology, 1974*, ed. J.D. Morris, W.G. Roll, R.L. Morris (Metuchen, NJ: Scarecrow Press).

Schneider, R., Binder, M., Walach, H. (2000), 'Examining the role of neutral versus personal experimenter–participant interactions: An EDA-DMILS experiment', *Journal of Parapsychology*, **64**, pp. 181–94.

Scott, C. et al. (1974), 'The Soal–Goldney experiments with Basil Shackleton: A discussion', *Proceedings of the Society for Psychical Research*, **56**, pp. 43–131.

Sheffield, F.D., Kaufman, R.S., Rhine, J.B. (1952), 'A PK experiment at Yale starts a controversy', *Journal of the American Society for Psychical Research*, **46**, pp. 111–17.

Smith, M.D. (in press), 'The psychology of the "psi-conducive" experimenter: Personality, attitudes towards psi, and personal psi experience', *Journal of Parapsychology*.

Soal, S.G., Goldney, K.M. (1943), 'Experiments in precognitive telepathy', *Proceedings of the Society for Psychical Research*, **47**, pp. 21–150.

Stanford, R. (1970), 'Extrasensory effects upon "memory"', *Journal of the American Society for Psychical Research*, **64**, pp. 161–86.

Stanford, R.G., Zenhausern, R., Taylor, A., Dwyer, M. (1975), 'Psychokinesis as psi-mediated instrumental response', *Journal of the American Society for Psychical Research*, **69**, pp. 127–34.

Taddonio, J.L. (1976), 'The relationship of experimenter expectancy to performance on ESP tasks', *Journal of Parapsychology*, **40**, pp. 107–14.

Thouless, R.H. (1949–1952), 'A report on an experiment in psychokinesis with dice and a discussion of psychological factors favouring success', *Proceedings of the Society for Psychical Research*, **49**, pp. 107–30.

Troffer, S.A., Tart, C.T. (1964), 'Experimenter bias in hypnotist performance', *Science*, **145**, pp. 1330–1.

Wagner, M.W., Monnet, M. (1979), 'Attitudes of college professors towards extra-sensory perception', *Zetetic Scholar*, **5**, pp. 7–16.

Watt, C. (2002), 'Experimenter effects with a remote facilitation of attention focusing task: A study with multiple believer and disbeliever experimenters', in *Proceedings of Presented Papers: The Parapsychological Association 45th Annual Convention*, ed. Watt, C. (ed.), pp. 306–18.

Watt, C., Baker, I. (2002), 'Remote facilitation of attention focusing with psi-supportive versus psi-unsupportive experimenter suggestions', *Journal of Parapsychology*, **66**, pp. 151–68.

Watt, C., Wiseman, R., Schlitz, M. (2002), 'Tacit information in remote staring research: The Wiseman–Schlitz interviews', *The Paranormal Review*, **24**, pp. 18–25.

Weiner, D.H., Zingrone, N.L. (1986), 'The checker effect revisited', *Journal of Parapsychology*, **50**, pp. 85–121.

West, D.J., Fisk, G.W. (1953), 'A dual ESP experiment with clock cards', *Journal of the Society for Psychical Research*, **37**, pp. 185–9.

White, R.A. (1976), 'The limits of experimenter influence on psi test results: Can any be set?', *Journal of the American Society for Psychical Research*, **70**, pp. 333–69.

Wiseman, R., Schlitz, M. (1997), 'Experimenter effects and the remote detection of staring', *Journal of Parapsychology*, **61**, pp. 197–207.

Wiseman, R., Schlitz, M. (1999), 'Experimenter effects and the remote detection of staring: An attempted replication', in *The Parapsychological Association 42nd Annual Convention Proceedings of Presented Papers*, ed. K. Dalton, pp. 471–9.

Wiseman, R., Smith, M.D. (1994), 'A further look at the detection of unseen gaze', in *The Parapsychological Association 37th Annual Convention Proceedings of Presented Papers*, ed. D.J. Bierman, pp. 465–78.

Wiseman, R. Smith, M.D., Freedman, D., Wasserman, T., Hurst, C. (1995), 'Two further experiments concerning the remote detection of an unseen gaze', in *The Parapsychological Association 38th Annual Convention Proceedings of Presented Papers*, ed. N.L. Zingrone, pp. 480–90.

Simon J. Sherwood and Chris A. Roe

A Review of Dream ESP Studies Conducted Since the Maimonides Dream ESP Programme

Abstract: *We review the dream ESP studies conducted since the end of the Maimonides research programme. Combined effect size estimates for both sets of studies (Maimonides r = 0.33, 95% C.I. 0.24 to 0.43; post-Maimonides r = 0.14, 95% C.I. 0.06 to 0.22) suggest that judges could correctly identify target materials more often than would be expected by chance using dream mentation. Maimonides studies were significantly more successful (p< 0.05) than post-Maimonides studies, which may be due to procedural differences, including that post-Maimonides receivers tended to sleep at home and were generally not deliberately awakened from REM sleep. Methodological shortcomings of some studies are discussed. Nevertheless, home dream ESP research has been successful and continues to be a less expensive and less labour-intensive alternative to sleep-laboratory-based research. We hope that interest in dream ESP research will be re-awakened.*

This paper aims to review studies of alleged dream extrasensory perception (ESP) conducted since the end of the Maimonides research programme and to compare and contrast their respective methodology and success.

As defined by Irwin (1999, p. 6), 'An *extrasensory experience* is one in which it appears that the experient's mind has acquired information directly, that is, seemingly without the mediation of the recognized human senses or the processes of logical inference'. ESP can be further classified: telepathy (information about the present obtained from another person); clairvoyance (information about present events or objects obtained from the environment); precognition (information about future events); retrocognition (information about past events).

Many spontaneous case reports of alleged ESP occur while the experients are in some kind of altered state of consciousness (ASC) (see Alvarado, 1998). Case

Correspondence:
Simon Sherwood, Division of Psychology, University College Northampton, Boughton Green Road, Northampton NN2 7AL, UK. *Email: Simon.Sherwood@northampton.ac.uk*

Journal of Consciousness Studies, **10**, No. 6–7, 2003, pp. 85–109

collections suggest that a large proportion, as much as 65% (Rhine, 1981), of spontaneous cases of ESP have occurred during dreams. Clients undergoing psychological therapy have also experienced dream ESP (e.g., see Krippner, 1991; Van de Castle, 1977).

Dreaming is an obvious ASC for researchers to focus on (Ullman & Krippner with Vaughan, 1973; 1989) because it is naturally occurring and contains features considered to be important facilitators of ESP (see Braud & Braud, 1975; Honorton, 1977). However, it has the disadvantage of being very time consuming and requires expensive EEG–EOG monitoring equipment and sleep laboratory facilities if participants are to be deliberately awakened from REM to report their dreams, and so researchers turned to using the Ganzfeld[1] technique during the 1970s. This technique is less expensive, less labour intensive, and was believed to induce a state similar to the hypnagogic (HG) state, i.e., the state that is entered just as one is falling asleep, a state also considered to include psi-conducive features of the sleep state. Although the Ganzfeld has been the dominant paradigm for ESP research since then, and has provided some of the best evidence (e.g., Bem & Honorton, 1994; Bem et al., 2001 — but see Hyman, 1994; Milton & Wiseman, 1999), the extent to which it induces an ASC is not clear (Alvarado, 1998). In fact, in a recent study, Wackermann et al. (2000) concluded that '[C]ontrary to the common belief, the ganzfeld does not necessarily induce a true hypnagogic state, and will surely not do so in most ganzfeld settings' (p. 302).

The Maimonides Dream ESP Studies

Psychiatrist Montague Ullman established a dream laboratory at the Maimonides Medical Center, Brooklyn, in 1962 (Krippner, 1991). Before the laboratory closed in 1978 (Krippner, 1991; 1993; Ullman et al., 1973; 1989), his research team had conducted thirteen formal dream ESP studies and three groups of pilot sessions (see Table 1). Of the thirteen formal studies, eleven were designed to investigate telepathy and two precognition. The pilot sessions were designed to investigate clairvoyance, telepathy and precognition, respectively (see Table 1)

The Maimonides procedure was developed and improved over time and a number of different procedural variations were explored. Thus, the following is intended as only a general description of a trial designed to investigate telepathy.[2] The receiver was attached to EEG–EOG monitoring equipment and slept in a sound-attenuated room in the laboratory. Once he or she was asleep, a target was randomly selected from among a set of targets (typically art prints), selected on the basis of emotional intensity, vividness, colour and simplicity. The target, in a sealed envelope, was given to the sender, who was then locked inside another sound-attenuated room in the building (or, in some studies, a different building). The experimenter monitored the receiver's EEG–EOG throughout the night and,

---

[1] A sensory habituation method that encourages the internal focusing of attention and minimizes sensory distractions while the participant is physically relaxed.

[2] It is possible that clairvoyance and/or precognition could also have operated.

once the receiver had entered REM sleep, signalled the sender (via a buzzer) to open the target envelope and begin sending the target. At the end of the REM period, the experimenter awakened the receiver via an intercom and asked him or her to describe any dream(s). Responses throughout the night and in the morning were tape-recorded and later transcribed. The sender heard the receiver's dream report via a loudspeaker, which may have reinforced his or her subsequent sending strategy. The receiver then went back to sleep. This process was repeated for each REM period with the same target being sent each time. In the morning, the receiver reported any associations to the dream mentation and guessed what the target might be. Receivers typically viewed between eight and twelve pictures, one of which was the target, gave a confidence rating for each picture[3] and also placed them in rank order according to the correspondence with their dream mentation, associations and/or guesses. Complete dream transcripts and target sets were also sent to independent judges who made similar judgements. The ratings/rankings from the two or three blind judges were combined. A trial was a 'binary hit' if the target picture had been ranked in the top half of the target set and a 'binary miss' if ranked in the bottom half. Performance was then evaluated to determine whether it was significantly higher or lower than mean chance expectations (MCE).

During most of the telepathy studies (see Table 1, A–H) the receivers' dreams were monitored and recorded throughout the night and the same target was sent during each REM period (Child, 1985). However, during two studies known as the 'Sensory bombardment' and 'Grateful Dead' studies (L, M), the sending periods did not occur regularly throughout the night and did not necessarily coincide with the receivers' REM periods. In the study with A. Vaughan, I. Vaughan, Harris and Parise (study O), some trials involved sending a different target during each REM period.

Studies using the same receiver across all trials often used the same sender, too (B, D, E, F), but not always. Successful sender and receiver pairings from the two screening studies (A, C) were used in later studies. Some studies used more than one sender (A, C, G, O), either across a series of trials with the same receiver or different receivers. There was not always a single sender for each receiver either; for some of the sensory bombardment (L) trials there was a single sender for two receivers; for the Grateful Dead trials a concert audience of about 2,000 people acted as senders. During precognition and clairvoyance trials there was no sender. The distance between the sender and receiver also varied across the studies (e.g., A & B vs. L & M).

Some studies employed 'multisensory' targets rather than just static art prints: in the second study with Erwin (F), the sender was provided with objects related to the art prints and asked to act out aspects of the scenes; in the first study with Bessent (I), Bessent spent an hour the following morning looking at a picture and immersing himself in a multisensory environment that accompanied this; in the second Bessent study (J), the targets were slide sequences with accompanying

---

[3] In the early studies (A–C — see Table 1) confidence ratings for the rankings were given on a five-point scale but from the Posin study (D) onwards a 100-point scale was used.

soundtracks. Slide sequences with a soundtrack were also used in the sensory bombardment study (L). In the final Maimonides study (Honorton *et al.*, 1975), films were used.

Maimonides dream ESP success

During his review, Child (1985) discovered that the only way the results could be analyzed across the Maimonides series was in terms of the number of binary hits and misses. For most studies, these data were available for both participants and independent blind judges but in some studies only blind judging was conducted (see Child, 1985, Table 1, studies F, I–K). Child used the data based upon judging of the whole dream transcripts (which included associations as well as the participants' guesses). Child (1985) concluded that:

> The outcome is clear. Several segments of the data, considered separately, yield significant evidence that dreams (and associations to them) tended to resemble the picture chosen randomly as target more than they resembled other pictures in the pool. (p. 1223).

A meta-analysis of 450 Maimonides ESP trials (based upon the blind judges' data) found the overall success rate to be 63% (MCE = 50%) with odds of 75 million to 1 against achieving such a result by chance (Radin, 1997, pp.71–2). This meta-analysis also found that the binary hit rate for 20 of the 25 sets of data analysed was above the MCE.

Statistical significance can provide an indication of the probability of obtaining such an outcome if the null hypothesis were true but it can not provide an indication of the magnitude of the effect. Whether or not a statistical test produces a significant outcome will depend upon the magnitude of the effect, the power of the test and the sample size. Conversion of a test statistic to a common effect size measure has the advantage over conventional significance testing in that it provides an indication of the magnitude of any effect and permits direct comparisons across studies with different sample sizes (Prentice & Miller, 1992). Thus, we have converted the test statistics for the judges' ratings/rankings (either z or t values) into an effect size measure[4] r (see Clark-Carter, 1997, pp. 550–1, 558) for the twelve formal studies[5] and three pilot studies listed in Table 1 of Child's (1985) review. A positive effect size indicates that performance was above chance expectations; a negative effect size indicates that performance was below chance. Cohen's (1977) rule of thumb suggests that r = 0.1 would be considered a small effect, r = 0.3 a medium effect and r = 0.5 or above a large effect.

For the fifteen sets of data, the effect size r[6] ranges from –0.22 to 1.10 (see Table 1). Interestingly, the studies with the largest effect sizes mostly involved

---

[4] The correlation coefficient r is one of the most commonly used effect size measures (Prentice & Miller, 1992).

[5] The Honorton *et al.* (1975) study was not included in Child's review and cannot be included here because complete statistical test results are not available.

[6] As with other correlation coefficient estimates, r should fall in the range –1 to +1. However, where z scores are large, it is possible for r to exceed this range.

	Study	Type of ESP	Trials	Test statistic	Effect size r
A	Ullman et al. (1966) study 1, first screening	Telepathy	12	z = 0.71	0.205
B	Ullman, et al. (1966) study 2, first Erwin study	Telepathy	7	z = 2.53	0.956
C	Ullman (1969), second screening	Telepathy	12	z = −0.25	−0.072
D	Ullman (1969), Posin study	Telepathy	8	z = 1.05	0.371
E	Ullman et al. (1973), Grayeb study	Telepathy	8	z = −0.63	−0.223
F	Ullman & Krippner (1969), second Erwin study	Telepathy	8	t = 4.93	0.881
G	Krippner & Ullman (1970), Van de Castle study	Telepathy	8	t = 2.81	0.728
H	Pilot sessions	Telepathy	67	z = 4.20	0.513
I	Krippner, et al. (1971), first Bessent study	Precognition	8	t = 2.81	0.728
J	Krippner et al. (1972), second Bessent study	Precognition	8	t = 2.27	0.651
K	Pilot sessions	Precognition	2	z = 0.67	0.474
L	Krippner et al. (1971), Sensory bombardment study	Telepathy	8	z = 3.11	1.100
M	Krippner et al. (1973), Grateful Dead study	Telepathy	12	z = 0.61	0.176
N	Pilot sessions	Clairvoyance	8	z = 0.98	0.346
O	Honorton et al. (1972), Vaughan, Harris, & Parise study	Telepathy	203	z = 0.63	0.044
	Honorton et al. (1975)	Telepathy	—	unknown	unknown

Table 1.

Results for the Maimonides dream ESP studies based upon the blind judges' data summarized by Child (1985)

gifted single participants who had been pre-selected (i.e., Erwin, Van de Castle, and Bessent) and two of the least successful Maimonides studies were the two screening studies (A, C) that identified successful senders and receivers for use in subsequent studies. The two precognitive studies and one pilot study (I–K) were very successful (effect size ranges from 0.47 to 0.73). The clairvoyance pilot sessions (N) were also successful but less so (r = 0.35). The most successful Maimonides dream ESP study (r = 1.10) was the sensory bombardment telepathy study (L); other studies that employed multisensory targets were also very successful (F, I, J) (r = 0.65 to 0.88).

Criticisms of the Maimonides studies

The main criticisms of the Maimonides studies are concerned with the lack of replication (see Hyman, 1986; Krippner, 1991; Parker, 1975, p. 90) and the number of statistical analyses, and by whom these were conducted (Child, 1985;

Parker, 1975, p. 89). Child (1985) encountered two main areas of difficulty when evaluating the Maimonides research findings: (1) the analysis had been passed to various consultants and the raw data were no longer available (this may explain some of the variation in data treatment and statistical analysis and inadequate description of analyses in some published reports); (2) in some earlier studies,

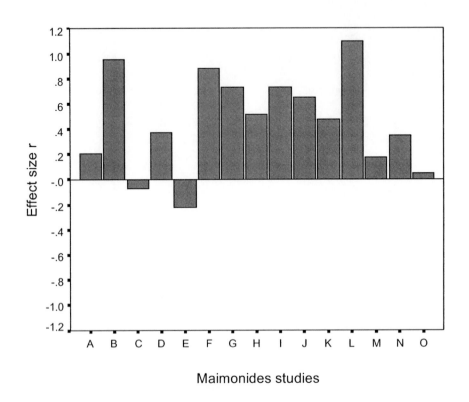

Figure 1.

Effect size r estimates based upon blind judges' data for the fifteen Maimonides data sets summarized by Child (1985)

the blind judges' judgements may not have been completely independent so that they might have derived clues to the target identity from other transcripts (Clemmer, 1986). However, this would not account for the successful results obtained from the participants' judgements or, in later studies, where transcripts were edited for potential cues and presented in random order (Krippner, 1991). Alcock (1981) criticized the studies for lacking a control group but the controls in such studies are the other non-target stimuli against which the transcript is also compared. Fraud has also been suggested as a possible explanation for the results (e.g., Clemmer, 1986) but no plausible mechanism for fraud has been put forward.

Attempted Replications of Maimonides Studies

This section addresses the issue of whether the Maimonides research has in fact been replicated. There have been two conceptual replications of individual performances within the Maimonides research programme. In terms of the effect sizes for blind judges, Erwin's performance in his first telepathy study was r = 0.96 compared with r = 0.88 in his second study; Bessent obtained an effect size of r = 0.73 in his first precognition study and r = 0.65 in his second.

During the 1960s and 1970s, there were six attempts,[7] by researchers at other laboratories, to replicate the Maimonides dream telepathy findings using EEG–EOG monitoring and deliberate awakening from REM sleep (Belvedere & Foulkes, 1971; Dement, 1974; Foulkes, et al., 1972; Globus et al., 1968; Hall, 1967; Strauch, 1970), though none of these can be considered exact replication attempts. The Foulkes et al. (1972) study cannot be considered an independent replication attempt because some of the investigators had been involved in a previous Maimonides study.

Three of the replication attempts are difficult to evaluate due to the limited amount of detail available in the published reports (Dement, 1974; Globus et al., 1968; Strauch, 1970). The first of these was a seventeen-night study involving a pair of friends (Globus et al., 1968). The sender viewed, imagined and acted out the activity portrayed in the target pictures during the sending periods. Judgements were based upon a combination of hypnagogic, non-REM and REM mentation (Parker, 1975; Strauch, 1970), which is unlike the Maimonides procedure. Although no specific details of the outcome nor any statistical analyses were reported, Globus et al. (1968, p. 365) concluded that 'A consensus of judges was unable to correctly designate the "target picture" more often than would be expected by chance; thus, the null hypothesis was not rejected'.

Strauch (1970) conducted a study with twelve female participants who reported good dream recall and previous parapsychological experiences. Each participant spent three nights at the laboratory but only on the latter two nights did the experimenter/sender attempt to send a randomly selected picture. Participants were awakened from REM sleep and reported their dreams. However, six independent judges did not identify the target pictures better than MCE. It is not known how the judges (one of whom was the receiver) performed individually but it has been reported elsewhere that 'the judges differed widely in their ratings' (Strauch, 1970, p. 50).

Dement (1974, pp. 58–9) described some pilot dream telepathy trials conducted in 1970–71 but the study itself is unpublished and only limited information about the methodology and results is provided. Six-hundred students attending one of Dement's classes were asked simultaneously to send a slide of an object to six participants as they entered a REM period at a sleep laboratory over a mile away. As Dement acknowledged, this experiment was very problematic, not least because

---

[7] Rechtschaffen (1970) also described some unpublished pilot dream telepathy trials but most of these involved the use of hypnotic waking dreams. As the majority of these trials did not involve dreams reported during sleep, it is not appropriate to discuss this pilot work here.

the senders were shown a photo of the receiver and then asked to decide which target they should send. Although the judging procedure is not described, Dement reported that none of the targets was manifested in the receivers' dreams.

A study by Hall (1967) has been cited as a successful replication of the Maimonides studies (see Krippner, 1975).[8] There were six male participants in this study, the most successful of whom was Van de Castle (see Van de Castle, 1989). Hall (1967) was able to identify a connection between the dream mentation and the target in 56 out of 121 dream transcripts and this was confirmed in 29 cases by judgements made by a large group of undergraduates. Although Hall (1967, p. 47) concluded 'This result shows that it is possible to influence dreams telepathically even under artificial experimental circumstances'. This could only be replication in a conceptual sense as the judging and analysis method used was unique to this study. However, this study lacked adequate controls against sensory leakage and involved arbitrary selection of data for analysis (see Parker, 1975; Strauch, 1970) and so cannot here be considered a successful replication of the Maimonides studies.

Van de Castle (1971) also acted as experimenter in a non-laboratory dream telepathy study involving a group of youth-camp members. However, the limited amount of information available in the published summary of this study makes it difficult to evaluate fully. Nevertheless, it is clear that, before midnight, Van de Castle selected a colour magazine picture and gave it to a camp staff member. Throughout the night this member of staff periodically acted as the sender. In the morning the picture was placed upon a table, along with four decoys, and the campers were asked to rank the pictures. Ranks of one or two were deemed a hit and ranks of four or five, a miss. This resulted in a total of 95 hits and 55 misses (p< 0.002). One problem is that handling of the target picture by the experimenter and sender prior to the judging may have left marks upon it that gave clues to the target identity. For this reason it is always advisable to use a duplicate set of materials for judging.

Belvedere and Foulkes (1971) attempted a replication (albeit not an entirely independent attempt) of the Van de Castle Maimonides study (Krippner & Ullman, 1970). Van de Castle again served as receiver and, using dreams plus associations to make judgements, obtained three binary hits and five misses. Judge 1 also obtained three hits and five misses; Judge 2 obtained four hits and four misses. This contrasted with the eight hits obtained by Van de Castle and six by the blind judges in the original study. Belvedere and Foulkes (1971) postulated that it could either be that the Maimonides result was spurious or that there were differences between the two studies that interfered with any anomalous communication processes that might have been operating. Belvedere and Foulkes (1971) acknowledged that there were some procedural variations: (1) Van de Castle had requested that colour magazine pictures be used instead of art prints; (2) that he should be awakened during rather than at the end of the REM periods; (3) the trials were conducted over a two-week rather than a 44-week

---

[8] Krippner (1975) also cites an unpublished study by Ross (1972) as being a successful replication but
     no details are available.

period; (4) the target pools may not have been sufficiently heterogeneous and not all in colour, as requested (see Van de Castle, 1989); (5) the psychological climate was not as conducive as before and; (6) Van de Castle did not have as much choice in terms of available senders. Van de Castle (1989) felt very strongly that the conditions in the replication study were far from conducive and that it should be deemed neither a replication attempt nor a failure. However, the onus is on parapsychologists to identify what the psi-conducive and psi-inhibitory factors are and to ensure that studies are designed to maximize the former and minimize the latter; simply saying, after the fact, that the conditions were not right can too easily be seen as attempt to salvage a favoured but unsupported hypothesis.

Belvedere and Foulkes, along with members of the original research teams (Foulkes *et al.*, 1972) attempted to replicate another Maimonides study, this time the sensory bombardment study (Krippner *et al.*, 1971). The consensus judging of the three judges resulted in five binary hits and three misses; this compares with eight binary hits and no misses from the three judges in the original study. However, again this study cannot be considered an exact replication attempt. As Foulkes *et al.* (1972, p. 734) pointed out, 'Our experiment deviated from the original in a number of ways. . . . It is not clear which set or sets of factors may have contributed to the discrepancy in results between the two studies'.

These deviations included that, in the original study, the sender was located at Masters and Houston's laboratory, fourteen miles away from the receiver located at the Maimonides laboratory; in the replication attempt he was located in Belvedere and Foulkes' laboratory, approximately 2,000 miles away. In the original study, two receivers were tested at a time; on three of the four nights there was only one sender for each pair but on the other night there were two senders each sending a different target to a different receiver. In the replication attempt, there was only one receiver per night and Bessent was the only sender used. Also, in the original study, the judges did not get to see the audio–visual sequences during judging and were only given a list of the sequence titles.

In summary, none of the five studies that used EEG–EOG monitoring and deliberate awakening can be considered exact replication attempts because of their variations in procedure. Four of them cannot be considered successful conceptual replications either, in that performance was not significantly better than MCE.

The Post-Maimonides Dream ESP Studies

We have seen that there were few replication attempts during the life of the Maimonides dream laboratory. The prohibitive costs of maintaining a sleep laboratory may have discouraged other researchers from replicating the Maimonides work. However, some researchers have continued to investigate dream ESP, albeit using less expensive and less labour-intensive methods.

It is a quarter of a century since the Maimonides laboratory closed and since their last formal dream ESP study was conducted (Honorton *et al.*, 1975). A search of the subsequent literature identified 22 formal reports of dream ESP studies (see Table 2). Unlike the Maimonides series, which focused mainly on

	Study	Type of ESP	Trials	Test Statistic	Effect Size r
1	Child et al. (1977) Experiment 1	Telepathy	8	t = 1.87 df = 7	0.58
2	Child et al. (1977) Experiment 2	Telepathy	5	t = 2.69 df = 4	0.80
—	Kanthamani et al. (1988) Preliminary	Clairvoyance	4	—	—
3	Kanthamani et al. (1988) Pilot	Clairvoyance	10	t = 0.75 df = 9	0.24
4	Kanthamani & Khilji (1990)	Clairvoyance	20	t = 1.79 df = 19	0.38
5	Kanthamani & Broughton (1992)	Clairvoyance	40 (20)	t = 3.52 df = 19	0.63
6	Braud (1977) Pilot	Telepathy	50	z = –1.90	–0.27
7	Braud (1977) Experiment 1	Telepathy	30	z = 1.29	0.16
	Braud (1977) Experiment 2	Telepathy	36		
—	McLaren & Sargent (1982)	Precognition	30	—	—
8	Sargent & Harley (1982)	Precognition	20	z = 0.30[a]	0.07
9	Harley (1989)	Clairvoyance	20	t = –2.45 df = 19	–0.49
10	Markwick & Beloff (1983)	Clairvoyance/ Telepathy	100	z = 1.87[a]	0.18
11	Markwick & Beloff (1988)	Clairvoyance/ Precognition	100	z = –0.39	–0.04
—	Hearne & Worsley (1977)	Telepathy	—	A = 1671 df = 7	—
—	Hearne (1981a)	Telepathy	2	—	—
12	Hearne (1981b)	Telepathy	—	$F_{(1,7)}$ = 0.00	0.00
13	Hearne (1987)	Telepathy	8	z = –0.39[a]	–0.14
14	Hearne (1989)	Telepathy	10	z = 0.31	0.10
15	Dalton et al. (1999)	Clairvoyance	32	z = 3.58	0.63
16	Sherwood et al. (2000)	Clairvoyance	28	z = 1.44	0.27
17	Dalton et al. (2000)	Clairvoyance	16	z = 2.35[a]	0.59
18	Eppinger (2001)	Clairvoyance	50	z = –0.07	–0.01
19	Roe et al. (2002)	Clairvoyance	31	z = 0.80	0.14
20	Sherwood et al. (2002)	Precognition	12	z = –1.16	–0.34
21	Weiner & McCain (1981)	Clairvoyance	12	t = 2.30 df = 11	0.57

[a] z score based upon ratings calculated by the auhtors (Sherwood & Roe)

Table 2. Results for the post-Maimonides dream ESP studies
(based mostly upon the combined judgements of participants and experimenters and/or senders).

telepathy, less than half of the post-Maimonides studies did so. The majority investigated clairvoyance, which is methodologically simpler in that it does not require a sender.

Braud (1977) studies

Among the first post-Maimonides studies were three telepathy studies conducted by Braud (1977) that differed from the Maimonides work in two basic ways; first, participants slept in their own homes, waking naturally and attempting to recall the content of their dreams; secondly, multiple participants were run on single trial nights. In the first study, 50 (mostly) 'friends and acquaintances' kept a dream diary for a specific date. Between 2:00 and 2:30 a.m. on that date, Braud sent a randomly selected target slide. Participants marked their dream impressions for the presence or absence of ten features. The target slides had been coded for the same binary features and Braud calculated the number of matches between the target and dream codings. Apparently, all 50 participants responded, but unfortunately only three of these correctly identified more than the MCE of five binary features. Participant majority votes resulted in only two matches with the target. When Braud restricted his sample to 10 'close friends' in the first of two confirmation studies, participants attempted to identify six different targets sent over three consecutive days. Three of the targets were sent at 10:00 p.m.; the remaining three targets were sent at 5:30 a.m. Braud (1977) did not report the performance for dream and hypnagogic (HG) mentation separately but only gave the overall mean majority vote score of 6.84, which was significantly greater than MCE. The second confirmation study used the same participants and procedure except that the sending times were changed to 10:30 p.m. and 6:00 a.m. Unfortunately, only seven respondents returned their protocols and, of these, three were incomplete. Participants who felt that they had not performed well might have decided not to return their data. This notwithstanding, the findings from the previous study were replicated and performance (mean score = 6.33) was again significantly better than MCE. Braud (1977) found that overall performance, for the two confirmation studies combined (mean score = 6.58), was significantly better than MCE. It was also apparent that HG performance (mean score = 7.33) was better than dream performance (mean score = 5.83) but not significantly so.

In summary, Braud's studies suggested that, although both HG and dream mentation might be conducive to telepathy, the HG state seems to be more conducive than the sleep state.[9]

Weiner and McCain (1981) study

Over 22 nights, 19 of McCain's friends recorded their dreams and coded them for the presence or absence of nine binary features (Weiner & McCain, 1981). Each night, Weiner randomly selected a target for each of two conditions: one was allocated to a single participant condition; the other was allocated to the remaining participants in the group condition. There were 12 individual and 22 sets of group dream reports. Performance in the individual condition was significantly

---

[9] It is also interesting to note that a content analysis of the transcripts from the first Maimonides study with Erwin as receiver revealed that hypnagogic and hypnopompic imagery, but not dream imagery, was significantly associated with the targets (White et al., 1971).

better than MCE. No figure is reported for the group majority vote condition, although performance was nonsignificantly lower than the individual condition. One potential problem with this study is that Weiner, who had determined the target sequence, independently judged the target and dream codings and compared her judgements with McCain to check for discrepancies; her memory of the target sequence might have influenced the resolution of any such discrepancies.

Child, Kanthamani and Sweeney (1977) studies

Child et al. (1977) conducted two telepathy experiments with Sweeney acting as the only percipient. Sweeney slept at home as Child selected and sent a randomly selected art print for ten minutes from 10:45 p.m. In experiment 1, judging took place after the series. Each of the three authors (i.e., including the sender) independently rated the eight dream transcripts against the eight pictures that had been selected as targets. No detail is given as to whether the order of targets and/or transcripts was randomized (which is essential because the sender knew the order in which the targets were selected and the receiver knew the order in which her dreams occurred) nor do the authors describe any controls to ensure that sender and percipient did not come into contact between sessions. Performance, based upon the combined judgements, was better than MCE (the mean SOR was 10.37 where MCE is 13.5) although this difference is not significant. In experiment 2, the procedure allowed the percipient and Kanthamani to make their judgements the following morning. Two of the seven sessions were later disregarded because Sweeney had not recalled any dreams. It is not clear why only seven trials were completed; it would have been better if the decision to exclude any trials had been made *a priori* in order to avoid accusations of optional stopping. The ranks awarded to targets were again combined to give a mean SOR of 8.85, which is significantly better than the MCE of 13. When the results of these two studies were combined, the cumulative result was significant. Child et al. (1977) reported that 'In subsequent months we carried out similar experiments with the agent in Connecticut and the participant in either Tennessee or Italy. These experiments showed little deviation from chance.' (pp. 92–3) but mentioned no further details. These replication attempts do not appear to have been published and are therefore unavailable for review.

Dream versus Ganzfeld ESP performance

Kanthamani conducted a number of further studies, but which investigated clairvoyance rather than telepathy. The first two experiments (Kanthamani et al., 1988) were intended to compare Ganzfeld and dream clairvoyance. One of the authors, Rustomji-Kerns served, as the sole percipient, as 'she had rich experience in dream work and in maintaining a dream journal' (p. 414). In the preliminary experiment she completed four Ganzfeld and four dream trials. The order of the conditions was not counterbalanced. After completing a Ganzfeld session, Rustomji-Kerns slept at home and suggested that she would wake in the night and write down her dreams. She added any further associations or impressions when she awoke the next morning. A common target was used for the two conditions in each trial, which may be problematic because the participant, when dreaming, would have knowledge of her own Ganzfeld experience so that the mentation for the two conditions may not have been independent.

The following morning, as a group, Rustomji-Kerns and the two experimenters judged first the Ganzfeld and then the dream mentation against four pictures in the target set, using ratings and rankings. However, the judges discussed any correspondences before making their judgements, which could have compromised the independence of these judgements. In the pilot experiment, involving ten trials per condition, a fourth judge also judged both types of mentation independently from the others in a counterbalanced fashion. Their ratings were used to compute combined z-scores of ratings for target pictures. Once the judging had been completed, the target envelope was opened. For the preliminary trials, the mean z-scores indicated that in the Ganzfeld condition the targets were rated slightly higher than the non-targets but the reverse was true in the dream condition. However, neither of these means nor the difference between them was statistically significant.

In the pilot experiment, Ganzfeld trials were not successful, giving a mean z score that was suggestively below MCE. The mean z score for dream judgements was positive but not significant. However, the difference between the conditions was suggestive. A secondary analysis using sum of ranks showed the dream protocol to be significantly better than the Ganzfeld protocol.

An attempted replication (Kanthamani & Khilji, 1990) involved a sample of ten participants who, in this case, each contributed two trials of each type, completed in a counterbalanced order. There were only two judges; the participant and the experimenter. Again, there was evidence of missing in the Ganzfeld condition and hitting in the dream condition and, although neither of these deviated significantly from MCE, the difference between the conditions was again significant. Analyses of the combined ranks confirmed earlier findings, but here dream performance was also significantly better than chance. However, we are not convinced about the validity of the t-test analyses conducted given that it would appear, from the reported degrees of freedom, that the two data points per participant in each of the two conditions were treated as independent.

A further confirmation (Kanthamani & Broughton, 1992) of the superiority of dream over Ganzfeld mentation involved 20 volunteers. Each participant contributed a Ganzfeld–dream trial pair followed by a dream–Ganzfeld pair, as this was the most successful order of presentation from the previous study. The study confirmed, once again, a significant difference between Ganzfeld and dreaming trials, with the latter being superior. Performance in the dream condition was significantly above MCE. The analysis for this study appears not to have repeated the error of treating participants' two data points in each condition as independent.

Sargent and Harley (1982) reported a pilot study that tested for precognition both in the Ganzfeld and in the dream state. In this study Sargent served as both participant and experimenter for all 24 Ganzfeld trials while Harley performed a similar role for all 20 dream trials.[10] Sargent and Harley did not analyze the two conditions separately, but rather combined performance for the two conditions, giving a sum of ranks of 101 that is below the MCE of 110. Although performance in both conditions was better than MCE, neither comes close to significance (SOR for Ganzfeld is 53, where MCE = 60; for dream trials SOR is 48, where MCE = 50). Ganzfeld performance was a little better than dream performance, however.

A more recent Ganzfeld versus dream clairvoyance study, using a repeated measures design, was conducted by Eppinger (2001). Fifty participants, pre-selected for their capacity for dream recall, completed a Ganzfeld and a dream clairvoyance trial in a counterbalanced order. Participants who could not remember their dreams from a given night were asked to repeat the trial with the same target. After a dream trial, the participant came into the laboratory with his or her dream report and rated and ranked four picture postcards. Unlike the Kanthamani studies, there were no additional independent judges. Although performance was lower than MCE in both conditions (dream SOR = 131, Ganzfeld SOR = 137, MCE = 125), it was marginally better in the dream condition.

Thus, in summary, four out of five clairvoyance studies found dream ESP performance to be superior to Ganzfeld performance, and three of these found this difference to be statistically significant. The other study by Sargent and Harley, which compared precognition performance under similar conditions, found a trend in the opposite direction; however, this study used an independent design for the two conditions and so the differences could have been due to individual differences between the two participants. The superiority of dream over Ganzfeld ESP performance evident here suggests that the former warrants the kind of further systematic investigation from which the latter has benefited.

Additional Sargent, Harley and McLaren studies

McLaren and Sargent (1982) conducted another dream precognition study with a single participant who kept a dream diary. Seventeen trials were overt precognition trials in which the participant was asked to rank a set of four pictures, determined by McLaren, against each dream record and to mark any dreams that he felt had been successful with 'CC' ('confidence call'). McLaren then randomly determined the target. The other thirteen trials were covert precognition trials in which the judging and determination of the target were carried out by Sargent. Only the results for the overt trials are reported (though in two places these appear to have been incorrectly labelled as 'CP' trials). Performance on the non-CC trials indicated significant psi-missing; performance was insignificantly better than chance on the CC trials. Unfortunately there is insufficient information provided concerning the methodological and security aspects of this study to evaluate their adequacy.

---

[10] The reader should be made aware of an exchange between Blackmore (1987) and Sargent (1987) concerning the protocol of some of Sargent's Ganzfeld sessions.

Harley (1989) conducted an exploratory dream clairvoyance study, with himself serving as participant and experimenter. Unlike the Maimonides studies, Harley 'tried to avoid associating to the dream, so that the transcript was as far as possible pure dream material' (p. 3). The independent judge rated the dream transcript against two sets of four pictures in order to look for possible displacement effects. Harley's rankings were suggestively poorer than MCE and his ratings were significantly poorer. An independent judge's performance was also significantly poorer than MCE. The author noted that none of the target pictures had strong emotional connotations, which may have been a contributing factor to failure here.

Markwick and Beloff studies

Markwick and Beloff (1983, 1988) conducted two 100-trial dream clairvoyance/telepathy (and clairvoyance/precognition) experiments with Markwick as participant, based in London, and Beloff as experimenter, based in Edinburgh. Randomly selected target pictures or objects were placed in a box by Beloff. Markwick only recorded 'selected dreams and hypnagogic imagery' (Markwick & Beloff, 1988, p. 77) and then ranked each duplicate set of five target possibilities. Some of the trial judgements were based upon multiple nights' dreams. In the first experiment (Markwick & Beloff, 1983), overall performance was significantly better than chance but seemed to decline after trial 64 following a crisis in Markwick's personal life. This significant finding is of particular interest given that 'It was obtained by a skeptically minded subject working under an ultrarigorous regime, with a reputed negative experimenter' (Marwick & Beloff, 1983, p. 229). Experiment two was similar except that only picture targets were used and two of the runs involved precognition rather than clairvoyance. Markwick's earlier success was not replicated and her performance was worse than chance, though not significantly. Markwick and Beloff (1988) speculated that the failure to replicate may have been due to a 'balancing out' of direct hits and extreme misses, which effectively cancelled each other out.

Hearne studies

In the first telepathy study by Hearne (Hearne & Worsley, 1977), eight sender–receiver pairs, half of whom were emotionally close, participated. While the receivers were in the third or fourth REM period of the night, the senders were presented (or not) with stimuli that both participants had a phobia about (e.g., a spider) during randomly sequenced experimental and control periods. It was hypothesized that information received concerning the phobic target would induce a fear response in the receiver and this would be indicated by an increase in heart rate. However, there were no significant differences in measures of heart rate or eye motility for the experimental versus control periods.

In an ingenious pilot study (Hearne, 1981a), the participant attempted to use ocular signalling during a lucid dream to communicate a four-digit target number being sent by the experimenter. Of nine nights spent in the sleep laboratory, only two yielded lucid dreams. During the first of these the participant awoke himself without having signalled; during the second, he saw several different numbers during his dream and made several aborted attempts to signal them. None of the numbers suggested were correct. The experimenter was not blind to the target because he also acted as the sender. If the signals in the EOG output were ambiguous, then interpretation could have been biased by knowledge of the targets. An independent blind judge ought to have interpreted the EOG traces.

In another study (Hearne, 1981b), eight emotionally close sender–receiver pairs participated in an experiment that investigated whether the receivers, in either a waking, NREM or REM sleep state, could detect when electric shocks were administered to the sender. There were no significant differences in the receivers' mean heart rate between the experimental and control periods in any condition. One pair seemed to demonstrate a difference in the waking condition but two replication attempts with this pairing failed.

In another single-participant telepathy study (Hearne, 1987), the participant, who had a history of writing about and interpreting dreams, slept at home and was awoken during REM by a home 'dream machine'. On eight non-consecutive nights, Hearne attempted to send a randomly selected magazine picture between 5:00 and 7:00 a.m. The participant recorded any dreams that she could remember upon awakening after 5:00 a.m. The following day, she ranked a duplicate set of eight pictures. However, it is not clear how the sender and receiver were prevented from communicating between the sending and judging periods. The participant scored below MCE. Hearne (1985) had earlier reported a case of ostensible precognition involving his dream machine but it is not clear whether this was part of any formal investigation and the report is not particularly impressive.

In another home dream telepathy study (Hearne, 1989) readers of a national newspaper attempted to dream about different randomly selected target pictures that Hearne sent each hour from midnight to 10:00 a.m. Readers recorded the most significant part of any dreams plus the time(s) that they awakened. There were 511 usable dream reports that were divided into ten piles according to the awakening time. Two judges viewed a different sample of dreams from each pile and judged whether each dream related to one of two possible targets or neither. Surprisingly, the judges were unable to allocate two-thirds of reports and these were consigned wastefully to an 'indeterminate' category and not included in the analysis. The judges matched 97 of the 171 (56%) allocated dreams to the correct target. The majority vote for each time/target period resulted in six hits and four misses (MCE = 5). No attempt was made to control for the stacking effect[11] or the fact that the number of dream reports differed across the different target/time periods.

---

[11] A stacking effect occurs when more than one participant is making judgements based upon the same target sequence (e.g., Milton & Wiseman, 1997, p. 93). In such circumstances, any chance coincidence of selection or judging biases can serve to artificially amplify or diminish hit rates.

Dalton, Sherwood and colleagues' studies

More recent work has concentrated on the question of whether consensus methods are superior to individual performance. With consensus judgement procedures, the responses from a number of individuals are combined to give a single judgement. This group-judging method is different from that implemented by Kanthamani and co-workers because here each participant gives ratings on the basis of their own dream transcript rather than a number of judges rating the same transcript.

Dalton *et al.* (1999) acted as experimenters and participants in an investigation of dream clairvoyance. The experimenters were blind to the target because an automated system randomly selected and played each target video clip repeatedly during the night (between 3:00 and 4:00 a.m.). During each of 32 trials, the participants slept at home and kept a record of any dreams. In the laboratory the following morning, participants viewed four video clips and individually rated and ranked the clips and then shared their night's dreams. These individual ranks were then combined to generate an objective consensus rank. The group consensus ratings and two of the three individuals achieved direct hit rates that significantly exceeded MCE. As expected, objective consensus performance was better than any of the individual performances, though no statistical examination of the difference was conducted. *Post hoc* inspection of the trial data suggested that the group had been more successful with emotional targets, particularly when they were negative. This is perhaps not surprising given that spontaneous cases of dream ESP often seem to feature negative life events (see Ullman *et al.*, 1989, Chapter 2). Although experimental waking ESP studies are equivocal with regard to the target emotionality issue (Delanoy, 1988) some studies do suggest that emotional target materials are more conducive than neutral materials (e.g., Bierman, 1997).

Sherwood *et al.* (2000) attempted to partially replicate these findings in a 28-trial study that also considered a 'discussion consensus judging procedure'. In order to reach a discussion consensus, the participants read each other's dream mentation and then discussed all of the material until they had reached a decision about the target identity. Results confirmed earlier findings, with a greater number of direct hits being obtained by using their objective consensus judgements than by using their own individual judgements. The discussion consensus was only marginally superior to the objective consensus. Effect sizes for the group were slightly smaller than the previous study but this may have been because the consensus judgements were based on two rather than three participants' responses. Again, a greater proportion of direct hits was obtained when the target was negative.

Dalton *et al.* (2000) reported a sixteen-trial extended replication attempt in which four undergraduate students acted as experimenter–participants. Again, dynamic targets were used but this study did not use a computer-controlled testing system. A major difference between this and earlier work was that the target for each trial was determined before the study began rather than on a trial-by-trial basis, which could raise security concerns. The primary analysis was of binary hits, with the group judgement giving rise to thirteen hits in sixteen trials, including seven direct hits, which was independently significant and superior to three of the four individuals. The choice of outcome measure is surprising, given that earlier studies by the lead author had used direct hits, although it is in keeping with the practice at Maimonides. The superiority of emotional over neutral targets was not confirmed by the group performance but three of the four individuals were more successful with emotional targets.

Sherwood et al. (2002) conducted an exploratory investigation of dream precognition using static targets. During twelve trial nights, three of the authors (Sherwood, Roe, Simmonds) slept at home and recorded their dream mentation. The following morning, they viewed four static pictures, and rated and rank ordered them. These individual rankings were combined to form an objective consensus judgement. Once judging was completed, the experimenter determined the target. The group and two of the individual participants scored below MCE in terms of direct hits while the other participant (SS) scored slightly above MCE. The results of this study did not provide much evidence for dream ESP nor any definite advantage of consensus over individual judging methods, in contrast to three previous studies. However, two of the participants in this investigation did not report having good prior dream recall, the static targets used were not especially engaging or emotional and there may have been problems with the randomization method used.

Roe et al. (2002) investigated dream clairvoyance and used dynamic targets selected for stronger emotional content. In this study, a distinction was made between the *emotional valence* and *emotionality* of targets. The procedure adopted was similar to Dalton et al. (1999) with aspects of the study controlled via an automated system. Contrary to predictions, neither the group nor any of the individual performances were significantly better than MCE. Group consensus judgements were more successful than two of the individuals but not significantly so. One individual (SS) again scored above chance, but this was counterbalanced by another individual (DL) who scored below chance with a similar effect size. There was a tendency for more emotional targets to be given lower ranks, and a suggestion that engaging clips were better than non-engaging ones, but these effects were generally quite small and with one exception did not achieve significance.

Post-Maimonides dream ESP success

It is somewhat difficult to assess the success of the post-Maimonides studies overall and in relative terms because they used different outcome measures (sometimes more than one) so there is no single metric that runs across all of the studies. As with the Maimonides studies, sometimes the full details of statistical analyses were not reported. In order to make comparisons across the studies we have again converted the statistical test results to the common effect size measure r, and these are given in Table 2 for each of the 21 sets of data for which the statistical test results were available (four studies did not provide the necessary information). Many of the post-Maimonides studies did not use independent blind judges but instead employed participant and experimenter/sender judging. However, as with the Maimonides studies, many of the post-Maimonides studies employed combined/consensus judging procedures and data from these judgements (which were mostly rankings) were used to calculate the effect size whenever possible. We can see (from Table 2 and Figure 2) that the effect sizes for the post-Maimonides studies range from –0.49 to 0.80. The majority of studies have a positive effect size, meaning that the targets were identified more often than chance expectations.

It is apparent that some of the most successful post-Maimonides studies were conducted by particular groups of researchers. The most successful post-Maimonides dream ESP studies were the two telepathy experiments (r = 0.58 and 0.80) conducted with Sweeney as receiver (Child *et al.*, 1977). Kanthamani and colleagues (Kanthamani *et al.*, 1988; Kanthamani & Khilji, 1990; Kanthamani & Broughton, 1992) and Dalton and colleagues (Dalton *et al.*, 1999; Sherwood *et al.*, 2000; Dalton *et al.*, 2000) also conducted series of successful clairvoyance studies (from r = 0.24 to r = 0.63). This suggests that

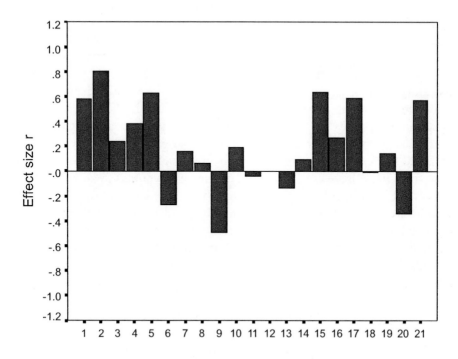

Figure 2.

Effect size r estimates based upon participants' and/or experimenter/senders' data
for 21 post-Maimonides data sets.

replication has been possible within laboratories and within a group of research-ers; however, independent replication across laboratories and across researchers is also required in order to demonstrate the validity of an effect.

Despite the differing numbers of studies it is clear that the three precognitive studies were the least successful (effect size range from $r = -0.34$ to 0.07, median -0.04); the telepathy (from $r = -0.27$ to 0.80, median 0.10) and clairvoyance studies were more successful (from $r = -0.49$ to 0.63, median 0.25). Investiga-tions of different types of ESP have resulted in different levels of success.

Differences Between the Maimonides and Post-Maimonides Dream ESP Studies

When the study effect sizes are combined[12] for the Maimonides ($r = 0.33$, 95% C.I. 0.24 to 0.43) and post-Maimonides studies ($r = 0.14$, 95% C.I. 0.06 to 0.22), respectively, we can see that performance was better than chance with medium and small effect sizes. We can be 95% confident that the true effect size is posi-tive and therefore better than chance expectations for both sets of studies. The Maimonides studies were significantly more successful than the post-Maimonides studies in terms of effect size ($t = 2.14$, df = 34, $p = 0.04$, two-tailed), although there are a number of differences between the two sets of studies that may have contributed to this. A meta-analysis of the studies that involves coding of the presence/absence or quality of particular features is needed to see whether the effect size covaries with particular variables.

For example, the vast majority of post-Maimonides studies did not involve laboratory monitoring of EEG–EOG (or some other physiological measure) or deliberate awakening from REM sleep in order to record dream recall (with the exception of Hearne, 1981a; 1981b). The advantage of awakening participants from REM sleep is that dream recall is much more likely, and can lead to more detail and longer overall reports. Reviews of studies involving laboratory awak-ening from REM have concluded that dreams are reported in about 75–80% of cases (see Empson, 2002; Goodenough, 1991). Spontaneous awakenings in the morning are less likely to lead to dream recall, and any dreams that are reported tend to be those from the last REM period only (Empson, 2002), or indeed may lead to no dreams being recalled. The Maimonides procedure tended to ask par-ticipants for their associations as well as their guesses, which means that the judges probably had more, and richer, information upon which to base their judgements.

Another potential advantage of the Maimonides procedure is that, in the telep-athy studies, sending efforts were synchronized with REM periods, whereas in post-Maimonides research the relationship was more haphazard. However, one way of increasing the likelihood of at least some overlap is to show or send the

---

[12] The combined effect size calculation involved the use of Fisher's transformed values of r (see Clark-Carter, 1997, pp. 558–9, 644–6). Due to the difficulty in carrying out a Fisher's transformation of an r greater than 1 for the sensory bombardment study (Study L), we have used the Fisher's trans-formation associated with a conservative r of 0.999.

target repeatedly for a period of at least 90 minutes (equivalent to one sleep cycle); this method was used in some successful post-Maimonides clairvoyance studies (e.g., 15, 16, 19).

The majority of post-Maimonides studies also involved the participants sleeping in their own homes (1–10, 13–21) rather than in a laboratory (11, 12). The advantages of having the participants sleep at home and awaken naturally are that they are likely to feel more comfortable and their sleep routines are disrupted less. This is why sleep laboratory studies try to allow one night for the participants to adjust before the experiment begins. It is very important to allow a few pilot nights per participant for home dream ESP experiments, too. We would also argue that it is important not to schedule trial nights too close together and to avoid consecutive nights because the latter can put pressure on participants and can compound any sleep disruptions.

Another difference, which is possibly confounded by the amount of information available for judging, is that the Maimonides programme tended to use independent blind judges whereas post-Maimonides studies tended to use participant judging. It is possible that some judges, by aptitude or through experience, may be better able to discriminate between 'normal' dream material and potentially psi-mediated material. Some recent post-Maimonides research has also suggested that consensus judgements might offer a slight advantage over individual judgements (e.g., 15–17).

Some senders and receivers, and certain pairings, might have been better than others, too. The Maimonides researchers went to some lengths to screen for 'effective' senders and receivers (including the recruitment of participants with prior success in psi studies) and to exploit conducive pairings. Post-Maimonides studies have tended not to screen so carefully or to use 'gifted' participants. It is clear that post-Maimonides studies did not always select participants even for having good dream recall (e.g., 20). This is crucial for studies that do not employ deliberate awakening from REM sleep.

The majority of Maimonides studies investigated telepathy whereas the majority of post-Maimonides studies investigated clairvoyance. The presence of a sender in many of the Maimonides studies may have contributed to the overall success of the research program. It could be that the sender plays some active role in the psi process or that there is simply a psychological effect in that the receiver feels more comfortable and/or optimistic. Certainly the Maimonides team felt that '[T]he active involvement of the agent [sender] is an important ingredient for success', (Ullman et al., 1973, p. 212). Nevertheless, many of the post-Maimonides studies did not use a sender (3–5, 8–11, 15–21) and, if they did, did not select them on the basis of prior success.

Van de Castle (1977; 1989), himself a participant in a number of dream ESP studies, has argued strongly that the laboratory climate is an important contributor to the success of a study. Further research is needed to try to operationalize the important environmental aspects, which might also be related to the characteristics of research personnel, so that these can be manipulated in future studies. One environmental variable that warrants further attention is the earth's geomagnetic field (GMF). Periods of lower GMF activity have been associated with reports of spontaneous precognitive dreams (Krippner *et al.*, 2000) and greater accuracy on experimental dream ESP trials (Dalton *et al.*, 1999; Krippner & Persinger, 1996; Persinger & Krippner, 1989 but see also Sherwood *et al.*, 2000). However, recent research suggests that the relationship between GMF and free-response ESP performance may depend on the Local Sidereal Time (LST) at the time of the trials (Spottiswoode, 1997).

Finally, target materials used by the Maimonides team were chosen because of their emotional intensity as well as for their vividness, colour and simplicity, and this was regarded as a crucial feature of the protocol (Ullman *et al.*, 1973; Van de Castle, 1977). Recent dream ESP research has supported the idea that emotional targets might be more conducive than neutral targets but the target pools used in post-Maimonides research do not seem typically to have been selected on their basis of emotionality characteristics.

Conclusion and Recommendations

Our review has shown that dream ESP remains a promising, if somewhat neglected, area for parapsychological research. Combined effect sizes for both Maimonides and post-Maimonides studies suggest that judges may be able to correctly identify target materials more often than would be expected by chance using dream mentation. There is evidence of conceptual replication within both sets of studies, although this seems to be concentrated within certain research teams. Overall, the Maimonides studies were more successful than the post-Maimonides studies but this may be due to procedural differences. There is a need for a meta-analysis of the experimental dream ESP literature, not only to provide an estimate of the overall effect size but also to identify process-oriented factors that might influence study outcomes. We hope that future researchers will also note some of the methodological shortcomings we have identified and address these in their study designs. Home dream ESP research is a less expensive and less labour-intensive alternative to sleep-laboratory-based research and merits further investigation. We hope that this review will help re-awaken interest in this neglected but promising paradigm.

References

Alcock, J.E. (1981), *Parapsychology: Science or Magic? A Psychological Perspective* (Oxford and New York: Pergamon).

Alvarado, C.S. (1998), 'ESP and altered states of consciousness: An overview of conceptual and research trends', *Journal of Parapsychology*, **62**, pp.27–63.

Belvedere, E., Foulkes, D. (1971), 'Telepathy and dreams: A failure to replicate', *Perceptual and Motor Skills*, **33**, pp. 783–9.

Bem, D.J., Honorton, C. (1994), 'Does psi exist? Replicable evidence for an anomalous process of information transfer', *Psychological Bulletin*, **115**, pp. 4–18.

Bem, D.J., Palmer, J. Broughton, R.S. (2001), 'Updating the ganzfeld database: A victim of its own success?', *Journal of Parapsychology*, **65**, pp. 207–18.

Bierman, D.J. (1997), 'Emotion and intuition I, II, III, IV & V: Unravelling variables contributing to the presentiment effect', *Proceedings of the 40th Annual Convention of the*

Parapsychological Association in conjunction with The Society for Psychical Research, Brighton, UK, pp. 49–62.

Blackmore, S. (1987), 'A report of a visit to Carl Sargent's laboratory', *Journal of the Society for Psychical Research*, **54**, pp.186–98.

Braud, W. (1977), 'Long-distance dream and presleep telepathy', in *Research in Parapsychology 1976*, ed. J.D. Morris, W.G. Roll, R.L. Morris (Metuchen, NJ: Scarecrow Press), pp.154–5.

Braud, W.G., Braud, L.W. (1975), 'The psi-conducive syndrome: Free response GESP performance following evocation of "left-hemispheric" vs. "right-hemispheric" functioning', in *Research in Parapsychology 1974*, ed. J.D. Morris, W.G. Roll, R.L. Morris (Metuchen, NJ: Scarecrow Press), pp.17–20.

Child, I.L. (1985), 'Psychology and anomalous observations: The question of ESP in dreams', *American Psychologist* **40**, pp.1219–30.

Child, I.L., Kanthamani, H., Sweeney, V.M. (1977), 'A simplified experiment in dream telepathy', in *Research in Parapsychology 1976*, ed. J.D. Morris, W.G. Roll, R.L. Morris (Metuchen, NJ: Scarecrow Press), pp. 91–3.

Clark-Carter, D. (1997), *Doing Quantitative Psychological Research: From Design to Report* (Hove, UK: Psychology Press).

Clemmer, E.J. (1986), 'Not so anomalous observations question ESP in dreams', *American Psychologist*, **41**, pp.1173–4.

Cohen, J. (1977), *Statistical Power Analysis for the Behavioral Sciences* (rev. ed.) (New York: Academic Press).

Dalton, K. Steinkamp, F., Sherwood, S.J. (1999), 'A dream GESP experiment using dynamic targets and consensus vote', *Journal of the American Society for Psychical Research*, **93**, pp.145–66.

Dalton, K., Utts, J., Novotny, G., Sickafoose, L., Burrone, J., Phillips, C. (2000), 'Dream GESP and consensus vote: A replication', *Proceedings of the 43rd Annual Convention of the Parapsychological Association, Freiburg, Germany*, pp.74–85.

Delanoy, D. (1988), 'Characteristics of successful free-response targets: Experimental findings and observations', *Proceedings of the 31st Annual Convention of the Parapsychological Association, Montreal, Quebec*, pp. 230–46.

Dement, W.C. (1974), *Some Must Watch While Some Must Sleep* (San Francisco, CA: W. H. Freeman).

Empson, J. (2002), *Sleep and Dreaming* (3rd ed.) (New York: Palgrave).

Eppinger, R. (2001), *'A Comparative Examination of Ganzfeld and Dream Reports in Free Response ESP Studies', Unpublished PhD thesis, University of Edinburgh.*

Foulkes, D., Belvedere, E., Masters, R.E.L., Houston, J., Krippner, S., Honorton, C., Ullman, M. (1972), 'Long-distance "sensory-bombardment" ESP in dreams: A failure to replicate', *Perceptual and Motor Skills*, **35**, pp. 731–4.

Globus, G., Knapp, P.H., Skinner, J.C., Healey, G. (1968), 'An appraisal of telepathic communication in dreams', *Psychophysiology*, **4**, p. 365.

Goodenough, D.R. (1991), 'Dream recall: History and current status of the field', in *The Mind in Sleep: Psychology and Psychophysiology* (2nd ed.), ed. S.J. Ellman, J.S. Antrobus (New York: John Wiley & Sons), pp.143–71.

Hall, C.E. (1967), 'Experimente zur telepathischen beeinflussung von träumen', *Zeitschrift für Parapsychologie und Grenzgebiete der Psychologie*, **10**, pp. 18–47.

Harley, T.A. (1989), 'Psi missing in a dream clairvoyance experiment', *Journal of the Society for Psychical Research*, **56**, pp. 1–7.

Hearne, K.M.T. (1981a), '"Lucid" dreams and ESP: An initial experiment using one subject', *Journal of the Society for Psychical Research*, **51**, pp. 7–11.

Hearne, K.M.T. (1981b), 'The effect on the subject (in waking, SWS and REM states) of electric shocks to the agent: An "ESP" experiment', *Journal of the Society for Psychical Research*, **51**, pp. 87–92.

Hearne, K.M.T. (1985), 'An ostensible precognition using a "dream machine"', *Journal of the Society for Psychical Research*, **53**, pp. 38–40.

Hearne, K.M.T. (1987), 'A dream-telepathy experiment using a home "dream machine"', *Journal of the Society for Psychical Research*, **54**, pp. 139–42.

Hearne, K.M.T. (1989), 'A nationwide mass dream-telepathy experiment', *Journal of the Society for Psychical Research*, **55**, pp. 271–4.

Hearne, K.M T., Worsley, A. (1977), 'An experiment in "telepathic" phobic fear and REM sleep', *Journal of the Society for Psychical Research*, **49**, pp. 434–9.

Honorton, C. (1977), 'Psi and internal attention states', in *Handbook of Parapsychology*, ed. B.B. Wolman (New York: Van Nostrand Reinhold), pp. 435–72.

Honorton, C., Krippner, S., Ullman, M. (1972), 'Telepathic perception of art prints under two conditions', *Proceedings of the 80th Annual Convention of the American Psychological Association*, **7**, pp. 319–20.

Honorton, C., Ullman, M., Krippner, S. (1975), 'Comparison of extrasensory and presleep influences on dreams: A preliminary report', in *Research in Parapsychology 1974*, ed. J.D. Morris, W.G. Roll, R.L. Morris (Metuchen, NJ: Scarecrow Press), pp. 82–4.

Hyman, R. (1986), 'Maimonides dream-telepathy experiments', *Skeptical Inquirer*, **11**, pp. 91–2.

Hyman, R. (1994). 'Anomaly or artifact — comments', *Psychological Bulletin*, **115**, pp. 19–24.

Irwin, H.J. (1999), *An Introduction to Parapsychology* (3rd ed.) (Jefferson, NC: McFarland).

Kanthamani, H., Broughton, R.S. (1992), 'An experiment in ganzfeld and dreams: A further confirmation', *Proceedings of the 35th Annual Convention of the Parapsychological Association, Las Vegas, NV*, pp. 59–73.

Kanthamani, H., Khilji, A. (1990), 'An experiment in ganzfeld and dreams: A confirmatory study', *Proceedings of the 33rd Annual Convention of the Parapsychological Association, Chevy Chase, MD*, pp. 126–37.

Kanthamani, H., Khilji, A., Rustomji-Kerns, R. (1988), 'An experiment in ganzfeld and dreams with a clairvoyance technique', *Proceedings of the 31st Annual Convention of the Parapsychological Association, Montreal, Quebec*, pp. 413–23.

Krippner, S. (1975), 'Paranormal communication: Dreams and other altered conscious states', *Journal of Communication*, **25**, pp. 173–82.

Krippner, S. (1991), 'An experimental approach to the anomalous dream', in *Dream Images: A Call to Mental Arms*, ed. J. Gackenbach, Anees A.S. (Amityville, NY: Baywood Publishing Company), pp. 31–54.

Krippner, S. (1993), 'The Maimonides ESP-dream studies', *Journal of Parapsychology*, **57**, pp. 39–54.

Krippner, S., Honorton, C., Ullman, M. (1972), 'A second precognitive dream study with Malcolm Bessent', *Journal of the American Society for Psychical Research*, **66**, pp. 269–79.

Krippner, S., Honorton, C., Ullman, M. (1973), 'An experiment in dream telepathy with "The Grateful Dead"', *Journal of the American Society of Psychosomatic Dentistry and Medicine*, **20**, pp. 9–18.

Krippner, S., Honorton, C., Ullman, M., Masters, R.E.L., Houston, J. (1971), 'A long-distance "sensory bombardment" study of ESP in dreams', *Journal of the American Society for Psychical Research*, **65**, pp. 468–75.

Krippner, S., Persinger, M. (1996), 'Evidence for enhanced congruence between dreams and distant target material during periods of decreased geomagnetic activity', *Journal of Scientific Exploration*, **10**, pp. 487–93.

Krippner, S., Ullman, M. (1970), 'Telepathy and dreams: A controlled experiment with electroencephalogram-electro-oculogram monitoring', *Journal of Nervous and Mental Disease*, **151**, pp. 394–403.

Krippner, S., Ullman, M., Honorton, C. (1971), 'A precognitive dream study with a single subject', *Journal of the American Society for Psychical Research*, **65**, pp. 192–203.

Krippner, S., Vaughan, A., Spottiswoode, S.J.P. (2000), 'Geomagnetic factors in subjective precognitive dream experiences', *Journal of the Society for Psychical Research*, **64**, pp. 109–17.

Markwick, B., Beloff, J. (1983), 'Dream states and ESP: A distance experiment with a single subject', in *Research in Parapsychology 1982*, ed. W.G. Roll, J. Beloff, R.A. White (New York: Scarecrow Press), pp. 228–30.

Markwick, B., Beloff, J. (1988), 'Dream states and ESP: A distance experiment featuring a pure clairvoyance, free-response design', in *Research in Parapsychology 1987*, ed. D.H. Weiner, R.L. Morris (London: Scarecrow Press), pp. 77–81.

McLaren, I., Sargent, C.L. (1982), 'Awareness of success in free-response dream ESP testing with a single subject', in *Research in Parapsychology 1981*, ed. W.G. Roll, R.L. Morris, R.A. White (Metuchen, NJ: Scarecrow Press), pp. 195–6.

Milton, J., Wiseman, R. (1997), *Guidelines for Extrasensory Perception Research* (Hatfield, UK: University of Hertfordshire Press).

Milton, J., Wiseman, R. (1999), 'Does psi exist? Lack of replication of an anomalous process of information transfer', *Psychological Bulletin*, **125**, pp. 387–91.

Parker, A. (1975), *States of Mind: Altered States of Consciousness and ESP* (New York: Taplinger).

Persinger, M.A., Krippner, S. (1989), 'Dream ESP experiments and geomagnetic activity', *Journal of the American Society for Psychical Research*, **83**, pp. 101–16.

Prentice, D.A., Miller, D.T. (1992), 'When small effects are impressive', *Psychological Bulletin*, **112**, pp. 160–4.

Radin, D. (1997), *The Conscious Universe: The Scientific Truth of Psychic Phenomena* (New York: Harper Collins).

Rechtschaffen, A. (1970), 'Sleep and dream states: An experimental design', in *Psi Favorable States of Consciousness*, ed. R. Cavanna (New York: Parapsychology Foundation), pp. 87–120.

Rhine, L.E. (1981), *The Invisible Picture: A Study of Psychic Experiences* (Jefferson, NC: McFarland).

Roe C.A., Sherwood, S.J., Luke, D.P., Farrell, L.M. (2002), 'An exploratory investigation of dream GESP using consensus judging and dynamic targets', *Journal of the Society for Psychical Research*, **66**, pp. 225–38.

Sargent, C.L. (1987), 'Sceptical fairytales from Bristol', *Journal of the Society for Psychical Research*, **54**, pp. 208–18.

Sargent, C.L., Harley, T.A. (1982), 'Precognition testing with free-response techniques in the ganzfeld and the dream state', *European Journal of Parapsychology*, **4**, pp. 243–56.

Sherwood, S.J., Dalton, K., Steinkamp, F., Watt, C. (2000), 'Dream clairvoyance study II using dynamic video-clips: Investigation of consensus voting judging procedures and target emotionality', *Dreaming*, **10**, pp. 221–36.

Sherwood, S.J., Roe, C.A., Simmonds, C.A., Biles, C. (2002), 'An exploratory investigation of dream precognition using consensus judging and static targets', *Journal of the Society for Psychical Research*, **66**, pp. 22–8.

Spottiswoode, S.J.P. (1997), 'Geomagnetic fluctuations and free-response anomalous cognition: A new understanding', *Journal of Parapsychology*, **61**, pp. 3–12.

Strauch, I. (1970), 'Dreams and psi in the laboratory', in *Psi Favorable States of Consciousness*, ed. Roberto Cavanna (New York: Parapsychology Foundation), pp. 46–54.

Ullman, M. (1969), 'Telepathy and dreams', *Experimental Medicine & Surgery*, **27**, pp. 19–38.

Ullman, M., Krippner, S. (1969), 'A laboratory approach to the nocturnal dimension of paranormal experience: Report of a confirmatory study using the REM monitoring technique', *Biological Psychiatry*, **1**, pp. 259–70.

Ullman, M., Krippner, S., Feldstein, S. (1966), 'Experimentally induced telepathic dreams: Two studies using EEG-REM monitoring technique', *International Journal of Parapsychology*, **2**, pp. 420–37.

Ullman, M., Krippner, S., with Vaughan, A. (1973), *Dream Telepathy: Experiments in Nocturnal ESP* (Jefferson, NC: McFarland).

Ullman, M., Krippner, S., with Vaughan, A. (1989), *Dream Telepathy: Experiments in Nocturnal ESP* (2nd ed.) (Jefferson, NC: McFarland).

Van de Castle, R.L. (1971), 'The study of GESP in a group setting by means of dreams', *Journal of Parapsychology*, **35**, p. 312.

Van de Castle, R.L. (1977), 'Sleep and dreams', in *Handbook of Parapsychology*, ed. Benjamin B. Wolman (New York: Van Nostrand Reinhold), pp. 473–99.

Van de Castle, R.L. (1989), 'ESP in dreams: Comments on a replication "failure" by the "failing" subject', in *Dream Telepathy: Experiments in Nocturnal ESP* (2nd ed.), ed. M. Ullman, S. Krippner, A. Vaughan (Jefferson, NC: McFarland), pp. 209–16.

Wackermann, J., Pütz, P., Büchi, S., Strauch, I., Lehmann, D. (2000), 'A comparison of ganzfeld and hypnagogic state in terms of electrophysiological measures and subjective experience', *Proceedings of the 43rd Annual Convention of the Parapsychological Association, Freiburg, Germany*, pp. 302–15.

Weiner, D.H., McCain, D.L. (1981), 'The use of the majority-vote technique in dream ESP: A pilot study', *Journal of Parapsychology*, **45**, pp. 156–7.

White, R.A., Krippner, S., Ullman, M., Honorton, C. (1971), 'Experimentally induced telepathic dreams with EEG-REM monitoring: Some manifest content variables related to psi operation', in *Proceedings of the Parapsychological Association, Number 5, 1968*, ed. W.G. Roll, R.L. Morris, J.D. Morris (Durham, NC: Parapsychological Association), pp. 85–7.

Adrian Parker

We Ask, Does Psi Exist?

But is this the right question and do we really want an answer anyway?

Abstract: *Although the question 'Does psi exist?' has become a recurrent and intransigent problem for psychological science, seen from a historical and social context, there appear to be reasons as to why no determined effort has been made to resolve the question. The sporadic exchanges from parapsychologists and critics appear only to reinforce the status quo: At most, it is agreed that some form of 'anomaly' has been established but there is no consensus about its nature. Yet such a defeatist stance shies away from the long tradition of research into spontaneous phenomena, as well as experimental research with dreams and hypnosis, all of which suggests that, if psi is real, it is not just an anomaly but has true information content and dynamic effects. This work is briefly reviewed and then, since much of the current controversy has centred on the ganzfeld technique, this is used as an example of the issues involved. The ganzfeld induces sleep-onset imagery during which randomly selected film clips are viewed by a sender as a source of psi-mediated information to be incorporated into the imagery. Our current development of the ganzfeld technique, known as the digital autoganzfeld, takes the work beyond 'anomaly status' since it enables real-time recordings to be made of apparently high-quality psi as it enters consciousness. Initial findings from this illustrate the complexity of the phenomena and the need for more adventurous designs in order to stimulate theory development. There is no doubt that technology now exists which would enable us to resolve the issues raised. Whether the area turns out to be a mixture of rampant fraud, artefact and subjective validation or to present genuine phenomena, a resolution of the issue may be seen as having unwanted implications for psychology — which may be one of the factors explaining why the controversy is left to continue as it is, unresolved. New questions are needed which take into account the natural context in which psi appears to occur, along with the support needed to reach clear answers.*

Correspondence: Adrian Parker, Dept of Psychology, University of Gothenburg, Box 500, SE 405 30 Gothenburg, Sweden. *Email: adrian.parker@psy.gu.se*

Journal of Consciousness Studies, **10**, No. 6–7, 2003, pp. 111–34

One person who would answer the questions that form this paper's title in the affirmative is, of course, the founder of modern experimental parapsychology, J.B. Rhine. A few weeks before he died in 1980, Rhine said to his interviewer: 'We overlooked many things. We failed to know how to convince people. We assumed it would all be accepted.' Then he asked: 'What does the world need to know to remove this blockage to acceptance?' (Berger, 1988). In fact, John Beloff had given him the answer in part, some years earlier when he wrote:

> Rhine succeeded in giving parapsychology everything it needed to become an accredited experimental science except the one essential: the *know-how* to produce positive results when and where required. (Beloff, 1973 p. 291).

Actually, Rhine fully accepted Beloff's critique but argued that progress would only come slowly by piecing together the variables that would eventually define the necessary and sufficient conditions for psi to occur. His disappointment lay in that he believed that sufficient evidence had been accrued to at least warrant the support of psychology in pursuit of this ideal (Rhine, 1972). Beloff's answer was thus for Rhine only a partial answer, but then I believe Rhine may have underestimated the complexity of the subject matter that he — and now we — are dealing with. To seek better questions and fuller answers is the quest of this article.

The Lessons from History

At least one part of the answer to Rhine's question actually comes in the form of the remit for writing this text. The editors felt that the JCS had been 'too favourable towards parapsychology' and 'this imbalance should be remedied'. Naturally, it might be asked why the status quo as regards parapsychology must *always* be maintained. The directive does also adds a rider: that there should be 'scholarly articles on both sides of the parapsychology/skeptic debate which properly reflect all facts and findings'. Even so, the implication remains that the accused will certainly get a fair trial before being hung or at least left hanging.

This is understandable from the pragmatic viewpoint since the study of consciousness is itself a controversial area which may be in danger of losing its current forward thrust if it be diverted into dealing with a difficult and, in some circles, suspect area. Seen in the historical context this reaction is also nothing new. Indeed, a historical overview of this area does lead to the impression of it being a forum where the scenes and players change but the roles are essentially the same, and the last scene always stays the same by letting the issue remain unresolved. However, it would be unwarranted to conclude as some critics have done (for example, Blackmore, 2001) that given no present agreement can be reached on the phenomena's existential status and that the phenomena demand a standpoint, then this standpoint should be that they probably do not exist. That contrasting and polarized views should exist among experts who have spent their lives studying the very same human experience may be dispiriting, but it is hardly unusual: there is, for instance, still little agreement among experts concerning the basic nature of hypnosis and dreams.[1] In the case of parapsychology, history suggests there may even be some powerful, and for some individuals, quite plausible reasons for maintaining this status quo, which is an issue we will later have cause to return to.

Virtually each century seems to have produced its doyens who would argue strongly that the phenomena were real while others would argue with equal conviction that they were illusory. Only certain Greek philosophers (notably the neoplatonists) seem to have been an exception by apparently having no problem whatsoever in seeing paranormal phenomena as part of a greater unseen natural order of the world (Dodds, 1971). By the 1600s paranormal abilities had come to be viewed in the context of witchcraft and apparitions but Joseph Glanvill, chaplain to Charles II, suggested that rather than demonic agencies being on the loose, some genuine paranormal ability lay behind all the superstition and thus he compiled the casebook: *Saducismus Triumphatus: Or, Full and Plain Evidence Concerning Witches and Apparitions* (1681). This was soon countered by Balthasar Bekker's *The World Bewitched* (originally published in Dutch in 1691 and in English in 1695) which revealed the magical tricks and natural causes leading to supernatural beliefs. Two classical works extending these themes were influential in the 1700s: Richard Baxter's book, *The Certainty of the Worlds of Spirits* (1691), and Charles Owen's *The Scene of Delusions*. In the 1800s, the physician John Ferriar wrote an impressive work, *An Essay Towards a Theory of Apparitions* (1813) which easily matches today's scepticism in seeking normal explanations of apparitions in terms of tricks, false memories and delusions. In 1848 came Catherine Crowe's much cited work *The Night Side of Nature,* documenting cases of apparent telepathic and apparitional experiences although not with the same critical ability that would come to characterize the work of the English Society for Psychical Research (SPR). Founded in 1882, the SPR is generally recognized as the first systematic attempt to bring some degree of objectivity to the subject by seeking witness testimony and evaluating the possible normal explanations for the experiences recorded. William James commented that were he asked 'to point to a scientific journal where hard-headedness and never-ending suspicion of sources of error might be seen in their full bloom, I think I should have to fall back on the *Proceedings of the Society for Psychical Research* (James, 1896/1972, p. 38).[2]

For some years psychology and psychical research shared a common platform. Henry Sidgwick, one of the founders of the SPR, was the president of the Second International Congress of Psychology in 1892 and presented there the recent findings of psychical research concerning crisis telepathy: the so-called Census of Hallucinations (Sidgwick *et al.*, 1894). It was not only William James but

---

[1] Compare, for example, the physiological theories of Hobson (1990) and Winson (2002) with the psychological theories of Van de Castle (1994) and Hartmann (1998). A good overview of the contrasting theories of hypnosis is to be found in Gauld (1992) and Kirsch and Lynn (1995).

[2] Although officially holding ' no corporate views', the SPR finally in 1990 issued their journal with a declaration saying ' for over a century the Society had published an impressive body of evidence for the existence of paranormal phenomena'.

many of the leading psychologists of the time such as McDougall, Freud, Coover and Boring, who had an interest in psychical research, yet, ultimately the two subjects went separate ways. The reasons for thus distancing psychology from psychical research and parapsychology probably reflects again, at least in part, the influence of political considerations: psychology could hardly be recognized as a normal science while it was tied to its occult double (Leahey, 1991). It was not until about a hundred years later,[3] at the 27th International Congress of Psychology held in Stockholm in 2000, that the subject was again reinstated, this time in the form of a symposium organized by Robert Morris, Koestler Professor of Parapsychology at the University of Edinburgh (Morris, 2001). Looking at this history, the above-mentioned remit for this paper may suggest that with the emergence of 'Consciousness Studies', the earlier strategy of dissociating the new subject from parapsychology is in danger of repeating itself.

It might be thought that by now laboratory investigations of the paranormal would have revealed if there is a residuum of phenomena not explicable by occult beliefs, cognitive errors and magical tricks, and if so, would have forced psychology to deal with them. Yet stripped of its occult and magical trappings, there is still no clarity about what we are dealing with. Two of the classic works in this area from the twentieth century are: *Extrasensory Perception* by J.B. Rhine (1967/72) which summarizes the research of the Duke laboratory using the card guessing paradigm from 1930 to 1950, and its antithesis: *ESP: A Scientific Evaluation* by Mark Hansel. Hansel's volumes (1966/1989) are still quoted by many critics as having effectively demolished all the work of Rhine and his co-workers. Yet in order to do so, Hansel had to devise scenarios by which at least four of Rhine's star subjects could, all individually and on their own initiative, have cheated. For some scenarios to work the list was extended to at least some of his co-workers. To be fair, Rhine was always much aware of the need to take precautions against fraud so that formal testing required two experimenter checks along with duplicate recordings. Fraud has undoubtedly occurred in parapsychology on several occasions (Rhine, 1974a; 1974b), although for some readers it may seem a little fanciful to believe that so many cheats all congregated at one time at the Duke laboratory, while for others the possibility may still seem a plausible alternative to psi. Yet it should be said, despite the replication problems, Rhine's work did not entirely stand alone, and similar findings had been obtained by some researchers in the US (Mauskopf & McVaugh, 1980) and in England (see West, 1962). The unfortunate consequence of Hansel's critique was that some critics such as David Marks (2000) still eagerly accept Hansel's scenarios without further ado as probable enough to totally discount Rhine's results.

Had Rhine's results been readily repeatable, the critics would have been silenced long ago, but then it might also be said that had the phenomena been so easily demonstrable and separable from magic and mystique then they would

---

[3] Alan Gauld (1968, p. 147) notes that the Society for Psychical Research was involved in presentations at Paris 1889, London 1892, Munich, 1896, Paris, 1900. With the exception of a minor presentation by Sidney Alrutz, (the founder of Swedish psychology) at Geneva in 1909, the subject seems to have vanished from the agenda until the Robert Morris symposium at Stockholm, 2000.

hardly have needed to be caught in the laboratory in the first place. As for reasons for this replication difficulty, assuming the Duke results were not due to an epidemic of fraud, then perhaps we need look no further than the first two volumes of the *Journal of Parapsychology*. These contain several experimental reports directly concerned with how the 'subject–experimenter relationship' influenced results. Rhine would first argue for the importance of rapport between subject and experimenter. Later in life, after his own workers had difficulties in repeating the results, he would concede that the spectacular success during this period may have been due the unique enthusiasm and team spirit that was present in the early Duke laboratory.[4] His co-worker Gaither Pratt described how in the initial testing period they discovered eight high-scoring subjects but two years later none were forthcoming. Pratt comments:

> The sense of excitement and the adventure of scientific discovery were missing for the testers and the tested. To achieve the psychological equivalent of the earlier work, the participants should have been able to feel that they were helping to solve a real scientific problem, such as the occurrence of ESP had been in earlier Duke research. (Pratt, 1974, p. 153)

By the time Duke University laboratory (the predecessor of what has now become the Rhine Research Center) became independent, whatever magic was necessary for high-scoring subjects had almost disappeared.[5]

Was Rhine correct in maintaining it was all down to the charisma of the experimenter in motivating subjects or was this merely an after-the-fact rationalization? Besides the experimental work, which supports Rhine's view (White, 1976a,b; 1977), history also speaks for it. The Duke laboratory was not, in fact, an entirely unique situation and whatever factors were responsible for its outstanding success, they were to reappear between 1962 and 1979 at the Maimonides Dream Research Laboratory in New York. Here again it is just possible that some difficult-to-define feature — at least in English — was at work. Indeed, the Scandinavian and German words *stämming* and *stimmung* may be more definitive ones since they refer to the atmosphere and feeling of a situation, and here the situation was such that a breakthrough in the current research paradigm appeared to be taking place. Naturally, the enthusiasm of the Ullman– Krippner–Honorton team, like that of Rhine and his co-workers before them, may have also been an important part of this successful atmosphere (Ullman *et al.*, 1974).[6]

---

[4] John Beloff (1993, p. 149) comments on this and it is interesting to compare Rhine (1948) and the Introduction to Rhine (1964).

[5] During the 1960s and 1970s some further three (Pavel Stepanek, Sean Harribance and Malcolm Bessent) were discovered by various laboratories and underwent extensive testing but unaccountably they were never used in any kind of demonstration in front of critics. My own experience of two apparently high-scoring subjects (Parker, 1974) unfortunately did not last long enough to achieve this goal but they did continue to score successfully for a short time in the presence of John Beloff and Brian Millar who had a psi-inhibitory reputation.

[6] The same could be said of the success of the remote viewing work carried out from 1972 to 1986 at Stanford Research Institute involving Russell Targ and Hal Puthoff and from late 1986 until 1995 at its successor, the Cognitive Sciences Laboratory, under the leadership of Edwin May (McMoneagle, 2000).

Of course, the critic might say new research paradigms merely introduce new sources of error, but the Maimonides studies have withstood the scrutiny of time, so much so that even Hansel, writing a later edition of his book (1989), appeared to have difficulties that may explain why he otherwise unaccountably persisted in claiming there were certain flaws in the procedure long after these has been shown to be non-existent (Child, 1985).

The Maimonides results are now usually simply ignored by the major critics such as Hyman (1996a; 1996b) and Marks (2000) or in the case of Alcock (1996), they are dismissed as non-replicable. Yet the 'failure to replicate' charge no longer seems to be well-founded. A recent review by Sherwood (2002) collected 21 reports of studies that could be seen as replication attempts of the Maimonides work concerning dream-ESP. Although as a whole the replication studies showed a lower effect size than the original work, there could be no doubt that the Maimonides findings were adequately replicated. There are naturally some weaknesses: Some studies included in the collection were not fully reported and most were conceptual replications with participants recalling their own dreams rather than, as in the original Maimonides studies, using the dream reports received through EEG-EOG awakenings. What is also again very obvious from Sherwood's analysis is that some experimenters were very successful, others not. All in all, the failure of the Maimonides work appears to be not so much a failure to replicate, but again a failure of further financing from mainstream science which would have been needed in order to make progress.

In the face of the pending closure of the Maimonides laboratory, Honorton began in the mid-1970s to work on a less expensive and less cumbersome technique than the EEG-EOG methodology. This became known as the *ganzfeld technique*, and the basic principle was much the same as with the dream telepathy studies: Spontaneous real-life experiences suggest that if telepathy occurs, it occurs most often when the 'receiver' is in an altered state (or at least in a relaxed state) and when there is an emotional crisis with the 'sender' (Stevenson, 1970). In the laboratory a homogeneous field of visual and auditory stimulation (the ganzfeld) induces a hypnagogic-like state in the receiver while the sender views an emotionally engaging film clip. Afterwards, the task is for the receiver or a judge to identify this film clip from decoy clips (usually three in number) that formed part of the set of four from which the clip was randomly chosen ($p = 0.25$).

The ganzfeld experiments began in 1964. They now number about a hundred studies, and have been conducted at some dozen different laboratories, so we should expect a clear answer to the question: Is the 'ganzfeld effect replicable? If we look superficially at all the experimental results, then the answer is an unequivocal, yes, but since not all the studies were done with the requisite controls against sources of error, inevitably the question becomes: Were all the successful studies merely replicating errors and were they open to fraud? It should be realised that very few studies were designed with the support of the resources needed to pay the double bill of being proof-orientated and replication-orientated. Nevertheless, in 1984 a constructive dialogue began between Charles

Honorton and the leading critic, Ray Hyman, resulting in a joint communiqué listing the more stringent criteria required for a replication to be declared as valid (Hyman & Honorton, 1986). It was important, for instance, to eliminate possibilities of multiple analyses, recording errors and, as far as possible, data manipulation. In what surely must be one of the most positive outcomes of any controversy in psychology, Honorton went back and redesigned the prototype manually operated ganzfeld, producing what is now known as the automated ganzfeld or *autoganzfeld* whereby these and other potential sources of error were eliminated. He and his colleagues then went on to carry out ten autoganzfeld studies with eight separate experimenters. These, the so-called PRL studies, took place at the Princeton Psychophysical Research Laboratory, and produced a 32 per cent hit rate where chance would be 25 per cent ($z = 2.89$, $p = .004$, two-tailed, with a small–medium effect size: $\eth = 0.59$) (Bem & Honorton, 1994).

It might be thought that the issue was now settled. However, the report by Daryl Bem and Charles Honorton detailing these findings, published in *Psychological Bulletin* shortly after Honorton's death, did little to attract funding or any interest from mainstream psychologists (Bem, quoted in Parker, 1994). Worse, the next 30 studies selected for a further meta-analysis by Julie Milton and Richard Wiseman not only failed to replicate the PRL effect by being overall non-significant, but produced a non-significant near-zero effect size (Milton & Wiseman, 1999). It may sound contrived but it is conceivable that many experimenters were by then tiring of straight replications so that by deviating too much from the original recipe, they failed to produce the requisite effect since there was a demonstrable lack of homogeneity both in the designs and in the results. Moreover, the overall statistical significance of the meta-analysis did return with the next ten replication studies, although the effect was still much smaller than with the original PRL studies. The homogeneity argument does, in fact, have strong empirical support in the form of an elegant study reported by Daryl Bem, John Palmer and Richard Broughton (Bem *et al.*, 2001). The authors recruited senior students to carry out blind ratings of the degree to which the post-PRL studies deviated from the standard ganzfeld procedure, and found a clear relationship between standardness and statistical significance, with the more standard studies showing a joint effect size compatible with the earlier studies.

The Return to the Status Quo

In 1995, the Clinton government commissioned Jessica Utts and Ray Hyman to assess the application value of parapsychological research findings. They concentrated on the research design known as *remote viewing* (localization and description of remote targets via ESP) and on research with the ganzfeld technique.

Both assessors agreed that there existed an *anomaly* in the sense that there was no apparent explanation for the results. Utts argued that psi ability had been established while Hyman insisted that all that could be concluded was that an anomaly existed in the form of an inexplicable finding, thereby avoiding admitting, along with the anomaly, the accompanying heavy baggage from psychical research. They differed in that Utts was of the opinion that more replications were meaningless while Hyman thought, given the ambiguity, they were still appropriate. Despite their differences both Hyman and Utts agreed on what else was needed. Utts (1996) wrote:

> Resources should be directed to the pertinent questions about how this ability works. I am confident that the questions are no more elusive than any other questions in science dealing with small to medium sized effects, and that if appropriate resources are targeted to appropriate questions, we can have answers within the next decade.

Hyman (1996) wrote:

> Despite better controls and careful use of statistical inference, the investigators seem to be getting significant results that do not appear to derive from the more obvious flaws of previous research. I have argued that this does not justify concluding that anomalous cognition has been demonstrated. However, it does suggest that it might be worthwhile to allocate some resources toward seeing whether these findings can be independently replicated. If so, then it will be time to reassess if it is worth pursuing the task of determining if these effects do indeed reflect the operation of anomalous cognition. This latter quest will involve finding lawful relationships between attributes of this hypothesized phenomenon and different independent variables.

In one respect Hyman may have been insufficiently critical. Some of the earlier pre-PRL work was carried out by Carl Sargent, a Cambridge University researcher whose results were considered suspect by a critic, Susan Blackmore. The debate was intensive and became a major reason for Blackmore's subsequent disillusionment with the field (Blackmore, 1987; Parker and Wiklund, 1987; Sargent, 1987). The issue was never fully resolved and both individuals have now left academic psychology for more lucrative work. Although these particular questionable results now make little difference to the results of the current meta-analysis, if we wish to reduce the possibility of the data manipulation and procedural errors then a separate analysis should be made of the high-quality autoganzfeld studies.[7] Unfortunately, the development of the *autoganzfeld* put the methodology back in the expensive and cumbersome class, so, following Princeton, only three laboratories in the world (the Rhine Research Center, and parapsychology laboratories at the Universities of Edinburgh and Amsterdam) have used it. Nevertheless, based on the list provided by Bem *et al.* (2001), it can be seen that there were eight such 'well-conducted' replication studies (scoring 7.0 on a seven-point scale of standardness) involving four teams which produced a Stouffers z of 3.06, $p = 2.2 \times 10^{-3}$ (two-tailed). What is again obvious from looking at the z values for the 'well-conducted' studies replications is that there are clear differences between research teams and experimenters, and much of the success is still dependent on particular experimenters.

---

[7]   I am aware that by this I am excluding some of my own successful ganzfeld work (Parker, 2000). Although we took reasonable precautions and the results were not dependent on any one experimenter, from the critic's point of view they do not have all the precautions included in the autoganzfeld.

Given this success, albeit a very limited one — but perhaps also an accredited one — and given the limited resources available, it would seem that Hyman's (1996a) demand for yet more replications has in principle been met during the five years following his report and that it is now time to look for lawful relationships. This is a conclusion even supported by the critics Milton and Wiseman (2001) in their latest comment about the outcome of the psi-ganzfeld meta-analyses in the *Psychological Bulletin* debate — a debate which began in 1994 and sporadically continues. In the same issue of that journal, Lance Storm and Suitbert Ertel (2001) maintained that the psi-ganzfeld database, seen as a whole, is now both consistent and convincing as regards to a replicable effect. In replying to this claim, Milton and Wiseman naturally questioned the quality of many of the studies but they also constructively suggested that the way forward was now to strive towards the Beloffian goal of being able to demonstrate psi where and when required. Claiming that nothing was actually known about the variables determining the occurrence of psi, Milton and Wiseman then suggested the next step 'would be to assess critically the experimental evidence for the effects of many variables that have been suggested as affecting outcomes in ganzfeld studies' and given this, a demonstrable 'replicable effect would be possible.' (Milton and Wiseman, 2001, p. 437)

Hyman (1996b) would say not even this would be enough:

> Even if . . . we were to find we could reproduce the findings under specified conditions, this would still be a far cry from concluding that psychic functioning has been demonstrated. You need a positive theory to guide you as to what needs to be controlled, and what can be ignored.

Of course, some readers might think that Hyman was now moving the goal posts, but for the moment what counts most is that there should be some forward movement of the play. This has not been the case. Despite Utts's strongly worded recommendation for university-based funding and Hyman's support in principle for theory-driven research, there has been no tangible response to this in the form of research grants or government-funded projects (Utts, 2002). Indeed, Hyman's remarks may instead have supplied a needed catch-22 to bring the debate back to status quo: the phenomena must first be given a theoretical explanation before research into their nature can be funded. A good illustration of this was found recently in a Swedish Science Research Council's assessment of a project that sought to look for some of Milton and Wiseman's 'lawful relationships' using psi in the ganzfeld. Although the application was approved, the project was given a low priority rating because information was first required about 'the mechanisms, which are the basis for the phenomena,' and about how 'that information is transferred between sender and receiver.' (SRC, 2001)

At the stage when the amount of work done in parapsychology has been calculated to be equivalent to no more than two months work in psychology (Schouten, 1998) the prior demands for precise and established theories are not only unrealistic but amount to little more than a catch-22. If efforts comparable to those in parapsychology had been deployed to areas of arguably comparable complexity, such as hypnosis or dream research, then at best we would have expected little more than we have here today: a *prima facie* case for the phenomenon's existence and the development of appropriate research methodologies to study it.

One of Hyman's main arguments for conceding the presence of an anomaly concerns an argument put forward by David Marks for a 'ten-year rule' of delay from the time from when strong psi findings are presented to when normal explanations for it are finally thought of. This division into parapsychologist and critic is an unfortunate one because it is places the critic forever in the role of a hacker who is given ten years to find a way of breaking into the computer security system. Even so, it is now twenty-five years since psi-ganzfeld research began and there exist other, older successful experimental designs such as Maimonides dream work (Ullman *et al.*, 1974) and hypnosis (Honorton & Krippner, 1969) which have stood an even longer test of time. Marks' argument fails then by virtue of its own criteria.

In taking a purist view by claiming all that has been demonstrated is an anomaly in the ganzfeld setup, it should be pointed out that critics such as Hyman are also ignoring that while much of the ganzfeld work has been process orientated, there are *proof-orientated psi experiments* (see, for example, Schmidt *et al.*, 1986) as well as the *conceptual replications* carried on psi in relation to other altered states (see Alvarado, 1998; Parker, 1976). The ganzfeld work has, moreover, an *ecological validity* in being an experimental analogue of themes re-occurring in the historic case collections of psychical research (Gauld, 1968; Stevenson, 1970; Roy, 1996). Case collections originally gave impetus to the ganzfeld and Maimonides designs by indicating that psi is most frequently associated with dream states rather than waking states, and ESP in the dream state has more information content (L. Rhine, 1962).

In down-playing the value of the well-documented case collections, leading critics such as Marks, Hyman and Alcock are naturally influenced by their backgrounds as social and cognitive psychologists. Certainly, many sceptics writing in the 1700s and 1800s knew about human proneness to self-delusions and imagination but today we have a greater precision in describing the sources of error through such terms as selective memory, contextual cues, fantasy proneness and subjective validation. James Alcock (2002) succinctly expresses this view as: 'If telepathy did not exist the human mind would need to invent it'. The problem, of course, with this statement is that some philosophers would say the same thing about the external world. Worse, there is a risk that cognitive psychologists, like psychoanalysts before them, have already begun to misuse terms like cognitive defences and subjective validation as (to borrow from what William James had to say about the Unconscious) 'the sovereign means for explaining away anything' that contradicts cognitive theory.[8]

In any case, although case collections are important, the primary thrust of parapsychology today is in laboratory experiments which produce quantitative evidence. Ironically, at least one critic seems to agree that the efforts to produce the above pure quantitative evidence may have contributed towards this distrust of what the findings actually mean. James Alcock (1996) lists eight reasons for being sceptical about ESP. Several of these actually concern the replication and methodological shortcoming discussed above, and a further two reasons concern the lack of theoretical understanding and progress, which will be discussed later. A final reason for being sceptical that Alcock gives relates to Hyman's refusal to concede more than a mere anomaly, in that: 'the best modern evidential claims are hidden from easy view in the world of statistical analysis' (Alcock, 1996, p. 249). Indeed, if ganzfeld psi is more than an anomaly and is indeed evidence for some form of little-understood communication, then obviously it should have information content. This consideration formed part of the impetus to develop a new form of ganzfeld experimentation which we have installed at the University of Gothenburg in Sweden and lately at the Institute for Frontier Areas of Psychology at Freiburg, Germany.

The Content of an Anomaly:
Recent Developments with the Ganzfeld Technique

In designing experiments, the above review suggests it is not enough to be solely technically orientated and that experimenter characteristics as well as participant factors are important. To see what factors must be included in psi experiments, let us use the example of the ganzfeld. Like Rhine before him, Honorton attributed his success with the ganzfeld to the importance of factors in the experimenter such as warmth and empathy towards the participants and the ability to motivate others (Terry & Honorton, 1976). Some of these statements might be regarded as after-the-fact rationalizations and indeed some critics (Milton & Wiseman, 2001) have asserted that nothing is known *empirically* about what makes a successful psi experimenter and what the psi-conducive factors are in experimentation. This would imply that 50 years later we must begin again where Rhine left off. Fortunately, several reviews of the empirically based research literature give strong support to the hands-on-based impressions of Rhine and Honorton (Kennedy & Taddonio, 1976; White, 1976a; 1976b; 1977). The assertion becomes more puzzling when it is well known that Wiseman has himself contributed to this literature (Wiseman & Schlitz, 1999), his own findings actually supporting Rhine's observations.

What appears to be known is that in some cases it seems that as well as a psi-conducive effect, a psi-inhibitory effect could also occur in which participants could consistently score significantly below chance — so-called

---

[8] The area of spontaneous cases is a relatively neglected by parapsychologists and more or less totally ignored by psychologists. Moreover, few of the traditional explanations from cognitive psychology would seem to apply to the better cases (Parker, 2002). For instance, Gauld and Cornell (1979, pp. 254–6) report evidence suggesting that witnesses over a long time period actually tone down rather than exaggerate their accounts. Neither are all mediumistic successes only so-called Barnum effects — general statements that that receive wide endorsements. Playfair and Keen (2003) report a contemporary mediumistic case which gave such specific information in terms of correct names and other specific details that the police reluctantly took her testimony seriously. Her identification of one the suspects was later confirmed by DNA testing.

psi-missing. This bi-directionality of psi effect is reminiscent of an effect found many years ago in psychotherapy — that the wrong therapeutic conditions could make patients significantly worse than a non-treatment condition (Truax & Carkhuff, 1967). Another apparently important factor finding concerns the *sheep–goat effect*, referring to the participants' degree of personal belief in psi and own experiences of the phenomena and how this has on many occasions been used as a predictor of scoring (Lawrence, 1993; Goulding & Parker, 2001).

The problem with such findings is that while they may appear to be at best necessary conditions, they never are sufficient conditions for psi to occur and, worse, they can be misused as an escape clause for explaining why experiments fail. Accordingly, in designing a program of research with the ganzfeld at Gothenburg, we intentionally selected individuals who scored high on the *sheep–goat scale* (of paranormal belief and experiences) with the expectation that those with more of their own psi-like experiences will score better, and because of the above considerations we always predict that experimenter effects will arise. Both these sets of predictions have found support in our analyses (Parker, 2000).

In 1995 our own attempt at replicating the PRL work was for financial reasons limited to using a manually operated video system of showing target film clips. Following the termination of the ganzfeld session, the participant would compare the mentation report with each of the target film clips previously recorded on a composite tape, and then make a direct forced choice as to which of the four clips was the target film clip. In the course of this work, by simply recording the mentation report along with the film track, we began to observe that some of the mentation reports of the imagery during ganzfeld appeared to be describing *in real time* whole sequences of the changing content of film clips. The critic in us would say this is merely our subjective validation in seeing what we wanted to see. Yet some descriptions were very accurate and the real time aspect seemed even harder to dismiss.

In order to document this, at the suggestion of a colleague, Dr Jan Dalkvist at the Psychology Department in Stockholm, a second video player was added which would copy the film clip as it was viewed and at the same time receive a sound recording from the ongoing mentation report of the participant in the ganzfeld state. The resulting audio-visual recording would then give us real-time recording of the film clip and mentation report and could be evaluated for real-time correspondences. Since the results of this set of five experiments were statistically highly significant ($z = 3.02$, $p = .0025$, two-tailed, ES = .25), it seemed legitimate to look at this content at least from the point of view of generating hypotheses about the lawful relationships sought after by critics and parapsychologists.[9] About one in five or six sessions would produce a mentation report which seemed to be describing the film clip in real time. We reasoned that

---

[9] To avoid a file drawer problem it should be mentioned that one further uncompleted study involved inviting back ten previously successful participants. Although immediate re-testing was very successful in our third ganzfeld study (Parker, 2000), this time only five hits in 29 trials were obtained but it should be said two years had now passed and many relationships had altered.

rather than studying an anomaly, this would provide an ideal opportunity for studying high-quality psi when it was actually happening. What speaks against simple subjective validation are the cases where not only unequivocal details are given but the mentation appears to follow the changing and unpredictable scenes in the film clip. For instance, in the session illustrated below, the receiver in ganzfeld gave a whole sequence of responses which not only correctly described a woman first in a marsh area and a forest with enormous trees but went on to give other responses that seemed to be misperceptions of the film content: a snowy effect (snow plough), the coloured wigs (coloured balls) her women assailants had on, and the boomerang-shaped stick she used to defend herself. All of these responses were in real time and culminated in the scene shown in Figure 1 when she said 'someone falls hitting their face on stony ground'. It should be added that the film has only music as a sound background, had not been used before and the participant had no prior access to it. Obviously, such illustrations are not meant as proof of psi but they might suggest there is more content to the anomaly than statistics.

It was these kinds of results that gave impetus to a co-worker, Dr Joakim Westerlund, and myself to develop what is now known as the digital ganzfeld. The digital ganzfeld has major improvements over the earlier autoganzfeld, in that it not only enables the real time recording of the mentation report with the film clip to be made, but the recording of the mentation report can also be super-imposed onto the decoy clips as well as onto the real target film (see Figure 1). This provides the opportunity of using the real time matches as an important aid

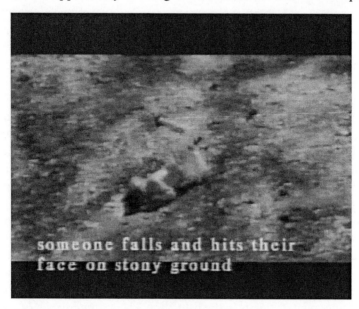

Figure 1

Video real time recording: The participant described accurately in real time with the film a whole sequences of events including: 'someone falls and hits their face on stony ground' at the exact moment when this took place.

in determining which is the target film. From the point of view of facilitating replications and involving mainstream psychologists in ganzfeld research, the procedure has something further to offer: The digital ganzfeld is a portable system
which, when placed on a laptop computer, can be used anywhere in the world.[10]

A legitimate use of such qualitative material is to generate hypotheses about
how psi enters consciousness. Initially we collected about 20 examples of what
seemed to be high-quality, real-time psi but what was more interesting, from the
point of view of hypotheses, were the near misses that interphased with sequences
of accurate descriptions. Very often these seemed to be evidence of *top-down processes* in which the participant was struggling to interpret vague information that
he had to work on and thus the process could be likened to normal sensory input during non-optimal conditions. It appeared to be the case
that the theme would be correct but interpretative mistakes would then
occur such as when the film clip suddenly focused on an imp-like
creature hidden amongst seaweed-covered rocks and the participant
responded with 'ivy-covered rocks with

Ongoing mentation via the microphone is digi-tally recorded on one sound card of the computer

The film is copied in visual basic as it is played along with the voice of the receiver describing imagery

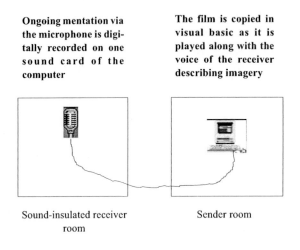

Sound-insulated receiver room

Sender room

Figure 2. The Digital Ganzfeld setup.

something in it' or such as when jumping white lemurs were seem as 'jumping
white lambs' (Parker *et al.*, 2000).

One of the difficulties in evaluating this kind of qualitative material is of
course its selective nature and clearly we cannot go much further until some
means of quantifying the material is developed. A major obstacle in reaching that
goal is that of dependency: If participants guessed correctly, for instance, that the
clip depicts a forest scene then some other features such as birds and paths, and
for some people even threatening scenes, like the one occurring in Figure 1,
might be expected to follow. Of course there are problems with using this kind of
argument to readily dismiss the above findings. Although such correspondences
are conceivable, as was mentioned earlier, it would seem unlikely that such correspondences would be constantly in real time, and the most impressive examples concern the correspondences between ganzfeld mentation reports and the
sudden and unexpected events in the film clips. The argument can, of course, also
backfire in that if the initial guess happens to be wrong, it can lead to a string of
wrong associative responses. Ironically, it is the complexity of this dependency

[10] However, when set up on a stationary computer system in order to prevent any leakage, we use the
extra precaution of separate sound cards for the recording of the mentation report and the film sound.

aspect that seems to have escaped the want-to-be critics. David Marks (2000) is the avowed spokesman for the concept of *subjective validation* in explaining away such coincidental 'hits' both in experimental work and real life. Clearly there is a need to support this with figures and Marks calculates that 4,950 pairs of events can be cross-matched for a given person in a given day. To arrive at this figure, he makes the gratuitous assumption that there are a hundred independent events experienced by a person in a given day, but like the content of films, surely few people hopefully have such entirely random lives.

A simple and better solution to the above problem, proposed by another of my colleagues, Dr Joakim Westerlund, is for a judge to first identify what *appear* to be sequences of real-time matches by the usual procedure of blind matching the mentation report against both targets and decoys. Further selections are then made amongst the apparent real-time matches: the matches have to be limited to a single phrase with a maximum of one best match per film clip. All such best matches in a given experimental series then form the collection which is used for further

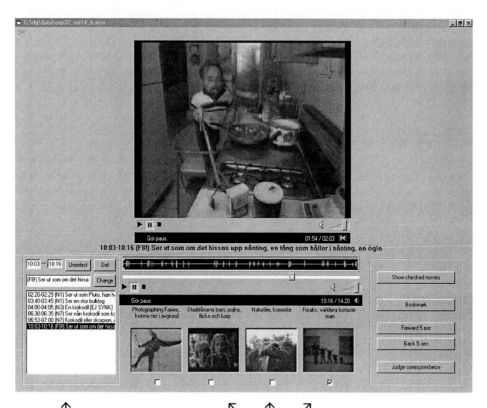

↑   ↖ ↑ ↗

List of bookmarks, each referenced   Film-clips can be activated here and
to selected sequences in the film-clips   compared one or two clips at
of what might be real time psi.   a time with the content of the mentation
report.

Figure 3
Real time digital recording:
Capturing psi (or is it capturing subjective evaluation?) when it happens.

quantitative study. If the matches are due to psi, rather than subjective validation, then we would expect the collection to be formed mostly from the target clips rather than from the decoys. This solution, although ingenious, has its limitations since by reducing the numerous striking correspondences found in good-quality hits to one singular phrase, a crude measure is produced involving a major loss of information, and even within single phrases some dependency can remain. The method is nevertheless a start and can be somewhat improved when objectively defined criteria are set up for rating the quality of real-time correspondences. The process of identifying the representative units for good hits is actually pro-grammed into digital ganzfeld by using a bookmarking system: The apparent real-time correspondences are listed so that when a particular item on the list is activated, the sound from the mentation record is recalled along with the corre-sponding part of the film clip. An example is found in Figure 3, where the partici-pant says: 'looks like something is being lifted, a tong which holds something'. The statement is synchronous with the five-second sequence in the film-clip when a handicapped man suddenly appears, lifting an object with the help of a type of tong.

To date, because of shortage of funding, only two main experiments have been run using this technique. An additional feature for these experiments was the use of two film clips, each lasting nearly 15 minutes per session; a modification which radically improves the statistical power of the procedure. In the first study (Goulding et al., 2003), 64 such double sessions were run, giving 128 trials (each having an expected 0.25 p value). Time restrictions meant that participant judg-ing (the usual procedure with ganzfeld which we used throughout our earlier studies) could only be carried out on half the sessions. The more systematic and time-consuming judging of the whole mentation report against each of the four (target and decoy) film clips had to be carried out by an external judge. One major purpose of the experimental design was to determine if this form of exter-nal judging with its more systematic use of bookmarks would be superior to par-ticipant judging.

Another of the main aims of the study was for other experimenters to inde-pendently replicate the earlier highly significant findings which my co-workers and I had previously obtained (Parker et al., 1997; Parker et al., 1998) using the same type of participant population. However, this time, the same method of par-ticipant judging gave scores *significantly below* chance expectation — a so-called psi-missing effect — with the direct hit rate lying at 14 per cent, (MCE 25 per cent), $z = 2.02$, $p = .05$ (two-tailed). External judging, which was the basis for the hypothesis of the experimenter, Anneli Goulding, was on the other hand close to chance with 23 per cent hits ($z = .041$). In accordance with the above method of quantifying the qualitatively good hits, a collection of 18 apparent real-time correspondences was formed. These were identified to occur more often with the target film than controls, although not significantly so: 33 per cent compared to the 25 per cent chance expectancy. When friends were in the role of being the sender, a *post-hoc* test of the judge's rankings gave a 45.5 per cent hit rate (chi-square = 7.2, df = 3, $p = .066$, two tailed) with the target ratings then showing a significant effect ($F = 4.54$, $p = .005$).

Clearly these type of results — and they are unfortunately all too common in parapsychology — can either be ignored, or dismissed as a peculiar statistical artefact, or we can try to make sense of them. If the psi-missing findings are a genuine effect, then it is conceivable that the systematic nature of the external judging did actually succeed in moving the rankings and ratings in a positive direction but not beyond the chance level. By using only the judge's blind identification of the best bookmarks, it might be that we had raised the receiver's original hit rate from 14 per cent to 33 per cent. Currently, we are assessing this qualitative material in order to determine whether the hits do in fact differ from misses in a quantifiable way.

In this particular case it is not difficult to think of possible causes of the apparent psi missing, such as the fact that the frustrating delays that occurred due to programming problems meant that experiments were run on a stressful, very tight time schedule.

The second study (Wright, 2003), which has just been completed at the time of writing, used only receiver judgments and produced a scoring rate more than twice as high compared to the above. The results were then in line with what has previously been claimed for the Ganzfeld: a 32–33 per cent direct hit rate and a small to medium effect size (Cohen's $r = 0.17$, $z = 1,48$, $p = .09$). Of particular relevance was the finding that one session per day trials gave a 45 per cent hit rate while those with two sessions per day gave a mere 19 per cent hit rate (chi^2 = 5.4, $p = .02$) thereby confirming a previous finding of Sandow (1979); findings that are consistent with the hypothesis that stress and tight schedules negatively effect psi performance.

These findings unfortunately also illustrate what appears to be an intractable problem in parapsychology. Until we can predict such outcomes *ahead of time*, the establishment of lawful relationships still evades us. What is very clear from the above review and from other more extensive reviews (e.g., White, 1976b) is that experimenter effects and psi-conduciveness are every bit as integral a part of the phenomena being studied as, say, placebo effects are in psychological treatment. But there is some evidence that they are even more so.

Returning the Magic to Psi?

In one respect it seems clear that Rhine underestimated the difficulties that lay ahead. For whatever reason the phenomena appear to have an *elusiveness* as a defining characteristic that makes them intrinsically difficult to capture in the laboratory in a stable, predictable and controllable fashion (Kennedy, 2001). There are many findings like the above where an expected significantly positive effect in an attempted replication suddenly reverses and becomes a mirror image of what is expected (see Parker, 1978 for a review).

That this elusiveness sounds almost magical may not be entirely facetious. It is just possible that the association of psi with magical practices and mediumship is not a sign of its being entirely illusory but that such ambiguous circumstances may actually be necessary psi-conducive conditions. The late Kenneth Batcheldor, as a chief consultant clinical psychologist with the National Health Service in England, had some credibility to risk when he claimed to have conducted many successful experiments in large-scale psychokinesis. Batcheldor would first produce some of the phenomena artefactually but then discovered that genuine phenomena would actually also spontaneously seem to occur. Success was attributed to the ambiguity around who was responsible for the phenomena which allowed the release of a creative psi ability in the participants (Batcheldor, 1994).

While this may seem a preposterous let-out, interesting in this context is endorsement of genuine psi by professionally experienced magicians, which is reported to be between 72 and 87 per cent (Truzzi, 1997; Hansen, 2001). This is a remarkable contrast to that of psychologists which, at an estimated, 34 per cent, must be a record low amongst scientists (Wagner & Monnet, 1979 quoted in Bem & Honorton, 1994). Although magicians can claim to be true experts in applied cognitive psychology, obviously even they can deceive themselves and be deceived by other magicians. However, given this expertise, such findings clearly warrant further thought since they may reveal something of central importance about the conditions conducive to psi. Might it just be that in pursuit of making psi clinically clean by bringing it to the laboratory, we are removing some of the essence of the phenomenon in terms of what makes it readily happen? Recently, Matthew Smith and Michael Gordon investigated the psychology of the 50 named 'psi-conducive and psi-inhibitory experimenters' and found by multiple regression of self-report questionnaires that 'higher psi-conduciveness scores were associated with belief in one's own PK [psychokinetic] ability and belief that it is possible to demonstrate ESP in an experimental study' (Smith & Gordon, 2001).[11]

The mention of such alleged phenomena as mind–matter interactions known as PK or psychokinesis may strain the reader's sense of what is credible. Nevertheless, the Rhine laboratory had already in the 1940s begun testing the claims of gamblers to be able to influence throws of the die and this became extended from the 1970s to influencing the output of random-number generators. The database from all these experiments is now, by parapsychological standards, so massive (597 studies) that meta-analysis produces enormous odds against chance whereas the control studies (235 studies) do as we might hope, confirm chance expectancy (Nelson & Radin, 1989). This sounds impressive, at least until one realises that the apparent PK effect is only about one per cent above the 50 per cent chance expectancy and might be taken as some unknown anomaly or artefact, were it not again for the occasional well-documented cases of large-scale spontaneous phenomena. Probably the most famous of these is the Rosenheim case, investigated by Hans Bender of Freiburg University, and concerned the numerous electrical disturbances and movements of objects that appeared to centre around a young woman. Such explanations as fraud seem rather facile when confronting the full force of German meticulousness and efficiency thrown into the case, a force which mustered police from the Criminal Investigation Department, staff and personnel from the Municipal Fire Service and Electricity

[11] Some empirical support is found in a review by Brian Millar (1979) who concluded that considering psi ability is rare, psi-conducive experimenters were themselves to be found over-represented as psi-conducive subjects!

Department as well as physicists from the Max Planck Institute. All of those involved in it failed to reveal anything suspicious or any normal explanation. In addition, there were about 40 first-hand witnesses to the events and there appear to have been brief film documentations of some of them (Bender,1974). If this was fraud, it would have to be one of many such inscrutable cases. Even Charles Honorton reported and filmed with the help of an amateur magician some apparently genuine PK effects by one of his former assistants, Felicia Parise, which resulted in the observable movement of objects (Honorton, 1993b).

Accepting PK would, of course, render the world a much more plastic place but it would also explain some of the inherent difficulties in producing phenomena to order, since not only do the expectancies of the experimenter but also his own psychic abilities become an important part of the experiment. J.B. Rhine to my knowledge rarely if ever commented publicly on the psi ability of the experimenter, but in 1975 in a private letter to me, he replied to my questioning by expressing the following viewpoint:

> I do not think the experimenter's own psi ability has shown up to be as an essential factor, but I still think we must assume that every experimenter has the ability and only needs to learn how he himself can liberate and register it. However, the very conditions that help the experimenter to liberate this might be the kind that would help him to induce his subjects to perform successfully (Rhine, September 5, 1975).

So perhaps Rhine, in his later years, did realise something of the complexity of the area that he had entered. Yet, this concept of psi as pervasive and elusive phenomena coupled to experimenter effects might suggest that psi, if it exists, is an intractable problem lying completely outside of science. This would be wrong. The experimental work and spontaneous case studies reviewed suggest that ESP-derived, definitive units of information are, as they enter consciousness, fully amenable to study, and the large-scale PK effects, if they are genuine, are quite tangible and offer an ideal opportunity to study mind–matter interaction. What we should not do is to be deterred if we still do not have the know-how to make psi happen at will. We should also not forget that at least some of the apparent elusiveness might simply be due to our ingenuity in always being able to find alternative explanations for psi, and thereby futilely pursuing the final crucial 'proof'. Of course, the extant evidence could still be an illusion, but this would seem to be an ambiguity, albeit remote, that we may have to live with in order to determine if progress can be made.

Perhaps if we were to do like Batcheldor and give our participants a mixture of correct and false-positive feedback, thereby creating an atmosphere where a 'miracle' is expected, effect sizes might soar. The very least we can learn from this work is the importance of being more adventurous in our experimental designs. Experimenters with charisma and charm rather than psychology degrees could be employed to run testing sessions whereas those with doctoral degrees retain responsibility for seeing that the formal controls inbuilt in the procedure are followed and ensure that the ethical standards for interactions are met.

Conclusion

Many critics and parapsychologists would agree that there is an anomaly to be investigated and hopefully at least some of these critics, after reading the above review, might even agree that the anomaly appears to have both information content and dynamic influence. Indeed, the divisions between critics and parapsychologists is a false one, nurtured in the past by dogmatic and dismissive statements rather than facts. However, if the balance or consensus that has been reached is to become a platform for progress rather than for maintaining the status quo, I would argue that there needs to be some realisation that we have come as far as we can in asking the question 'Does psi exist?' and need to ask new ones. The question that would appear to be most appropriate to critic and parapsychologists alike becomes: Assuming ESP ability exists, can we make its occurrence more likely and thereby learn something about its nature?

Given the complexity of the phenomena, two further prerequisites for progress would be the development of new designs that capitalize on psi's apparent elusiveness and the deployment of appropriate resources needed for such research programmes.

Regrettably, there are many reasons for supposing this scenario will not happen, not the least the unlikely alliance between science and religion in seeing the claims of the occult as at worst a mutual enemy, and at best an unwelcome guest. It might easily be thought that religion would have much to gain from research in this area — and indeed one leading critic (Alcock, 1987) depicted parapsychology as 'the search for the soul'.[12] Paradoxically, many of the claims of the paranormal are still seen as either a devilish challenge to Christianity or as an affront to Humanism. Some scientists may even have a hidden agenda in defending one or the other or both of these faiths, resulting in the absurd situation where some critics, as Honorton (1993a) aptly puts it, are more inclined to believe in angels than in psi.

There may be other, more subtle reasons for the failure to resolve the challenge presented by parapsychology. Ray Hyman (1996), for instance, partly justifies his scepticism on the basis of a rewrite of contemporary physics being required in order to accommodate the phenomena (although I fail to see why advances in one area of science have to be constantly held congruous with knowledge in other areas). Ironically, in terms of rewriting, the opposite may be true. Given that parapsychology has arguably survived the most intensive and prolonged scrutiny that any area of psychology has been subjected to, then such a declaration should imply that human self deception is so devious and pervasive that much of psychology, and perhaps even parts of natural science, should by rights come into question. Rupert Sheldrake (1998) surveyed papers published in leading science journals for their attention to experimenter effects and blind assessments of data. The highest proportion was by far to be found in parapsychology (85 per cent) followed by medical sciences (six per cent) and psychology (five per cent). Many

---

[12] One leading parapsychologist, Charles Tart (1987) in the peer debate with James Alcock (1987) found nothing at all wrong with this arguing that many major enterprises in science had begun with a search for something.

findings considered established in psychology, such as the classical Asch experiments influence of group pressure on conformity judgments, suffer from replication problems (reviewed in Alcock *et al.*, 1998). It would therefore seem inescapable that if the same criteria used for rejecting parapsychology are applied to psychology, then many, if not most, areas would fall. It would be strange then if there were not strong forces that wish to maintain the status quo and let the issue remain, as it is, unresolved.

The alternative scenario, that genuine phenomena exist, may be seen as equally unwelcome since it may open the door to psychical research with its whole troop of unwelcome phenomena from mediumship to apparitional experiences — or worse, New Age — although the paradox is that experimental parapsychology provides the means of dealing with the unbidden guests by explaining away most of them as forms of psi from the living. This scenario is obviously not without its risks but has some potential benefits as regards the status of psychology amongst the sciences: Many authorities (e.g., Tart, 1997) agree this would bring about a re-evaluation of the function of consciousness in nature and provide new perspectives on the mind–body relationship.

Clearly, the possibility of developing theories which will resolve the issue *does* lie within the grasp of our generation. As shown earlier the advance of technology enables us now to study what at least appears to be high-quality psi. Considering the complexity of factors involved, further experimentation with the backing of mainstream psychology might or might not make the kind of rapid progress that Jessica Utts (as quoted earlier) foresees but there is no doubt it would resolve, once and for all, the basic issue of what we are dealing with. Of course, the apparent elusiveness and experimenter-psi effects make the phenomena unique in science, but to argue that this is beyond science is to repeat what was once said about psychology little over a century ago. It probably only means we have to be more sophisticated and ingenious.

Alan Gauld concludes his scholarly review of the history of hypnosis with poetically eloquent advice that might apply equally well to parapsychology:

> The mysterious domain [of hypnosis] emerges, then, as a kind of fairy palace, less than real, but more than illusion. It has, one may say, sufficient substance in its foundations to have deceived mortals rather well. Especially has it ensnared savants of past generations, who in turn have misled the media and the public at large. But from our vantage point of the end of the twentieth century we can begin to see that there is no one path by which it may be reached, no one material of which it is built, no one hidden chamber containing all its secrets, no one key that will open all its doors, and no simple formula by which it may be dispelled. Those who set out to investigate it should be beware of the bafflements to come. (Gauld, 1992 p. 624)

The reassuring aspect is that with sufficient persistence and backing, progress does now seem to have been reached with hypnosis (Kirsch & Lynn, 1995; Oakley, 2002). So if we are serious about wanting to understand psi, the above-reviewed findings may give us reason to believe that by liberating ourselves from simplistic questions, and applying efforts and a technology appropriate to the complexity of the task, we can at last come further than our immediate predecessors, or even our ancestors, at understanding the nature of these phenomena. High-scoring subjects and successful experimenters are to be found and a technology is available.

Acknowledgements
I would like to thank The Institute für Grenzgebiete der Psychologie und Psychohygiene, Freiburg (the Astrid Holler Fund) and the BIAL Foundation for the financial support of this paper. Thanks also to Dr Alan Gauld, Dr Annekatrin Puhle, Dr Joakim Westerlund, Anneli Goulding and Dr Jan Dalkvist for helpful comments on an earlier draft of the manuscript.

References

Alcock, J.E. (1987), 'Parapsychology: Science of the anomalous or search for the soul?' *Behavioral and Brain Sciences*, **10**, pp. 553–643.

Alcock, J.E. (1996), 'Extrasensory perception', in *The Encyclopedia of the Paranormal*, ed. G. Stein (Amherst, NY: Prometheus Books).

Alcock, J.E. (2002), Personal communication.

Alcock, J.E., Carment, D.W., Sadava, S.W. (Eds.) (1998), *A Textbook of Social Psychology* (Scarborough, ON: Prentice Hall).

Alvarado, C. (1998), 'ESP and altered states of consciousness: An overview of conceptual and research trends', *Journal of Parapsychology*, **62**, pp. 27–64.

Batcheldor, K. (1994), 'Notes on the elusiveness problem in relation to a radical view of paranormality', *Journal of the American Society for Psychical Research*, **88**, pp. 90–115.

Baxter, R. (1691), *The Certainty of the Worlds of Spirits fully evinced by Unquestionable Histories* (London: T. Parkhurst and J. Salusbury).

Bekker, B. (1691), *Te betoouerde Weereld. (Leuward).* In German (1693) *Die bezauberte Welt* (Amsterdam) and in French (1694).

Beloff, J. (1973), *Psychological Sciences* (Norwich: Fletcher & Son).

Beloff, J. (1993), *Parapsychology: A Concise History* (Cambridge: Cambridge University Press).

Bem, D., Honorton, C. (1994), 'Does psi exist? Replicable evidence of an anomalous process of information transfer', *Psychological Bulletin*, **115**, pp. 4–18.

Bem, D., Palmer, J., Broughton, R. (2001), 'Updating the ganzfeld database: A victim of its own success?', *Journal of Parapsychology*, **65**, pp. 207–18.

Bender, H. (1974), 'Modern poltergeist research — A plea for an unprejudiced approach', in *New Directions in Parapsychology*, ed. J. Beloff (London: Elek Science).

Berger, A. (1988), *Lives and Letters in American Parapsychology, 1850–1987* (Jefferson, NC: McFarland).

Blackmore, S.J. (1987), 'A report of a visit to Carl Sargent's laboratory', *Journal of the Society for Psychical Research*, **54**, pp. 186–98.

Blackmore, S.J. (2001), 'What can the paranormal teach us about consciousness', *Skeptical Inquirer*, **25** (2), pp. 22–7.

Child, I.L. (1985), 'Psychology and anomalous observations', *American Psychologist*, **40**, pp. 1219–30.

Crowe, C. (1848/2000), *The Night Side of Nature* (2000 edition: Ware, UK: Wordsworth)

Dodds, E.R. (1971), 'Supernormal phenomena in classical antiquity', *Proceedings of the Society for Psychical Research*, **55**, pp. 189–271.

Ferriar, J. (1813), *Toward A Theory of Apparitions* (London: Cadell and Davies).

Gauld, A. (1968), *The Founders of Psychical Research* (London: Routledge & Kegan Paul).

Gauld, A. (1992), *A History of Hypnotism* (Cambridge: Cambridge University Press).

Gauld, A., Cornell, A.D. (1979), *Poltergeists* (London, Boston & Henley: Routledge & Kegan Paul).

Glanvill, J. (1681), *Saducismus Triumphatus: Or, Full and Plain Evidence concerning Witches and Apparitions* (London: S Lownds).

Goulding, A., Westerlund, J., Parker, A. (2003), Paper in preparation to be submitted. *Journal of Parapsychology*.

Goulding, A., Parker, A. (2001), 'Finding psi in the paranormal: Psychometric measures used in research on paranormal beliefs/experiences and in research on psi-ability', *European Journal of Parapsychology*, **16**, pp. 73–101.

Hansel, M. (1966), *ESP: A Scientific Evaluation* (New York: Scribner's).

Hansel, M. (1989), *The Search for Psychic Power: ESP and Parapsychology Revisited* (Buffalo, NY: Prometheus).

Hansen, G. (2001), *The Trickster and the Paranormal: Magicians who have endorsed psychic phenomena* (Philadelphia: Xlibris Books).

Hartmann, E. (1998), *Dreams and Nightmares: The New Theory of the Origin and Meaning of Dreams* (New York: Plenum Trade).

Hobson, J.A. (1990), *The Dreaming Brain* (London: Penguin Books).

Honorton, C. (1993a), 'Rhetoric over substance: the impoverished state of scepticism', *Journal of Parapsychology*, **57**, pp. 191–214.

Honorton, C. (1993b), 'A moving experience', *Journal of the American Society for Psychical Research*, **87**, pp. 329–40.

Honorton, C., Krippner, S. (1969), 'Hypnosis and ESP performance: A review of the experimental literature', *Journal of the American Society for Psychical Research*, **63**, pp. 214–52.

Hyman, R. (1996a), 'Evaluation of program on anomalous mental phenomena', *Journal of Scientific Exploration*, **10**, pp. 31–58.

Hyman, R. (1996b), 'The evidence for psychic functioning: claims versus reality', *Skeptical Inquirer*, **20**, pp. 24–6.

Hyman, R., Honorton, C. (1986), 'A joint communiqué: The psi ganzfeld controversy', *Journal of Parapsychology*, **50**, pp. 350–64.

James, W. (1896/1972), 'What psychical research has accomplished'. *Proceedings of the Society for Psychical Research*, **XII**. Reprinted in *Psychology and Extrasensory Perception*, ed. R. Van Over (1972). (Scarborough, ON: Mentor).

Kennedy, J.E. (2001), 'Why is psi so elusive? A review and proposed model', *Journal of Parapsychology*, **65**, pp. 219–46.

Kennedy, J., Taddonio, J, (1976), 'Experimenter effects in parapsychological research', *Journal of Parapsychology*, **40**, pp. 1–33.

Kirsch, I., Lynn, S.J. (1995), 'The altered state of hypnosis', *American Psychologist*, **50**, pp. 846–58.

Lawrence, T.R. (1993), 'Gathering in the sheep and goats. A meta-analysis of forced-choice sheep–goat ESP studies 1947–1993'. *Presented Paper. Proceedings of the 36th Annual Convention of the Parapsychological Association*, pp. 75–86.

Leahey, T.H. (1991), *A History of Modern Psychology* (Englewood Cliffs, NJ: Prentice Hall).

Marks, D (2000), *The Psychology of the Psychic* (Buffalo, NY: Prometheus).

Mauskopf, S.H., McVaugh, M.R. (1980), *The Elusive Science: Origins of Experimental Psychical Research* (Baltimore, MD: Johns Hopkins University Press).

McMoneagle, J, (2000), *Remote Viewing Secrets, A Handbook* (Charlottesville, VA: Hampton Roads).

Millar, B. (1979), 'The distribution of psi', *European Journal of Parapsychology*, **3**, (1), pp. 78–110

Milton, J., Wiseman, R. (1999), 'Does psi exist? Lack of replication of an anomalous process of information transfer', *Psychological Bulletin*, **125**, pp. 387–91.

Milton, J., Wiseman, R. (2001), 'Does psi exist? Reply to Storm and Ertel', *Psychological Bulletin*, **127**, pp. 434–8

Morris, R. (2001), 'Research methods in experimental parapsychology: problems and prospects', *European Journal of Parapsychology*, **16**, pp. 8–18.

Nelson, R., Radin, D. (1989), 'Statistically robust anomalous effects: Replication in random event generator experiments', in *Research in Parapsychology*, ed. L. Henckle, R.E. Berger (Metuchen, NJ: Scarecrow Press), pp. 23–6.

Oakley, D.A. (2002), 'Hypnosis and consciousness: A structural model', *Hypnos: Swedish Journal of Hypnosis in Psychotherapy and Psychosomatic Medicine*, **XXIX**, pp. 69–76.

Owen, C. (1712), *The Scene of Delusions* (London), In German (1715) as *Schauplatz der Betrügereyen* (Leipzig).

Parker, A (1974), 'Some success at screening for high-scoring ESP subjects', *Journal of the Society for Psychical Research*, **47**, pp. 336–70.

Parker, A. (1976), *States of Mind* (New York: Taplinger)

Parker, A. (1978), 'A holistic methodology in psi and ASC research', in *Psi and Altered States*, ed. B. Shaplin, L. Coly (New York: Parapsychology Foundation), pp. 42–52.

Parker, A. (1994), 'The status of the Ganzfeld: What has been achieved and what remains to be achieved', symposium in *Proceedings of the ParapsychologicalAssociation*, Amsterdam.

Parker, A. (2000), 'A review of the Ganzfeld work at Gothenburg University', *Journal of the Society for Psychical Research*, **64**, pp. 1–15.

Parker, A. (2002), 'Cognitive psychology's day in court: An essay review of Houran and Lange's Haunting and Poltergeists: Multidisciplinary Perspectives', *European Journal of Parapsychology*, **17**, pp. 97–109.

Parker, A., Wiklund, N. (1987), 'The Ganzfeld: Towards an assessment', *Journal of the Society for Psychical Research*, **54**, pp. 261–5.

Parker, A., Frederiksen, A., Johansson, H. (1997), 'Towards specifying the recipe for success with the Ganzfeld', *European Journal of Parapsychology*, **13**, pp. 15–27.

Parker, A., Grams, D., Pettersson, C. (1998), 'Some further variables to psi in the Ganzfeld', *Journal of Parapsychology*, **62**, pp. 27–45.

Parker, A., Persson, A., Haller, A. (2000), 'Using qualitative Ganzfeld research for theory development: Top down processes in psi-mediation', *Journal of the Society for Psychical Research*, **64**, pp. 65–81.

Playfair, G.L., Keen, M. (2003), 'A possibly unique case of psychic detection', *Journal of the Society for Psychical Research*, Submitted.

Pratt, J.G. (1974), 'Some notes for a future Einstein of parapsychology', *Journal of the American Society for Psychical Research*, **68**, pp. 133–55.

Rhine, L.E, (1962), 'Psychological processes in ESP experiences. Part II: Dreams', *Journal of Parapsychology*, **27**, pp. 172–99.

Rhine, J.B. (1948), 'Conditions favoring success in psi tests', *Journal of Parapsychology*, **12**, pp. 58–75.

Rhine, J.B. (1964), *Extrasensory Perception* (Boston, MD: Bruce Humphries).

Rhine, J.B. (1967/72), 'A parapsychologist reviews seventy years of psychology', Invited address at the Annual Convention of the American Psychological Association. Reprinted 1972 in *Psychology and Extrasensory Perception*, ed. R. Van Over (Scarborough, ON: Mentor Books), pp. 161–87.

Rhine, J.B. (1974a), 'Security versus deception in parapsychology', *Journal of Parapsychology*, **38**, pp. 99–121,

Rhine, J.B. (1974b), 'A new case of experimenter unreliability', *Journal of Parapsychology*, **38**, pp. 218–25.

Roy, A, (1996), *Archives of the Mind* (Stansted, UK: SNU Publications).

Sandow, N. (1979), 'Effects of associations and feedback on psi in the Ganzfeld: Is there more than meets the judge's eye?', *Journal of the American Society for Psychical Research*, **73**, pp. 123–43.

Sargent, C. (1987), 'Sceptical fairytales from Bristol', *Journal of the Society for Psychical Research*, **54**, pp. 208–18.

Schmidt, H., Morris, R.L., Rudolph, L. (1986), 'Channeling evidence for PK effects to independent observers', *Journal of Parapsychology*, **50**, pp. 1–16.

Schouten, S. (1998), 'Are we making progress?', in *Psi Research Methodology: A Re-examination*, Proceedings of an International Conference, ed. L. Coly, J. McMahon (New York: Parapsychology Foundation), pp. 295–322.

Sheldrake, R. (1998), 'Could experimenter effects occur in the physical and biological sciences?' *Skeptical Inquirer*, **May/June**, pp. 57–8.

Sherwood, S.J. (2002), 'ESP during Sleep: Sweet dreams or a nightmare', invited paper presented at 45th Annual Convention, Parapsychological Association, Paris.

Sidgwick, H., and Committee (1894), 'Report on Census of Hallucinations', *Proceedings of the Society for Psychical Research*, **X**, pp. 25–422.

Smith, M.,D., Gordon, M. (2001), 'The psychology of the psi-conducive experimenter', *Proceedings of 45th Annual Convention, Parapsychological Association*.

SRC, (2001), 'Protocol from the Science Research Council Assessments', Vetenskapliga Rådets Protokoll (Stockholm. FO905/2001).

Stevenson, I, (1970), *Telepathic Impressions: A Review and Report of 35 New Cases* (Charlottesville, VA: The University of Virginia Press).

Storm L., Ertel S. (2001), 'Does psi exist? Milton and Wiseman's (1999) meta-analysis of ganzfeld research', *Psychological Bulletin*, **127**, pp. 424–33.

Tart, C. (1987), 'Is searching for the soul unscientific?', *Behavioral and Brain Sciences*, **10**, p. 612.

Tart, C. (Ed.) (1997), *Body, Mind, Spirit* (Charlotesville, VA: Hampton Roads).

Terry, J., Honorton, C. (1976), 'Psi information retrieval in the Ganzfeld: Two confirmatory studies', *Journal of the American Society for Psychical Research*, **70**, pp. 207–18.

Truax, C., Carkhuff, R. (1967), *Toward Effective Counselling and Psychotherapy* (Chicago, IL: Aldine).

Truzzi, M. (1997), 'Reflections on the sociology and social psychology of conjurors and their relations with psychical research', in *Advances in Parapsychological Research*, ed. S. Krippner (Jefferson, NC: McFarland).

Ullman, M., Krippner, S., Vaughan, A. (1974), *Dream Telepathy* (Baltimore, MD: Penguin Books).

Utts, J. (1996), 'An assessment of the evidence for psychic functioning', *Journal of Scientific Exploration*, **10**, pp. 3–30.

Utts, J (2002), Personal communication.

Van de Castle, R. (1994), *Our Dreaming Mind* (New York: Ballatine).

West, D.J. (1962), *Psychical Research Today* (Harmondsworth, UK: Penguin Books).

White, R.A. (1976a), 'The influence of persons other than the experimenter on the subject's scores in psi experiments', *Journal of the American Society for Psychical Research*, **69**, pp. 133–66.

White, R.A. (1976b), 'The limits of experimenter influence on psi test results: Can any be set?', *Journal of the American Society for Psychical Research*, **70**, pp. 335–69.

White, R.A. (1977), 'The influence of the experimenter motivation, attitudes and methods of handling subjects in psi test results', in *Handbook of Parapsychology*, ed. B.Wolman (New York: Van Nostrand Reinhold), pp. 273–301.

Winson, J. (2002), 'The Meaning of dreams', *Scientific American, Special Edition: The Hidden Mind*, pp. 54–61.

Wiseman, R., Schlitz, M. (1999), 'Experimenter effects and the remote detection of staring', *Journal of Parapsychology*, **61**, pp. 197–207.

Wright, T. (2003), 'Går det att förbättra sin ESP Prestation genom upprepade digitala ganzfeldsessioner?', Master of Social Science Dissertation, Department of Psychology, Göteborg University.

Stanley Jeffers

Physics and Claims for Anomalous Effects Related to Consciousness

Abstract: *A minority of physicists has endorsed some claims made for anomalous effects related to consciousness. A smaller number have attempted experiments to establish the veracity of such claims. The nature of these claims, in particular those for psychokinesis, is reviewed. Most of the experimental work bearing on these claims conducted by professional scientists has not yielded convincing evidence in their support. What are frequently stated to be the most credible claims are not, in fact, persuasive and furthermore the appeals to quantum mechanics by way of explanation are questionable.*

Brief Historical Background

The field of claims for anomalous phenomena related to consciousness embraces many areas including psychokinesis, clairvoyance, out of body experiences and reincarnation. This large array of claims has been the subject of a recent book, *The Conscious Universe — The Scientific Truth of Psychic Phenomena* (Radin, 1997). However, this essay will only be concerned with claims for psychokinetic effects and the purported relationship between such claims and physics. Other anomalous phenomena related to consciousness, such as clairvoyance, will not be discussed. The reader is referred to Radin's book for a comprehensive review of these particular claims. There is now substantial interest in the possible application of quantum mechanics to understand consciousness-related phenomena other than the anomalous phenomena usually subsumed under the term parapsychology. These areas include biological quantum models of consciousness, the relation of consciousness to time and physical reality and are the subject of a recent major conference on Quantum Approaches to Consciousness (Northern Arizona University, July 1999). This article will focus on assessing claims specifically for psychokinetic phenomena. A small number of physicists have taken an interest in claims for anomalous effects related to consciousness. These include Sir William Crookes whose contributions to science include the

Correspondence:
S. Jeffers, Department of Physics and Astronomy, York University, Toronto, Ontario, Canada.

Journal of Consciousness Studies, **10**, No. 6–7, 2003, pp. 135–52

discovery of the element thallium and notable research in the physics of low-pressure discharges (Medhurst, 1972). He built devices in order to detect putative psychic influences. The noted scientists Lord Rayleigh and J.J. Thompson were active members of the Society for Psychical Research. In the modern era, a number of physicists have engaged in speculations concerning the relationship between physics and psychology — these include Bohr, Pauli and Jordan. However as far as this author is aware none of these had any interest in parapsychological phenomena *per se*. Jordan, for example, is quoted as stating that 'we ourselves produce the results of measurement' (Jammer, 1974). This means that the process of measurement by a sentient being actualizes what can only, according to the orthodox account of quantum mechanics, be described as having potential existence prior to the act of measurement. This clearly cannot imply that the assumption of different states of intentionality will produce different statistical outcomes when a large number of measurements are made. This particular assertion comprises the basic claims of Schmidt (1978) and Jahn and Dunne (1986).

Nobel Laureate Wigner is frequently quoted in this context (Wigner, 1962). However, as argued below, the references to Wigner's speculations cannot be used to justify parapsychological claims. Stapp (1993) is an example of a modern theoretical physicist who has argued extensively that a fundamental connection exists between quantum mechanics and consciousness. He takes a very pragmatic view of scientific theories as instruments we use to bring order to our experiences rather than providing a mental or mathematical reflection of an external world. Nobel Laureate Brian Josephson has given his support to claims for parapsychological phenomena (Josephson and Pallikari-Viras, 1991; Josephson, 1988).

Is Classical Physics Relevant to Claims for Anomalous Effects due to Consciousness?

By classical physics we mean the physics of macroscopic phenomena as embodied in the great classical theories of mechanics, electromagnetism, gravitation and thermodynamics. If, as claimed by some authors (Jahn and Dunne, 1988), psychokinetic effects have been demonstrated at the macroscopic level then one would have to attempt to explain these observations using classical theories. Jahn and Dunne (1988) have described experiments involving the dropping of thousands of polystyrene balls through a rectangular array (10' × 6') of pegs thus generating to first order a Gaussian distribution. It is claimed that human observers when instructed to shift this distribution either to the left or right, using the power of their minds alone, can in fact succeed at this task. The experiment is run with a tri-polar protocol, i.e. a shift to the left or right or the generation of baseline data where the operator is instructed to ignore the apparatus. Many authors try to appeal to the putative role for consciousness in quantum mechanics in explaining claimed anomalies observed in experiments of this type. In the case of this particular experiment, it is easy to show that any such claims are entirely inappropriate. Assuming a mass for the balls of around 5 g and an average speed as they drop through the array of 10 m/ sec then the de Broglie wavelength associated with the balls is of the order of 10^{-32} m. Since this is orders of magnitude smaller than the size of a nucleus there is no possibility of detecting any wave-type phenomena associated with these objects. They can only be treated classically. If the experimental data were credible then one would be forced to postulate that the consciousness of the observer actually radiates a form of energy that produces an identifiable force that acts on the balls. One could postulate that the brain of the observer was emitting some form of electromagnetic energy, for example, that produced this effect. However there is a clear problem with such a suggestion, as was realized by Einstein.

> Einstein once said that he would not believe in extra sensory perception (ESP) unless it was observed to fall off with distance. This view was based on the well-established physical principle of energy conservation. If a mind is radiating some form of 'psychic energy' in all directions, then that energy should spread out over an area that increases with the square of the distance from the source. (Stenger, 1995)

Jahn and Dunne (1988), however, have advanced the claim that their experiments with an electronic random event generator (REG), described in more detail below, do in fact show that the claimed psychokinetic effects are not only independent of distance but perhaps, more surprisingly, independent of the time at which the operator is attempting to influence the device, which may or may not be operating at that time. It is not at all clear how any observed effect could be causally related to anyone's intentionality if these claims are accepted. Recently Costa de Beauregard (1998), has advanced the view that classical physics may indeed embrace paranormal phenomena such as precognition, telepathy, psychokinesis and teleporting. He comes to this conclusion by considerations derived from special relativity, Bayesian accounts of probability and the equivalence of information with negentropy. However, the paper makes no quantitative predictions. The lack of any quantitative predictions characterizes all attempts to appropriate quantum mechanics to account for the claims of parapsychology. Indeed, as argued below, proponents of parapsychology more frequently make post- rather than pre-dictions in contrast to normal scientific practice.

Is Quantum Physics Relevant to Claims for Anomalous Effects due to Consciousness?

Numerous authors have invoked a role for consciousness in quantum mechanical phenomena (von Neumann, 1955; Wigner, 1962; London and Bauer, 1939; Zweifel, 1974; Cochran, 1971; Jahn and Dunne, 1986; Josephson, 1994; Goswami, 1993). The Orthodox Interpretation of quantum mechanics is usually invoked in which the state of a quantum system (unless it happens to be an eigenstate of the appropriate operator) is indeterminate prior to an observation being made. The quantum system exists as a linear superposition of possible states until an observation (i.e. the registration of a pointer reading in the consciousness of a sentient being) is made. The relative statistical weights in the linear superposition are determined by repetition of the experiment. Upon observation, one of these instantaneously assumes a value of unity (corresponding to the actual state of affairs) and the rest zero. This is the famous 'collapse of the wave function'. For Wigner (1962), it is the 'entering of an impression into our consciousness which alters the wave function because it modifies our appraisal of the probabilities for different impressions which we expect to receive in the future. It is at this point that the consciousness enters the theory unavoidably and unalterably.' Thus new knowledge changes the mathematical formalism used to predict future possibilities. If the wave function is interpreted as a mathematical description of possible states of affairs then Wigner's argument is not relevant to claims of any consciousness-related anomalous effects. For the argument to be relevant to these claims, one has to assume that the wave function has objective existence and, furthermore, that consciousness can affect it insofar that the assumption of different states of intentionality modifies the wave function. From this perspective consciousness would then have to be considered as primary and matter secondary. Wigner (1962) does appear to advocate this position when he writes 'it will remain remarkable, in whatever way our future concepts may develop, that the very study of the external world led to the conclusion that the content of the consciousness is an ultimate reality'. This philosophical idealist position is precisely that advocated strongly by physicist Goswami in his book *The Self-Aware Universe* (Goswami, 1993) and equally strongly argued against by physicist Stenger in his book *The Unconsciouness Quantum* (Stenger, 1995). If wave functions have real existence, rather than being abstract mathematical entities, then there are severe difficulties in accounting for their actual collapse, as the collapse process appears to take place instantaneously and thus violates Special Relativity. The collapse cannot be described by the Schrodinger Wave Equation and cannot be explained by quantum mechanics. There are some viable accounts of quantum phenomena however in which no collapse takes place and in which the wave/particle dualism of Complementarity is replaced by a wave/particle unity (Bohm and Hiley, 1993; Goldstein, 1998a and b). Proponents of parapsychology either ignore these accounts, misrepresent them or attempt to go beyond them, as in the case of Sarfatti (1996).

The prototypical quantum mechanical experiment is the famous double slit experiment. The early discussions of this experiment frequently asserted that any attempts to ascertain through which slit the particles pass inevitably introduces an uncontrollable disturbance of the paths of the particles which smears out the trajectories and consequently the interference fringes. This was the early account (prior to 1935 and the publication of the famous article by Einstein, Podolsky and Rosen, 1935) given by Bohr and Heisenberg of the double slit experiment. Clearly such an account maintains a realist ontology. One would have to assert that the particles actually do have trajectories through the interferometer but that it would not be possible to ascertain the exact trajectory of a given particle. In the light of the criticism from Einstein, Podolsky and Rosen, Bohr abandons this ontological position and asserts that the interaction between a quantum mechanical system and the measuring apparatus used to probe it is unanalysable in principle. From this perspective, any further analysis of what might actually go on inside an interferometer is simply ruled out. Thus Bohr (1949) writes:

> In commenting on Einstein's views as regards the incompleteness of the quantum mechanical mode of description, I entered more directly on questions of terminology. In this connection I warned especially against phrases, often found in the physical literature such as 'disturbing of phenomena by observation' or 'creating physical attributes to atomic objects measurements'. Such phrases, which may serve to remind of the apparent paradoxes in quantum theory, are at the same time apt to cause confusion, since words like 'phenomena' and 'observations', just as 'attributes' and 'measurements' are used in a way hardly compatible with common language and practical definition. As a more appropriate way of expression I advocated the application of the word phenomenon exclusively to refer to the observations obtained under specified circumstances, including an account of the whole experimental arrangement.

Wooters and Zurek (1979) have given a detailed analysis of Einstein's version of the double slit experiment in which Einstein argued that, in principle, one could use the momentum transferred to the screen by a photon passing through one of the slits to determine unambiguously through which slit the particle had traversed. Wooters and Zurek discuss the intermediate case whereby some information may be obtained regarding path taken and interference fringes with some contrast ($< 100\%$) may be observed. In their analysis, one can have correct information with respect to the path 75% of the time and still observe fringes with 88.6% contrast. Even with correct path information 99% of the time the observed contrast will be reduced to 20% according to their analysis. The Complementarity Principle is discussed in information-theoretic terms thus 'the more clearly we wish to observe the wave nature of light, the more information we must give up about the particle properties'. In a recent remarkable experiment conducted by Professor L. Mandel of the University of Rochester (Zou et al., 1991), two beams are brought together and interfere. However each beam is accompanied by a secondary beam — these two beams are generated by parametric down conversion whereby light from a laser is incident on a crystal which acts to produce two photons (a signal and an idler photon) per incident photon. In principle, the photons in the secondary beams may be used to determine which path the individual photons in the interfering beams actually took. This may be achieved either by blocking one of the secondary beams or by deliberately misaligning the secondary beams. In either case, neither of the interfering beams is disturbed. However, attempts to extract path information using one of these procedures do in fact result in the reduction of the contrast of the interference fringes. To quote from Zou et al. (1991) '... the disappearance of the interference pattern here is not the result of a large uncontrollable disturbance acting on the system, in the spirit of the Heisenberg gamma-ray microscope, but simply a consequence of the fact that the two possible paths have become distinguishable. In quantum mechanics, interference is always a manifestation of the intrinsic indistinguishability of the photon paths . . . .'. Whether or not this auxiliary measurement is actually made, or whether the detector which could make this auxiliary measurement is even in place, appears to make no difference. It is sufficient that it could be made, and that the photon path would then be identifiable, in principle, for the interference to be wiped out. Given that the Orthodox Interpretation of quantum mechanics rules out any mechanistic analysis of interference phenomena, one would have to argue that it is the possibility of information with respect to the path taken entering into the consciousness of the observer that correlates with the reduction in contrast of the fringes. A double slit experiment has been conducted (Ibison and Jeffers, 1998) in which people attempt to extract path information by using any mental stratagem they wish. Success would presumably lead to a reduction in the contrast of the fringes if the claims of parapsychology have merit. This experiment is described in more detail below but has not yielded any evidence for the abilities of humans to succeed at gaining information by any anomalous means.

Popper (1985) has argued that since the Copenhagen Interpretation prohibits a causal space-time (hence particle-like behaviour) analysis of the physical processes which occur inside an interferometer when high contrast interference fringes (hence wave-like behaviour) are observed, then the Copenhagenist is forced to assert that it is the entering into the consciousness of the observing subject of information with respect to the path taken by the radiation that is inversely correlated with the contrast of the interference fringes. Popper has used similar arguments in the context of the Einstein, Podolsky and Rosen paradox. Here many pairs of particles are formed such that their momenta are correlated. Their subsequent positions and momenta remained correlated. In Popper's version of this experiment, a slit is placed in one beam (say A on the right) and narrowed. This beam diffracts such that the slit width and spread in momenta of the diffracted particles are inversely related. Popper (1985) argues that the Copenhagen interpretation forces one to conclude that by this procedure *knowledge* gained of the *position* of the particles on the right must imply that the particles on the *left* are also diffracted! Thus:

> a particle possesses sharp position and momentum, and thus a trajectory: and our knowledge of a particle's position cannot, qua knowledge, disturb its momentum: the particle's momentum continues to exist. It remains a particle, having position and momentum and a trajectory, a path. But the Copenhagen interpretation wishes us to accept that our knowledge of the position of B on the left (obtained by measuring A on the right) must make the momentum of B 'indeterminate' since no particle can have both. If this is so then our knowledge would make the momenta on the left scatter, upon repetition.

On this interpretation, it is the entering of knowledge into the consciousness of the observer of either position or momentum which 'causes' the conjugate variable to become less well determined. This follows since no causal, space-time analysis is possible according to the Copenhagen Interpretation. This is consistent with Bohr's general philosophical position of emphasizing epistemology as opposed to ontology. The customary view of invoking an 'uncontrollable disturbance' due to the interaction between a photon and a particle implies that the particle after the interaction does in fact still have a trajectory (but it cannot be determined). This is not consistent with the Principle of Complementarity which asserts mutual exclusiveness between the wave and particle descriptions.

Of course, other interpretations of quantum mechanics exist in which there is no role for the observer. Bohm (1988), for example, has given a realist interpretation that includes a quantum potential which is derived from a real wave. Particles then move under the influence of the quantum potential and thus have real trajectories. The pattern of trajectories does reproduce the flux of particles observed in a double slit experiment. Bohm has characterized the quantum potential as being the carrier of active information. However the use of the word information here does not imply an observer who becomes informed but rather implies a signal which the particle can decode and respond to. This does not impute consciousness to the particle (see also Bohm & Hiley, 1993). This author finds it surprising that Bohm's account of quantum mechanics has not, in general, been embraced by the physics community since it does indeed reproduce all the predictions of quantum mechanics while maintaining a realist ontology. No wave function collapse with all its philosophical difficulties occurs in Bohm's account. Bohm's account offers scant comfort to those who propose paranormal phenomena, as pointed out by Stenger (1995) when he quotes Bohm:

> Our basic assumption has actually nothing to do with consciousness. Rather it is that the particles are the direct manifest reality, while the wave function can be 'seen' only through its manifestations in the motions of particles. This is similar to what happened in ordinary field theories (e.g. the electromagnetic), on which the fields likewise manifest themselves only through the forces that they exert on particles. (The main difference is that the particles can be the sources of fields, whereas, in the quantum theory, particles do not serve as sources of the wave function.) Moreover the conclusion that after an irreversible detection process has taken place, the unoccupied packets will never manifest themselves in the behaviour of the particles follows, as we have seen, from the theory itself, and has nothing to do with our not being conscious of these packets. (Bohm and Hiley, 1993)

Sarfatti (1996) has proposed a modified version of the Bohm interpretation in which he proposes that the particles react back on the quantum potential (back action) and that the particle plus quantum *potential* form a 'self-organising feed back loop' and it is this which is consciousness. Presumably this model could embrace parapsychological effects.[1]

---

[1] Prosser (1976) and Jeffers *et al.* (1992) have analysed the double slit experiment from a classical point of view in solving Maxwell's equations for this diffracting geometry with the double slit barrier acting to impose boundary conditions on the solutions. The solutions yield the amplitude, phase and Poynting vector for the diffracted radiation. Prosser (1976) has interpreted the Poynting vector field which is symmetric with respect to the line of symmetry between the slits as implying that none of the electromagnetic energy which passes through a given slit actually crosses the axis of symmetry. This feature of his analysis is similar to the Bohm (1988) quantum potential model. Further work on the Prosser interpretation has, however, invalidated it (Jeffers *et al.*, 1994).

Physics and Claims for Anomalous Effects

In his book *The Conscious Universe* Dean Radin makes some comments regarding the highly dismissive attitude of most physicists regarding claims of paranormal effects. He quotes approvingly from the late Euan Squires:

> If conscious choice can decide what particular observation I measure, and therefore into what states my consciousness splits, might not conscious choice also be able to influence the outcome of the measurement? One possible place where mind may influence matter is in quantum effects. Experiments on whether it is possible to affect the decay rates of nuclei by thinking suitable thoughts would presumably be easy to perform and might be worth doing. (Squires, 1987)

Radin also complains 'Given the distinguished history of speculations about the role of consciousness in quantum mechanics, one might think that the physics literature would report a substantial number of original experiments on this topic. Surprisingly, a search revealed only three studies.' These are described as (i) the experiments of Hall, Kim, McElroy and Shimony (1977) who conducted experiments to investigate if the rate of radioactive decay was affected if the radioactive system had been previously observed. The results of these experiments showed that the observed number of 'hits' was exactly at the level expected from chance. (ii) Radin claims that another experiment previously conducted at MIT showed a 60% hit rate where chance expectation was 50%. However Radin does not point out in his text that this study remains unpublished (Smith, 1968). (iii) The third study referred to is the extensive research programme conducted by Jahn and Dunne and discussed in more detail below. Radin comments: 'Thus, of three relevant experiments reported in mainstream physics journals, one described results exactly at chance and two described positive effects. Given the fantastic theoretical implications of such an effect, it seems rather strange that no further experiments of this type can be found in the physics literature.' Are physicists then not interested in anomalous effects? Of course they are. Anomalous effects are of great interest to the physics community as they may signal the limiting conditions under which a particular theoretical framework can be applied. A famous example of such an anomaly is the well-known advance of the perihelion of Mercury or, in the present era, the claims made for anomalous production of excess energy from so-called cold fusion reactions.

In 1859 Le Verrier determined that the orbital plane of Mercury was precessing at a rate of 43 arc seconds per century. This is an extremely small amount and completely at variance with Newtonian mechanics. The modern accepted value of the precession is 43.11 +/− 0.21 arc seconds per century, an effect of the order of 200 standard deviations. The General Theory of Relativity predicts a value of 42.98 arc seconds per century, in phenomenal agreement with observation. It is characteristic of attempts to appropriate quantum mechanics to provide a theoretical basis for parapsychological phenomena that these attempts do not yield any quantitative predictions.

In his review of parapsychological research conducted by physicists, Radin fails to mention the experiments conducted by this author and discussed in more detail below (Ibison and Jeffers, 1998; Jeffers and Sloan, 1992) which have not yielded any convincing evidence to support parapsychology.

Experiments Conducted by Physicists on Psychokinetic Effects

The study of ostensibly anomalous phenomena typically involves human operators attempting to bias the output of a device whose performance is probabilistically determined, typically Gaussian. Schmidt and Pantas (1972) and Jahn and Dunne (1986) have made claims for a positive effect. The claimed effect is marginal but highly significant statistically. Schmidt and Pantas (1972) have reported extensively on the use of electronic random event generators triggered by the random radioactive decay of strontium 90. Jahn (1982) has employed primarily a Random Event Generator that counts noise pulses from a diode. Both groups have reported results that defy chance expectations by large margins ($p < 2.10^{-9}$ Schmidt; $p < 2.10^{-6}$ Jahn). The results of both groups have been criticized both in terms of the methodology and the statistical analysis employed (Alcock, 1981; Jeffreys, 1990). Both groups claim that some operators can bias the probability distributions of randomly governed events in accord with pre-declared intention.

The idea that consciousness could play an active role in the determination of physical phenomena is not alien to physics but has been seriously considered by a number of authors, primarily in the context of attempting to resolve the paradoxes of quantum mechanics (Feynman, 1951; Wigner, 1962). Radin and Nelson (1989) have published a meta-analysis of hundreds of experiments in this area published in a wide variety of journals and have concluded 'it is difficult to avoid the conclusion that under certain circumstances, consciousness interacts with random physical systems'.

Jahn (1982) and others have suggested that the claimed effect exists at the level of 'information', i.e. it is the statistical distribution of possible outcomes from the apparatus that is affected by the operators intentions and thus the claimed effect is not seen as purely physical. In a similar vein, Eccles (1986) has suggested that intention may influence neural events in the brain by analogy with the probability fields of quantum mechanics. If true, then any process governed by probabilistic laws should be amenable to demonstrating the claimed effect.

A simple optical experiment based on the phenomenon of single slit diffraction to examine these claims has been conducted (Jeffers and Sloan, 1992). The normalized diffracted intensity distribution can be interpreted as the probability of locating a photon in the observation plane. The experiment yields high data-rates in computer compatible form and has been designed to meet methodological criticisms that have been levelled at other work in this area. In particular, the calibration methods adopted by other workers against the claimed effect has been singled out (Alcock, 1981). The essential claim which has been advanced is that some human operators can produce a statistically significant shift of the mean of a given distribution generally in accord with intention. The other moments of the statistical distribution remain unaffected. In our experiment, the relevant distribution is the digitally recorded single slit diffraction pattern. This is recorded with high accuracy with a short integration time.

Diffraction phenomena have been studied at very low flux levels (corresponding to the passage of, on average, one photon at a time through the apparatus). Most of these studies (Taylor, 1909; Pipkin, 1978) with the exception of reports from Panarella and Dontsov and Baz (Panarella, 1985; Dontsov and Baz, 1967) have concluded that diffraction occurs even at the level of one photon. Several studies aimed at checking the claims of Panarella have failed to confirm his findings (Jeffers *et al.*, 1987; Sinton *et al.*, 1985; Ohtake *et al.*, 1985).

In the experiments of Jahn (1982), a commercial microelectronic noise diode is used. The output noise is sampled at pre-set regular intervals. If the signal is greater (smaller) than its mean, a positive (negative) pulse is output. Typically 200 such pulses will be counted and only those with a regular alternation of positive and negative. Data are accumulated in runs that comprise typically 50 trials at attempting to bias the machine's behaviour. A series typically consists of 2500 or 5000 trials in blocks of 50 or 100 runs or 3000 trials in blocks of 3 runs corresponding to no effort at biasing or biasing high or low. For a series of 3000 trials per intention, the total number of binary bits accumulated during the series is of the order of 2.10^8. This is considered to be the minimum database at which the claimed effect can be discerned. A complete series typically may take a week or so to complete. Some of their 'best' data, based on 5000 trials (see Jahn and Dunne, 1986, pp. 101–2), yields a baseline mean and standard deviation of 99.898 and 7.053, a mean and standard deviation of trials biased towards high output of 100.279 and 7.043 and a mean and standard deviation of efforts to bias towards a low output of 99.571 and 7.036. The probability against chance separation of the high and low efforts is minimally 3.10^{-7}. Data are accumulated in either a volitional or instructed mode. In the volitional mode, the operator declares their preference for the sequence of trials ahead of time, whereas in the instructed mode the computer randomly assigns the experimental sequence. In the latter mode, the experiment may not yield equal numbers of trials for each type of effort. In particular, baseline trials (no operator effort) are not equi-spaced temporally, which makes it difficult to evaluate any short-term drift in the instrumental performance. Long runs (typically overnight) are performed to check on the baseline performance of the instrument. These yield results consistent with expected Gaussian statistics but only averaged over many hours.

The statistical distribution employed in the diffraction experiment is the single slit diffraction pattern produced by illuminating (using an incandescent bulb powered by a stabilized power supply) a commercially available slit (5 microns wide). The Fraunhofer diffraction pattern falls onto a linear photodiode array (Princeton Applied Research Model #1453A with 1024 diodes) controlled by a micro-computer. The entire experiment is software controlled. Complete details are given in Jeffers and Sloan (1992).

Calibrations of the apparatus have established that the statistical distribution of repeated measures of the patterns centroid do indeed conform to a Gaussian distribution and that any displacement of the order of 0.0062 pixels should be unambiguously recovered from our data corresponding to a linear offset of 1.6×10^{-5} cm. The data published by Jahn *et al.* show a separation of the 'high' and 'low' distributions which amounts to 4.5% of the full width at half maximum of the baseline distribution. For the diffraction experiment, this would translate into a linear shift separating the 'right' and 'left' distributions of 12 pixels or a separation of the order of 6 pixels between either 'left' or 'right' and the no effort distributions. The sensitivity of the diffraction experiment to the claimed effect is three orders of magnitude better than this.

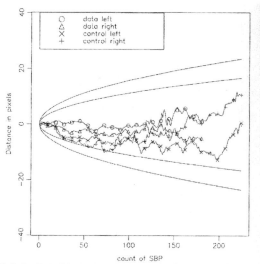

Fig. 11. Plot of the cumulative sum of the SBP for all 20 experimental subjects along with the same parameter for the 25 control runs taken on the same days as the experimental runs. Also plotted are the random walk probability envelopes for 5% and 1% terminal probability.

Figure 1.   Reproduced from Jeffers and Sloan (1992) with permission from the *Journal of Scientific Exploration* (*Journal of Scientific Exploration*, P.O. Box 5848, Stanford, CA 94309-5848 USA. http://www.jse.com

Data from twenty experimental subjects, together with data from control experiments, is shown above and yields no evidence for any anomalous effect.

The Double Slit Experiment

Another experiment has been conducted which bears a more direct relationship to the claims that have been advanced by some authors that quantum mechanical phenomena inevitably involve a role for the consciousness of a sentient being able to remotely abstract information. This is the famous double slit experiment.

Interference effects are seen at flux levels corresponding to the passage of a single photon/particle through the apparatus. The wave model accounts for the observed fringes seen in the observation plane behind the slits but cannot yield information with respect to which slit the photon actually passed. Feynman has stated that the double slit experiment 'has in it the heart of quantum mechanics; in reality it contains the only mystery' (Feynman, 1951). When physical phenomena are poorly understood then a wide range of possible accounts are advanced. The most extreme positivistic accounts of quantum mechanical phenomena envisage an active role for human consciousness in microphysics phenomena. Thus, it has been claimed (Wigner, 1962) that the conscious act of observation causes the 'collapse of the wave function', i.e. the entity under examination exists potentially everywhere (is spatially distributed as a wave) but becomes spatially localized as a particle by the very act of observation. At the other end of the philosophical spectrum, realist (local and non-local) accounts of the double slit experiment have been advanced (Bozic, Maric and Vigier, 1992; Bohm & Hiley, 1993; Prosser, 1976) that deny the Principle of Complementarity and assert the simultaneous existence of wave and particle.

The original account of the famous double slit invoked the Heisenberg Uncertainty Relations to assert the impossibility of simultaneously observing interference fringes with 100% contrast and determining, with absolute certainty, through which slit the particle actually passed. This was asserted to be true given that the interaction of the photon of light used to illuminate the particle would disturb the path of the particle by imparting its momentum to the particle. Recent two beam interference experiments have been carried out in which, in principle, path information may be obtained without introducing any uncontrollable disturbance in the interfering beams in the sense implied by the Uncertainty Relations (Zou et al., 1991). However, any attempt to extract this information from the experimental apparatus does in fact result in the reduction of the contrast of the interference fringes. Thus the Principle of Complementarity has a deeper foundation than the Uncertainty Relations. It follows that, if it were possible, *by any means*, to extract path information from a two-beam interference experiment then this would be manifest in a reduction of the contrast of the fringes. A double slit experiment has been conducted in which participants have been invited either to exert their intentionality in consciously directing the energy preferentially through one path or to abstract at any time the nature of the energy flow. A drop in the fringe contrast would indicate success at either task. This experiment could then in principle detect any anomalous transfer of information from the interferometer to the observer or if the consciousness of the observer has affected the nature of the energy flow in the interferometer.

The experiment is a simple two-beam set-up which uses a low power He-Ne laser to illuminate a commercially available double slit comprising a stainless steel disc in which two slits (10 microns wide) are cut. The slits are separated by 10 microns. Complete details are givien in Ibison and Jeffers (1998). Detection of the resulting interference fringes is achieved using a linear diode array (Princeton Applied Research Model #1453 with 1024 diodes).

Given the reciprocal relationship between contrast and path information in an interferometer, one anticipates from the results of recent interference experiments that if information concerning the path could be abstracted from the experimental situation by direct or indirect means that this would be readily manifest in a corresponding reduction in the contrast of the interference fringes. Repeated calibrations of the equipment yield typically measured values for the fringe contrast of 0.991 with a standard deviation of 0.001.

Experiments of this nature have been run at York University and at Princeton University in the laboratory of Professor R. Jahn. In these experiments the operators are presented with some feedback — the CRT displays a large vertical bar whose height is a measure of the current value of the fringe contrast. The protocol in this experiment is bi-polar — the operators are either attempting to abstract path information or not. The experiment runs for some 25 minutes during which time 200 measures with each protocol are obtained. The experiments run at York University have revealed no evidence that humans can produce any effect on the fringe contrast. The experiments conducted with this apparatus at Princeton have yielded results at the marginal level of $p = 0.05$ but as discussed below, Mathews (1999) has argued this cannot be accepted as convincing.

A two-beam interference experiment has been conducted which tests for the capacity of human operators to either remotely abstract information or to actively and preferentially collapse wave functions. The experiment has not yielded any convincing evidence that the human operators tested can succeed in either task.

Are the Best Experiments Convincing?

The longest running programme of experiments on anomalous phenomena has been conducted by Professor R. Jahn, leader of the Princeton Engineering Anomalies Research (PEAR) Group. The primary experiment as described above has been conducted using the Random Event Generator. The essential claims advanced as of 1987 have been that (i) operators can bias the outcome in accord with intention; (ii) the performance of the REG is entirely in accord with expectations from random statistics in the absence of operators; (iii) the experimental data exhibit 'baseline bind', a condition described where the data obtained when the operators are (presumably) ignoring the equipment turns out to be too good to be true. The essential claims that have been advanced in experiments conducted with this device have been that the cumulative deviations from chance expectations when operators are invited to attempt to increase/decrease the mean count rate do indeed exceed that from chance alone when this is defined to be a terminal probability of less that $p = 0.05$ (i.e. a standard deviation of 1.64). Such a criterion is typical of work is this area but is substantially less stringent than that employed in the physical sciences where a deviation of the order of several standard deviations are more typical. Furthermore Matthews (1999) has drawn attention to the fact that the use of p-values routinely exaggerate the true significance of experimental data. According to Mathews:

> There are serious flaws in this line of reasoning. To begin with, the cut-off of $p = 0.05$ is entirely arbitrary, having its origins in nothing more statistically justifiable than a mathematical coincidence concerning the Normal Distribution. More worrying and contrary to appearances, a p-value of 0.05 does not imply that the probability of the results being a fluke is 1 in 20. Rather it means that assuming chance alone is at work, there is a 1 in 20 probability that repetitions of the experiment will produce results at least as impressive as those seen.

Matthews argues from the perspective of Bayesian analysis that if the initial level of scepticism for a claimed effect is high (which is true for parapsychological claims) then a maximum p-value for 'significance' is nothing like 0.05 but more like 0.000005. This latter value comes close to that recently claimed by the PEAR group for a review of twelve years of their data on the REG experiment.

In previous reports (Jahn and Dunne, 1988) cumulative deviation plots are shown (see for example Fig II–5, p. 105) where the terminal probabilities for the data presumably influenced by operator intention do accumulate to less than 0.05 whereas the baseline data (accumulated in the presence of the operator but when the operator is instructed to ignore the apparatus) lies close to the horizontal axis and well within the p = 0.05 envelope.

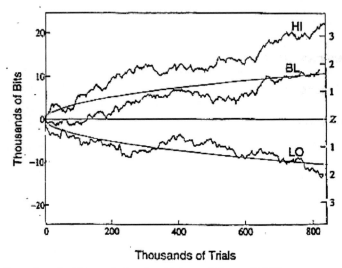

Figure 2.   Reproduced with permission from Jahn and Dunne (1988).

Several claims are advanced in this work, e.g. the shape of the cumulative deviation plots is operator specific and constitute 'signatures' and the baseline measures are too good to be true. The latter claim rests on an analysis of seventy six baseline series of which seven or eight may be expected to exceed the p = 0.05 terminal probability criterion simply by chance. However none of the baseline cumulative deviation plots actually do. This is described as 'baseline bind' and is presented as evidence that some operators may have a conscious (or even sub-conscious!) intention to produce a baseline plot that is better than chance expec-tations. It is further claimed that baseline measures in the physical absence of the same operators do indeed conform to chance expectations. If true this could be cited as evidence for a distance dependent effect which, if validated, would be of great significance. However, in the related work involving remote perception, claims are advanced that the ability to acquire information remotely does not depend on distance up to several thousand miles nor is it correlated with time to within a few days.

There are, however, apparent contradictions in some of these claims with those advanced in a more recent publication (Jahn *et al.*, 1997). This particular paper presents a compendium of all the data produced by REG experiments at PEAR over a twelve year period. Of particular concern are the cumulative deviation plots reproduced in Fig 2. The terminal probabilities assessed for attaining the separation between high and low intentions is cited as 6.99×10^{-5}. Furthermore, it is asserted in the Summary that claimed effects with the REG are indeed independent of distance and the time at which the operator is expressing a particular intention that may be quite different from the time at which the device is operated. If true, it is not clear to this author how any causal relationship could be claimed between device operation and anyone's intention expressed at anytime. The most parsimonious account of the lack of such correlation is that the device is operating independent of anyone's intention.

Consider the behaviour of the baseline cumulative deviation plot as shown in Fig 2. The terminal probability for this baseline plot accumulates to slightly less than $p = 0.05$ (one-tailed distribution).

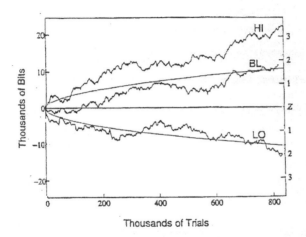

Thousands of Trials

Cumulative deviation graphs of benchmark REG results for HI, LO, and BL operator intentions. Parabolic envelopes are one-tail 95% confidence intervals about the theoretical chance mean. The scale on the right ordinate refers to the terminal z-scores.

Figure 3.   Reproduced from Jahn *et al.* (1998) with permission from the *Journal of Scientific Exploration* (*Journal of Scientific Exploration*, P.O. Box 5848, Stanford, CA 94309-5848 USA. http://www.jse.com

This is substantially at variance with the previous claims concerning baseline behaviour (Jahn and Dunne, 1998). Surprisingly there is no commentary in the 1997 paper concerning the baseline behaviour and the conflict with previous claims. The naive interpretation of this plot is that the behaviour of the REG when examined over a twelve year baseline shows evidence of a slow but imperceptible drift, indicating that it is not a random device as claimed. Doubt must then be cast on the claimed terminal probabilities for the cumulative deviation plots with expressed operator intention.

The only other alternative is to assume that even though the operators are instructed not to interact with the device they actually do in some way that is not specified a priori. To this author, this seems to be arbitrary and ad hoc. In response to these criticisms Professor Jahn has offered the following remarks (Jahn, 1999):

1. The baseline data from experiments such as these never should be regarded as calibration data. They comprise a third condition of experimenter intention (albeit possibly somewhat subconscious), and display many of the structural features of the high- and low-intention data, including mean shifts, higher moment aberrations, gender disparities, and count population regularities. For example, virtually all of the baseline mean shift displayed in Figure 2 is contributed by female operators; a separate graph for male operators would show no such trend. Also, various experiments display characteristically different baselines even though the same equipment is employed.

2. The proper comparison standards for the active data (and for the baseline data) and for qualification of the equipment, are the calibration data, taken with no operators (or anyone else) in the experimental room. As clearly noted in Table I of this paper, these calibration data are totally indistinguishable from theoretical chance expectations — so much so that we simply use theoretical values as our comparison standards for the empirical data.

3. All of this notwithstanding, the baseline trend, in fact, does not have 'a p value of a little less than 0.05'. As also noted in Table I, baseline and calibration data must be treated as two-tailed, hence p = 0.09 is the proper value. Thus, we do not claim it as a significantly aberrant baseline. (There are, however, particular operators who consistently produce such.)

4. Operator-specific baseline displacements are even more strongly displayed in our Random Mechanical Cascade experiments, where again a striking male (chance baselines) vs. female (displaced baselines) disparity is observed.

With respect to statement 2, it is surprising that no calibration data (with no one near the device) is obtained for *every* experimental run which would be methodologically preferable. Rather such calibrations are made intermittently. With respect to statement 1, surely the whole idea of a tri-polar protocol is to provide data against which any putative effect can be assessed. The claim that operators actually do influence the device when asked not to do so constitutes a post-diction, and an inconsistent one at that, given that up to 1987 the claimed effect was such as to produce too good a baseline measure whereas in 1998 it is claimed that operators produce much larger effects and may be doing this even sub-consciously!

Summary

Contrary to previous assertions most of the experimental work conducted by physicists concerning claims for psychokinetic effects have yielded no convincing evidence in support of these claims. Proponents of parapsychology typically offer 'post-' rather than pre-dictions in contrast to normal scientific practice. An assessment of some of the more credible claims reveals inconsistencies that diminish the impact of these claims.

Acknowledgements

The author gratefully acknowledges the help and generous support he has received from Professor Robert Jahn and his colleagues at the PEAR laboratory during the period that he has taken an interest in the subject of this paper. He has benefited from numerous discussions with members of the PEAR group and also Professor Jim Alcock of Glendon College, York University, Toronto and Professor Morris Freedman of the University of Toronto.

References

Alcock, J.E. (1981), *Parapsychology: Science or Magic?* (Elmsford, NY: Pergamon Press).
Bell J.S. (1988), *Speakable and Unspeakable in Quantum Mechanics* (Cambridge: Cambridge University Press).
Bohm D. (1988), *Microphysical Reality and Quantum Formalism*, ed. A. van der Merwe *et al.* (Dordrecht: Kluwer Academic Publishers), pp. 3–18.
Bohm, D. and Hiley, B.J. (1993), *The Undivided Universe: An Ontological Interpretation of Quantum Mechanics* (London: Routledge).
Bohr, N. (1949), in *Albert Einstein: Philosopher-Scientist*, ed. P.A. Schilpp, The Library of Living Philosophers (Evanston), pp. 200–41.
Bozic, M., Maric, Z. and Vigier, J.-P. (1992), 'De Broglian probabilities in the double slit experiment', *Foundations of Physics*, **22** (11), pp. 1325–44.
Bunge, M. (1991), *New Ideas in Psychology*, **9**, p. 2.
Cochran, A.A. (1971), 'Relationships between quantum physics and biology', *Foundations of Physics*, **1**, p. 235.
Costa de Beauregard, O. (1998), *Journal of Scientific Exploration*, **12** (2), pp. 315–20.
Dontsov, P. and Baz, A.I., Sov. (1967), *Phys JETP*, **25**, p. 1.
Eccles, J.C. (1986), 'Do mental events cause neural events analagously to the probability fields of quantum mechanics?', *Proc. R. Soc. Lond.* B, **227**, pp. 411–28.
Einstein, A., Podolsky, B. and Rosen, N. (1935), 'Can quantum mechanical reality be considered to be complete?', *Phys. Rev.*, **47**, p. 777.
Feynman, R.P. (1951), *Proceedings of the Second Berkeley Symposium on Mathematical Statistics and Probability* (Berkeley, CA: University of California Press).
Gardner, M. (1981), *Science, Good, Bad and Bogus* (Buffalo, NY: Prometheus Books).
Goldstein, S. (1998a), 'Quantum theory without observers, Part One', *Physics Today* (March 1998).
Goldstein, S. (1998b), 'Quantum theory without observers, Part Two', *Physics Today* (April 1998).
Goswami, A. (1993), *The Self Aware Universe — How Consciousness Creates The Material World* (G.P. Putnam's Sons).
Hall, J., Kim, C., McElroy, B. and Shimony, A. (1977), 'Wave packet reduction as a medium of communication', *Foundations of Physics*, **16**, pp. 759–67.
Hyman, R. (1987), *Behavioural and Brain Sciences*, **10** (4), pp. 593–4.
Ibison, M. and Jeffers, S. (1998), 'A double slit diffraction experiment to investigate claims of consciousness-related anomalies', *Journal of Scientific Exploration*, **12** (4), pp. 543–50.
Jahn, R.G. (1982), 'The persistent paradox of psychic phenomena — an engineering perspective', *Proc. IEEE*, **70**, pp. 136–70.
Jahn, R.G. (1999), private communication.
Jahn, R.G. and Dunne, B.J. (1986), 'On the quantum mechanics of consciousness with applications to anomalous phenomena', *Foundations of Physics*, **16**, pp. 101–2.
Jahn, R.G. and Dunne, B. (1998), *Margins of Reality — The Role of Consciousness in the Physical World* (New York, San Diego: Harcourt Brace Jovanovich).
Jahn, R.G., Dunne, B.J., Nelson, R.D., Dobbins, Y.H. and Bradish, G.J. (1997), 'Correlations of random binary sequences with pre-stated operator intention: a review of a 12-year program', *J. Sci. Exp.*, **11** (3), pp. 345–67.
Jammer, M. (1974), *The Conceptual Development of Quantum Mechanics* (Woodbury, NY: Tomash Publishers).
Jeffers, S. (1994), 'Intentionality and complementarity: what might the double slit experiment tell us about consciousness?', presented at Toward a Science of Consciousness II, Tucson, Arizona.
Jeffers, S., Hunter, G. and Wadlinger, R. (1987), in *Quantum Uncertainties — Recent and Future Experiments and Interpretations*, ed. W.M. Honig, D.W. Kraft and E. Panarella (Plenum Press), pp. 197–202.
Jeffers, S., Prosser, R., Hunter, G. and Sloan, J. (1992), 'Classical electromagnetic theory of diffraction and interference: edge, single and double slit solutions', presented at the Waves and Particles Meeting, Trani, Italy.

Jeffers S.,Prosser R.D.,Berseth W.C.,Hunter G.,Sloan J. (1994), Contribution to *Ultra-Wideband Short-Pulse Electromagnetics 2*, ed. L.Carin and L.B.Felsen (New York: Plenum Press), pp 371–7.

Jeffers, S. and Sloan, J. (1992), 'A low light level diffraction experiment for anomalies research', *Journal of Scientific Exploration*, **6** (4), p. 333.

Jeffreys, W.H. (1990), 'title', *Journal of Scientific Exploration*, **4** (2), pp. 153–69.

Josephson, B.D. (1994), 'To err is mechanical', *Times Higher Educational Supplement* (Nov. 4).

Josephson, B.D. (1988), 'Limits to the universality of quantum mechanics', *Foundations of Physics*, **21**, pp. 1195–204.

Josephson, B.D. and Pallikari-Viras, F. (1991), 'Biological utilisation of quantum non-locality', *Foundations of Physics*, **21**, pp 197–207.

Lande, A. (1975), 'Quantum fact and fiction IV', *Am. J. Phys.*, **43**, p. 701.

London, F. and Bauer, E. (1939), 'La theorie de l'observation en mecanique quantique', No.775 of *Actualites Scientifiques et industrielles: Exposes de physique generales* (Paris: Hermann).

Mandel, L. (1993), 'An operational account of Schrodinger's cat paradox', in *Physics and Probability*, ed. W.T. Grandy, Jr. and P.W. Milloni (Cambridge:Cambridge University Press).

Matthews, R.A.J. (1999), *Journal of Scientific Exploration*, **13** (1), pp. 1–7.

Medhurst, R.G. (1972), *Crookes and the Spirit World* (New York: Taplinger).

Milloni, P.W. (1984), 'Wave particle duality of light: a current perspective', in *The Wave-Particle Dualism* (D. Reidel Publishing Co).

Ohtake, Y., Mizobuchi, Y. and Sugiyama, M. (1985), *Spec. Sci. Tech.*, **9** (4), pp. 279–86.

Panarella, E. (1985), *Ann. de la Found. Louis de Broglie*, **10** (1), pp. 1–35.

Pipkin, F.M. (1978), in *Advances in Atomic and Electron Physics*, ed. D.R.Bates, **14**, p. 294.

Popper, K. (1985), *Open Problems in Quantum Physics*, ed. G.Tarrozzi and A. van der Merwe (Dordrect: Reidel).

Prosser, R.D. (1976), *Int. J. Theor. Phys.*, **15**, p. 169.

Prosser, R.D., Jeffers, S., Hunter, G. and Sloan, J. (1994), 'Maxwellian analysis of the pulsed microwave double slit experiment', paper presented at the Second International Conference on Ultra-Wideband Short-Pulse Electromagnetics, Polytechnic University, New York City.

Radin, D. (1997), *The Conscious Universe — The Scientific Truth of Psychic Phenomena* (Harper Collins).

Radin, D.I. and Nelson, R.D. (1989), 'Evidence for consciousness-related anomalies in random physical systems', *Foundations of Physics*, **19** (12), pp. 1499–514.

Sarfatti, J. (1996), 'What is Back-Reaction?', a discussion between J. Sarfatti and S. Jeffers on the interpretation of Bohm s account of quantum mechanics at
   http://www.teleport.com/~rhett/quantum-d/posts/rhett_2-19-96.html

Schmidt, H. (1978), *Foundations of Physics.*, **8** (5/6), pp. 463–81.

Schmidt, H. and Pantas, L. (1972), 'PSI tests with internally different machines', *Journal of Parapsychology*, **36**, pp. 222–32.

Sinton, A.M., Gardenier, P.H. and Bares, R.H.T. (1985), *Spec. Sci. Tech.*, **9** (4), pp. 269–78.

Smith, R. (1968), unpublished manuscript (MIT).

Stapp, H.P. (1993), *Mind, Matter and Quantum Mechanics* (Springer-Verlag).

Stapp, H.P. (1994), 'Theoretical model of a purported violation of the predictions of quantum theory, *Phys. Rev. A*, **50**, (1).

Stenger, V.J. (1995), *The Unconscious Quantum — Metaphysics in Modern Physics and Cosmology* (Prometheus Books).

Squires, E.J. (1987), 'Many views of one world — an interpretation of quantum theory', *European Journal of Physics*, **8**, p. 173.

Squires, E. (1988), *The Mystery of the Quantum World* (Adam Hilger Ltd.).

Taylor, G.I. (1909), 'Interference fringes with feeble light', *Proc. Cambridge Philos. Soc.*, **15**, p. 114.

Uffink, J. and Hilgevoord, J. (1988), 'Interference and distinguishability in quantum mechanics', *Physica B*, p. 151.

Vigier, J.P. (1987), 'Theoretical implications of time-dependant double resonance neutron interferometry', in *Quantum Uncertainties — Recent and Future Experiments and Interpretations*, ed. W.M. Honig, D.W. Kraft and E. Panarella (Plenum Press).

von Neumann, J. (1955), *Mathematical Foundations of Quantum Mechanics* (Princeton, NJ: Princeton University Press).

Wheeler, J.A. and Zurek, W.H. (1983), *Quantum Theory and Measurement* (Princeton, NJ: Princeton University Press).

Wigner, E. (1962), *The Scientist Speculates*, ed. I.J. Good (London: Heinemann).

Wooters, W.K. and Zurek W.H. (1979), 'Complementarity in the double slit experiment: quantum non-separability and a quantitative statement of Bohr's principle', *Phys. Rev. D*, **19** (2), p. 473.

Zou, X.Y., Wang, L.J. and Mandel, L. (1991), 'Induced coherence and indistinguishability in optical interference', *Phys. Rev. Letts.*, **67** (3), p. 318–21.

Zweifel, P.F. (1974), *Int. J. Theor. Phys.*, **10**, p. 67.

Christopher C. French

Fantastic Memories

The Relevance of Research into Eyewitness Testimony and False Memories for Reports of Anomalous Experiences

Abstract: Reports of anomalous experiences are to be found in all known societies, both historically and geographically. If these reports were accurate, they would constitute powerful evidence for the existence of paranormal forces. However, research into the fallibility of human memory suggests that we should be cautious in accepting such reports at face value. Experimental research has shown that eyewitness testimony is unreliable, including eyewitness testimony for anomalous events. The present paper also reviews recent research into susceptibility to false memories and considers the relevance of such work for assessing reports of anomalous events. It is noted that a number of psychological variables that have been shown to correlate with susceptibility to false memories (e.g., hypnotic susceptibility, tendency to dissociate) also correlate with the tendency to report paranormal and related anomalous experiences. Although attempts to show a direct link between tendency to report anomalous experiences and susceptibility to false memories have had only limited success to date, this may reflect the use of inappropriate measures.

I: Introduction

In all cultures throughout the world, there have always been occasional reports of strange, even miraculous, events. Today, such events are often labelled as 'paranormal' to indicate that, if they really did occur as reported, conventional science is incapable of explaining them. Such reports have always aroused intense controversy. Believers in the paranormal see them as proof of the limitations of the scientific worldview, whereas sceptics often dismiss them as being the result of fraud, stupidity or madness. How should a fair-minded, intelligent, rational person respond to such reports?

Correspondence:
Christopher C. French, Anomalistic Psychology Research Unit, Dept of Psychology, Goldsmiths College, University of London, New Cross, London SE14 6NW, UK. *Email: psa01ccf@gold.ac.uk*

Journal of Consciousness Studies, **10**, No. 6–7, 2003, pp. 153–74

In 1748, Hume published *Of Miracles*, an essay that is particularly relevant to this question (Grey, 1994). Hume presented a strong argument that one would never be rationally justified in believing that a miracle had occurred. He defined a miracle as an event that violates a law of nature, a definition that would be taken by many as including paranormal events. It is important to realise that Hume was not claiming to have proved that miracles have never occurred, only that we would never be justified in believing that they have. He proposed the following principle:

> No testimony is sufficient to establish a miracle unless that testimony be of such a kind that its falsehood would be more miraculous than the fact which it endeavours to establish.

Although this principle allows for the possibility that the evidence in favour of a miracle might outweigh the evidence against it, in practice, Hume argued, this never happens. Several factors undermine the credibility of miraculous claims, not least of which is the problem of witness reliability. Is it more likely that the person or persons making the claim are deceivers, or else themselves deceived, or that a law of nature has been violated? Whereas the evidence supporting violations of laws of nature is sparse, possibly even non-existent, we are surrounded by evidence that people sometimes lie and sometimes make mistakes.

This article will focus on the reliability of accounts of anomalous events from individuals who are sincere in presenting those accounts. This is not to deny that deliberate hoaxes and fraud are present in the world of the paranormal, but to accept that many — probably most — reports are made in good faith. Even so, sincerity is no guarantee of accuracy. Empirical support for such scepticism comes from both classic experiments on eyewitness testimony and more recent research on the formation of false memories. The evidence will be considered under four headings. (1) Cases where a normal episode is generally agreed to have taken place, but eyewitnesses disagree over details of what happened. (2) Cases where an apparently paranormal episode is generally agreed to have taken place, but eyewitnesses disagree over details of what happened. (3) Cases where there is a doubt as to whether a sincerely remembered normal episode ever took place at all. (4) Cases where a sincerely 'remembered' episode can be shown never to have taken place, but is entirely the product of an experimental procedure of one kind or another.

In the light of this survey, and accompanying analysis of the ways in which sincere memories can be inaccurate, the role of unreliable memory as a source of genuinely held belief in paranormal events will be considered. The motivation for this investigation is that sceptics are often challenged to offer a natural explanation for some alleged paranormal event as described by an individual who claims to have witnessed the event firsthand. However, if memory research supports the idea that such an account may not be an accurate reflection of an actual past event, then in the absence of objective evidence that the event really did occur as described, this is a challenge that should not be accepted. It is possible that the 'event' is either a distorted account of an episode that did occur or even a false memory with no basis whatsoever in objective reality.

II: Evidence of Unreliable Testimony

1. Eyewitness testimony (normal events)

A great deal of research has been directed towards understanding factors affecting the reliability of eyewitness testimony for normal events, particularly in forensic contexts. A full review of this topic is beyond the scope of the current paper (for more detailed consideration, the reader is referred to, e.g., Cohen, 1989; Loftus, 1979). Studies have typically involved assessing the recall of eyewitnesses for staged events, either using live action or video presentation. When we are able to assess witness reports against some form of objective record, it becomes clear that both perception and memory are constructive processes, influenced not only by input from the senses ('bottom-up' influences) but by our own knowledge, belief and expectations about the world ('top-down' influences).

Some of the findings from this body of research are consistent with our everyday intuitions about how memory works. Our memory is less accurate for peripheral details compared to those upon which our attention is focussed. Our memories are poorer for stimuli presented briefly under imperfect viewing conditions compared to extended viewing under ideal conditions. Our memories are most accurate when we are neither under-aroused (e.g., drowsy) nor over-aroused (e.g., frightened).

However, it is worth noting that our intuitions about memory are often wrong. For example, even under perfect viewing conditions, our memories of what we saw may be highly influenced by our view of what we think we must have seen. French and Richards (1993) showed participants an ordinary clock face with Roman numerals under perfect viewing conditions for an extended period. Participants were asked to draw the clock face from memory. They tended to represent the four as 'IV' in line with their general expectations of Roman numerals. In fact, however, the four on clocks and watches is almost always represented as 'IIII'. Most people are quite surprised when this is first pointed out to them, as they reflect upon the literally thousands of occasions they must have looked at clocks and watches without noticing this oddity. Even thousands of exposures to a simple stimulus under perfect viewing conditions may not be enough to lead to accurate recall.

Schema theory provides a useful framework for considering eyewitness testimony. As Cohen (1989, p. 71) points out:

> It can account for the fact that many of our experiences are forgotten, or are reconstructed in a way that is incomplete, inaccurate, generalised, or distorted. Schema theory emphasises the role of prior knowledge and past experience, claiming that what we remember is influenced by that which we already know. According to this theory, the knowledge we have stored in memory is organised as a set of schemas, or knowledge structures, which represent the general knowledge about objects, situations, events, or actions that has been acquired from past experience.

Loftus (1979) has drawn attention to the potentially distorting effects on memory of the use of leading questions in post-event interviews. Classic examples from her research include the fact that, following the viewing of a film of two cars colliding, witnesses give much higher estimates of speed if they are asked how fast they were travelling when they 'smashed into' each other than if the word 'contacted' is used. Furthermore, witnesses were more likely to report seeing a broken headlight (even though there wasn't one) if they were asked, 'Did you see *the* broken headlight?' as opposed to 'Did you see *a* broken headlight?' (emphasis added). There are real concerns that interviews carried out by investigators with very strong motivations to find evidence supporting their beliefs may often unintentionally lead witnesses in similar fashion.

Another potential source of socially encountered misinformation is that of fellow eyewitnesses. Understandably, investigators often have more faith in an eyewitness account if it appears to be supported by an account of the same incident from another eyewitness. However, it is very likely to be the case that witnesses will have discussed the incident amongst themselves before ever being formally interviewed by investigators. In the light of findings from research on conformity, we might expect that witnesses will influence each other's reports to a greater or lesser extent. Recent experimental work (e.g., Gabbert *et al.*, in press, submitted) has shown that this is indeed the case. In a sense, such research on misinformation effects provides a link between that dealing mainly with naturally arising memory distortions for witnessed events and that dealing primarily with false memories for events that never actually took place at all.

2. Eyewitness testimony (apparently paranormal events)

The focus of this section is on the reliability of eyewitness accounts of apparently paranormal events in circumstances where we can be fairly certain that paranormal forces were not at work. In many of the studies reviewed below, we can be absolutely certain of this, as the situations employed were entirely under the control of the investigators concerned.

As long ago as 1887, Davey had experimentally demonstrated the unreliability of eyewitness accounts of séances. Hyman (1985, p. 27) offers the following account:

> Davey had been converted to a belief in spiritualistic phenomena by the slate-writing demonstrations of the medium Henry Slade. Subsequently, Davey accidentally discovered that Slade had employed trickery to produce some of the phenomena. Davey practised until he felt he could accomplish all of Slade's feats by trickery and misdirection. He then conducted his well-rehearsed séance for several groups of sitters, including many who had witnessed and testified to the reality of spiritualistic phenomena. Immediately after each séance, Davey had the sitters write out in detail all that they could remember having happened during his séance. The findings were striking and very disturbing to believers. No one realized that Davey was employing tricks. Sitters consistently omitted crucial details, added others, changed the order of events, and otherwise supplied reports that would make it impossible for any reader to account for what was described by normal means.

Similar findings were reported by Besterman (1932) and, more recently, by Wiseman *et al.* (1995) and Greening (2002).

Such studies do not allow us to distinguish between the possibilities that distortions occurred during the actual perception of the events as opposed to subsequent recall, but the end result is the same. It is likely that both stages of information processing are affected. The actual perception of the séance is likely to be affected by the mental set that is adopted by the observer. A sceptic is likely to adopt a 'problem-solving' approach, intent on trying to figure out how any effects are being achieved. Someone who believes that the effects might be genuinely paranormal is more likely to just sit back and enjoy them, without a critical eye for crucial details.

Such an account is supported by Wiseman and Morris (1995) who compared believers and disbelievers in the paranormal in terms of their accuracy of recall for pre-recorded 'pseudo-psychic demonstrations' — in other words, conjuring tricks, such as bending a key ostensibly using psychic powers. Overall, believers tended to rate the demonstrations as being more 'paranormal' than disbelievers. They also tended to be less accurate in remembering information that was crucial to explaining how the deception had occurred (e.g., the fact that the key disappeared from view was important because a bent key was switched for the original straight key).

Jones and Russell (1980) exposed participants to either a 'successful' demonstration of ESP or a 'failed' demonstration. In the former case, the experimenters used a marked deck of cards to ensure 60 per cent accuracy, whereas performance was at the chance level of 20 per cent in the latter demonstration. Results again showed accurate recall by disbelievers regardless of whether the results supported their belief, but a strong tendency for believers to remember both demonstrations as successful.

Many of the factors associated with poor reliability of eyewitness testimony are commonly (although not universally) associated with ostensibly paranormal events (see, e.g., Loftus, 1979). These include poor viewing conditions (e.g., darkness or semi-darkness), altered states of consciousness (e.g., due to tiredness, biological trauma, engaging in particular rituals or drug abuse), emotional arousal, and either the ambiguous and unexpected nature of the event on the one hand (in spontaneous cases) or a high level of expectation and will to believe on the other (e.g., in a séance). It should not be surprising, therefore, that the often schema-driven accounts given by eyewitnesses to ostensibly paranormal events are typically distorted versions of the actual events in question. French (1992; 2001a) discusses further the role of beliefs and expectations in perception and interpretation of anomalous experiences.

3. Questionable normal memories

Loftus (1993) presents evidence showing that autobiographical memories for entire episodes can often be open to doubt, even in the absence of any deliberate attempt by others to implant such memories. For example, she describes a study by Pynoos and Nader (1989) in which the investigators had assessed children's memories for a sniper attack on an elementary school playground. Interestingly, children who had not, in fact, been present during the attack provided apparently sincere first-hand accounts of the event, presumably based upon accounts provided by actual witnesses:

> One girl initially said that she was at the school gate nearest the sniper when the shooting began. In truth she was not only out of the line of fire, she was half a block away. A boy who had been away on vacation said that he had been on his way to the school, had seen someone lying on the ground, had heard the shots, and then turned back. In actuality, a police barricade prevented anyone from approaching the block around the school. (Pynoos & Nader, 1989, p. 238)

Another relevant example is provided by so-called 'flashbulb memories' (Brown & Kulik, 1977). It was once believed that certain highly emotional events could lead to memories that were highly vivid and accurate. Classic examples include people's highly confident reports of where they were, whom they were with and what they were doing when they learned of some dramatic news story, such the assassination of John F. Kennedy. Subsequent research in which participants were questioned soon after such dramatic events, and then again after a long delay, has shown that even flashbulb memories can often be inaccurate, no matter how confidently they are described (see, e.g., Neisser & Harsch, 1993, pp. 9–31, for a study of flashbulb memories of the Challenger disaster).

Loftus (1993) provides numerous other examples of situations where confidently held autobiographical 'memories' appear to be based upon no event that the claimant ever actually witnessed first-hand. Such examples should lead us all to be somewhat less confident concerning the accuracy of our autobiographical memories, no matter how clear and vivid they may appear to be. There are very few real-life contexts in which we are forced to question the accuracy of apparent memories, either our own or those of others. But it appears likely that many such memories, whether for natural or paranormal events, could be false memories even without any deliberate attempt by others to implant such a false memory.

4. Implanted false memories

Although psychologists have long recognised that eyewitness accounts of witnessed events were unreliable, it is only within the last decade or so that much research has been directed at the possibility that people may sometimes have rich and detailed memories for events that they have never actually witnessed at all. The main reason for this explosion of research into false memories was the sudden increase in cases of alleged recovered memories of childhood sexual abuse, especially in the USA (see, e.g., Lindsay & Read, 1995; Loftus, 1993; Loftus & Ketchum, 1994; Ofshe & Watters, 1994). Worryingly, surveys of some professionals who were using such techniques as hypnotic regression in attempts to recover memories of abuse revealed a very poor understanding of the relationship between hypnosis and memory. In Yapko's (1994, p. 163) words:

> Survey data regarding hypnosis and suggestibility indicate that while psychotherapists largely view hypnosis favourably, they often do so on the basis of misinformation. A significant number of psychotherapists erroneously believe, for example,

that memories obtained through hypnosis are more likely to be accurate than those simply recalled, and that hypnosis can be used to recover accurate memories even from as far back as birth. Such misinformed views can lead to misapplications of hypnosis when attempting to actively recover memories of presumably repressed episodes of abuse, possibly resulting in the recovery of suggested rather than actual memories.

Experimental psychologists tended to doubt the accuracy of the memories recovered via hypnosis and related techniques (e.g., Spanos, 1996; Wagstaff, 1989, pp. 340–57). A considerable amount of experimental evidence shows that the hypnotic regression procedure is such that it provides a context in which individuals often produce an account mixing fantasy with pre-existing knowledge and expectations — and may then come to believe with total conviction that the account reflects events that really took place (McConkey *et al.*, 1998, pp. 227–59). Recent reviews by Kebbell and Wagstaff (1998) and Lynn and McConkey (1998) conclude that there is little or no evidence to support the claim that hypnosis can reliably enhance the accuracy of eyewitness memory.

Indeed, experimental psychologists have expressed doubts about the very concept of repression itself. The idea that the unconscious mind can somehow automatically take over and hide away memories for traumatic events is not supported by any convincing experimental evidence (Holmes, 1990, pp. 85–102). However, it must also be recognised that convincing experimental evidence for repression would be almost impossible to produce for ethical reasons. The severity of the traumatic intervention which clinicians suspect would be required to produce repression is far more extreme than the experimental manipulations that any ethics committee would approve.

Data are available from real-life contexts supporting the claim that some people experience traumatic events and subsequently appear to be unable to recall those events. Williams (1994), for example, showed that many women with a documented history of childhood sexual abuse did not report the abuse when interviewed twenty years later. Loftus *et al.* (1994) reported that 19 per cent of their sample of women reporting childhood sexual abuse felt that they had forgotten the abuse for periods of their life, only for the memory to return later. There are numerous difficulties in interpreting the findings from such studies as they relate to the concept of repression. Loftus *et al.* (1994) consider a number of these, including the fact that some such events would elude recall due to childhood amnesia and, in other cases, the ordinary mechanisms of forgetting. Furthermore, it is possible that some women may actually remember the abuse but choose not to reveal this to the interviewer. Femina *et al.* (1990), in a study of childhood physical abuse, found that some interviewees with documented abuse histories simply denied ever having been abused. However, when confronted with the evidence of abuse during a second follow-up interview, the interviewees admitted they could remember the abuse. Reasons for initially denying the abuse included 'embarrassment, a wish to protect parents, a sense of having deserved the abuse, a conscious wish to forget the past, and a lack of rapport with the interviewer' (p. 229).

To a large extent, whether or not repression ever occurs, in the sense of an active, unconscious, automatic and involuntary suppression of traumatic memories, is not centrally important to the issues addressed in this paper. Readers are referred to collections edited by Conway (1997), Davies and Dalgleish (2001), Lynn and McConkey (1998), Pope and Brown (1996) and Schacter (1995), for a range of views on the wider issues surrounding this debate. For our purposes, it is sufficient that the controversy led to increased research activity in the area of false memories.

In the early days of the controversy, those who believed that recovered memories were largely accurate would sometimes object that, although memory for peripheral details of a witnessed event might be distorted, there was little evidence that people were prone to false memories for episodes that had never actually occurred at all. In fact, we now know that it is alarmingly easy to implant false memories in a sizeable minority of the population using well-established experimental techniques.

There is now a considerable amount of experimental literature available regarding false memories. However, it is unclear whether different experimental approaches lead to different types of false memory and as yet no single theory can fully account for all of the available data. Intuitively, some experimental approaches appear to be of greater relevance to assessing the likely reliability of accounts of anomalous events than others. The different approaches described below vary in a number of important ways. Some approaches involve studying distortions of memory for events that were actually witnessed, whereas more recently attempts have been made to implant false memories for entire episodes that were never witnessed at all.

Some commentators would include the extensive literature on the so-called 'misinformation effect' established by Loftus and colleagues in the 1970s (e.g., Loftus et al., 1978) within the false memory framework. In general, such studies have involved showing participants slides or video clips of events such as traffic accidents or criminal acts and subsequently reading text which includes misleading information about the witnessed event. Participants frequently incorporate the misinformation into their memory for the event as demonstrated in recall or recognition tasks. Studies investigating the effects of leading questions upon recall and recognition (e.g., Loftus, 1975), as described above, can also be considered within the misinformation framework insofar as they involve a deliberate attempt to distort a memory for an actual witnessed event. The actual events in question may range from the trivial (e.g., falsely recalling single words) to the mildly traumatic (e.g., getting lost as a child in a shopping mall).

Roediger and McDermott (1995) replicated an effect first demonstrated by Deese (1959) in which participants were presented with a list of words all strongly semantically related to a critical non-presented word. For example, the words *thread, pin, sewing, point,* and so on, were presented, but the word *needle* was not. Subsequently, the critical lure word (in this example, *needle*) was falsely recalled or recognised with great confidence by many participants.

Arguably of more direct relevance to reports of anomalous events are those studies that have attempted to implant false memories for entire episodes that in all probability never occurred. Loftus and Pickrell (1995), for example, found that partial or complete false memories for a plausible but false childhood event (i.e., getting lost in a shopping mall) could be implanted in around 25 per cent of their participants. This was achieved by repeatedly interviewing the participants and getting them to try to recall as much detail as possible for four childhood events, three of which had actually occurred (according to other family members) plus the false event. Similar results were reported by Hyman *et al.* (1995). Other techniques that have been successfully used to implant false memories rely upon the use of other forms of false feedback to convince participants that events that they initially cannot remember must have actually taken place. Mazzoni and Loftus (1998) found that telling participants that the contents of their dreams indicated that certain events must have taken place before the age of three led to a dramatic increase in reports of corresponding memories.

Orne (1979) is one of a large number of investigators to show that suggestions made to hypnotically susceptible individuals following a hypnotic induction procedure will often lead to those individuals reporting memories for events that never occurred (e.g., being woken up in the night by a loud noise). However, numerous studies have now demonstrated that simply imagining events that never occurred can also lead to the formation of false autobiographical memories, a phenomenon that is known as 'imagination inflation' (Loftus, 2001). For example, Garry *et al.* (1996) had participants indicate which of a number of childhood events had or had not happened to them personally. Two weeks later, participants were asked to imagine some of the events that they had indicated had not happened to them. Subsequently, their confidence that these events had actually taken place was significantly increased relative to similar events that had not been imagined.

Further research is needed on the relationship between laboratory-based measures of susceptibility to false memories and susceptibility to false memories in more ecologically valid contexts. In general, experimenters adopt a single measure of false memory formation and so it is not clear whether or not the different measures would all inter-correlate, supporting the notion of a general susceptibility to false memories. Alternatively, it may be more accurate to think in terms of a number of distinct susceptibilities, each of which are related to different underlying brain mechanisms. It is worth noting, however, that Platt *et al.* (1998) reported that susceptibility as assessed using Roediger and McDermott's (1995) word-list technique was positively correlated with susceptibility to false autobiographical memories.

A full discussion of different theoretical approaches to false memories is beyond the scope of the current article (see Brainerd *et al.*, 2000, pp. 93–127, for further details). Although some apparent false memories can be accounted for in terms of demand characteristics and participants actually reporting accurate memories for misinformation (McCloskey & Zaragoza, 1985), it is now generally accepted that false memories really can be produced using the paradigms described above. Early 'single-trace' theories assumed that only one memory trace was laid down for each event and that this trace had to be overwritten or distorted in some way for a false memory to result. However, such theories have largely been supplanted by 'multiple-trace' theories in which more than one memory trace is associated with each event and false memories occur when there is confusion regarding which traces are accurate.

One influential theory of false memory development is that put forward by Hyman and Kleinknecht (1999, pp. 175–88). They proposed that three processes are involved in the development of false memories. First, the presented information is judged with respect to plausibility. Such judgements will be dependent upon the source of the information and the pre-existing beliefs of the individual. Second, an event memory must be constructed on the basis of schematic knowledge plus personal experiences, suggestion and current situational demands. Finally, the individual must commit a source monitoring error in which the constructed memory is accepted as reflecting the initial event rather than misinformation presented following the event.

Several other models of false memory also assume that errors of source monitoring underlie false memories. Source monitoring refers to the ability to accurately determine the original source of information (Johnson *et al.*, 1993) where the original sources could represent any number of internal or external sources. Internal sources might include imagination, dreams or hallucinations. External sources might include written text, pictures, verbal utterances (by a range of speakers) and so on. One particular aspect of source monitoring which is of potentially great relevance to the topic of this paper is that of reality monitoring, i.e., the more general ability to distinguish between memories based upon external events and those generated by internal mental processes (Johnson & Raye, 1981). Indeed, a number of experimental techniques have been developed to allow measurement of reality monitoring ability in which participants are presented with some stimuli and asked to internally generate others, for example by imagining them. The number of errors made in subsequently deciding which stimuli were presented and which were simply imagined provides an index of reality monitoring ability. Several commentators view errors in which imagined items are confused with presented items as themselves being false memories and have used standard reality monitoring tasks to assess susceptibility to false memories (e.g., Blackmore & Rose, 1997).

III: Further Examples of Probable False Memories for Anomalous Events

Section II.2 above dealt with several instances where one could be certain that the situations concerned did not involve paranormal forces because they were entirely under experimental control and objective records existed of the events involved. It is often the case, however, that the only source of evidence is the allegedly first-hand report itself. In the case of alien abduction claims and past-life regressions, a strong circumstantial case can be made that we are indeed often dealing with instances of false memory.

1. Alien abduction claims

It appears that the circumstances under which detailed reports of alien abduction are produced are exactly those that one would expect to lead to the formation of false memories. Blackmore (1994, p. 30) provides the following report of an alleged alien abduction. It is a fictional composite account based upon her investigations of numerous cases:

> I woke up in the middle of the night and everything looked odd and strangely lit. At the end of my bed was a four-feet-high grey alien. Its spindly, thin body supported a huge head with two enormous, slanted, liquid black eyes. It compelled me, telepathically, to follow and led me into a spaceship, along curved corridors to an examination room full of tables on which people lay. I was forced to lie down while they painfully examined me, extracted ova (or sperm) and implanted something in my nose. I could see jars containing half-human, half-alien foetuses and a nursery full of silent, sickly children. When I eventually found myself back in bed, several hours had gone by.

Those who believe that alien abduction accounts accurately reflect events that really occurred often argue that the aliens involved are generally capable of rendering their victims almost totally amnesic with respect to the episode. The abductee may, for example, only remember waking up in his or her bedroom and being unable to move. Alternatively, the abductee may remember nothing at all, and simply be aware of a period of 'missing time'. Such experiences are open to various more conventional explanations, but some ufologists (e.g., Hopkins *et al.*, 1992) insist that they actually indicate a high probability that the victim was abducted. If such an explanation appears to offer a plausible explanation to the person who experienced it, that person may be interviewed by a therapist specialising in alien abduction cases to see if they can recover further details. Spanos *et al.* (1994, p. 438; see also, Spanos, 1996) comment as follows:

> Frequently, the interviews include two phases. In the first phase background information is obtained and clients are asked about unusual or inexplicable experiences that have occurred during their life. These include 'missing time' experiences, unusual or bizarre dreams, and experiences that suggest hypnagogic imagery or sleep paralysis (e.g., having seen a ghost, strange lights, or a monster). Such experiences are defined as distorted memories of alien abduction that call for further probing (Jacobs & Hopkins, 1992). Moreover, making such experiences salient enhances the likelihood that some of their characteristics (e.g., paralysis, feelings of suffocation) will be incorporated into any abduction memories that are recalled in Phase 2. Phase 2 typically involves hypnotic or non-hypnotic guided imagery employed to facilitate recall. This may involve leading questions (Baker, 1992), or the subject may be pressed repeatedly for more details (Jacobs, 1992). In addition, subjects may be informed that some material is so deeply hidden that several such interviews are required. Subjects who have difficulty 'remembering' some or all of their abduction are defined as 'blocking' and are provided with strategies for facilitating recall. These include asking subjects to imagine a curtain and then to peek behind it to view their abduction, or to imagine a movie screen on which they see their abduction replayed (Jacobs & Hopkins, 1992).

The creation of false memories is clearly implicated in UFO abduction claims, but several other factors are also involved (see, e.g., Appelle *et al.*, 2000, pp. 253–82; French, 2001b, pp. 102–16; Holden & French, 2002), although discussion of such additional factors is beyond the scope of this article.

2. Hypnotic past-life regression

Some believers in reincarnation believe that it is possible to hypnotically regress individuals not only back to childhood, but back to previous incarnations. A Cardiff-based hypnotherapist, Arnall Bloxham, was the subject of a BBC documentary and subsequently featured in a book by Iverson (1977). At first sight, it appeared that Bloxham had used hypnotic regression to produce incontrovertible proof of reincarnation. One of his cases in particular, that of a Welsh housewife referred to as Jane Evans, appeared to be very impressive. She provided details of six previous incarnations, many with a wealth of historically correct background information. In one life, she was a maid in the house of a wealthy French merchant named Jacques Couer in the fifteenth century.

Although Iverson felt that the case for reincarnation was established, subsequent investigation by Harris (1986) proved him wrong. In fact, in both of these cases and others, there were significant errors in the accounts produced. For example, Jane Evans reported that Couer was single with no children. In fact, he was married with five children — something that most maids would notice. Such errors provided the clue to the source of the story. A novel by Thomas B. Costain entitled *The Moneyman* was based upon Couer's life but the author had taken the literary liberty of deliberately omitting Couer's family as they kept getting in the way of the plot development. It appears that Evans had read the book and then forgotten reading it. During the hypnotic sessions these details had re-emerged and had been taken to be real memories.

In the case of Jane Evans and many other similar claims, it is generally believed that no deliberate hoax was involved. Instead, these are seen as being cases of cryptomnesia (literally, 'hidden memories'; see Baker, 1992). It is argued that an individual can store away information from a variety of sources during his or her life, such as from novels, films, history books, or wherever, without later being aware of the source of the information. When the information is later recalled under hypnosis, perhaps elaborated upon by the individual's own fantasies, the memories can be taken to be veridical.

Spanos and colleagues (1994) summarise some of their own studies of past-life regression. It appears that a particular type of personality is very prone to producing detailed accounts of past lives under hypnosis. Such individuals score highly on measures of fantasy-proneness. They are highly imaginative individuals with a rich fantasy life and sometimes have difficulty separating fantasy from reality. They become engrossed in works of fiction to the extent that they lose themselves. Elsewhere, Spanos *et al.* (1991) have reported the results of studies in which individuals were hypnotised and regressed into past lives and then asked for details of their past life. Information that any individual living at the time would be aware of (e.g., the country's currency, ruler, etc; is the country at war?) is usually not known by the participant. Whether or not participants subsequently accept their past-life memories as evidence of reincarnation depends upon whether they believe in the possibility of reincarnation and the expectations built up by the experimenter.

IV: Is There a Link Between Susceptibility to False Memories, Paranormal Beliefs and Tendency to Report Paranormal Experiences?

Within the last few years, attention has turned to the issue of why some individuals seem to be more prone to false memories than others. A number of psychological factors have been identified as being correlated with such susceptibility and the degree to which such factors have been found to correlate with the tendency to report anomalous experiences is of considerable interest. If common factors were found linking both susceptibility to false memories and tendency to report anomalous experiences, this would strengthen the *prima facie* case that at least some reports of anomalous experiences may be based upon false memories. Not surprisingly, the link between paranormal belief and reports of personal experience of ostensibly paranormal phenomena is already well established. Those who feel they have had personal experience of the paranormal are understandably far more likely to believe in the paranormal.

Dobson and Markham (1993) and Markham and Hynes (1993) reported that participants with vivid visual imagery were more likely to make source-monitoring errors. Hypnotic suggestibility has been found to correlate with number of false memories reported by a number of investigators (e.g., Barnier & McConkey, 1992; Laurence & Perry, 1983; Sheehan *et al.*, 1991). Heaps and Nash (1999) found that susceptibility to imagination inflation was correlated with indices of hypnotic suggestibility and dissociativity, but not with vividness of imagery or interrogative suggestibility. However, a subsequent study by Horselenberg *et al.* (2000) did find a correlation between imagination inflation and imagery ability, using a different measure of the latter. Tomes and Katz (1997) assessed habitual susceptibility to misinformation by presenting participants with three events involving misinformation. They found it to correlate with vivid visual imagery (as well as spatial dexterity and emotional empathy for others). Eisen and Carlson (1998) reported that susceptibility to misinformation was positively correlated with both absorption and dissociation. *Absorption* has been described by Tellegen and Atkinson (1974) as 'a disposition for having episodes of single "total" attention that fully engage one's representational (i.e., perceptual, enactive, imaginative and ideational) resources'. It is commonly measured using the Tellegen Absorption Scale (Tellegen & Atkinson, 1974).

Hyman and Billings (1998) attempted to implant false childhood memories in participants using a similar approach to that employed by Loftus and Pickrell (1995). Using this technique, susceptibility to false memories was found to correlate with scores on the Creative Imagination Scale (CIS; a measure of both hypnotisability and imagery) and dissociativity, but not with absorption or social desirability. Platt *et al.* (1998) used two measures of memory distortion in their study: scores on Roediger and McDermott's (1995) word task (described above) and naturally occurring distortions of autobiographical memory. Only one significant correlation was found between either of the two memory measures and measures of absorption, dissociativity and fantasy-proneness: absorption was negatively correlated with accuracy of autobiographical memory. Although no significant correlations were found between the word task and personality measures in this study, a previous investigation by Winograd *et al.* (1998) had found significant correlations between both dissociativity and vivid imagery and susceptibility to false memories. CIS scores were not correlated with proneness to false memories in this study.

A number of psychological factors have thus been found to correlate with susceptibility to false memories, although there is considerable variation across studies. It is likely that this reflects, to some extent, the use of different measures of susceptibility, suggesting that different types of false memory may well depend upon different mechanisms. As stated, if the same psychological factors also correlate with paranormal belief and reports of anomalous experiences, it would strengthen the argument that at least some such reports may depend upon false memories.

Imagery ability has also been found to correlate with paranormal beliefs (Finch, 2002; Greening, 2002; Diamond & Taft, 1975). Furthermore, although people who report out-of-body experiences (OBEs) do not score higher than non-OBEers on standard imagery questionnaires (e.g., Blackmore, 1982; Irwin, 1981a), they do seem to be superior in terms of using spatial imagery to create novel perspectives (e.g., Blackmore, 1986, pp. 108–11; Cook & Irwin, 1983).

A number of studies have demonstrated a small but significant correlation between hypnotic susceptibility and belief in the paranormal (e.g., Diamond & Taft, 1975; Palmer & Van Der Velden, 1983; Wagner & Ratzenberg, 1987), although some studies have failed to find such a relationship (e.g., Groth-Marnat *et al.*, 1998–99; Pekala *et al.*, 1995). Atkinson's (1994) study is exceptional in finding a relatively large correlation ($r = .53$) between hypnotic susceptibility and belief in the paranormal. Other investigators have shown that groups of highly hypnotisable participants report higher levels of paranormal belief than those with less susceptibility (Nadon *et al.*, 1987; Pekala *et al.*, 1992; Pekala *et al.*, 1995; see Kumar & Pekala, 2001, pp. 260–79, for a thorough technical review of this area).

Hypnotic susceptibility has also been found to correlate with a range of reported paranormal and anomalous experiences (e.g., Atkinson, 1994; Nadon & Kihlstrom, 1987; Palmer & Van Der Velden, 1983; Pekala *et al.*, 1995; Spanos & Moretti, 1988; Wagner & Ratzeberg, 1987; Wickramasekera, 1989, pp. 19–35), although once again there are occasional studies that fail to find such a relationship (e.g., Persinger & De Sano, 1986). Richards (1990, p. 35) reported 'low and marginally significant' correlations between hypnotic susceptibility and self-reports of psychic experiences. Studies have also compared groups differing in hypnotic susceptibility and have found differences in the degree to which anomalous/paranormal experiences are reported (e.g., Pekala *et al.*, 1992; 1995).

Absorption correlates moderately with paranormal belief (Palmer & Van Der Velden, 1983), subjective paranormal experiences (e.g., Irwin, 1981a) and mystical experiences (Spanos & Moretti, 1988). Both Irwin (1981b) and Myers *et al.* (1983) found that students who reported OBEs also demonstrated higher levels of absorption than those who did not. Irwin (1985) showed that the need for absorption was higher in experients than non-experients for a wide range of subjective paranormal experiences.

Dissociativity has often been shown to be correlated with paranormal belief (e.g., Greening, 2002, Study 2.2; Irwin, 1994; Pekala *et al.*, 1995; Wolfradt, 1997), but some studies have failed to find such a relationship (Greening, 2002, Study 2.1; Groth-Marnat *et al.*, 1998–99). Makasovski and Irwin (1999) present data suggesting that pathological dissociation predicts belief in parapsychological and spiritual concepts, but that non-pathological dissociative tendencies (absorption) do not correlate with paranormal belief. Rattet and Bursik (2001) reported that dissociative tendencies were related to paranormal belief, but not to self-reported precognitive experiences. Dissociativity has been shown to be related to the tendency to report a wide range of paranormal and anomalous experiences (Pekala *et al.*, 1995; Richards, 1991; Ross & Joshi, 1992; Ross *et al.*, 1991). Powers (1994) has shown that a group of alleged alien abductees showed higher levels of dissociativity than a matched sample of non-abductees. Children reporting past-life memories have been shown to have higher levels of dissociative tendencies in both Sri Lanka (Haraldsson *et al.*, 2000) and Lebanon (Haraldsson, 2002). Greyson (2000) has reported that although people reporting near-death experiences (NDEs) are psychologically healthy, some do show non-pathological signs of dissociation. The possibility that at least some reports of NDEs may be based upon false memories was raised by French (2001c) in a commentary on a prospective study of NDEs by van Lommel *et al.* (2001). The latter investigators interviewed a number of patients two years after they had suffered cardiac arrests that they had reported at the time were not associated with NDEs. At the two-year follow-up interviews, however, four of the 37 patients now reported that they had indeed experienced NDEs during their cardiac arrest.

In summary, it appears that there are numerous studies supporting an association between paranormal beliefs and reports of anomalous experiences on the one hand and a range of psychological factors thought to be associated with increased susceptibility to false memories on the other. It is important at this point to emphasise, however, that this pattern of correlations is also consistent with an alternative interpretation, one that is taken seriously by many parapsychologists. It is possible that individuals who score highly on such measures as dissociativity, hypnotic susceptibility and so on have the right psychological profile to experience genuine paranormal phenomena (if they actually exist). Of course, the false-memory hypothesis and the psi hypothesis are not mutually exclusive. The correct interpretation of the pattern of findings will only be resolved by empirical investigation.

Having established a *prima facie* case for a link between false memories and paranormal beliefs and tendency to report anomalous experiences, we shall now review the relatively few studies that have investigated the postulated link directly. Haraldsson (1985) reported a low but significant correlation between suggestibility (as measured by the Gudjonsson Suggestibility Scale) and global paranormal beliefs (as measured by Tobacyk's Paranormal Belief Scale, PBS). Of the seven sub-scales of the PBS, only those measuring belief in witchcraft, spiritualism and precognition were significantly correlated with suggestibility.

Blackmore and Rose (1997) tested the hypothesis that susceptibility to false memories would be correlated with paranormal belief using a reality-monitoring task. Participants were initially shown simple drawings of objects or asked to imagine drawings of objects. Over subsequent sessions spanning a number of weeks, they were questioned regarding their memory of the pictures (both real and imagined). In a final session, they were asked to indicate whether each draw- ing had initially been presented or imagined. A false memory was recorded every time a picture that had only been imagined was recorded as having been pre- sented. No correlation was found between susceptibility to false memories and paranormal belief. Three similar experiments by Rose and Blackmore (2001) also failed to find the predicted relationship. Greening (2002), using a similar methodology, did find a significant correlation in the predicted direction, but was unable to replicate the effect in two follow-up experiments.

Clancy *et al.* (2002) used the word list paradigm of Roediger and McDermott (1995) in a study comparing people with recovered memories of alien abduction, people who believed they had been abducted but without such memories, and people who denied having been abducted by aliens. The group with memories of abduction were shown to be more susceptible to false memories than the control participants. Furthermore, false recognition and recall were correlated with hyp- notic susceptibility, depressive symptoms and schizotypic features.

V: Directions for Future Research

It is clear that direct attempts to prove a link between susceptibility to false mem- ories and reports of anomalous experiences have so far met with only limited success. However, this may reflect the methods that have been used to date to test the hypothesis. It is unlikely that all of the different measures of susceptibility to false memory are measuring the same thing. It would therefore be advisable if future studies concentrated mainly upon those techniques that would appear to be most relevant to the possibility that memories for certain types of event may sometimes be false. Intuitively, naturally occurring distortions of autobiographi- cal memory and susceptibility to implanted memories of entire episodes would seem to be the most relevant. Measurements of reality monitoring errors would appear to be of less relevance unless it could be shown that errors made in the task used by Blackmore and Rose (1997) generalise to more serious confusions (such as between daydreams and reality). Susceptibility to misinformation is of some relevance, but one assumes that in everyday life it would be relatively rare for another individual to try to deliberately manipulate someone else's memory. Unintentional distortion by discussion with another individual is always a possibility, however. Finally, it is ironic that the word list paradigm is one of the few which seem to have been successful in discriminating between a group who had reported a particular anomalous experience and control groups (Clancy *et al.*, 2002), given the apparent lack of ecological validity of the task itself. This important finding awaits replication, however.

Another possible reason for the inconsistency in results to date is that many investigations have focussed upon belief in anomalous phenomena rather than reported experiences of anomalous phenomena. Although one of the most common reasons given for belief in the paranormal is personal experience, it is by no means the case that all believers have had such personal experience. There are many other reasons for belief in anomalous phenomena including media reports, personal accounts from trusted others, and so on. Clearly, one would expect a higher correlation between susceptibility to false memories and actual reports of particular anomalous experiences rather than belief in those anomalous phenomena. A further recommendation for future research in this area is that greater emphasis should be placed upon searching for correlates of the tendency to report anomalous phenomena as opposed to simply believing in them.

As is usually the case when considering psychological factors associated with paranormal and related beliefs, the studies reviewed above are generally quasi-experimental in nature. Participants cannot be randomly assigned to high and low paranormal belief groups. It is possible that susceptibility to false memories causes people to come to believe they have had a paranormal experience (even if they have not) which then produces or reinforces their belief in some particular aspect of the paranormal. On the other hand, it is reasonable to argue that pre-existing beliefs play a causal role in the acceptance of potential false memories as authentic. According to Hyman and Kleinknecht (1998), plausibility is an important factor in making such decisions. Whereas a fleeting memory of an ostensibly anomalous experience might be dismissed as probably being the memory of a dream by a sceptic, a believer is more likely to accept that it may reflect something that actually happened. Further reflection and elaboration may then lead to a more detailed and vivid 'memory'.

It must be emphasised, however, that memory distortion and the formation of false memories can never provide a complete explanation for all reports of anomalous events, nor is it intended to do so. A wide range of other factors needs to be taken into account (see, e.g., Cardeña *et al.*, 2000; French, 1992; Roberts & Groome, 2001; Zusne & Jones, 1989). To take but one example, a sincere report of having seen a ghost may well actually be a more or less accurate report of an hallucinatory experience. It is possible that the intense emotion generated by the experience may lead to less reliable testimony (e.g., Loftus, 1979) but the report is best understood by considering primarily the psychology of hallucinations (Bentall, 2000, pp. 85–120).

It is possible that much of what we take to be our personal autobiographical history is based upon false, or at least distorted, memories. This usually is not drawn to our attention because no one is likely to challenge mundane memories of ordinary everyday events unless one person's memory actually directly contradicts another. With respect to paranormal and related claims, however, the situation is entirely different. A listener may decide that a particular account must be inaccurate simply because the account contradicts that person's understanding of what is and what is not possible. Is it reasonable that such a person, without any claim whatsoever to first-hand knowledge of the events in question, should feel justified in adopting this sceptical position? On the basis of the evidence reviewed above, the answer has to be affirmative.

The review of recent developments in the area of false memory research suggests that a *prima facie* case can be made for a possible link between susceptibility to false memories and tendency to report anomalous experiences. One of the most important factors associated with paranormal and related beliefs is alleged personal experience of anomalous events and thus an indirect link may exist between susceptibility to false memories and level of belief. Alternatively, as described above, it may be that pre-existing beliefs play an important role in determining whether potential false memories are accepted as records of events that really occurred. They may also play a role in determining the content of such memories, as schema-driven distortions are likely to occur. To date, the few direct tests of the postulated links between susceptibility to false memories, reports of anomalous experiences, and level of paranormal and related beliefs have met with only limited success, but further research, taking into account the issues discussed above, is certainly warranted.

References

Appelle, S., Lynn, S.J., & Newman, L. (2000), 'Alien abduction experiences', in *Varieties of Anomalous Experience: Examining the scientific evidence*, ed. Cardeña, E., Lynn S.J., & Krippner, S. (Washington, DC: American Psychological Association).

Atkinson, R.P. (1994), 'Relationship of hypnotic susceptibility to paranormal beliefs and claimed experiences: Implications for hypnotic absorption', *American Journal of Clinical Hypnosis*, 37, pp. 34–40.

Baker, R.A. (1992), *Hidden Memories: Voices and Visions from Within* (Buffalo, NY: Prometheus).

Barnier, A.J., & McConkey, K.M. (1992), 'Reports of real and false memories: The relevance of hypnosis, hypnotizability, and test control', *Journal of Abnormal Psychology*, 101, pp. 521–7.

Bentall, R.P. (2000), 'Hallucinatory experiences', in *Varieties of Anomalous Experience: Examining the scientific evidence*, ed. Cardeña, E., Lynn, S.J., & Krippner, S. (Washington, DC: American Psychological Association).

Besterman, T. (1932), 'The psychology of testimony in relation to paraphysical phenomena: Report of an experiment', *Proceedings of the Society for Psychical Research*, 40, pp. 363–87.

Blackmore, S.J. (1982), *Beyond the Body: An Investigation of Out-of-the-Body Experiences* (London: Heinemann).

Blackmore, S.J. (1986), 'Where am I? Perspectives in imagery, memory, and the OBE', in *Research in Parapsychology 1985*, ed. Weiner, D.H, & Radin, D.I. (Metuchen, NJ: Scarecrow Press).

Blackmore, S. (1994), 'Alien abduction: The inside story', *New Scientist*, No. 1952, 19 November, pp. 29–31.

Blackmore, S.J., & Rose, N. (1997), 'Reality and imagination: A psi-conducive confusion?' *Journal of Parapsychology*, 61, pp. 321–35.

Brainerd, C.J., Reyna, V.F., & Poole, D.A. (2000), 'Fuzzy-trace theory and false memory: Memory theory in the courtroom', in *False-Memory Creation in Children and Adults: Theory, Research and Implications*, ed. Bjorklund, D.F. (Mahwah, NJ: Erlbaum).

Brown, R., & Kulik, J. (1977), 'Flashbulb memories', *Cognition*, 5, pp. 73–99.

Cardeña, E., Lynn S.J., & Krippner, S. (eds.) (2000), *Varieties of Anomalous Experience: Examining the scientific evidence* (Washington, DC: American Psychological Association).

Clancy, S.A., McNally, R.J., Schacter, D.L., Lenzenweger, M.F., & Pitman, R.K. (2002), 'Memory distortion in people reporting abduction by aliens', *Journal of Abnormal Psychology*, **111**, pp. 455–61.

Cohen, G. (1989), *Memory in the Real World* (London: Erlbaum).

Conway, M.A. (ed.) (1997), *Recovered Memories and False Memories* (Oxford: Oxford University Press).

Cook, A.M., & Irwin, H.J. (1983), 'Visuospatial skills and the out-of-body experience', *Journal of Parapsychology*, **47**, pp. 23–35.

Davies, G., & Dalgleish, T. (eds.) (2001), *Recovered Memories: Seeking the Middle Ground* (Chichester: Wiley).

Deese, J. (1959), 'On the prediction of occurrence of particular verbal intrusions in immediate recall', *Journal of Experimental Psychology*, **58**, pp. 17–22.

Diamond, M.J., & Taft, R. (1975), 'The role played by ego-permissiveness and imagery in hypnotic responsivity', *International Journal of Clinical and Experimental Hypnosis*, **23**, pp. 130–8.

Dobson, M., & Markham, R. (1993), 'Imagery ability and source monitoring: Implications for eyewitness memory', *British Journal of Psychology*, **84**, pp. 111–18.

Eisen, M.L., & Carlson, E.B. (1998), 'Individual differences in suggestibility: Examining the influence of dissociation, absorption, and a history of childhood abuse', *Applied Cognitive Psychology*, **12**, pp. S47–61.

Femina, D.D., Yeager, C.A., & Lewis, D.O. (1990), 'Child abuse: Adolescent records vs. adult recall', *Child Abuse and Neglect*, **14**, pp. 227–31.

Finch, S.E. (2002), 'Daydream believers? Fantasy-proneness, transliminality and reality monitoring: A search for vulnerability factors in false memory creation', unpublished PhD thesis, Goldsmiths College, University of London.

French, C.C. (1992), 'Factors underlying belief in the paranormal: Do sheep and goats think differently?' *The Psychologist*, **5**, pp. 295–9.

French, C.C. (2001a), *Paranormal Perception? A Critical Evaluation* (London: Institute for Cultural Research. Monograph Series, No. 42).

French, C.C. (2001b), 'Alien abductions', in *Parapsychology: The Psychology of Unusual Experience*, ed. Roberts, R., & Groome, D. (London: Arnold).

French, C.C. (2001c), 'Dying to know the truth: Visions of a dying brain, or false memories?' *Lancet*, **358**, pp. 2010–11.

French, C.C., & Richards, A. (1993), 'Clock this! An everyday example of a schema-driven error in memory', *British Journal of Psychology*, **84**, pp. 249–53.

Gabbert, F., Memon, A., & Allan, K. (in press), 'Memory conformity: Can eyewitnesses influence each other's memories for an event?', *Applied Cognitive Psychology*.

Gabbert, F., Memon, A., & Allan, K. (submitted), 'Say it to my face: Examining the effects of socially encountered misinformation'.

Garry, M., Manning, C.G., Loftus, E.F., & Sherman, S.J. (1996), 'Imagination inflation: Imagining a childhood event inflates confidence that it occurred', *Psychonomic Bulletin & Review*, **3**, pp. 208–14.

Greening, E.K. (2002), 'The relationship between false memory and paranormal belief', Unpublished PhD thesis, University of Hertfordshire.

Grey, W. (1994), 'Philosophy and the paranormal. Part 2: Skepticism, miracles, and knowledge', *Skeptical Inquirer*, **18**, pp. 288–94.

Greyson, B. (2000), 'Dissociation in people who have near-death experiences: Out of their bodies or out of their minds?' *Lancet*, **355**, pp. 460–3.

Groth-Marnat, G., Roberts, L., & Ollier, K. (1998–99), 'Hypnotizability, dissociation, paranormal beliefs', *Imagination, Cognition and Personality*, **18**, pp. 127–32.

Haraldsson, E. (1985), 'Interrogative suggestibility and its relationship with personality, perceptual defensiveness and extraordinary beliefs', *Personality and Individual Differences*, **6**, pp. 765–7.

Haraldsson, E. (2002), 'Children who speak of past-life experiences: Is there a psychological explanation?' Paper presented to the Parapsychological Association Congress, Paris, August 2002.

Haraldsson, E., Fowler, P.C., & Periyannanpillai, V. (2000), 'Psychological characteristics of children who speak of a previous life: A further field study in Sri Lanka', *Transcultural Psychiatry*, **37**, pp. 525–44.

Harris, M. (1986), *Sorry, You've Been Duped! The Truth Behind Classic Mysteries of the Paranormal* (London: Weidenfeld and Nicolson).

Heaps, C., & Nash, M. (1999), 'Individual differences in imagination inflation', *Psychonomic Bulletin & Review*, **6**, pp. 313–18.

Holden, K.J., & French, C.C. (2002), 'Alien abduction experiences: Clues from neuropsychology and neuropsychiatry', *Cognitive Neuropsychiatry*, **7**, pp. 163–78.

Holmes, D.S. (1990), 'The evidence for repression: An examination of sixty years of research', in *Repression and dissociation: Implications for personality theory, psychopathology, and health*, ed. Singer, J.L. (Chicago and London: University of Chicago Press).

Hopkins, B., Jacobs, D.M., & Westrum, R. (1992), *Unusual personal experiences: An analysis of the the data from three national surveys conducted by the Roper Organisation* (Las Vegas, NV: Bigelow Holding Corporation).

Horselenberg, R., Merckelbach, H., Muris, P., Rassin, E., Sijsenaar, M., & Spaan, V. (2000), 'Imagining fictitious childhood events: The role of individual differences in imagination inflation', *Clinical Psychology and Psychotherapy*, **7**, pp. 128–37.

Hyman, I.E., Jr., & Billings, F.J. (1998), 'Individual differences and the creation of false childhood memories', *Memory*, **6**, pp. 1–20.

Hyman, I.E., Jr., Husband, T.H., & Billings, F.J. (1995), 'False memories of childhood experiences', *Applied Cognitive Psychology*, **9**, pp. 181–97.

Hyman, I.E., Jr., & Kleinknecht, E.E. (1999). 'False childhood memories: Research, theory, and applications', in *Trauma and Memory*, ed. Williams, L.M., & Banyard, V.L. (Thousand Oaks, CA: Sage).

Hyman, R. (1985), 'A critical historical overview of parapsychology', in *A Skeptic's Handbook of Parapsychology*, ed. Kurtz, P. (Buffalo, NY: Prometheus).

Irwin, H.J. (1981a), 'The psychological function of out-of-body experience: So who needs the out-of-body experience?' *Journal of Nervous and Mental Disease*, **169**, pp. 244–8.

Irwin, H. J. (1981b), 'Some psychological dimensions of the out-of-body experience', *Parapsychology Review*, **12**(4), pp. 1–6.

Irwin, H.J. (1985), 'Parapsychological phenomena and the absorption domain', *Journal of the American Society for Psychical Research*, **79**, pp. 1–11.

Irwin, H.J. (1994), 'Paranormal belief and proneness to dissociation', *Psychological Reports*, **75**, pp. 1344–6.

Iverson, J. (1977), *More Lives than One?* (London: Pan Books).

Jacobs, D.M. (1992), *Secret Life: Firsthand Accounts of UFO Abductions* (New York: Simon & Schuster).

Jacobs, D.M., & Hopkins, B. (1992). 'Suggested Techniques for Hypnosis and Therapy of Abductees', Unpublished manuscript, Temple University, Philadelphia.

Johnson, M.K., Hashtroudi, S., & Lindsay, D.S. (1993), 'Source monitoring', *Psychological Bulletin*, **114**, pp. 3–28.

Johnson, M.K., & Raye, C. (1981), 'Reality monitoring', *Psychological Review*, **88**, pp. 67–85.

Jones, W.H., & Russell, D. (1980), 'The selective processing of belief disconfirming information', *European Journal of Social Psychology*, **10**, pp. 309–12.

Kebbell, M.R., & Wagstaff, G.F. (1998), 'Hypnotic interviewing: The best way to interview eyewitnesses?', *Behavioral Sciences and the Law*, **16**, pp. 115–29.

Kumar, V. K., & Pekala, R.J. (2001), 'Relation of hypnosis-specific attitudes and behaviors to paranormal beliefs and experiences: A technical review', in *Hauntings and Poltergeists: Multidisciplinary Perspectives*, ed. Houran, J. & Lange, R. (Jefferson, NC: McFarland & Co).

Laurence, J.R., & Perry, C. (1983), 'Hypnotically created memory among highly hypnotizable subjects', *Science*, **222**, pp. 523–4.

Lindsay, D. S., & Read, J.D. (1995), '"Memory work" and recovered memories of childhood sexual abuse: Scientific evidence and public, professional, and personal issues', *Psychology, Public Policy, and the Law*, **1**, pp. 846–908.

Loftus, E.F. (1975), 'Leading questions and the eyewitness report', *Cognitive Psychology*, **7**, pp. 560–72.

Loftus, E.F. (1979), *Eyewitness Testimony* (Cambridge, MA: Harvard University Press).

Loftus, E.F. (1993), 'The reality of repressed memories', *American Psychologist*, **48**, pp. 518–37.

Loftus, E.F. (2001), 'Imagining the past', *The Psychologist*, **14**, pp. 584–7.

Loftus, E.F., Garry, M. & Feldman, J. (1994), 'Forgetting sexual trauma: What does it mean when 38% forget?' *Journal of Consulting and Clinical Psychology*, **62**, pp. 1177–81.

Loftus, E.F., & Ketcham, K. (1994), *The Myth of Repressed Memory: False Memories and Allegations of Sexual Abuse* (New York: St. Martin's Press).

Loftus, E.F., Miller, D.G., & Burns, H.J. (1978), 'Semantic integration of verbal information into a visual memory', *Journal of Experimental Psychology: Human Learning and Memory*, **4**, pp. 19–31.

Loftus, E.F., & Pickrell, J.E. (1995), 'The formation of false memories', *Psychiatric Annals*, **25**, pp. 720–5.

Loftus, E.F., Polonsky, S., & Fullilove, M.T. (1994), 'Memories of childhood sexual abuse: Remembering and repressing', *Psychology of Women Quarterly*, **18**, pp. 67–84.

Lynn, S.J., & McConkey, K.M. (eds.) (1998), *Truth in Memory* (New York & London: Guilford Press).

Makasovski, T., & Irwin, H.J. (1999), 'Paranormal belief, dissociative tendencies, and parental encouragement of imagination in childhood', *Journal of the American Society for Psychical Research*, **93**, pp. 233–47.

Markham, R., & Hynes, L. (1993), 'The effect of vividness of imagery on reality monitoring', *Journal of Mental Imagery*, **17**, pp. 159–70.

Mazzoni, G.A.L., & Loftus, E.F. (1998), 'Dream interpretation can change beliefs about the past', *Psychotherapy*, **35**, pp. 177–87.

McCloskey, M., & Zaragoza, M.S. (1985). 'Misleading post-event information and memory for events: Arguments and evidence against memory impairment hypotheses', *Journal of Experimental Psychology: General*, **114**, pp. 1–16.

McConkey, K.M., Barnier, A.J., & Sheehan, P.W. (1998), 'Hypnosis and pseudomemory: Understanding the findings and their implications', in *Truth in Memory,* ed. Lynn, S.J., & McConkey, K.M. (New York & London: Guilford Press).

Myers, S.A., Austrin, H.R., Grisso, J.T., & Nickeson, R.C. (1983), 'Personality characteristics as related to the out-of-body experience', *Journal of Parapsychology,* 47, pp. 131–44.

Nadon, R., & Kihlstrom, J.F. (1987), 'Hypnosis, psi, and the psychology of anomalous experience', *Behavioural and Brain Sciences,* 10, pp. 597–9.

Nadon, R., Laurence, J.R., & Perry, C. (1987), 'Multiple predictors of hypnotic susceptibility', *Journal of Personality and Social Psychology,* 53, pp. 948–60.

Neisser, U., & Harsch, N. (1993), 'Phantom flashbulbs: False recollections of hearing the news about Challenger', in *Affect and Accuracy in Recall: Studies of 'flashbulb memories',* ed. Winograd, E., & Neisser, U. (New York: Cambridge University Press).

Ofshe, R., & Watters, E. (1994), *Making Monsters: False Memories, Psychotherapy, and Sexual Hysteria* (New York: Scribner).

Orne, M.T. (1979), 'The use and misuse of hypnosis in court', *International Journal of Clinical and Experimental Hypnosis,* 27, pp. 311–41.

Palmer, J., & Van Der Velden, I. (1983), 'ESP and "hypnotic imagination": A group free-response study', *European Journal of Parapsychology,* 4, pp. 413–34.

Pekala, R.J., Kumar, V.K., & Cummings, J. (1992), 'Types of high hypnotically susceptible individuals and reported attitudes and experiences of the paranormal and the anomalous', *Journal of the American Society for Psychical Research,* 86, pp. 135–50.

Pekala, R.J., Kumar, V.K., & Marcano, G. (1995), 'Anomalous/paranormal experiences, hypnotic susceptibility, and dissociation', *Journal of the American Society for Psychical Research,* 89, pp. 313–32.

Persinger, M.A., & De Sano, C.F. (1986), 'Temporal lobe signs: positive correlations with imaginings and hypnosis induction profiles', *Psychological Reports,* 58, pp. 347–50.

Platt, R.D., Lacey, S.C., Iobst, A.D., & Finkelman, D. (1998), 'Absorption, dissociation, fantasy-proneness as predictors of memory distortion in autobiographical and laboratory-generated memories', *Applied Cognitive Psychology,* 12, pp. S77–89.

Pope, K.S., & Brown, L.S. (1996), *Recovered Memories of Abuse: Assessment, Therapy, Forensics* (Washington, DC: American Psychological Association).

Powers, S.M. (1994), 'Dissociation in alleged extraterrestrial abductees', *Dissociation,* 7, pp. 44–50.

Pynoos, R.S., & Nader, K. (1989), 'Children's memory and proximity to violence', *Journal of the American Academy of Child and Adolescent Psychiatry,* 28, pp. 236–41.

Rattet, S.L., & Bursik, K. (2001), 'Investigating the personality correlates of paranormal belief and precognitive experience', *Personality and Individual Differences,* 31, pp. 433–44.

Richards, D.G. (1990), 'Hypnotic susceptibility and subjective psychic experiences: A study of participants in A.R.E. conferences', *Journal of Parapsychology,* 54, pp. 35–51.

Richards, D.G. (1991), 'A study of the correlations between subjective psychic experiences and dissociative experiences', *Dissociation,* 4, pp. 83–91.

Roberts, R., & Groome, D. (eds.) (2001), *Parapsychology: The Psychology of Unusual Experience* (London: Arnold).

Roediger, H.L, III, & McDermott, K.B. (1995), 'Creating false memories: Remembering words not presented on lists', *Journal of Experimental Psychology: Learning, Memory, and Cognition,* 21, pp. 803–14.

Rose, N., & Blackmore, S.J. (2001), 'Are false memories psi-conducive?' *Journal of Parapsychology,* 65, pp. 125–44.

Ross, C.A., & Joshi, S. (1992), 'Paranormal experiences in the general population', *Journal of Nervous and Mental Disease,* 180, pp. 357–61.

Ross, C.A., Ryan, L., Voigt, H., & Eide, L. (1991), 'High and low dissociators in a college student population', *Dissociation,* 4, pp. 147–51.

Schacter, D.L. (ed.) (1995), *Memory Distortion: How Minds, Brains, and Societies Reconstruct the Past* (Cambridge, MA & London: Harvard University Press).

Sheehan, P.W., Statham, D., & Jamieson, G.A. (1991), 'Pseudomemory effects and their relationship to level of susceptibility to hypnosis and state instruction', *Journal of Personality and Social Psychology,* 60, pp. 130–7.

Spanos, N.P. (1996), *Multiple Identities and False Memories: A Sociocognitive Perspective* (Washington, DC: American Psychological Association).

Spanos, N.P., Burgess, C.A. & Burgess, M.F. (1994), 'Past-life identities, UFO abductions, and Satanic ritual abuse: The social construction of memories', *International Journal of Clinical and Experimental Hypnosis,* 42, pp. 433–46.

Spanos, N.P, Menary, E., Gabora, N.J., DuBreuil, S.C. & Dewhirst, B. (1991), 'Secondary identity enactments during hypnotic past-life regression: A sociocognitive perspectiv'', *Journal of Personality and Social Psychology,* 61, pp. 308–20.

Spanos, N.P., & Moretti, P. (1988), 'Correlates of mystical and diabolical experiences in a sample of female university students', *Journal for the Scientific Study of Religion,* 27, pp. 105–16.

Tellegen, A., & Atkinson, G. (1974), 'Openness to absorbing and self-altering experiences ("absorption"), a trait related to hypnotic susceptibility, *Journal of Abnormal Psychology*, **83**, pp. 268–77.

Tomes, J.L., & Katz, A.N. (1997), 'Habitual susceptibility to misinformation and individual differences in eyewitness memory', *Applied Cognitive Psychology*, **11**, pp. 233–51.

Van Lommel, P., van Wees, R., Meyers, V., & Elfferich, I. (2001), 'Near-death experience in survivors of cardiac arrest: A prospective study in the Netherlands', *Lancet*, **358**, pp. 2039–45.

Wagner, M.W., & Ratzeberg, F.H. (1987), 'Hypnotic suggestibility and paranormal belief', *Psychological Reports*, **60**, pp. 1069–70.

Wagstaff, G.F. (1989), 'Forensic aspects of hypnosis', in *Hypnosis: The cognitive–behavioral perspective,* ed. Spanos, N.P., & Chaves, J.F. (Buffalo, NY: Prometheus).

Wickramasekera, I. (1989), 'Risk factors for parapsychological verbal reports, hypnotizability and somatic complaints', in *Parapsychology and Human Nature*, ed. Shapin, B., & Coly, L. (New York: Parapsychology Foundation).

Williams, L.M. (1994), 'Recall of childhood trauma: A prospective study of women's memories of child sexual abuse', *Journal of Consulting and Clinical Psychology*, **62**, pp. 1167–76.

Winograd, E., Peluso, J.P., & Glover, T.A. (1998), 'Individual differences in susceptibility to memory illusions', *Applied Cognitive Psychology*, **12**, pp. S5–27.

Wiseman, R., & Morris, R.L. (1995), 'Recalling pseudo-psychic demonstrations', *British Journal of Psychology*, **86**, pp.113–25.

Wiseman, R., Smith, M., & Wiseman, J. (1995), 'Eyewitness testimony and the paranormal', *Skeptical Inquirer*, **19**(6), pp. 29–32.

Wolfradt, U. (1997), 'Dissociative experiences, trait anxiety and paranormal beliefs', *Personality and Individual Differences*, **23**, pp. 15–19.

Yapko, M.D. (1994), *Suggestions of Abuse* (New York: Simon & Schuster).

Zusne, L., & Jones, W.H. (1989), *Anomalistic Psychology: A Study of Magical Thinking* (Hillsdale, NJ: Erlbaum).

Geoffrey Dean and Ivan W. Kelly

Is Astrology Relevant to Consciousness and Psi?

Abstract: *Many astrologers attribute a successful birth-chart reading to what they call intuition or psychic ability, where the birth chart acts like a crystal ball. As in shamanism, they relate consciousness to a transcendent reality that, if true, might require a re-assessment of present biological theories of consciousness. In Western countries roughly 1 person in 10,000 is practising or seriously studying astrology, so their total number is substantial. Many tests of astrologers have been made since the 1950s but only recently has a coherent review been possible. A large-scale test of persons born less than five minutes apart found no hint of the similarities predicted by astrology. Meta-analysis of more than forty controlled studies suggests that astrologers are unable to perform significantly better than chance even on the more basic tasks such as predicting extraversion. More specifically, astrologers who claim to use psychic ability perform no better than those who do not. The possibility that astrology might be relevant to consciousness and psi is not denied, but such influences, if they exist in astrology, would seem to be very weak or very rare.*

Introduction

Astrology has one sure thing in common with parapsychology — a highly visible outpouring of market-driven nonsense that threatens to bury the work of serious researchers. Just as parapsychology means ghost busting and psychic phonelines to the ordinary person, so astrology means sun signs and newspaper columns. Here we ignore the latter view in favour of serious astrology, the study of purported relationships between the heavens and earthly affairs. The case for astrology was lucidly put by Charles Carter (1925), the leading British astrologer of his day, as follows:

> Practical experiment will soon convince the most sceptical that the bodies of the solar system indicate, if they do not actually produce, changes in: 1. Our minds. 2. Our feelings and emotions. 3. Our physical bodies. 4. Our external affairs. (p. 14)

Correspondence:
Professor I.W. Kelly, Department of Educational Psychology, 28 Campus Drive, University of Saskatchewan, Saskatoon, Canada S7N 0X1. *Email: ivan.kelly@usask.ca*

Journal of Consciousness Studies, **10**, No. 6–7, 2003, pp. 175–198

However, the appeal to 'practical experiment', or experience, is not as straight-forward as it may seem. Astrology can be applied to anything that is born or begins independent existence, such as a person, company, ship, nation, animal or idea; and the astrologer begins by calculating the birth chart or horoscope, a stylized map of the heavens at the moment of birth (think of a wheel covered in strange symbols) as seen from the place of birth. Then comes the interpretation. But after twenty centuries of practice, astrologers still cannot agree on what a birth chart should contain, how it should be interpreted, or what it should reveal. Nor do they agree on how astrology should be tested, or even (despite what Charles Carter says) on whether it can be tested in the first place. As a result, even to astrologers, 'astrology is almost as confused as the earthly chaos it is supposed to clarify' (Dobyns and Roof, 1973, p. 4).

For our present purpose this disagreement and confusion are of little concern. As we shall see, what matters is that some astrologers claim that astrology involves an altered state of consciousness, and many more claim that astrology involves some degree of psi. So if astrologers can perform as they claim, we might be on to something. We look first at the claims (these occupy roughly half of what follows) then at the empirical studies.

Astrology and Consciousness

We know that brain processes are related to consciousness, the difference between being awake and being asleep. But is consciousness a biological process needing a biological brain, or is it merely a by-product of complexity needing only sufficient complexity, as in some futuristic computer program? As yet nobody knows for sure. But if astrological links with human behaviour are real, they might provide clues.

Unfortunately astrologers themselves provide more confusion than clues. For example some astrologers see astrology as describing 'the mind stuff which shapes and informs all of life and consciousness' (Harvey and Harvey, 1999, p. 31). Others see consciousness as just one more thing shown by the birth chart; for example the quintile aspect 'introduces a new dimension of consciousness' so you 'experience subtleties of thought transcending the usual', while Jupiter leads to 'expansions of consciousness' (Moore and Douglas, 1971, pp. 586, 707). Precisely what all this means is hard to say, for such talk raises more questions than it answers.

Our best clue concerning consciousness comes from horary astrology, where a client's question is said to be answered in the birth chart calculated for when the astrologer receives the question. Ordinary astrology sees the birth chart as exist-ing independently of the astrologer, whereas an horary birth chart does not exist until the astrologer becomes involved by receiving the question. Some astrolo-gers such as Jeff Mayo (1964) find it is:

> sheer nonsense for anyone to believe that a question . . . has its correct answer
> wrapped neatly in cosmic vibrations tuned in to when the letter is opened on

Wednesday 9:03 am — or, if the recipient's train was held up on the way to his office, at 9:14 am. Horary astrology makes a mockery of a serious subject. (p. 184)

But for British astrologer Geoffrey Cornelius (1994), a teacher and practitioner of divinatory astrology, the actual involvement of the astrologer, as opposed to being a mere interpreter, suggests that astrological 'connections' are less a gift of nature and more a product of the astrologer's mind; that is, of consciousness. In this 'all in the mind' view of astrology there is nothing actually 'out there' that involves planets. Instead what matters is the mental state of the astrologer. The technique used for reading the chart is then merely a ritual that leads to the right mental state. Just as astrologers differ, so will techniques, but all techniques will necessarily work no matter how much they may seem to disagree.

British astrologer Charles Harvey (1994) points out that such a view has the advantage of elevating the internal confusions of astrology above criticism, and the disadvantage of denying any way for astrology to be improved over, say, tea-leaf reading, or to have been discovered in the first place. He argues that there can be a psi component to astrology (a point most astrologers would agree with, see later), but not to the extent claimed by Cornelius, simply because some computer-generated chart readings 'can prove remarkably to the point' (p. 398). Nevertheless, despite the disagreement, such a view provides a clue too good to ignore. To see how astrology might be nothing more than the right mental state, we can look at shamanism.

Parallels with Shamanism

To shamans or medicine men, purportedly obtaining information from the spirit world to benefit their community, everything provides knowledge about every-thing else, but only via symbols that have to be interpreted to make sense. In shamanism:

> Symbols . . . serve as keys that unlock the door to . . . another order of reality . . . The image-schemas [symbol systems] of shamanic practitioners were especially adept when prediction was demanded. Game needed to be located, weather patterns needed to be forecast, enemy movements needed to be anticipated . . . the shamanic fine-tuning of image-schemas through heightened perception and/or changed states of consciousness may have assisted this assignment (Krippner, 2000, pp. 102, 114).

Astrologers work in a similar world of symbolism and 'image-schemas', where everything interacts with everything else and has to be interpreted to make sense. In place of the frenzied dancing, drumming and mushroom-eating used by shamans to achieve their 'shamanic consciousness', there is concentration on the birth chart and its highly complex symbolism based on analogy, mythology, numerology, sympathy and ancient ideas generally, with each symbol being applicable at different levels such as inner, outer and physical, which in turn will depend on age, maturity, gender and so on. The complexity of the birth chart is thus almost without limit, which is why the best readings are said to require the aid of psi to sort out the confusion. For many astrologers a chart reading involves no more than ordinary concentration, so 'shamanic consciousness' hardly applies to them. But for others it is different.

Consider what American clinical psychologist Ralph Metzner (1971), a former editor of *Psychedelic Review*, says in his book *Maps of Consciousness*. For six years he explored 'the extraordinary inner worlds opened up for me by the psychedelics' (these worlds are similar to shamanic experiences), after which he began to see how astrology and other divinatory systems 'were originally intended to be used as maps for the path of the evolutionary development of consciousness' (p. vii). He is careful to distinguish between a model (simulates how you behave) and a map (try it and see how you feel) (p. 10). More to the point:

> Like . . . other mantic [divinatory] procedures, astrological horoscope casting is in one way a framework for intuitive perception. I know of one clairvoyant astrologer who simply looks at the actual horoscope diagram [birth chart] and then begins to 'see' the inner life, the thought forms, and emotional patterns of her client, almost as if she were gazing into a crystal ball (p. 111).

Consider also how American astrologer Jane Evans (1979) describes reading the birth chart as 'a ritual carrying a magic dimension', with clear shamanic parallels:

> As the astrologer works with the ancient symbology giving it interpretation more suitable to this age, it becomes an active entering-into, a deep participation with those symbols and the personality/Self of the [horoscope's owner] . . . When that participation is achieved there is a breakthrough. The astrologer can be taken . . . inward to realization. Like a lightning flash that reveals a whole landscape formerly in darkness, insight suddenly illuminates the horoscope giving pattern and meaning to what was hitherto just a collection of symbols . . . A door opens to communication with the Inner Self, whether your own or that of the person whose horoscope is being studied (p. 5).

Much the same applies to this description of reading the birth chart by British astrologer Rose Elliot (1974):

> First of all, I like to absorb the chart completely; like to look at it, not analysing it but allowing the different factors to sink into my subconscious. When the time comes actually to interpret the chart, I concentrate on the centre of the chart, which appears as a kind of golden orb; concentrating on this point in the chart, I feel as if I am *inside* the chart, standing in the centre, with all the planetary forces around the chart playing on me like the rays of the sun . . . At a certain point the golden orb I have described opens out, and I find myself standing in a sort of corridor. This corridor represents time . . . I can look back down this corridor into the past, and forward to the future. As I do so, certain 'rooms' which open off the corridor, become lit up and I look into them and see a picture, like a cinema . . . These always have a bearing on the chart (pp. 12–13).

Elliot would not be your usual everyday astrologer. Her experiences could of course arise not from shamanic ecstasy but merely from a fantasy-prone personality (one that fantasizes vividly during much of waking life). But proneness to fantasy seems to be an essential ingredient of shamanism (Krippner, 2000, p. 96), so for our purpose it may not matter. The point is, both groups (shamans and astrologers) relate consciousness to a transcendent reality that, if true or even partly true, might require a re-assessment of present biological theories of consciousness. Just as shamanism can be seen as relevant to consciousness, so might astrology, especially as our principal concern here is validity, which seems to be rarely considered in shamanic studies.

Furthermore, Freeman and Núñez (1999, p. xi) note that the mind–body split stems from the magic–science split in world views, typified by astrology on the one hand and Newtonian physics on the other. So astrology might lead us to useful pre-split insights. At which point we move on to consider psi.

Astrology and Psi

The parapsychologist John Beloff (1994) argues that the existence of psi suggests that the mind can 'extract information from objects other than its own brain'. Similarly, whether the heavens actually correlate with human behaviour, or are merely a means of attaining the right mental state, as variously claimed by astrologers, it suggests that minds might be affected by things other than brains (and vice versa). It might also be evidence for paranormal happenings that might be related to psi.

As a bonus, astrology brings advantages shared with parapsychology — testability (at least in principle), promise of new knowledge and (according to astrologers) positive results. Many methodological and conceptual problems are common to both, for example compare the psi review articles and commentaries in *Behavioural and Brain Sciences* (1987) with their astrological equivalent in *Correlation* (1994–8).

The bonus would be even better if astrologers had genuine psychic ability, which they see as a gift synonymous with intuition that mysteriously pops things into their minds. They know without knowing how they know (and without knowing that they could very well be wrong). However, only psychic ability, if it exists, is without a scientific explanation, whereas intuition may be due to the unconscious processing of previous experience (Eysenck, 1995, pp. 170–201; Myers, 2002). But here the distinction is less important than establishing whether something unusual is happening.

Do Astrologers have Psychic Ability?

Sigmund Freud was a corresponding member of the Society for Psychical Research from 1911 until his death in 1939. In 1921 he told how a patient of his had given a birth date to a renowned lady astrologer in Munich, who predicted that after a few months the person would die of crab or oyster poisoning. In fact the prediction was wrong, although the person had almost died of crab poisoning at the same time a year earlier (which might be unremarkable if the person often ate crabs). As shown by the following quote, Freud says he doubts whether astrology could discover anything as specific as crab poisoning:

Let us not forget how many people are born on the same day. Is it conceivable that ... the date of birth would include such details? ... On the other hand, her client did possess this information. The occurrence can be fully explained if we are willing to assume that ... thought transference exists ... the purpose of the astrologer's work was to divert her own intra-psychic forces, and to occupy them innocuously. This made it possible for her to become receptive and permeable to the impact of the thought of others (Freud, 1921/1955, pp. 181–3).

Fifty years later much the same view was put forward by psychic researcher Alan Vaughan (1973), who comments 'My own small experience with astrologers has given me the impression that their best hits are psychic rather than astrological, though in truth it is very difficult to separate the one from the other' (p. 103).

Most astrologers would not disagree with this view. A chart is so complex that American astrologer Doris Chase Doane (1956) says 'it is almost impossible to read a birth-chart ... without exercising in some degree, Extra-sensory Perception' (p. 3). According to Moore and Douglas (1971) 'some astrologers are clairvoyantly gifted. Using the horoscope as a psychometric tool, they may be spectacularly successful in describing the specific details of a person's life' (p. 8). Cornelius (1994) argues that some unknown element 'is involved in the astrological interpretation ... [and] is broadly but consistently characterized by astrologers and researchers alike, as either ESP or intuition' (p. 70). A survey of two hundred and fifty astrologers, mostly American, found that over half claimed to use psychic ability in their chart readings (Moore, 1960, p. 127). Like Freud, astrologer Dal Lee (1964) concludes that astrological meanings are too broad to allow specific statements unless some ESP faculty is used, and that some astrologers have ESP at least some of the time, often getting a perfect hit but hardly knowing where it comes from. Let us look more closely.

Hidden Persuaders

Examples of what seem to be perfect hits are seeing abuse at age thirteen, seeing the location of a lost shawl in a French restaurant (Phillipson, 2000, pp. 64, 71) and guessing sun signs correctly. Such hits lead to the claim that astrologers proudly and repeatedly make, that astrology is unassailable because it is based on experience, which echoes our opening quote from Charles Carter. But the claim is untenable because astrologers are generally unaware of the many hidden persuaders that can make them see hits where none exist (Dean, Mather and Kelly, 1996, pp. 89–93). Examples are the Barnum effect (reading specifics into generalities), cognitive dissonance (seeing what you believe), cold reading (let body language be your guide), nonfalsifiability (nothing can count against your idea) and operant conditioning (heads you win, tails is irrelevant). There are many more. Technically these hidden persuaders can be described as 'statistical artifacts and inferential biases'.

When hidden persuaders are prevented, the hits generally disappear, as for an American astrologer who publicly challenged sceptics to test his predictions of appearance (Ianna and Tolbert, 1984), a French astrologer who claimed to diagnose medical conditions (Gauquelin, 1987), and when guessing sun signs was found to depend on cue leakage (Dean, 1983). Offering cash prizes of up to $US5,000 did not improve the hit rate (Dean, Mather and Kelly, 1996, p.71). As an example, in 1927 thousands of astrologers attempted to win $US1,000 (then roughly the average annual wage) by correctly describing three people from their birth data, but the result was conspicuous disagreement — 'they not only contradicted themselves, they were unanimously unsuccessful in describing the three people' (Miller, 2002). Such a situation will be familiar to any investigator of paranormal claims.[1]

Of course this does not deny the possibility that astrologers could have genuine psychic ability. Indeed, most astrologers aggressively ignore such problems in favour of seeing astrology less as a set of rules and more as something akin to divination, where 'its reliability depends on the quality of the astrologer's intuition' (Phillipson, 2000, p. 167). Some even see astrology as a link to the spirit world, a view we now explore.

Help from Spirit Guides

Some astrologers claim they are helped by spirit guides, for example they will feel somehow 'directed' to focus on particular chart factors, or something in a birth chart will suddenly jump out at them. American astrologer Gary Keen (1988) describes the effect of such guidance on the astrologer:

> He knows he has stepped across a divide that separates the material from the mental or unknown [spirit] world . . . He will attempt to develop some form of association with this unseen magical power that resides within, around and above the horoscope he holds in his hand (pp. 19–20).

Such effects explain why some astrologers see the birth chart as a mandala or magical diagram, a means to contact spirit powers that guide and direct a person.

---

[1] The same hidden persuaders explain how phrenology, once more popular and far more influential than astrology is today, could be accepted as completely valid even though it is now known to be completely invalid (Dean, 1998). The point is, hidden persuaders are generally not noticed, yet they can be totally compelling. For example Aphek and Tobin (1989), in a survey of fortune-telling techniques, cite a case where a young lady PhD in psychology was amazed when an astrologer told her things that the astrologer 'could not possibly have known'. But on analysing the tape recording she realized that 'in every case she had herself supplied the cues that enabled the seer to proceed' (p. 180).

Interestingly, it is not uncommon for astrologers to make a seemingly accurate reading for a client only to discover later that it was based on the wrong birth chart. For example one British astrologer notes how it has 'happened to a lot of astrologers. Some of the best readings have been with wrong charts.' But he ignores the logical conclusion (that astrology is dominated by hidden persuaders, so any chart will do), adding only: 'I think a lot of what you get from astrology is actually psychic ability' (in Phillipson, 2000, p. 118).

The power of hidden persuaders to lead us astray is illustrated by American psychologist Ray Hyman (2003, p. 22), who as a teenager began reading palms to earn extra income. He was highly praised for his accuracy, even on specific matters such as health, and became a staunch believer. But when he gave readings that were the opposite of what the palm indicated, his accuracy was as highly praised as before. Dean (1987) found the same for reversed birth-chart readings. Clearly no sensible person will consider a paranormal explanation of astrology and palmistry hits unless hidden persuaders have been eliminated. For more on how seers capitalize on hidden persuaders see Hyman (1977) and Steiner (1989).

Note again the parallel with shamanism, where 'practitioners deliberately alter or heighten their conscious awareness to enter the so-called "spirit world", accessing material that they use to help and to heal members of the social group that has acknowledged their shamanic status' (Krippner, 2000, p. 98). Indeed, American astrologer Barbara Clow (1988) emphasizes the astrologer's 'shamanistic duty' to place a client in contact with spirit forces, thus making the chart 'a unified energy field of consciousness' (p. xv).

According to Burgoyne (1889/1982, p. 84), an astrologer and medium, to really learn astrology one must be able to contact spirits and thus receive occult knowledge. Of nine randomly-selected lecturers at a major American astrology convention in 1988, seven claimed to have spirit guides or were spiritists, and another was involved with spiritistic literature (Ankerberg and Weldon, 1989, p. 219). Some astrology books have purportedly been dictated by spirit guides, and some have been dedicated to spirit guides, for example Joan Hodgson's *Reincarnation Through the Zodiac* (1978) is dedicated 'with deep love and gratitude' to her spirit guide White Eagle. When the seer Edgar Cayce was asked if it was proper to study astrology, his spirit guide answered: 'When studied aright, very, very, very much so' (Gammon, 1973, p. 15). Even John Addey, the leading British astrologer and empirical investigator of his time, was of the view that planets are 'spiritual existences or substances and their influence is universal' (Addey, 1996, p. 9).[2]

In short, such views hold that spirits are the real basis of astrology, and that planetary 'energies' are really spirit energies, whatever that means. Spirits might of course be psi in disguise, which would make them open to the same objections, for example the absence of criteria for deciding whether psi is present or absent (Alcock, 1987, 1990), and the severe incompatibility of psi with the findings of neuroscience (Beyerstein, 1987; Kirkland, 2000). In effect they replace one mystery with another and thus make the situation worse for astrology rather than better.

* * *

To recap, we have seen how various astrologers claim that consciousness, psi and spirit guides are relevant to astrology. In general they provide no evidence for such claims, only speculation, and are unaware that their claims are confounded by hidden persuaders and fantasy-prone personality. Nevertheless let us accept that astrologers may use some sort of intuition or psychic ability when reading a birth chart. Also, because the incidence of astrologers and serious students of astrology is roughly 1 in 10,000 of the general population (Dean, Mather and

---

[2] Having a spirit guide would seem to be a private matter not readily disclosed, like tax evasion, so that estimating the proportion of astrologers with spirit guides is a risky business. In our experience it is not high. Nevertheless many examples of such astrologers are given by Ankerberg and Weldon (1989, pp. 201–55), while former astrologer Charles Strohmer (1988, p. 61), unaware of hidden persuaders, claims that evil spirits (not just spirits) lie behind the hits in every system of divination including astrology. Furthermore the incidence of fantasy-prone personality in the general population (about 4%) is much higher than the incidence of astrologers (about 0.01%). So who knows?

Kelly, 1996, p. 60), it is not inconceivable that astrologers might form some sort of 'psychic elite' where the chance of detecting psi and anomalous states of consciousness is correspondingly increased — an opportunity not to be lightly passed by. But before we look at the empirical evidence, we must ask why astrology has been generally neglected by psi researchers, even those who do not confuse astrology with sun signs.

Why has Astrology been Neglected by Psi Researchers?

The answer seems simple enough. Astrology is based on the untenable *Principle of Correspondences*, so it is not worth the bother.[3] It is like believing in fairies. There is also the question of evidence. In his 1930 presidential address to the Society for Psychical Research, in the days before the advent of sun signs, Dr Walter Franklin Prince put it this way:

> I myself, at the risk of appearing ridiculous even to my colleagues, have for fourteen years held my archives open for astrological evidence, and have collected many exhibits of what was offered as evidence by supposed experts . . . [I know] of no evidence which is not the result either of a forced application of the rules to human careers already known, or of a careful culling of 'hits' from preponderating numbers of 'misses'. I do not think that any psychical researcher in forty-eight years [since the SPR began in 1882] has given attention to the claims of astrology and has not definitely cast the pretended science on the dust heap (Prince, 1930, p. 294).

---

[3] The Principle of Correspondences, once widely accepted, was discredited after the seventeenth century. It involves argument by analogy, the assumption that things similar in some respects are also similar in other respects. Thus the changeable Moon indicates a changeable person, the number four and the fourth planet have the same qualities, and Aries indicates ramlike impulsivity. Such analogies have great flexibility, which astrologers see as a strength, for example the astrological element Water might relate to ambergris, breasts, crabs, fluctuation, gardens, ink, insecurity, the Moon, music, navigation, Neptune, pearls, poetry, pumpkins, sensitivity, tridents and turquoise, to mention only a few. But the Principle is untenable. The height of John Smith tells us nothing about the height of John Brown. No longer do we believe with Aristotle that death can occur only at low tide. No longer do midwives open the door to ease a painful labour. Nor do we have any immediate way of choosing between opposing correspondences. The Moon was male to the Babylonians but female to the Greeks. Is Mars unfortunate because red = blood (war) or fortunate because red = blood (life)? No wonder the Principle of Correspondences survives in Western education only as an example of fallacious reasoning packed with hidden persuaders.

We should not confuse the Principle of Correspondences with the physical analogies so useful in science, as when the analogy between the behaviour of light and the behaviour of waves led to the discovery of diffraction and other optical phenomena. But confusing them is easy because the first is experienced from infancy whereas physical analogies are not. To the child it may be the roundness of the pebble that makes it sink, or the yellowness of the Moon that stops it falling. In effect the Principle of Correspondences is something we have to unlearn in order to make sense of the world, which explains its appeal — it encourages us to do what in childhood cames naturally, like believing in Santa Claus. Remnants can survive in subtle ways. If you visit the Middle East, should you be more worried about dying in a terrorist attack than about dying generally? Is social collapse due to drug barons more likely than social collapse generally? Most people answer yes to both. But the second alternative includes the first, so the correct answer is no. The addition of a plausible correspondence has led our reasoning astray. Other remnants are less subtle, as when red hair is considered hot-tempered, or when dice are rolled vigorously to coax a high number, or when Eastern beliefs threaten rhinos with extinction, see Zusne and Jones (1989), Gilovitch and Savitsky (1996).

Prince was quite properly ignoring unsupported claims in favour of empirical research. To him the evidence (of which he had 'collected many exhibits') was clearly negative. More recently the same emphasis on empirical research has been made by the parapsychologist Carl Sargent (1986), but with a new twist:

> Almost nothing can be concluded from this [present accumulation of empirical] research, since independent replications with standardized procedures are wholly lacking. For a sound research programme which does justice to the complex and dynamic interplay of horoscope factors which traditional astrologers emphasize, it would be necessary . . . to poll astrologers on which predictor variables would best predict a limited range of criterion variables (e.g., extraversion, aggressiveness, manifest anxiety) . . . and use multiple regression techniques . . . At present such a research programme has not been implemented (p. 348).

In other words the neglect of astrology by psi researchers might or might not be justified, but the appropriate tests had not been made. That was in the early 1980s. Today, thanks to advances in research, that situation no longer applies.

The Revolution in Astrological Research

Very few empirical studies of astrology existed before 1950. However, by 1975 there were more than one hundred studies in astrology journals and psychology journals, most of them little known. So Alan Vaughan (1973) could say 'it seems astonishing to me that so few experiments in astrology have been attempted' (p. 104). Today the number of empirical studies exceeds five hundred. They have revolutionized our understanding of astrology, but because about 80% of studies are not accessible via computerized abstracts such as PsycINFO, they are still generally unknown.[4]

Unfortunately this revolution in understanding has had little effect on astrological practice, simply because astrologers rely solely on experience, or what psychologists call 'personal validation'. Garry Phillipson (2000, p. 168), after interviewing more than thirty leading astrologers, found that many (not all) regarded scientific studies as misguided. As British astrologer Roy Alexander (1983) puts it: 'I take it for granted that astrology works, and that we have enough cumulative experience to know that it works, whether the computer studies and the scientists agree with us or not' (p. xii). Similarly the parapsychologist Dean Radin (1997) notes that 'Parapsychologists have certainly learned the folly of ignoring human experience just because current scientific theories cannot adequately explain those experiences' (p. 179).

Indeed, as the journalist Neil Spencer found in his survey of modern astrology, so powerful is experience that astrologers carry on despite having 'no rational

---

[4] Nor will you find them in most astrology books. Even for astrologers, 'anyone used to reading books on or around our subject must have a mind which positively aches with the effort of keeping it open: a reader put off by *non sequiturs*, evidence which isn't evidence at all, irrationality and eccentricity will not get halfway along the first shelf [at any astrology bookshop]' (Parker, 1991). For comprehensive critical surveys of astrology, its problems and associated scientific research, including non-technical accounts for the general reader, see annotated entries in the list of references or visit http://www.astrology-and-science.com/

reason why it should work' (Spencer, 2000, p. 245). But experience is precisely where hidden persuaders operate, whose hidden nature might explain the apparent absence of any reason why astrology should work, especially as astrologers are generally unaware that hidden persuaders exist. Which brings us back to empirical studies.

Measuring Astrological Performance

As we noted earlier, if astrologers can perform as they claim, we might be on to something. In what follows we measure performance in terms of *effect size*, expressed as a correlation or similar measure, where 0 means no effect, 1 means perfect effect, and −1 means perfect inverse effect. We also submit sets of effect sizes to meta-analysis, which subtracts the sampling and measurement variability (something not possible with an individual effect size) to see if there is a genuine residual effect (Utts, 1991). The whole point of meta-analysis is that it reaches better conclusions than those reached in individual studies.

In astrology an effect size of, say 0.4, which is equivalent to 70% hits when 50% is expected by chance, would mean that birth charts can tell us something useful about people, albeit not very much. Similarly an effect size of, say 0.05 or 0.1, equivalent to 51% or 52% hits when 50% is expected by chance, would mean that birth charts are worthless except perhaps as a celestial inkblot test, even though it might still be evidence of something paranormal.[5] Effect sizes even closer to zero (we shall be seeing plenty of these) have an additional problem because the sample size required to reliably measure effect size r varies roughly as $1/r^2$, so one-tenth the effect size requires one hundred times the sample size. Furthermore they are sensitive to the assumption that zero effect sizes and perfect randomness can exist in real data (which assumption may not be justified, see Gilmore, 1987), and they are also sensitive to artifacts (something spurious that mimics a genuine effect).

Artifacts in Astrology

As shown by the other articles in this *JCS* issue, the controversy over psi is largely about artifacts, or whether the allegedly paranormal phenomena could have non-paranormal explanations. Artifacts in astrology, just as in parapsychology, can be surprisingly subtle and resistant to detection, compared to which the everyday hidden persuaders are child's play. Some examples follow below, some of which became famous in their day as the best claimed evidence for astrology.

A claimed correlation between planetary positions and radio propagation quality (Nelson, 1951) was due to the close but unequal spacing of planet days, which meant that the positions were bound to occur close to disturbed radio days

---

[5] We should not confuse a tiny *effect* with a tiny effect *size*. Although gravity has only a tiny effect on the bending of light, the effect size is 1, that is, if we know the gravity we can exactly predict the bending. Nor should we confuse contexts. A tiny but reliable effect size equivalent to 2% more hits than an expected 50% is of no use whatever if we wish to make accurate statements from a client's birth chart, but to a casino turning over millions of dollars a year it could mean the difference between profitability and ruin.

(Meeus, 1982; Martens and Trachet, 1998, pp. 174–9). Apparent support for astrology in the birth charts of married couples (Jung, 1960) arose because the charts had come from the files of an astrologer whose advice to the couples had nudged the sample into conformity; the effect did not replicate with artifact-free data (Dean, 1996). Claimed success in matching charts to case histories (Clark, 1961) was consistent with the use of tiny samples, typically ten birth charts, whose disproportionately huge sampling variations were mistaken for genuine effects (Eysenck and Nias, 1982, pp. 86–7), a point confirmed by later studies and meta-analysis (Dean, 1986). An apparent correlation between sun signs and extraversion (Mayo, White and Eysenck, 1978; Smithers and Cooper, 1978) disappeared in later studies when the subjects had no prior knowledge of astrology, which showed that prior knowledge can nudge a person's self-image in the direction of astrology (Eysenck and Nias, 1982, pp. 50–60; van Rooij, 1999). A tiny but consistent surplus or deficit of rising or culminating planets at the birth of eminent professional people in the nineteenth and early twentieth centuries (Gauquelin, 1983) was consistent with parents adjusting birth data to suit popular beliefs, which in those days could easily be done without detection (Dean, 2002). Many more examples could be cited.

The existence of artifacts does not deny the possibility of genuine effects. But unless research can confirm such effects when artifacts are controlled (which so far is not the case), we have good reason to suspend belief. Of course we can never be sure about failing to find tiny effect sizes of around 0.01, just as we can never be sure about failing to find whether surfing in Hawaii affects the waves in Australia; but we can be sure about failing to find effect sizes commensurate with astrological claims, say not less than 0.5, just as we can be sure about failing to find a cat in a shoebox.[6]

The above artifacts have effect sizes around 0.04 to 0.1, which are comparable with the effect sizes reported in parapsychology, albeit with ongoing controversy over their interpretation, for example 0.02 for throwing dice and guessing random numbers, 0.06 for distantly affecting skin conductivity, 0.08 for ESP, and 0.11 for telepathy under conditions of sensory deprivation (converted from the hit rates of Radin, 1997, pp. 141, 134, 154, 106, 88). So it is doubly essential to avoid artifacts in astrology lest they be seen as possible evidence for psi. Effect sizes in controversial areas that differ significantly from expectancy (in this case zero) must always raise worries about artifacts. In what follows we look first at the performance of astrology, for which the definitive test is time twins, and then at the performance of astrologers.

---

[6] An effect size commensurate with astrological claims can be estimated in two ways. Via astrologer estimates of chart accuracy, which translate to a mean of roughly 0.5 (Dean, 1986, p. 43), and via studies of people judging sets of data, which show that correlations have to exceed about 0.4 before they are detected by the average person (Jennings, Amabile and Ross, 1982; Oates, 1982). Even correlations around 0.7, which are considered strong by psychologists, are missed by one person in four. Only when correlations reach 0.85 are they detected by almost everyone. Astrologers claim to see correlations in every birth chart, so a commensurate effect size of not less than 0.5 does not seem unrealistic. Effect sizes are conspicuously absent from the writings of astrologers.

Time Twins, the Definitive Test of Astrology

Suppose that heavenly conditions correlate with earthly happenings to the strong extent claimed by most astrologers ('there is no area of human existence to which astrology cannot be applied' say Parker and Parker, 1975, p. 60). At one moment the heavens signify that people born at that moment will have trait *A*, the next moment it is trait *B*, and so on. Time twins (people born at the same moment) should therefore be more alike than expected by chance. Time twins are thus the definitive test of astrology because errors or uncertainties of birth chart interpretation are avoided.

How far apart can time twins be before they cease to be time twins? According to John Addey (1967), in perhaps the most extensive survey of time twins made by an astrologer, 'one would expect to find *really exceptional* [his emphasis] similarities of life and temperament only in those born almost exactly at the same time [within a few minutes] and in the same locality', nevertheless 'the tendency for similarities to appear in the lives of those born on the same day must remain strong and well worth investigating' (p. 14). So births more than a day apart might not qualify.

Time twins are surprisingly numerous. The spacing of human births in a large population is described by a Poisson distribution, which shows that every year in a city of one million people about 4,000 pairs of time twins are born 5 minutes apart or less. The number increases very rapidly as the city size or time interval increases; in a population of ten million the annual number of pairs is about 100,000, same as the number born 60 minutes apart or less in a population of one million. Increasing the interval to 24 hours pushes the total to many millions, but even this is only a tiny fraction of all possible birth pairs each year, which explains why the above survey by John Addey managed to locate only a few dozen pairs of time twins. Time twins are like needles in a haystack (there are very many needles but it is a huge haystack).

So time twins are not easy to find. Nevertheless the number of time twins that exist in Western history alone is so enormous (hundreds of millions or even more, depending on how time twins are defined) that many striking similarities in personality and events will occur by chance alone. Historically the most famous case is that of the prosperous London ironmonger Samuel Hemmings and King George III, said to have shared the same birth and death hours after lives showing many similarities such as being married on the same day. But chance is not the explanation here — a check of contemporary records showed that only the simultaneous death could be verified, and that the other events were most likely fabricated by astrologers (Dean, 1994).

Tests of Time Twins

The first systematic study of time twins was reported by British astrologers Peter Roberts and Helen Greengrass (1994). With help from the media they managed to collect a total of 128 people born on average just over an hour apart on six dates during 1934–1964, or 1% of the 13,000 people then being born every six days in the UK. After interviewing 17 born on the same day (which gave 18 pairs born one hour apart or less) they found some evidence of similarities in interests and occupation, for example two born 15 minutes apart were respectively a bassoon player and a clarinet player, but there were no clear similarities in appearance, handwriting, names or life events. The strong similarities predicted by astrology were simply not there. Nevertheless the authors claimed that, in the full sample of 128 people (which gave 1,400 pairs born one day apart or less), the proportion of 'close resemblers' increased as the birth interval decreased. This suggests that only a few percent of time twins are similar, which would nevertheless provide some support for astrology, albeit not as generally conceived by astrologers. However an independent re-analysis found that the effect was due to procedural artifacts (French, Leadbetter and Dean, 1997). When these artifacts were controlled, the effect disappeared, see Table 1.

	Original study (1994)				French *et al.* (1997)			
Mean hours between births	0.3	3.2	11.5	21.5	1.5	5.2	10.2	17.8
N = No of time twin pairs	98	493	688	121	360	341	352	347
Close resemblers, pairs	4	15	17	2	10	12	11	5
Close resemblers) as %	4.1	3.0	2.5	1.7	2.8	3.5	3.1	1.4
Next closest) of N	9.2	15.8	16.1	12.4	13.3	17.0	15.6	15.0

Table 1
A claimed astrological effect in 128 time twins born <1 day apart disappeared on re-analysis

Original analysis and re-analysis of Roberts and Greengrass's (1994) sample of 128 time twins, which gave 1,400 pairs of time twins born <1 day apart. **Left:** The claimed effect is in the fourth line — as the mean interval between births increases from 0.3 to 21.5 hours, the proportion of close resemblers (the most alike pairs*) decreases smoothly from 4.1% to 1.7% in the direction predicted by astrology. But the numbers underlying the 4.1% and 1.7% are much too small for comfort, and (last line) the effect is reversed for the next-closest resemblers, so the result might be a statistical artifact. **Right:** Suspicion confirmed. When the 1,400 pairs are re-analysed with less variable N's, the effect disappears and (last line) it stays that way. French *et al.* found it was no better for individual scores (*a, b, c* or *d*) or for tests of serial correlation.

* Close resemblers, 3% of the 1,400 pairs, are those with $\sqrt{(a^2+b^2+c^2+d^2)}<3$, where *abcd* are the scores (each out of 12) for extraversion, neuroticism (emotional stability), psychotisim (tough–tender), and social conformity on the short form Eysenck Personality Questionnaire (Eysenck, Eysenck and Barrett, 1985). The next closest, 15% of 1,400 pairs, are 3 to 4.9. For all 1,400 pairs the mean is 7.8, standard deviation 2.9.

A more powerful test was made possible by data from a study unconnected with astrology (Dean, forthcoming) involving 2,101 persons born in London during 3–9 March 1958. They were born on average 4.8 minutes apart, so they were precisely those for which Addey had predicted '*really exceptional* similarities of life and temperament'. Measurements at ages 11, 16 and 23 had provided for each person 110 relevant variables including test scores for IQ, reading and arithmetic; teacher and parent ratings of behaviour such as anxiety, aggressiveness and sociability; physical data such as height, weight, vision and hearing; self-ratings of ability such as art, music and sports; and various others such as occupation, accident proneness and marital status; all of which are supposed to be shown in the birth chart. Included as a control were sixteen variables for the mother such as age, blood pressure and length of labour; seven leading astrologers agreed unanimously that these sixteen variables would definitely not be shown in the birth chart of the child.

About 92% of birth times had been recorded to the nearest 5 minutes, the rest to the nearest minute. Before analysis the subjects were arranged in chronological order of birth. This gave 2,100 successive pairs of time twins; 73% were born 5 minutes apart or less, and only 4% were born more than 15 minutes apart. The similarity between time twins for each variable was then measured as the serial correlation between successive pairs *AB*, *BC*, *CD* and so on. Here serial correlation is a direct measure of effect size and is extremely sensitive due to the large sample size. Unlike the Roberts and Greengrass approach (count each time twin against every other time twin within one day, which would have produced nearly 600,000 pairs), serial correlation counts each time twin once only, thus minimizing the risk of artifacts. So the test conditions could hardly have been more conducive to success. But the results are uniformly negative, see Table 2. The effect size due to astrology is 0.00 ± 0.03.

The above result is consistent with empirical studies of signs, aspects and so on, which when free of artifacts have consistently failed to find effects commensurate with astrological claims (Eysenck and Nias, 1982; Culver and Ianna, 1984; Dean, Mather and Kelly, 1996; Martens and Trachet, 1998; Dean et al., 2002). It disconfirms the idea of sun signs (2,101 Pisceans evidently had few similarities) and Jung's idea of synchronicity. Here, however, such a result is actually good news, because if artifact-free tests of astrologers are found to give positive results it might suggest the existence of human abilities of interest to parapsychologists.

Source of variables	Variables N	Mean subjects	Serial correlation in original data and two controls					
			Original data		Randomized		Equated every	
			Mean	sd	Mean	sd	50th	25th
Mother	16	2066	0.001	0.029	−0.001	0.022	0.017	0.038
Subject	110	1393	−0.003	0.028	−0.001	0.028	0.018	0.036

Mean subjects is less than 2,101 due to missing data. Randomized means are for 2,000 replications.
Equated = every 50th or 25th subject is made the same as the next to simulate astrological effects.

Table 2
Astrological effects for 110 variables were not detectable in 2,101 time twins born 5 minutes apart

According to astrology the serial correlation in this data should be strongly positive for subject variables and zero for mother variables. But both **original** means are effectively zero. The difference (−0.004) is in the wrong direction and non-significant ($p = 0.56$ by t-test). Nor do the 110 individual serial correlations (not listed) show any support for astrology — 5 are significant at the $p = 0.05$ level vs 5.5 expected by chance. The **randomized** means and standard deviations agree with the expected values $-1/(s-1)$ and $1/\sqrt{s+1}$ respectively, where s is the number of subjects, so the data are well-behaved. There is nothing here that would deny the previous indication. Furthermore the **equated** means after equating every nth subject are in good agreement with the expected increase $1/n$, which confirms that the test is sensitive and working. A serial correlation of 0.001 is equivalent to getting 50.05% hits when 50% is expected by chance.

Tests of Astrologer Accuracy and Client Discrimination

Tests of astrologers can be divided into tests of accuracy, discrimination, agreement, intuition and confidence. In parapsychology, tests of accuracy (as in counting hits) are generally too insensitive to reliably detect weak effects, at least not without huge sample sizes, whereas tests of reaction time (as in recognizing words with and without someone else thinking about them) promise greater sensitivity (Hines, Lang and Seroussi, 1987). But interpreting a birth chart is not the same as recognizing words, so tests of reaction time seem inapplicable in astrology, at least as presently practised.

Tests of accuracy generally involve astrologers matching birth charts with information such as personality profiles or case histories. To date more than forty studies have been reported totalling nearly 700 astrologers and 1,150 birth charts. Meta-analysis gives a mean effect size of 0.051, standard deviation 0.118, for which $p = 0.66$. Visual plots indicate the existence of a publication bias against negative results, which probably accounts for the weak positive direction (Dean and Kelly, 2001, p. 198; Dean, Mather and Kelly, 1996, p. 76). There is clearly nothing here to suggest that astrologers can perform usefully better than chance, once hidden persuaders are controlled.

Tests of discrimination involve subjects picking their own chart interpretation from typically three to five others, all of which must be free of give-away cues such as dates and planetary positions. Selection can be biased by generality (the statement cannot fail to fit) and social desirability (we are generous, they are extravagant). But when each interpretation doubles as a control, as is usual, such biases tend to cancel out. To date ten studies totalling nearly 300 subjects have been reported in which give-away cues such as sun sign descriptions were reliably absent. Meta-analysis of first choices gives a mean effect size of 0.002, standard deviation 0.038 (Dean, Mather and Kelly, 1996, pp. 74–5). There is nothing here to suggest that your own chart interpretation fits you better than someone else's.

Tests of Astrologer Agreement

The failure of astrologers to get correct answers when reading birth charts under blind conditions could of course be the result of asking the wrong questions. (It could not, as some astrologers claim, be due to some property of astrology that makes it untestable by science, because this would immediately deny their experience that astrology works, just as our experience that a TV set works would be denied if we could not tell *works* from *does not work*.) However, correctness is irrelevant when testing agreement among astrologers, just as using feet or metres is irrelevant when testing agreement among surveyors. Because problems of correctness are avoided, tests of agreement are more straightforward than tests of accuracy. This is a valuable advantage.

To date twenty-five studies have been reported involving a total of nearly 500 astrologers. Meta-analysis gives a mean agreement (as an effect size) of 0.101, standard deviation 0.064 (Dean and Kelly, 2001, p. 200; Dean, Mather and Kelly,

1996, p. 78), which is essentially no agreement at all. By contrast, tests intended for application to individuals, as astrology traditionally is, are generally frowned upon by psychologists unless the agreement between test and re-test, or between one practitioner and another, is 0.8 or better. Perfect agreement would of course be 1. We say more on agreement later, under 'Tests of Astrologer Confidence'.

Tests of Reported Intuition

To date the most systematic investigation of astrologer variables including the reported use of intuition is that of Dean (1985), who had 45 astrologers from the USA, UK, Australia and Europe predict the direction (+ or –) of E and N in 160 extreme subjects as measured by the Eysenck Personality Inventory (Eysenck and Eysenck, 1964).[7] To make each direction clear-cut, the subjects were the top and bottom *fifteenths* from a sample of 1,198 students and ordinary people ranked by E or N score, which well exceeds the usual approach in psychology of taking the top and bottom *thirds*. Their mean age was 30 (range 15–66), 46% were university students, and 72% were female. Each extreme (E+, E–, N+, N–) had 40 subjects, total 160, of which 40 were E only, 40 were N only, and 80 were both E and N, so each astrologer had to make a total of 240 judgments. The mean score of the (+) extremes was typically 7 standard deviations from the mean score of the (–) extremes, so in each case the direction (+ or –) was exceptionally clear-cut. As in the previous test of time twins, the conditions could hardly have been more conducive to success. Some of the results were not reported in Dean (1985) and are published here for the first time.

On average the 45 astrologers had ten years of experience (range 1–36 years), spent nearly 5 minutes on each judgment (range 0.5–15), and were generally confident of success (only 21% of judgments were made with low confidence). But despite these encouraging signs, the mean effect size for hits was only 0.01, less than the 0.14 for judgments made using the subject's age (based on the slight decrease in E and N with increasing age, namely 'if over 35 years then E– and N–, else E+ and N+'); and less even than the 0.02 for 45 controls making the same judgments without birth charts, showing if anything that judgments were made worse by looking at birth charts. The reported use of intuition (or what astrologers saw as intuition) had no effect, see Table 3.

---

[7] This follows the convention among psychologists. E is extraversion (sociability) and N is neuroticism (emotional stability). N is not the same as *N* (in italics), which is the sample size. Both E and N exist as a continuum between (+) and (–). E+ is sociable and outgoing, E– is quiet and reserved. N+ is emotional and easily upset, N– is calm and not easily upset. (Also, later, P is psychoticism, where P+ is tough-minded and uncaring, P– is tender-minded and caring.) E and N were chosen because they are among the most major and enduring of known personality factors (Eysenck and Eysenck, 1985). Thus they emerge from personality and laboratory tests of all types, even those without E and N in mind; and they are found in all cultures including non-Western cultures. Furthermore they are visible in ancient personality descriptions such as the four temperaments (which match the astrological elements fire, earth, air and water), which makes them even more suitable for testing astrology. Indeed, in a separate survey, 86 astrologers had rated E and N as respectively easy and moderately easy to discern in birth charts (Dean, 1986, p. 20). Note how this fits the earlier 'sound research programme' of Carl Sargent, where he had suggested the testing of manifest anxiety (same as N) and extraversion (obviously the same as E), and the polling of astrologers.

Reported use of intuition	Number of astrologers	Effect size for hits and agreement			
		Is the subject an extreme (+) or (−)?			
		Extraversion		Neuroticism	
None	9	−0.00	0.12	0.02	0.04
Hardly any	16	0.01	0.17	0.03	0.05
Some	13	−0.01	0.17	−0.01	0.02
Lots	5	0.02	0.17	0.01	0.00
Hits, 1st vs 2nd half	45	−0.13	—	0.02	—

Table 3
Use of intuition did not improve judgments by 45 astrologers of E and N in 160 extreme subjects

First figure in each pair is the mean effect size for hits, second figure is the mean agreement between astrologers. Because both E and N are said to be easily discernible in birth charts, we expect good hits and agreement. But both are negligible. The agreement is slightly better for E, in keeping with its higher rated discernibility, but that is all. In the last line, contrary to what the use of intuition might predict, astrologers getting high scores for the first half of their judgments show no tendency to get high scores for the second half. With or without intuition, these astrologers could not tell one extreme from another. An effect size of 0.01 it equivalent to getting 50.5% hits when 50% is expected by chance.

Of course the reported use of intuition does not mean that intuition or psychic ability was genuinely present. Nevertheless a genuine presence might be most likely where judgments show good agreement. But when the judgments were ranked by agreement, the effect size for E hits was a negligible 0.01 for the top third (mean agreement 0.38), hardly different from −0.01 for the bottom third (mean agreement −0.01). The effect sizes for N hits were no better. Note that if astrology (or anything) is false, then it cannot provide valid data for unconscious processing, so any success would by definition be due to psychic ability rather than intuition.

Scores on the Eysenck Personality Questionnaire were available for 41 of the 45 participating astrologers. Those reporting use of intuition tended to be N+ (effect size 0.33, $p = 0.04$) and P+ (0.31, $p = 0.05$) but not especially E+ (0.02), whereas values of 0.15–0.20 are typically reported between E+ and apparent ESP performance (Utts, 1991, pp. 376–7). The correlation between time taken and perceived difficulty was surprisingly low (0.29, $p = 0.07$). Compared to the 15 male astrologers, the 26 female astrologers tended to be more N+ (0.25) and more P− (0.14), which is in accordance with previous gender findings (Eysenck and Eysenck, 1985). In accordance with the popular stereotype they also reported using more intuition, albeit only slightly (0.12). But in mean effect size for hits, females (0.01) hardly differed from males (−0.00).

Tests of Astrologer Confidence

If we have a genuine judgment skill, psychic or non-psychic, our accuracy should increase as our experience-based confidence increases. In the present study, each astrologer had indicated their confidence (high, medium, low) for each of their 240 judgments. But judgments made with high confidence were no more accurate than those made with low confidence, see Table 4. Judgments of the 80 subjects who were extreme on both E and N showed negligible correlation (0.02) between E hits and N hits, which correlation should exist even if astrology worked only for some people, but not if astrology did not work at all. By contrast, the correlation between E confidence and N confidence was highly significant (0.34, $p = 10^{-90}$), and persisted even when birth charts were not used (0.27, $p = 10^{-55}$), suggesting that it was more a product of the astrologers' imagination than of anything in the birth chart.

Rated confidence	Mean number of judgments	Effect size for hits and agreement			
		Is the subject an extreme (+) or (−)?			
		Extraversion		Neuroticism	
Low	1125	0.00	—	0.05	—
Medium	2430	0.03	—	0.02	—
High	1845	−0.02	—	−0.04	—
Mean agreement on confidence		—	0.02	—	0.00

Table 4
Confidence did not improve judgments by 45 astrologers of E and N in 160 extreme subjects

Same study as Table 3. All effect sizes are again negligible. We might expect effect size to increase with confidence but if anything it goes the other way, which is incompatible with these astrologers having valid judgment skills whether psychic or non-psychic. In the last line, the mean agreement on confidence is negligible, less even than the negligible mean agreement on judgments (which is 0.16 for E and 0.04 for N). When variables as fundamental as E and N produce consistently negligible effect sizes and agreement, it suggests there is no hope for more complex variables such as those that fill astrology books.

The above tests of agreement and confidence overcome any concerns about the validity of E and N for testing astrologers. Even if E and N were meaningless, this is of no consequence provided E and N are held to be discernible in birth charts — and the astrologers would hardly have proceeded if it were otherwise. The point is, we might conceivably explain away poor effect sizes for hits, but not poor agreement or the inconsequence of confidence. If astrologers cannot agree on what a birth chart indicates, or on their confidence in that indication, then what price astrology and the supposed intuitions of astrologers?

When Astrologers Receive Everything They Ask For

The same inconsequence of confidence was found in matching tests where the astrologers received everything they asked for. In an American test they received subjects with diverse backgrounds, certified birth times precise to 5 minutes or better, case files that included results from two personality tests, responses to their own 61-item questionnaire covering everything from height and hobbies to favourite colours and family deaths, and two photographs of the subject. Six professional astrologers selected for competence by their peers matched case file to birth chart for 23 subjects, all aged 30–32 years to avoid age cues, which took each astrologer 12–24 hours of work. Their confidence was generally high but the mean effect size for hits was a negligible 0.02 and the mean agreement between astrologers was an equally negligible 0.03. One non-astrologer tried the matchings and scored three hits, the same as the best astrologer (McGrew and McFall, 1990).

In a similar Dutch test involving seven birth charts, 5,000 Dutch guilders (about $US3,000) was offered to any astrologer who could successfully match all charts to their owners. Of the 44 astrologers who took the test, at least half had read more than one hundred charts and were very experienced, while one-third were frequently paid for their services. Half expected 100% hits and only six expected less than 60%, so again their confidence was high. But their mean effect size was –0.04, not even in the right direction, and the mean agreement between astrologers was 0.01. The best astrologer scored three hits, as did one non-astrologer (Nanninga, 1996).

In both of these tests the astrologers' confidence presumably included their confidence in intuition or spirits or psychic ability, whose role they would have maximized by their method of working. So the results allow no reason to suppose that astrology capitalizes on or focuses such influences, which (if they exist) would seem to be either very weak or very rare. This does not deny the possibility that shaman-type superstars may exist as cited under 'Parallels with Shamanism', but until they come forward for testing we should remain sceptical.[8]

Support for such a view is provided by the Dutch parapsychologist Hendricus Boerenkamp (1988). He monitored a total of more than 130 readings by twelve of the Netherland's top psychics, and then rated their accuracy against matched groups of non-psychics who were given the same task as the psychics. Typically each reading involved 60–90 statements spread over personality (35%), general circumstances including occupation (25%), relationships (15%) and physical matters such as health (25%), much the same as for a typical astrology reading. Nearly 10,000 statements were obtained, of which 10% were sufficiently specific to be tested, of which 14% turned out to be correct; that is, only 1.4% of all

[8] Is there a sidereal connection? Spottiswoode (1997) looked at the location and start time of all available remote viewing and ganzfeld trials. The effect size showed a reproducible four-fold peak within a two-hour window centred on 13.5 hours local sidereal time, which is roughly when the constellation Virgo (or tropical sign Libra) is overhead. Are emanations, or lack of them, from Virgo/Libra causing something? (An astrologer might ask why Libra and not Pisces, the sign usually connected with intuition and psychic ability.) But if the Spottiswoode effect is real, and if astrologers are as psychic and as attuned to the stars as they claim, we might expect the effect to have entered astrological tradition, say as a rule that urges astrologers to work only when Virgo/Libra is overhead. But we found no hint of such a rule in astrology books. For example, in his 850-page *Christian Astrology*, the renowned British astrologer William Lilly (1659/1985) gives students detailed advice on chart interpretation 'and whatever else is fit for the Learner to know before he enter upon judgment'. His advice includes the need to be mentally prepared: 'be thou humble . . . form thy minde according to the image of Divinity', which of course may merely reflect his need to escape censure by showing how astrology was compatible with Christianity (hence his title). But he says nothing about the best time to 'enter upon judgment', even though his reputed success in horary astrology might imply a psychic ability potentially open to Spottiswoode effects. In fact his practice would have been much too busy to allow restricting it to the 2 or 3 hours in every 24 when Virgo/Libra was overhead.

statements were both specific and correct, and for every such statement there were six that were both specific and incorrect. Unknown to the psychics, the same person was sometimes the target in two successive readings, but no psychic noticed it, and the second reading was often in conflict with the first. Furthermore there was no appreciable difference in hit rate between psychics and non-psychics, which would seem to deny that psychic ability (or at least claimed psychic ability) could play a role in astrology. Boerenkamp concluded that the accuracy of psychics was no better than that of non-psychics, but their sensitivity to human ills and their huge experience (their own lives were often traumatic) made them useful counsellors.

Conclusion

Our concern in this article has been to measure the performance of astrology and astrologers. A large-scale test of time twins involving more than one hundred cognitive, behavioural, physical and other variables found no hint of support for the claims of astrology. Consequently, if astrologers could perform better than chance, this might support their claim that reading specifics from birth charts depends on psychic ability and a transcendent reality related to consciousness. But tests incomparably more powerful than those available to the ancients have failed to find effect sizes beyond those due to non-astrological factors such as statistical artifacts and inferential biases. The possibility that astrology might be relevant to consciousness and psi is not denied, but if psychic or spirit influences exist in astrology, they would seem to be very weak or very rare. Support for psychic claims seems unlikely.

References

Articles marked with an asterisk are available at http://www.astrology-and-science.com/ as either an extended abstract (*) or an expanded article (**).

Addey, J. (1967), 'Astrological twins', *Astrological Journal*, **9** (1), pp. 14–29.

Addey, J.M. (1996), *A New Study of Astrology* (London: Urania Trust).

Alcock, J.E. (1987), 'Parapsychology: science of the anomalous or search for the soul?', *Behavioural and Brain Sciences*, **10**, pp. 553–65.

Alcock, J.E. (1990), *Science and Supernature: A Critical Appraisal of Parapsychology* (Amherst, NY: Prometheus Books).

Alexander, R. (1983), *The Astrology of Choice* (New York: Weiser).

Ankerberg, J. and Weldon, J. (1989), *Astrology: Do the Heavens Rule Our Destiny?* (Eugene, OR: Harvest House). With 350 references. Excellent critique by Bible scholars who have done their homework.

Aphek, E. and Tobin, Y. (1989), *The Semiotics of Fortune-Telling* (Amsterdam: Benjamins).

Behavioural and Brain Sciences (1987), **10**. Target papers on psi by Rao and Palmer (pp. 539–51) and Alcock (pp. 553–65) with nearly 50 commentaries (pp. 566–643 and 1990, **13**, pp. 383–91).

Beloff, J. (1994), 'Minds and machines: a radical dualist perspective', *Journal of Consciousness Studies*, **1** (1), pp. 32–7. With a rejoinder by Bierman, D.J., in 1996, **3** (5–6), pp. 515–16.

Beyerstein, B. (1987), 'Neuroscience and psi-ence', *Behavioural and Brain Science*, **10**, pp. 571–2.

Boerenkamp, H.G. (1988), *A Study of Paranormal Impressions of Psychics* (The Hague: CIP-Gegevens Koninklijke). Also published in *European Journal of Parapsychology* from 1983 to 1987.

Burgoyne, T.H. (1889/1982), *The Light of Egypt or the Science of the Soul and the Stars* (Albuquerque, NM: Sun Publishing, 2 vols.).

Carter, C.E.O. (1925), *The Principles of Astrology* (London: Theosophical Publishing House).

Clark, V. (1961), 'Experimental astrology', *In Search*, Spring, pp. 101–12.

Clow, B.H. (1988), *Chiron: Rainbow Bridge Between Inner and Outer Planets* (St Paul, MN: Llewellyn).

Cornelius, G. (1994), *The Moment of Astrology* (Penguin Arkana).

Correlation (1994–8)*, Target papers and commentaries on crucial issues in astrology research, **13** (1), pp. 10–53; **14** (2), pp. 32–44; **15** (1), pp. 17–52; **17** (2), pp. 24–71. The first is on the relevance of science to astrology, with 33 commentaries. For back issues, email astrological.association@zetnet.co.uk

Culver, R.B. and Ianna, P.A. (1984), *The Gemini Syndrome: A Scientific Evaluation of Astrology* (Amherst, NY: Prometheus Books). With 280 references. A clear and very readable critique by astronomers with much useful information including their classic survey of 3,011 astrological predictions.

Dean, G. (1983), 'Can self-attribution explain sun-sign guessing?', *Correlation*, **3** (2), pp. 22–7.

Dean, G. (1985), 'Can astrology predict E and N? 2: the whole chart', *Correlation*, **5** (2), pp. 2–24. The findings have been summarized by Martens and Trachet (1998), pp. 193–6, who describe the study as 'unequalled in its range, carefulness, thoroughness, and extensiveness' (p. 192).

Dean, G. (1986), 'Can astrology predict E and N? 3: discussion and further research', *Correlation*, **6** (2), pp. 7–52. With 110 references. Includes meta-analyses of astrological studies.

Dean, G. (1987), 'Does astrology need to be true? Part 2', *Skeptical Inquirer*, **11** (3), pp. 257–73.

Dean, G. (1994), 'Samuel Hemmings and George III', *Correlation*, **13** (2), pp. 17–30 and **14** (2), pp. 23–7. An abstract is available on www.astrology-research.net

Dean, G. (1996), 'A re-assessment of Jung's astrological experiment', *Correlation*, **14** (2), pp. 12–22.

Dean, G. (1998), 'Meaningful coincidences: parallels between phrenology and astrology', *Correlation*, **17** (1), pp. 9–40. With 70 references. Includes a detailed look at validity.

Dean, G. (2002)*, 'Is the Mars effect a social effect?', *Skeptical Inquirer*, **26** (3), pp. 33–8. See also **27** (1), pp. 57–9, 65 for a critique and rejoinder.

Dean, G. (forthcoming), 'Does birth induction affect the subsequent life?'.

Dean, G. and Kelly, I.W. (2001), 'Does astrology work? Astrology and skepticism 1975–2000', in *Skeptical Odysseys*, ed. P. Kurtz (Amherst, NY: Prometheus Books, pp. 191–207). Reviews the progress of research into astrology since 1975. Includes meta-analyses, effect size comparisons and artifacts.

Dean, G., Kelly, I.W. and Mather, A. (1999), 'Astrology and human judgment [cognitive and perceptual biases]', *Correlation*, **17** (2), pp. 24–71. A comprehensive review with 160 references.

Dean, G., Kelly, I.W., Smit, R. and Mather, A. (2002), 'Astrology' and 'Sun sign astrology', in *The Skeptic Encyclopedia of Pseudoscience*, ed. M. Shermer (Chicago: ABC-CLIO). For the general reader.

Dean, G., Loptson, P. and Kelly, I.W. (1996), 'Theories of astrology', *Correlation*, **15** (1). pp. 17–52. A comprehensive review with 84 references. Includes Jung's synchronicity.

Dean, G. and Mather, A. (1996)**, 'Sun sign columns: an armchair invitation', *Astrological Journal*, **38**, pp. 143–55. Includes history of sun sign columns, results of tests and views of astrologers.

Dean, G. and Mather, A. (2000)**, 'Sun sign columns: response to an invitation', *Skeptical Inquirer*, **24** (5), pp. 36–40. A follow-up to the previous reference.

Dean, G., Mather, A. and Kelly, I.W. (1996), 'Astrology', in *The Encyclopedia of the Paranormal*, ed. G. Stein (Amherst, NY: Prometheus Books), pp. 47–99. A comprehensive scientific survey with 15 secondary references. Includes meta-analyses, effect size comparisons and artifacts.

Doane, R.C. (1956), *Astrology 30 Years Research* (Hollywood, CA: Professional Astrologers).

Dobyns, Z.P. and Roof, N. (1973), *The Astrologer's Casebook* (Los Angeles: TIA Publications).

Elliot, R. (1974), 'Astrology and the psychic faculty', *Astrological Journal*, **16** (3), pp. 12–17.

Evans, J. (1979), *Twelve Doors to the Soul: Astrology of the Inner Self* (Wheaton, IL: Theosophical Publishing House).

Eysenck, H.J. (1995), *Genius: The Natural History of Creativity* (Cambridge: Cambridge University Press).

Eysenck, H.J. and Eysenck, S.B.G. (1964), *Manual of the Eysenck Personality Inventory* (London: University of London Press). 1968 update (San Diego, CA: Educational and Industrial Testing Service).

Eysenck, H.J. and Eysenck, M.W. (1985), *Personality and Individual Differences: A Natural Science Approach* (New York: Plenum). With 1,200 references. Readable, very relevant to testing astrology.

Eysenck, H.J. and Nias, D.K.B. (1982), *Astrology Science or Superstition?* (New York: St Martin's Press). Also a Pelican paperback (1984). With 230 references. Clear, sympathetic and very readable critique by psychologists. Somewhat dated but still valid, later research tends to be even more negative.

Eysenck, S.B.J., Eysenck, H.J. and Barrett, P. (1985), 'A revised version of the psychoticism scale', *Personality and Individual Differences*, **6**, pp. 21–9. Includes the short form EPQ.

Freeman, W.J. and Núñez, R. (1999), 'Restoring to cognition the forgotten primacy of action, intention and emotion', *Journal of Consciousness Studies*, **6** (11–12), pp. ix–xix.

French, C.C., Leadbetter, A. and Dean, G. (1997), 'The astrology of time twins: a re-analysis', *Journal of Scientific Exploration*, **11** (2), pp. 147–55, with comments through p. 161.

Freud, S. (1921/1955), 'Psychoanalysis and telepathy', in *The Standard Edition of the Complete Psychological Works of Sigmund Freud*, ed. J. Strachey (London: Hogarth Press and the Institute of Psycho-Analysis), Vol. 18, pp. 173–94.

Gammon, M.H. (1973), *Astrology and the Edgar Cayce Readings* (Virginia Beach, VA: ARE Press).

Gauquelin, F. (1987), 'How Guy de Penguern's medical predictions came out', *Astro-Psychological Problems*, **5** (2), pp. 10–14.

Gauquelin, M. (1983), *The Truth about Astrology* (Oxford: Blackwell).

Gilmore, J.B. (1987), 'Axioms in science, classical statistics, and parapsychological research', *Behavioural and Brain Science*, **10**, pp. 577–81.

Gilovich, T. and Savitsky, K. (1996), 'Like goes with like: the role of representativeness in erroneous and pseudoscientific beliefs', *Skeptical Inquirer*, **20** (2), pp. 34–40.

Harvey, C. (1994), Book Review of Cornelius (1994), *Astrological Journal*, **36**, pp. 396–8.

Harvey, C. and Harvey, S. (1999), *Principles of Astrology* (London: Thorsons).

Hines, T.M., Lang, P. and Seroussi, K. (1987), 'Extrasensory perception examined using a reaction-time measure', *Perceptual and Motor Skills*, **64**, pp. 499–502.

Hodgson, J. (1978), *Reincarnation Through the Zodiac* (Reno, NV: CRCS Publications).

Hyman, R. (1977), 'Cold reading: how to convince strangers that you know all about them', *The Zetetic* (now *Skeptical Inquirer*), **1** (2), pp. 18–37.

Hyman, R. (2003), 'How not to test mediums', *Skeptical Inquirer* **27** (1), pp. 20–30. Hyman has devoted more than half a century to the study of psychic and other readings, and why they can seem so compelling.

Ianna, P.A. and Tolbert, C.R. (1984), 'A retest of astrologer John McCall', *Skeptical Inquirer*, **9**, pp. 167–70. Hits were at chance level in matching appearance to birth time, the same as in an earlier test.

Jennings, D.L., Amabile, T.M. and Ross, L. (1982), 'Informal covariation assessment: data-based versus theory-based judgments', in *Judgment under Uncertainty: Heuristics and Biases*, ed. D. Kahneman, P. Slovic and A. Tversky (New York: Cambridge University Press, pp. 211–38).

Jung, C.G. (1960), 'The structure and dynamics of the psyche', in *The Collected Works of C.G. Jung*, ed. H. Read, M. Fordham and G. Adler (London: Routledge & Kegan Paul), Vol. 8, pp. 459–84.

Keen, G. (1988), in *Spiritual, Metaphysical and New Trends in Modern Astrology*, ed. J. McEvers (St Paul, MN: Llewellyn).

Kelly, I.W. (1997)**, 'Modern astrology: a critique', *Psychological Reports*, **81**, pp. 1035–66. With 131 references. Includes a brief survey and listing of major critical works.

Kelly, I.W. (1998), 'Why astrology doesn't work', *Psychological Reports*, **82**, pp. 527–46. 58 references.

Kirkland, K. (2000), 'Paraneuroscience?', *Skeptical Inquirer*, **24** (3), pp. 40–3.

Krippner, S. (2000), 'The epistemology and technologies of shamanic states of consciousness', *Journal of Consciousness Studies*, **7** (11–12), pp. 93–118.

Lee, D. (1964), 'Impact of ESP on astrology', *Astrological Review*, **36** (2), pp. 12–17 and **37** (2), pp. 9–16. Two later articles in **38** (2) and **39** (2) are much less informative.

Lilly, W. (1659/1985), *Christian Astrology* (London: Regulus).

Martens, R. and Trachet, T. (1998), *Making Sense of Astrology* (Amherst, NY: Prometheus Books). Very readable, includes studies published since the review by Eysenck and Nias (1982).

Majo, J. (1964), *Teach Yourself Astrology* (London: Teach Yourself Books).

Mayo, J., White, O. and Eysenck, H.J. (1978), 'An empirical study of the relation between astrological factors and personality', *Journal of Social Psychology*, **105**, pp. 229–36.

McGrew, J.H. and McFall, R.M. (1990), 'A scientific inquiry into the validity of astrology', *Journal of Scientific Exploration*, **4**, pp. 75–84. Further details appear in *Correlation* (1992), **11** (2), pp. 2–10.

Meeus, J. (1982), 'On the "correlation" between radio disturbance and planetary positions', *Skeptical Inquirer*, **6** (4), pp. 30–3.

Metzner, R. (1971), *Maps of Consciousness* (New York: Collier).

Miller, R. (2002), 'Hugo Gernsback, skeptical crusader', *Skeptical Inquirer*, **26** (6), pp. 35–9. Gernsback used his many popular magazines to challenge all kinds of pseudoscientific beliefs including astrology.

Moore, M. (1960), *Astrology Today: A Socio-Psychological Survey*, Astrological Research Associates Research Bulletin No. 2 (New York: Lucis).

Moore, M. and Douglas, M. (1971), *Astrology, The Divine Science* (York Harbor, ME: Arcane).

Myers, D.G. (2002), *Intuition: Its Powers and Perils* (New Haven, CT: Yale University Press).

Nanninga, R. (1996), 'The astrotest: a tough match for astrologers', *Correlation*, **15** (2), pp. 14–20. Followed by J. van Rooij, 'Astrologers failing the astrotest: an analysis', pp. 21–5.

Nelson, J.H. (1951), 'Shortwave radio propagation correlation with planetary positions', *RCA Review*, March, pp. 26–34.

Oates, M. (1982), 'Intuiting Strength of Association from a Correlation Coefficient', *British Journal of Psychology*, **73**, pp. 51–6.

Parker, D. (1991), Book Review, *Astrological Journal*, **33**, pp. 264–5.

Parker, D. and Parker, J. (1975), *The Compleat Astrologer* (London: Mitchell Beazley).

Phillipson, G. (2000), *Astrology in the Year Zero* (London: Flare Publications). With 135 references including 32 critical works. Explores issues via interviews with astrologers and (**) scientific researchers. The best single source of in-depth views from both sides. The only book of its kind.

Prince, W. (1930), Address, *Proceedings of the Society for Psychical Research*, **39**, pp. 273–304.

Radin, D.I. (1997), *The Conscious Universe* (San Francisco: Harper Edge).

Roberts, P. and Greengrass, H. (1994), *The Astrology of Time Twins* (Bishop Auckland: Pentland Press).

Sargent, C. (1986), 'Parapsychology and astrology', in *Hans Eysenck: Consensus and Controversy*, ed. S. Modgil and C. Modgil (Lewes: Falmer Press), pp. 339–55.

Smithers, A.G. and Cooper, H.J. (1978), 'Personality and season of birth', *Journal of Social Psychology*, **105**, pp. 237–41. Findings support those of the immediately preceding study by Mayo *et al.* (1978).

Spencer, N. (2000), *True as the Stars Above: Adventures in Modern Astrology* (London: Gollancz).

Spottiswoode, S.J.P. (1997), 'Association between effect size in free response anomalous cognition experiments and local sidereal time', *Journal of Scientific Exploration*, **11**, pp. 109–22.

Steiner, R.A. (1989), *Don't Get Taken! Bunco and Bunkum Exposed: How to Protect Yourself* (El Cerrito, CA: Wide-Awake Books). A critical look at hokum and confidence tricks.

Strohmer, C.R. (1988), *What Your Horoscope Doesn't Tell You* (Wheaton, IL: Tyndale House).

Utts, J. (1991), 'Replication and meta-analysis in parapsychology', *Statistical Science*, **6**, pp. 363–403.

van Rooij, J.J. (1999), 'Self-concept in terms of astrological sun-sign traits', *Psychological Reports*, **84**, pp. 541–6. With 14 references. Confirms the effect of sun-sign knowledge on self-concept.

Vaughan, A. (1973), *Patterns of Prophecy* (New York: Hawthorn).

Zusne, L. and Jones, W. (1989), *Anomalistic Psychology: A Study of Magical Thinking*, 2nd edn. (Hillsdale, NJ: Erlbaum).

Fotini Pallikari

Must the 'Magic' of Psychokinesis Hinder Precise Scientific Measurement?

Abstract: *Although evidential reports of paranormal phenomena (psi for short) have been accumulating over the last 50 years, scepticism within the scientific community at large against the very existence of psi has not retreated in proportion. Strong criticism has been voiced and it is worth taking it under serious consideration while attempting to understand psi. This article reviews the micro-psychokinesis phenomenon, aiming to reconcile evidence that favours it with other evidence that seems to refute it. To achieve this challenging task, some seemingly irrelevant observations will be invoked — such as the often observed decline and differential effects, the ten-year-old statistical balancing effect, the longstanding reports for the experimental evidence of PK, the recent large-scale failure to replicate the conventional PK hypothesis — alongside the austere arguments against PK. This paper argues that the evidence can withstand this serious criticism.*

I: Introduction: The Micro-PK Hypothesis

Psychokinesis, or PK for short, describes the ability to mentally modulate a physical system by intention or volition alone (Glossary, 2001). The physical system can be either a macroscopic object, in which cases we refer to macro-PK, or a probabilistic system consisting of the outcomes of a random process, in which case the phenomenon is termed micro-PK. According to the conventional hypothesis of micro-PK volition, focussed intention modulates the probabilistic system by shifting the process' statistical average off the value expected by chance. This microscopic effect is assumed to become amplified enough to produce macroscopic effects, as in macro-PK, causing the movement of objects by thought alone.

This assertion not only challenges our everyday experience of a solid, concrete world around us — objects do not fly around by wish alone — but also contradicts the observations of the majority of experimental scientists, one of whom is the author. Physical constants can still be measured with an ever-increasing

Correspondence: F. Pallikari, Physics Dept, Athens University, Panepistimiopolis, Zografos, Athens 15784, Greece. *Email: fpallik@phys.uoa.gr*

Journal of Consciousness Studies, **10**, No. 6–7, 2003, pp. 199–219

accuracy even if they may be found to change over very long periods of time and geographical coordinates. Precise experimental measurements are still possible (Anderson, 1991) in well-calibrated, controlled and repeatable experiments.

It is a fact that there is still no generally accepted theory to predict conscious-ness-related anomalies such as micro-PK, regardless of some attempts in that direction (Josephson & Pallikari, 1991; Oteri, 1975; Stapp, 1994). This may be one of the main reasons why the scepticism against micro-PK has not retreated in proportion to the claimed accumulating evidence over the last 50 years (Jahn, 1982; Radin & Nelson, 2002). A prediction-making theory, or a model, that describes physical reality, while taking into account some element of conscious-ness in its gears, would help to alleviate the obvious discrepancy: perceiving physical reality through consciousness while excluding consciousness from the scientific framework that it describes so accurately. As Erwin Schrödinger pointed out many years ago (Schrödinger, 1958, p. 37):

> Without being aware of it and without being rigorously systematic about it, we exclude the subject of Cognizance from the domain of nature that we endeavour to understand.

In recent years, within the biomedical and psychological sciences, the use of meta-analyses has become a valuable and widespread instrument for the study of contradictory evidence regarding single studies of poor repeatability. The same applies apparently to the experimental evidence regarding micro-PK. Two of these meta-analyses (Radin, 1997; Radin & Nelson, 2002) have given evidence in favour of the conventional micro-PK hypothesis. They report all known stud-ies with random-number generators done since 1959. These comprise an unbal-anced contribution of 515 micro-PK experiments and only 235 related control studies. The authors claim that the evidence in favour of PK reaches an incredi-bly high significance, namely a probability $1:10^{50}$, that the result was achieved by just pure chance. A third, most recent meta-analysis also concludes in favour of the micro-PK hypothesis, however, reporting a much weaker strength of effect (Steinkamp et al., 2002). A weakening of observed effect with newer analyses may, however, make the issue of repeatability and prediction questionable. Pre-diction is indeed the key word that would give credibility to the phenomenon (Gell-Mann, 1994, p. 78).

When it comes to assessing the possibility of an effect one must look at all evi-dence, not only that in its favour but also (perhaps especially, according to falsificationists) against it. Useful information may be gained even from appar-ent failures to replicate the conventional PK hypothesis. If an effect is real, what causes it sometimes to make itself apparent, i.e., mean shifts to be observed in sampled RNG outcomes in the direction of intention (Jahn, 1982), yet at other times fail to register, i.e., sampling distributions of RNG outcomes conform within chance expectation (Jahn et al., 2000), although experimenters have used identical protocols to generate similar large databases? A number of possible biases could either show an apparent micro-PK effect, although no effect actu-ally exists; or, alternatively, intensify an existent effect that is weak; for example,

(a) the number of runs are not fixed in advance,[1] (b) different PK-RNG machines are used, (c) most significant results obtained by one operator, (d) data selection and optional stopping are employed, (e) no measures are taken against data tampering.[2] We can return to this discussion later, but we can note in passing that although possibility (e) cannot be excluded it seems unlikely to explain away the effect, as this condition would accompany failures as well as successes.

One may naturally ask if a micro-PK effect exists when it fails to replicate its conventional hypothesis within a very large database. It may be premature, nonetheless, to conclude that it does not, simply because the conventional hypothesis — that volition alters the long-run statistics of random processes — may have been formulated incorrectly in the first place.

This article will deal with the case of micro-PK and try to weigh the claims in its favour alongside the major scientific arguments against it. It will reflect on the possibility that common ground may be found, fruitfully reconciling the two opposed positions. If one follows all the evidence in favour of PK while respecting the serious criticism against it, a surprisingly new light may be shed on the question 'what is the mechanism of micro-PK?'

II: Statistical Balancing in Micro-PK

One approach towards the understanding of the micro-PK mechanism, originated some twelve years ago, is statistical balancing, which will be presented in this section. Micro-PK experiments carried out by the author during the years

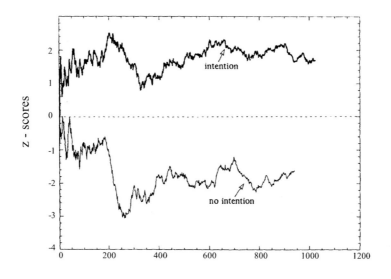

Figure 1

A plot of z values in bipolar tests against sample size. (Pallikari-Viras, 1997). Details in text.

---

[1] In the Princeton Engineering Anomalies Research (PEAR) database the number of trials per run is fixed in advance.

[2] For an extended review on experimental biases, see Alcock (1987; 1990).

1990–92 using Helmut Schmidt random number generator (RNG) machines (for an overview see Schmidt, 1974) have registered the following peculiar result. Generated data that were pooled according to the condition of mental effort to influence the statistical outcome of the RNG machine exhibited a positive deviation of the statistical mean from the expected chance value (Pallikari, 1998). On the other hand, pooled data generated within a couple of minutes after and sometimes before those sessions in an interspersed fashion and under exactly the same conditions (mode of operation and number of generated data) except for avoiding the psychological condition to consciously attempt to influence, also exhibited a mean shift from chance but in the opposite direction. In other words, the magnitude of the two z-scores in this binary experiment were numbers of opposite sign, a situation that was maintained as the size of sets grew up to several thousand data in each group, and even reached what is considered to be a statistically significant value: see Figure 1. Adding more data to each pool by consecutive sessions has had the result (apparently unfortunate for the psi hypothesis) of decreasing the magnitude of the two z-scores symmetrically down to statistically non-significant values. It was this bizarre observation that motivated the author to search in the parapsychology literature to learn if other researchers had come across it, and also to establish if mathematics and physics provided a ready explanation for this effect, that appeared at first sight to be a trivial one. Note that we are not seeing a straightforward random walk, which tends to bring cumulative anomalies back to the mean. These data show that if values *rise* significantly in the experimental condition, they tend to *fall* significantly in the control condition, and vice versa.

The bizarre effect was termed by the author 'Statistical Balancing' due to its function of rendering to chance level any deviations from the mean that may have been observed in one half of the data set. The search into the literature of parapsychology revealed that this statistical balancing effect indeed exhibited distinct similarities with previously reported PK research results, noted below as (A), (B) and (C).

(A) The decline effect: In one of Rhine's many reports on the decline effect he states (Rhine, 1969, p. 2):

> if he is able to do so [psi hitting] for a time, this can well be followed by a period of missing that will cancel his earlier gains.

Psi-missing, a tendency to score below chance, would set out around the middle of a long run to render the overall score to chance and erase the previous psi-hitting success (Rhine, 1971, p. 113):

> ... it was found that under certain conditions the subject would consistently score below the chance average. When showing such a trend he would go about as far below 'chance' as he had normally gone above.

and in Rhine's textbook of parapsychology (Rhine & Pratt, 1957, p. 90):

> It has indeed created disruptively abnormal effects for the parapsychologist; as for example when a subject participating in long runs of trials develops at the mid-point or thereabouts (as some have done) a sort of cumulative strain that induces a psi-missing tendency for the rest of the run. The score total will be dismissed as a

chance result, yet there may well be a highly significant decline distribution within the run.

It is worth noting that Rhine realised the importance of his finding yet he could not attribute to it a psychological explanation, such as tiredness or boredom. He writes (Rhine, 1969, p. 18):

> Probably to understand what goes wrong in psi-missing will bring us closer to grasping what goes right in psi-hitting

and also (Rhine, 1969, p. 6):

> The negative motivation idea, however, did not last long as a general hypothesis of what causes negative deviations.

The decline effect was accompanied by a reduction of variance and it is worth quoting Rhine again because we shall refer to this later (Rhine, 1969, p. 27):

> Moreover, the very idea of significantly small variance (i.e., very little fluctuation of scores) as an experimentally induced effect is a challenging one.

Opposite to Rhine's own opinion, a more recent study of the decline effect attributes mainly a psychological cause to it (Dunne et al., 1994).

(B) The differential effect (Rao, 1965): When people were asked to produce a PK effect in two different conditions (perhaps with two types of targets that were being compared or two test conditions) they tend to score above chance in the one (psi-hitting) and below chance in the other (psi-missing). The result of this would be that the overall effect was null.

(C) Within the large PK-RNG database of the Princeton Engineering Anomalies Research (PEAR) it was observed that when all PK-intention data (PK^+, PK^-) were analyzed together with no-intention data (baseline, as they are termed) they yielded the theoretically expected Gaussian curve, even if the statistical mean of each of the two separate distributions of PK-intention data were shifted from their chance expectation value (Jahn & Dunne, 1987). The interpretation given for this 'fascinating and suggestive feature of the data', as the authors admit, is clearly indicative of a statistical balancing underway which supports the interpretation that will be attempted here. They actually state (Jahn & Dunne, 1987, p. 119):

> In other words, without deforming the global chance behavior of their total results, the operators somehow dispose the system to correlate subsets of the output scores with their intentions.

Statistical balancing has also been observed in experiments performed independently. Since the time it was first presented by the author, there have been similar reports of it in quite diverse circumstances (Bierman & Van Gelderen, 1994; Houtkooper, 2002), while on a couple of occasions observations of statistical balancing were privately communicated to the author that have not appeared in publication, to the best of the author's knowledge. It seems worthwhile combining all this diverse evidence into a workable hypothesis, one that accords with our current scientific framework. The hypothesis will be derived from the field of science with which the author is familiar — physics. It is, however, acknowledged that a psychologist would be more inclined to give a solely psychological interpretation to the evidence of statistical balancing, which is idiosyncratic to some individuals (Dunne *et al.*, 1994). The psychology of the operators should be relevant to the understanding of this mind–matter problem, yet if the understanding of mind requires psychology, to understand the behaviour of a physical system requires a physical theory. But before a physical explanation is attempted, it is pertinent to give a brief outline of the results of a fractal analysis of PK-RNG data, which will shed quite a different light on the problem.

III: Fractal Analysis of PK-RNG Data

A better picture of a potential micro-PK mechanism was realized through the additional information obtained from a fractal analysis of the PK-REG time series. The central theme of this section will be this alternative data analysis. The author subjected two micro-PK datasets to the rescaled range, or R/S, fractal analysis. The datasets were generated over two different experiments, one carried out by the author using Helmut Schmidt machines (Pallikari & Boller, 1999) and the other (Pallikari *et al.*, 2000; Pallikari, 2001) on part of the data within a

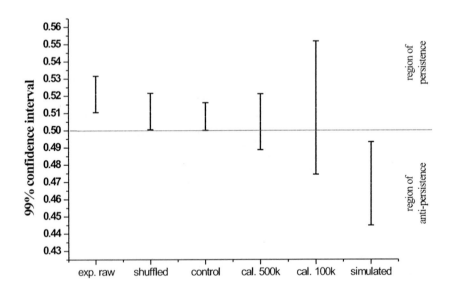

Figure 2

A graph displaying the results of the Hurst analysis of PK-data (PEAR replication experiment, Pallikari *et al.*, 2000) as confidence intervals within which the Hurst exponents of five PK datasets lie at a probability of 99%. The horizontal line at 0.5 divides the graph into two regions: a region of persistent long-range correlations (H > 0.5) and a region of anti-persistent long-range correlations (H < 0.5). Experimental PK data display clear persistence, which they lose after being shuffled. The control and the two calibration data sequences (of 500,000 and 100,000 units) are random sequences (H = 0.5). Finally, computer-simulated random sequences display clear anti-persistent long-range correlations. See also Table 1. (Pallikari, 2000)

File	H	99% Confidence Interval	df	σ_H
Experimental raw 450,000	0,521	0.510 to 0.532	62	0,004
Experimental shuffled 450,000	0,511	0.500 to 0.522	62	0,004
Control 450,000	0,508	0.500 to 0.516	62	0,003
Calibration 500,000	0,505	0.489 to 0.521	37	0,006
Calibration 100,000	0,513	0.474 to 0.552	28	0,014
Simulated[3] 450,000	0,469	0.455 to 0.493	5	0,006

Table 1

Hurst exponents, confidence intervals, degrees of freedom and associated standard deviation values as plotted in Figure 1 (PEAR replication experiment, Pallikari *et al.*, 2000). According to Hurst theory the Hurst exponent for random data is $H = 0.5$.

very large dataset generated in order to replicate the old PEAR results (Jahn *et al.*, 2000).

Hurst first introduced the rescaled range technique, R/S, some fifty years ago. It has since then been extensively applied by a large number of independent researchers in the search for hidden long-run and short-run correlations in time series of records of natural phenomena, in a vast variety of the fields of science. The R/S analysis is indeed considered as a very sensitive tool for such a purpose (Gammel, 1998).

Applied on PK-RNG data, the R/S analysis revealed subtle, persistent, long-range correlations (Hurst exponent, $H > 0.5$) in the accumulated departure from the mean of experimental data, according to the fractional Brownian model, fBm (Feder, 1988), both in the early as well as the recent study (Figure 2 and Table 1). If the data sequences were independent, (data representing the length of

(a)
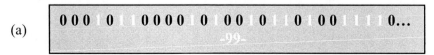

(b)
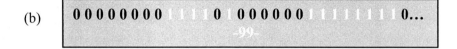

Figure 3

A rudimentary example to illustrate a 200-bit RNG sequence (a) without the gluing effect and (b) with the gluing effect underway. The (a) sequence consists of 99 ones and 101 zeros, while the (b) sequence consists also of 99 ones and 101 zeros, but due to the gluing effect, naturally occurring runs of bits are sustained for a little longer. In both cases the sum of bits is the same, yielding the same statistical distributions. Both sequences can occur by chance without the necessity of a biasing process underway.

[3] Weighted average from six separate files of computer-simulated RNG data and associated standard error.

independent steps in a random walk), the Hurst exponent would be, $H = 0.5$. Experimental data are generated during attempts of operators to mentally modulate the statistical outcome in predetermined directions. The control data are generated in between the experimental sessions at the same conditions except for the attempted mental influence. Calibration data are generated over sessions of very long, uninterrupted duration in the absence of attempts to mentally influence the random process. The experimental data are also termed intention data. According to the PEAR lab protocol calibration data are called control.

The mechanism for the observed persistence in experimental data ($H > 0.5$) was interpreted under the light of Jungian synchronicity as a gluing effect that sustained naturally occurring runs of binary events of the same kind (Pallikari, 2000). The gluing mechanism was considered as the manifestation of a mind–matter process. It is enhanced by immediate feedback and the freedom operators have to control the duration of breaks between runs, which will be called here 'optional stopping', and works as follows. Should the ongoing run yield an unfavourable outcome, i.e., an unfavourable statistical fluctuation, the operator can postpone the collection of further data. The possibility of selective timing based on sensory acquisition of information is entirely different from selecting the timing to start a run on the basis of precognition. Both possibilities will be considered next.

Looked at from the level of bits, the gluing caused longer runs of the same kind of bit to occur slightly more frequently than chance predicts, equally so for both ones as well as zeros, with the result that in the very long bit sequences generated in one session (200 bits x 100 trials = 20,000 bits per trial in a single effort) there resulted, on average, a statistical balance of bits. The statistical mean of the distribution of RNG outcomes was therefore within chance expectation; see the illustration of Figure 3. Control data sequences exhibited weaker, not statistically significant persistence while calibration data sequences were consistent with the behaviour of a random process of independent outcomes (Figure 2 and Table 1).

IV: The Role of Statistical Balancing and the Gluing Effect in Micro-PK

A recent meta-analysis and the law of large numbers

On the basis of the law of large numbers,[4] the statistical balancing hypothesis predicts that the statistical average of large enough PK data time-series will be within chance expectation. It also implies that if a micro-PK mechanism exists then it is more likely to be captured by sampling *short sequences of PK data* rather than long ones. Can this assertion be supported by experimental evidence?

A recent meta-analysis considering 712 experimental micro-PK studies and 158 control runs[5] (Steinkamp *et al.*, 2002) revealed the following interesting

---

[4] In repeated, independent trials with the same probability, p, of success in each trial, the chance that the percentage of successes differs from p by more than a fixed positive amount, e >0, converges to zero as the number of trials, n, goes to infinity, for every positive e.

[5] These were further reduced to 357 experimental (as in Figure 4) and 142 control studies of similar micro-PK conditions.

result: the smaller the size of a study — that is, the fewer binary data it refers to — the larger the deviation of effect reported, as a proportion of successes, from chance. Even in a study as comparatively small as 100,000 experimental/intention binary events collected, the proportion of successes was already collecting around a chance outcome (Figure 4). Still smaller studies (1,000 or 100 bits) exhibited stronger deviations from chance, yet in either direction, scattering considerably about the chance value, both in the direction of intention as well as in the contrary direction. This result, obtained from all the appropriate available micro-PK studies to date, reinforces the statistical balancing prediction after a careful evaluation. There are, admittedly, more studies falling in the psi-hitting side of the graph (effect size above 0.5) and they refer to relatively stronger effects than the ones falling in the psi-missing side. This is to be expected since a result is (a) more likely to be published (and the author be motivated to submit) if it reports a statistically significant effect and (b) if it reports a confirmation of a hypothesis rather than its refutation. This is the so-called publication bias. Often, estimates to correct this artefact are given in the form of the 'file-drawer effect' (Hunter & Schmidt, 1990, p. 510), but the validity of this approach is often challenged and debatable (Scargle, 2000). 'A result which clearly challenges the file-drawer analyses carried in prior meta-analyses,' Steinkamp *et al.* conclude (2002, p. 265) and continue: 'It is worrying that just a few small experiments are necessary to change the whole overall picture'.

Interestingly enough, the tendency of the law of large numbers to erase subtle psychophysical effects was stated some fifty years ago by one of the brilliant

Funnel plot of all 357 studies

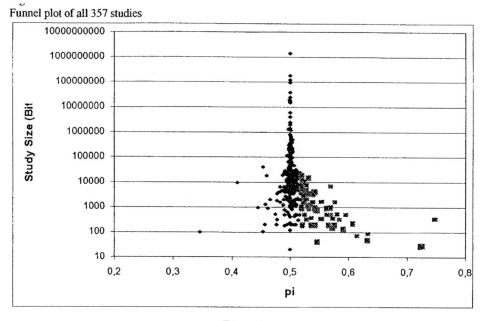

Figure 4

A plot of the study size of experimental/intention data only (in bits) against the effect size for 357 PK experimental studies of a recent meta-analysis (Steinkamp *et al.*, 2002).

mid-twentieth-century school of physicists, who helped to lay the foundations of quantum theory, Wolfgang Pauli (1900–58). The eminent physicist, inspired by the work of C.G. Jung on synchronicity, writes to his assistant Markus Fierz on June 3rd of the year 1952[6] (Pauli, 1996):

> The synchronistic phenomena (Σ) as considered by Jung in a narrow sense cannot be captured by the natural laws because they are not reproducible, i.e., they are unique and they get blurred by the statistical laws of large numbers.

Pauli referred to those phenomena that, according a common property in terms of the meaning one gives to them, occasionally cluster in one's life; they are synchronistic, as Jung has named them, and Pauli symbolised them by Σ. This cluster-inducing persistence gets blurred in the long run, Pauli says, falling victim of the law of large numbers. Pauli recognized and accepted the spontaneity and the non-reproducibility of the psychophysical, synchronistic phenomena, and their unavoidable dilution in the sea of all other life's events owing to our inability to control them: no overall biasing mechanism underway, yet a clear consciousness-induced effect.

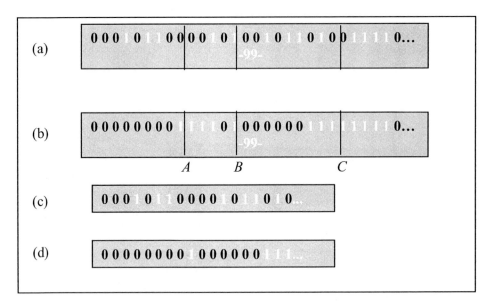

Figure 5

Same RNG as in Figure 2, but now fewer bits are collected per PK effort; first up to A and then from B to C, etc. and smaller databases are generated per experiment. If no PK-synchronistic effect is underway then the sum of 18 bits is 7, (c) but if a PK-synchronistic effect is underway the sum of 18 bits is 4, (d), in which case the frequency of zeros or ones deviates largely from chance expectation value.

---

[6] We are grateful that email messages had not been invented at the time; otherwise we would not be able to appreciate Pauli's ingenious thoughts on this matter through his letters.

The five postulates of the micro-PK mechanism

Let us now organize all that was previously discussed regarding the micro-PK mechanism into five postulates consistent with current evidence, as follows:

(a) A PK-gluing/synchronistic effect weakly sustains the direction of naturally occurring statistical fluctuations. It is as if human agent intention infuses some kind of glue onto events generated by the random process, which share a common property introducing a non-zero correlation, a situation reminiscent of Jungian synchronicity. The nature of the gluing mechanism is currently unknown.

(b) The micro-PK mechanism operating in closed systems[7] in which binary events are generated at the same bias-free probability, (e.g., ones and zeros, hits and misses, success or failures) does not distinguish between the two types of binary events, yielding an equally likely clustering of each type.

(c) Naturally occurring fluctuations in a binary stochastic process sustained/glued by PK become a slow, decaying 'tide' of a PK-induced clustering which may modulate the arrangement of neighbouring bit sequences in a time series (such as the controls), even if a PK condition is not applied.

(d) Depending upon the size of a database, the statistical average of experimental data (data pooled according to the pre-stated condition of PK mental influence) may significantly deviate from chance. Studies of smaller size are more likely to exhibit such deviation than larger ones.

(e) If a significant mean shift occurs in experimental data, then all remaining data of comparable size[8] that have been regularly generated in between experimental sessions according to the same protocol (same small run lengths, same machine used) will display an equally significant mean shift, yet in a direction symmetric to the previous one about the chance expectation.

Postulate (e) is actually the direct consequence of the law of large numbers while it also defines statistical balancing in micro-PK. A big question arises: how does the gluing, synchronistic effect favour deviations from chance occurring in small databases, as they often do and in the direction of pre-stated intention?

Let us first hypothesize that small databases are likely to arise from a collection of shorter data sequences per effort, called 'runs' according to the PEAR experimental protocol, since it is doubtful that a small database has been produced in only one long sitting, or by at least a very few, very long mental effort 'runs', but by many pooled short 'runs'. For the majority of PK studies, therefore, we will assume on the basis of the recent meta-analysis by Steinkamp *et al.* that shorter 'runs' were generated. Conventional non-psi tests measuring properties of a system's macro-states require studies shorter than 100,000 repetitions in order to predict the only evolution possible of a system. In such cases no consistent deviations in the direction of attempted mental influence have been reported

---

[7] Closed in the sense of the 'organizational closure' as discussed by Walter von Lucadou (1995).

[8] Data rejection is not permitted throughout the study, from the pre-stated beginning till the end, for whatever reason.

and there are many experimenters who would wish their measurements had yielded a different result. There are also other types of experiments which test theories applied on a collection of events that constitute a probabilistic system in order to predict its several possible evolutions and to assign a probability to each (Ruhla, 1992, p. 4). Such are the statistical distributions of photon counts or the disintegrations of radioactive sources, for instance. When a very large number of measurements is concerned in a very large probabilistic system, no deviations determined by mental effort have been reported. In the realm of very small probabilistic systems and very few measurements, on the other hand, nature behaves in an unexpected way, violating fundamental statistical laws, as will be discussed below. To illustrate the mechanism for the PK gluing effect onto shorter sequences we shall invoke the example discussed in the previous section, see Figure 5.

An example of how the gluing/synchronistic mechanism works

In this rudimentary example only nine bits (symbolic of a short run) are generated per PK effort, the first one from the start of bit collection up to point A, the next one from point B to C, and so on. Any bits generated between PK effort sessions such as from A to B and from C onwards are either (i) rejected as exploratory runs, faulty trials etc., (ii) some of them are recorded as control runs and the rest are rejected as in the first case (i), or (iii) all of them are collected as control runs and analysed. If no gluing synchronistic effect were underway, case (a), pooling the bits per effort would yield a sequence in which the proportion of either binary event does not deviate significantly from chance expectation value, Figure 5(c). In the presence of a PK-synchronistic effect, on the other hand, the following will happen: (a) pooling the bits per effort could yield a sequence in which the proportion of either bit is more likely to deviate significantly from chance expectation value, Figure 5(d). In other words, the experimental data sequences could exhibit a significant mean shift from chance.

For this to work, the involvement of the psychological component is essential. According to the gluing scenario, it is the psychological component — the mind — that is considered to trigger the mechanism upon the physical system — the random process. Via feedback, not precognition, the gluing is directed over a favourable bit upsurge or otherwise rests idle. The ability to control such a mechanism during short-duration tests, even with the aid of feedback, is a matter of a capricious 'psychic skill'. In general, through a psychic skill, weak imbalances in excess of the *same* type of binary event may come about in experimental sessions. The difference between their sum and chance expectation makes an array of small numbers falling on the same side about the chance average. Such a 'glued' array of small numbers yields a decrease of their variance, whereas, if small numbers alternated more about chance their variance would have been larger. One should remember that the example given here is meant only to depict the situation in simple terms, easily illustrated in one page, as in Figure 5. In real terms much longer sequences of binary events are generated, many more bits are

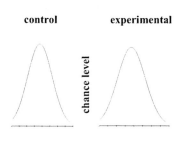

control   experimental

chance level

Figure 6

Distributions of PK-experimental and control data in an ideal balancing of statistical averages about the chance expectation.

sampled and the balancing math is better illustrated in terms of a statistical language.

What would happen if the number of bits generated per PK effort decreased from longer to shorter sequences? Shortening the sequence makes the likelihood of a bit imbalance more prominent as shorter runs of the same bit are naturally more frequent than longer ones. The specific example given in Figure 5 has favoured zeros. It is equally likely that it could have favoured the opposite bit to display psi-missing, but whatever the outcome, psi-hitting or psi-missing, this would have come about sooner in the presence of a synchronistic/gluing effect which sustains longer run lengths. Generally speaking, the gluing effect can temporarily beat the law of large numbers even in relatively larger databases, while in its absence they would already have settled into statistical balance for that size. To dilute the mean-shifting effect of longer runs within a sequence and even out the created imbalances, many more runs per effort will be required.

Should a deviation from chance be found in data that have been pooled by PK experimental condition, and since the whole of the large dataset displays no statistical deviation from chance, according to the previously stated evidence and the above illustration we shall expect the following. If the remainder of all the generated bits are collected as control data, from A to B and from C onwards (Figure 5) one would expect that their statistical average will also deviate from chance, conforming to the postulates (c) and (e) above, but in the opposite direction; i.e., symmetrically about chance expectation value to that of the experimental data, provided the size of experimental and control data is comparable and adequately large (see Figure 6). This is the basic prediction of the statistical balancing in micro-PK under the conditions earlier described.

Alternatively, if some of the data sequences generated during the experiment are excluded, the likelihood of a statistical balancing of averages of the two parts becomes smaller. The balancing can also be destroyed by a different procedure. If a control data collection with the same RNG is performed separately, independent of a given experiment, this will be equivalent to a random data sampling as in case (a) of Figures 4 and 5, so it is more likely that it will produce no mean shift from chance (the longer the generated sequence of bits, of course).

It should be emphasized that micro-PK is basically manifested through different types of 'selection' schemes. Data are selected from the time series of RNG records and pooled according to the pre-stated psychological condition into 'experimental', control, etc. (see example of Figure 5). The 'as-generated' time series of RNG outcomes is thus broken into segments so that non-adjacent segments generated under the same psychological label brought from diverse locations in the time series are merged together. While long original time series would show no mean shift from chance, the pooling together of shorter segments each marked by weak micro-PK may collectively result in a stronger effect conforming to intention if selective timing (i.e., optional stopping) is applied. The peak of the control distribution would then balance the experimental about chance (Figure 6). Without the selective timing and a psychic skill the experimental peak could either turn out to be within chance prediction, or even opposite to intention, if short and few segments of the time series were collected. In that case, a psi-hitting or a psi-missing outcome in experimental data will be a matter of 50/50 chance.

Explaining the micro-PK evidence on the basis of the gluing/synchronistic effect

Based on the above description, the reason why meta-analyses of PK experimental data usually produce impressive mean shifts from chance in the direction of intention and only chance scores in control data is as follows. First, under this hypothesis we assume that they carry the publication bias: (i) researchers will publish them if they have an effect to show, (ii) they publish them if they have a positive effect to show, i.e., confirmation of the conventional micro-PK hypothesis.[9] Secondly, the majority of studies are done in smaller databases according to current evidence — and if we assume these consist of shorter sequences — as illustrated above, they are more likely to produce high effect sizes, especially if a gluing process is underway. Thirdly, we assume they carry the optional stopping bias (unrestricted duration of breaks between the end of a PK effort to the beginning of the next one). In experiments that sample very short sequences per mental effort, optional stopping can easily control the final score, not necessarily by precognition, but more likely via immediate feedback (Palmer, 1978) if the latter is also provided. Suppose the bits generated are not the desired ones. The operator can then stop for a while and repeat at a later time when the random process goes through an upsurge of favourable bit generation. Starting a bit collection later may result in an upsurge of 'good' bits. During the favourable bit upsurge a gluing/clustering effect has a better chance to enhance the sequence 'goodness' and produce a 'better' score. Control studies, on the other hand, nicely yield no mean shift from chance, since not only are there consistently fewer of them published (although we would expect them to equal the number of experimental studies for a case of statistical balance), but they are also performed separately and independent of this PK-experimental data sampling. What about all other micro-PK experiments generating larger data sequences per effort, as with the large PEAR database?

To begin with, recall that such very large databases still exhibit statistical balancing, as mentioned at the end of Section 3. It has even been acknowledged that whatever mechanism was responsible for those mean shifts, it still preserved the

---

[9] This only describes a general tendency and of course there are exceptions to this rule, which is why there exist reports of negative scores, albeit fewer in number.

chance behaviour of the overall data distribution, as if 'without deforming the global chance behavior of their total results the operators somehow dispose the system to correlate subsets of the output scores with their intentions' (Jahn & Dunne, 1987, p. 119). In this reference, however, the chart of RNG distributions for high and low intentions clearly shows the separation of peaks above and below chance results. According to the illustration given previously (Figures 4 and 5) no mean shifts would be expected in these larger mental effort sequences and databases, as the failure to replicate[10] them has later confirmed (Jahn et al., 2000). It is worth noting that this was not the only case where such large databases have failed to be replicated (Jeffers & Sloan, 1992) and the law of large numbers confirmed as the balancing effect predicts.

One could not make correct suggestions as to the reasons of the previous PK success in those larger databases unless one has had the chance to examine closely all the subtle factors involved throughout these experiments either as an observer or a participant. Lacking such familiarity, one must follow other routes of speculation about the apparent success.

One view is that the micro-PK mechanism operates as a psychophysical organizational closure (Lucadou, 1995) in which the relevant parameters controlling the effect are associated with the operator on the one hand, as well as with the characteristics of the random process on the other. In that sense, the state of mind of the operator participating in the data-generation process would be highly relevant to the strength of the effect according to existing critique (Alcock, 1987; 1990), perhaps enough to overcome the obliterating effect of the law of large numbers within the limits of the applied experimental protocol. How so? In larger runs involving immediate feedback, in which the pursuit of a high score cannot greatly benefit from optional stopping in between 'runs',[11] as argued earlier, it is up to the operator's skill to apply or not apply the micro-PK/ synchronistic effect during the upsurge of a bit run, depending on whether or not it is favourable. This is perhaps the trick that makes a 'psi-gifted' operator. Even more so, should the number of 'runs' per session not be fixed in advance, operators may stop any time they wish and the scores will display a clear positive effect in the pre-stated direction. What of ESP card-guessing tests in which the decline was first observed? Here again, as in the micro-PK case, it is the arrangement of statistical outcomes — the basic balanced unit is a hit or a miss — that is modulated by the gluing/synchronistic process. It is featured as a persistence of hits balanced by a persistence of misses, and the overall score is rendered to chance. It must be pointed out that statistical balancing is not restricted to only PK random data. It can manifest in any random, unbiased, PK-free database. Yet, there is still a chance to distinguish PK random data from all other random data by plotting the graph of Figure 4. The PK gluing will have broadened the plot, as compared to that of a PK-free, control database.

---

[10] Failure to replicate does not devalue the importance of prior evidence in the PEAR database, but only instructs the scientist to consider alternative hypotheses to the understanding of micro-PK.

[11] Due to the law of large numbers.

The suggestion that the micro-PK mechanism will not change the statistics of the random process (of the parent distribution), in agreement with the statistical balancing hypothesis, has been separately proposed under an entirely different background (May *et al.*, 1995a; 1995b) as the Decision Augmentation Theory (DAT for short). The DAT suggests that any observed shifts of the mean in sub-sets of output sequences are the result of selection based on precognition. The operator applies precognition to 'see' a favourable oncoming bit sequence and by the pressing of a button begins the data sampling, which turns out to be suc-cessful. On the basis of the DAT it has been shown that micro-PK is not mediated by PK force acting on each binary event, which results in an undisturbed parent distribution. The random process statistics are thus conserved; the world remains unchanged, surviving from the biasing impact of this selective process. There has been serious criticism against the applicability of the DAT mathematical analysis on specific databases (e.g., Dobyns & Nelson, 1998; Dobyns, 2000), yet here we shall be concerned with the question whether a selection by precognition mechanism is at all viable. We shall attempt to review DAT from the perspective of the approach introduced in this article and clarify this point: Can the DAT hypothesis account for the mass of facts that surround micro-PK?

V: Could a Data-selection Process Based on Precognition Account for the Evidence for Micro-PK?

How could selection by precognition explain the finding that the effect size goes down as the size of study increases? We shall attempt to offer the following inter-pretation *à la* DAT: The operator 'senses' by precognition a favourable sequence and initiates the data sampling session. Yet, such favourable outcomes cannot by nature be sustained over very long sequences. A long sequence of random events is more likely to yield a chance outcome, against intention, due to the law of large numbers, something the precognition skill cannot overcome. Naturally, one can conclude that the effect of selection by precognition will be stronger if shorter sequences are sampled, as in shorter studies. If, as we have assumed, shorter studies use shorter sequences, the DAT selection hypothesis can account for the evidence regarding the relationship between effect size and study size. Yet one may have second thoughts. Even if a modest consistent DAT selection mecha-nism existed, then the effect will be expected to increase as the sampling of short sessions are repeated again and again; that is, as the study size grows larger and larger through pooling successful short mental effort data sequences. But this is contrary to the current evidence and the DAT selection mechanism loses ground.

How then can DAT explain psi-missing? Does the operator, by some twist of psychological complication, wish all of a sudden to select a sequence, which yields a score opposite to the pre-stated intention? And even if we allowed for this unlikely circumstance to be true, why does this twist of psychological com-plication occur around the middle of a long run? One can readily argue, then, against the hypothesis of selection by precognition. It is less easy to do so when it comes to the main results of the DAT mathematical analysis: these make sense.

So, we can conclude that although a lot of selection takes place to yield mean shifts in PK-RNG sequences (e.g., pooling by pre-stated psychological condition, timing based on feedback), the DAT suggestion cannot on its own account for the effect.

Both perspectives of (a) the gluing, exhibiting statistical balancing and (b) the selection by precognition PK mechanisms imply that there is no PK force making the statistical average of the parent distribution from which the trials are sampled to shift beyond chance. The gluing mechanism would further predict no statistically significant mean shifts in very large statistical systems. If such very large systems refer to many particle macroscopic bodies, the average of their macroscopic properties will not change due to PK. In that sense, micro-PK does not bring about physical changes easily felt in the world around us. This conclusion is in agreeement with an abundance of evidence. The solid, robust world around us confirms it, experimental physics confirms it and even the failures to replicate micro-PK confirm it. In contrast, the selection by precognition approach cannot account for the disagreement between the conventional PK hypothesis and the abundance of evidence. The DAT suggestion that only the correct timing to start the bit collection process accounts for the PK mechanism can be understood simply as an inexorably proposed solution to accommodate the implications of its reasonable as well as valuable mathematical analysis.

The most recent micro-PK meta analysis indicates that violations of fundamental statistical laws and evidence for micro-PK effects are stronger in small systems, as shown in Figure 4. Just by chance the sampling distribution of proportions is expected to have a mean equal to 0.5 and a standard deviation equal to $0.5/\sqrt{N}$, where N is the size of sample. (Spiegel, 1961, p. 142). The gluing mechanism suggests that the frequency of certain run lengths, as well as their associated variance (Von Mises, 1964, pp. 184–92), will have increased in a series of measurements. Increase of variance enhances the blurring of precision regarding the measured property, enabling violations of statistical laws the shorter the run length. Such deviations occur in small-size PK studies where the experimental/intention data fall well outside the envelope of 95% confidence (proportion of hits $= 0.5 \pm 1.96 \times 0.5\sqrt{N}$), both for psi hitting as for psi missing, as in Figure 4. Is this anomaly improbable according to orthodox scientific standards? Hardly. It has been observed by independent 'orthodox' scientific experiments that nature behaves not as it would be expected to in the realm of smaller systems or shorter timescales, and violations of fundamental laws have been recorded (Wang et al., 2002), admittedly in much smaller statistical systems than Figure 4 refers to. 'Such violations may play a role in how life itself functions', the authors of the aforementioned reference acknowledge, which must also be highly relevant to the prospect of identifying the micro-PK mechanism.

VI: Discussion

In accordance with the above discussion, we can safely predict that physical reality is well protected from micro-PK attempts to influence the long-run statistics of random processes. However, to explain the evidence of high hitting and missing scores that can occur in short studies we shall have to accept that a micro-PK mechanism exists; more likely a gluing/synchronistic effect. Can such a mechanism be supported within our scientific framework?

The suggestion of an ongoing micro-PK mechanism implies that the states of two remote systems, of the brain and of the random process, have been somehow coupled. That is, the state of the one determines the state of the other and vice versa. The scientific term for this condition is 'entanglement'. Could entanglement play a role in micro-PK or is it too far-fetched? Perhaps not. Much thought has been given to the subtle aspects of quantum theory, such as the non-local interactions between entangled remote systems, also to account for psi phenomena (Josephson and Pallikari-Viras, 1991), which is sometimes described, perhaps for enriching scientific folklore, as 'telepathic'. Brain neurophysiology research is growing fast, on the other hand, and earlier indication of synchronous brain patterns between two distant brains (Richards et al., 2000) may be finally confirmed to occur via 'paranormal' means as well. There is even indication that hot large molecules could sustain entanglement (Nairz et al., 2000) — could this also be achieved with brain molecules?

Progress in areas of research relevant to consciousness promises to further contribute positively to a real working micro-PK mechanism. We can anticipate it being demonstrated in a well-controlled experiment. By analogy: just because we have not yet attained room-temperature superconductivity, this does not mean that it cannot ever be achieved. At the moment, one can be content that some light has been shed on this mechanism.[12] Moreover, we do not need to explicitly describe the finest design of the micro-PK mechanism right at the start, but simply understand the regular patterns it exemplifies — a situation we often put up with in science.

VII: Conclusions

The micro-PK mechanism operating in an organizational mind–matter closure does not present a threat to precise scientific measurement in very large systems. In smaller systems it either stays idle, or it is activated as a non-dissipative process: one that conserves the statistical equilibrium of the parameters that define the physical system. If the system were described in terms of statistical physics, the micro-PK would be seen to sustain 'spontaneous' fluctuations from equilibrium of the isolated system's parameters, where equilibrium means a state of well-defined statistics. Any spontaneous deviation from equilibrium would bring about such processes within the physical system, which would render it back to equilibrium, according to the Le Châtelier principle (Reif, 1965).[13] Yet, in the realm of very small systems, a not yet well-understood micro-PK mechanism could modulate the system's fluctuations against its natural development, as the fluctuation theorem predicts (Evans et al., 2001) and evidence supports

---

[12] The author intends to publish a mathematical model of micro-PK, which accounts for all current evidence.

[13] 'When a system is in stable equilibrium, any perturbation that changes its parameters must bring about processes which tend to restore equilibrium.'

(Wang *et al.*, 2002). The fluctuation theorem basically quantifies the probability of observing Second Law violations in small systems observed for a short time. It further predicts that in the long run any physical system, such as the statistical system of micro-PK or ESP outcomes could be, will obey the laws of nature. On such occasions the psychological component of the mind–matter closure 'the operator' will 'subjectively' attribute the equilibrium-seeking process (decline effect) to psychological causes, for instance to negative attitude. According to the gluing/ synchronistic approach, however, the decline effect is mainly due to the non- dissipative nature of the micro-PK mechanism, and to the inherent tendency of an isolated statistical system to conserve its statistics, as the law of large numbers predicts. Finally, evidence for micro-PK and ESP does not seem to support either the sensory or extrasensory-based selection hypotheses alike.

Life is but a big game that spans classical and quantum multiplayer systems (Lee and Johnson, 2002). In the micro-PK game we are the players against nature, obeying rules that we do not fully understand. The gluing/synchronistic approach to the mind–matter problem in combination with the micro-PK statistical balancing attempts a description of a rule in which nature, apparently bound by the observer, gets locked into one of its available binary states. Scientists are familiar with a similar rule of a game, called the Quantum Zeno Effect, where rapid-fire rate of observations on a quantum system may lock it in one of its available states and delay its natural evolution (Wunderlich *et al.*, 2001). If the gluing/synchronistic rule of the micro-PK game against nature can account for much of the evidence around the mind–matter problem, it still remains highly speculative if not risky, as these phenomena are lacking a detailed predictive physical theory.

Let us, therefore, before closing this article, risk a prediction as far as the current evidence allows. Let us assume a single micro-PK study consisting of N random binary events and a related control study of the same size. Further assume that a proportion of hits against misses has been registered in the former, which is different from chance expectation at a given acceptable level of statistical significance (α), while the control data outcome conforms with chance at the same level of significance. This difference between the PK and control outcomes will fail to register as their size grows larger than 1,000,000 binary random events (assuming that there has been no data selection/rejection). Perhaps this risk is too daring for a physicist to take. But Lee and Johnson (2002) are encouraging: 'Life is full of risks and life, after all, is just a game'.

Acknowledgements
I would like to express special thanks to Eberhard Bauer for his invaluable and enriching contribution to my literature search and his comments from which this manuscript has greatly benefited. Special thanks to Dr. Damien Broderick who had the patience not only to read through the manuscript and smooth the style but also to offer his helpful comments. Keith Chandler offered a few but important comments and corrections on the proofs, and a great deal of encouragement, both of which are very much appreciated.

References

Alcock, J.E. (1987), 'Parapsychology: Science of the anomalous or search for the soul?, *Behavioral and Brain Sciences*, **10**, pp. 553–643.

Alcock, J.E. (1990), *Science and Supernature* (New York: Prometheus Books).

Anderson, P. (1991), 'Letter to the editor', *Physics Today*, October issue, p. 146.

Bierman, D.J., Van Gelderen, W.J.M. (1994), 'Geomagnetic activity and PK on a low and high trial-rate RNG', in *Proceedings of the 37th Annual Convention of the Parapsychological Association*, ed. D.J. Bierman, pp. 50–56.

Dobyns, Y.H. (2000), 'Overview of several theoretical models', *Journal of Scientific Exploration*, **14** (2), pp. 163–94.

Dobyns, Y.H., Nelson, R.D. (1998), 'Empirical evidence against decision augmentation theory', *Journal of Scientific Exploration*, **12** (2), pp. 231–57.

Dunne, B.J., Dobyns, Y.H., Jahn, R.G., Nelson, R.D. (1994), 'Series position effects in random event generator experiments', *Journal of Scientific Exploration*, **8** (2), pp. 197–215.

Evans, D.J., Searles, D.J., Mittag, E. (2001), 'Fluctuation theorem for Hamiltonian systems — Le Chatelier's principle', *Physical Review E: Statistical, Nonlinear, Soft Matter Physics*, **63**, 051105 (4) [online citation].

Feder, J. (1988), *Fractals* (New York: Plenum Press).

Gammel B.M. (1998), 'Hurst's rescaled range analysis for pseudorandom number generators used in physical simulations', *Physical Review E*, **58** (2), pp. 2586–97.

Gell-Mann, M. (1994), *The Quark & the Jaguar: Adventures in the Simple and the Complex* (London: W. H. Freeman).

Glossary (2001), *Journal of Parapsychology*, **65** (4), pp. 429–32.

Houtkooper, J.M. (2002), 'A pilot experiment with evoked psychokinetic responses circumventing cognitive interference?', in *Proceedings of the 45th Annual Convention of the Parapsychological Association*, ed. C. Watt, pp. 104–15.

Hunter, J.E., Schmidt, F.L. (1990), *Methods of Meta-Analysis* (Newbury Park, CA: Sage Publications).

Jahn, R.G. (1982), 'The persistent paradox of psychic phenomena: An engineering perspective', *Proceedings IEEE*, **70** (2), pp. 136–70.

Jahn, R.G., Dunne, B.J. (1987), *Margins of Reality: The Role of Consciousness in the Physical World* (Orlando: Harcourt Brace Jovanovich).

Jahn, R., Mischo, J., Vaitl D., *et al.* (2000), 'Mind/machine interaction consortium: PortREG replication experiments', *Journal of Scientific Exploration*, **14** (4), pp. 499–555.

Jeffers, S., Sloan, J. (1992), 'A low-light-level diffraction experiment for anomalies research', *Journal of Scientific Exploration*, **6** (4), pp. 333–52.

Josephson B.D., Pallikari-Viras, F. (1991), 'Biological utilisation of quantum nonlocality', *Foundations of Physics*, **21**, pp. 197–207.

Lee, C.F., Johnson, N. (2002), 'Let the Quantum Games Begin', *Physics World*, **15** (10), pp. 25–9.

Lucadou, v. W. (1995), 'The model of pragmatic information', *European Journal of Parapsychology*, **11**, pp. 58–75.

May C.E., Utts M.J., Spottiswoode J.P. (1995a), 'Decision Augmentation Theory: Toward a model of anomalous mental phenomena', *Journal of Parapsychology*, **59**, pp. 195–220.

May E.C., Utts J.M., Spottiswoode J.P. (1995b), 'Decision Augmentation Theory: Applications to the number generator database', *Journal of Scientific Exploration*, **9** (4) pp. 453–88.

Nairz, O., Arndt, M., Petschinka, J., Voss-Andreae, J., van der Zouw, G., Keller, C., Zeilinger, A. (2000), 'Coherence and decoherence in de Broglie interference of fullerenes', *Conference Digest IQEC 2000*, Nice, p. 115.

Oteri, L. (ed. 1975), *Quantum Physics and Parapsychology* (New York: Parapsychology Foundation).

Pallikari, F. (1998), 'On the balancing effect hypothesis', in *Research in Parapsychology 1993*, ed. N. Zingrone (Metuchen, NJ: Scarecrow), pp. 102–3.

Pallikari, F. (2001), 'A study of the fractal character in electronic noise processes', *Chaos, Solitons & Fractals*, **12** (8), pp. 1499–507.

Pallikari-Viras, F. (1997), 'Further evidence for a statistical balancing in probabilistic systems influenced by the anomalous effect of conscious intention', *Journal of Society for Psychical Research*, **62**, pp. 114–37.

Pallikari, F., Boller, E. (1999), 'A rescaled range analysis of random events', *Journal of Scientific Exploration*, **13**, pp. 25–40.

Pallikari, F., Boller, E., Bösch, H. (2000), 'Jungian synchronicity sheds light on the micro-PK mechanism', in *Proceedings of the 43th Parapsychological Association Convention*, ed. F. Steinkamp, pp. 210–22.

Palmer, J. (1978), 'Extrasensory perception: Research findings', in *Advances in Parapsychological Research 2: Extrasensory Perception*, ed. S. Krippner (New York: Plenum Press), pp. 59–243.

Pauli, W. (1996), Scientific correspondence with Bohr, Einstein and others, IV, part I, 1950–52, ed. by K.V. Meyenn (Berlin, Heidelberg: Springer).

Radin, D.I. (1997), *The Conscious Universe* (San Francisco: HarperEdge).

Radin D., Nelson, R. (2002), 'Meta-analysis of mind–matter interaction experiments: 1959 to 2000', in *Spiritual Healing, Energy, Medicine and Intentionality: Research and Clinical Implications*, ed. W.B. Jonas (Edinburgh: Harcourt Health Sciences).

Rao, K.R. (1965), 'The bidirectionality of psi', *Journal of Parapsychology*, **29**, pp. 230–50.

Reif, F. (1965), *Fundamentals of Statistical and Thermal Physics* (New York: McGraw Hill).

Rhine, J.B. (1969), 'Psi-missing re-examined', *Journal of Parapsychology*, **33** (1), pp. 1–38.

Rhine, J.B. (1971), *New World of the Mind* (New York: Morrow, Orig. Publication in 1953).

Rhine, J.B., Pratt, J.G. (1957), *Parapsychology: Frontier Science of the Mind* (Springfield, IL.: Thomas).

Richards, T.L., Standish, L.J., Johnson, L.C. (2000), 'EEG coherence and visual evoked potentials: Investigation of neural energy transfer between human subjects', *Proceedings of Conference: Towards a Science of Consciousness*, University of Arizona at Tucson, April.

Ruhla, C. (1992), *The Physics of Chance. From Blaise Pascal to Niels Bohr* (Oxford, New York, Tokyo: Oxford University Press).

Scargle, J.D. (2000), 'Publication bias: The "file-drawer" problem in scientific inference', *Journal of Scientific Exploration*, **14** (1), pp. 91–106.

Schmidt, H. (1974), 'Instrumentation in the parapsychology laboratory', in *New Directions in Parapsychology*, ed. J. Beloff (London: Elek Science), pp. 13–37.

Schrödinger, E. (1958), *Mind and Matter* (Cambridge, UK: Cambridge University Press).

Spiegel, M.R. (1961), *Theory and Problems of Statistics* (New York: Schaum Publishing Company).

Stapp H.P. (1994), 'Theoretical model of a purported empirical violation of the predictions of quantum theory', *Physical Review A*, **50** (1), pp. 18–22.

Steinkamp, F., Boller, E., Bösch, H. (2002), 'Experiments examining the possibility of human intention interacting with random number generators: A preliminary meta-analysis', in *Proceedings of the Parapsychological Association 45th annual Convention*, ed. C. Watt, pp. 256–72.

Von Mises, R. (1964), *Mathematical Theory of Probability and Statistics* (New York and London: Academic Press).

Wang, G.M., Sevick, E.M., Mittag, E., Searles, D.J., Evans, D.J. (2002). 'Demonstration of Violations of the Second Law of Thermodynamics for Small Systems and Short Time Scales', *Physical Review Letters*, **89**, PhysRevLett.89.050601.

Wunderlich, Chr., Balzer, Chr., Toschek, P.E. (2001), 'Evolution of an atom impeded by measurement: The quantum Zeno effect', *Zeitschrift fuer Naturforschung*, **56a**, pp. 160–4.

Peter Brugger and Kirsten I. Taylor

ESP

Extrasensory Perception or Effect of Subjective Probability?

This paper consists of two parts. In the first, we discuss the neuropsychological correlates of belief in a 'paranormal' or magical causation of coincidences. In particular, we review experimental evidence demonstrating that believers in ESP and kindred forms of paranormal phenomena differ from disbelievers with respect to indices of sequential response production and semantic-associative processing. Not only do believers judge artificial coincidences as more 'meaningful' than disbelievers, they also more strongly suppress coincidental productions (i.e. repetitions) in their generation of random sequences. These findings illuminate the cognitive mechanisms underlying the formation and maintenance of paranormal beliefs for which the right cerebral hemisphere is hypothesized to play a central role. These same right hemispheric semantic-associative processing characteristics are centrally implicated in the creative thought process as well as the genesis of delusional (pathological) beliefs (e.g. ideas of reference).

The second part of the paper highlights how fundamental limitations in the concept of randomness constrain the analysis and interpretation of forced-choice experiments in the field of parapsychology. Relevant proposals have periodically been forwarded during the past century (key names: Goodfellow, Brown, Gatlin). These suggest that (1) as human subjects' guesses are highly non-random and (2) as no finite sequence of target alternatives is free of bias, above-chance matching of guesses to targets simply reflects the amount of sequential information common to both target and guess sequences. The importance of such a non-causal model has been regularly downplayed by conservative parapsychologists, especially those who insist that ESP involves a *transfer* of information. Moreover, statistically significant relationships between guessing accuracy and personality factors and/or experimental manipulations most likely do *not* reflect a transfer of information, but are to be expected if subjects' sequential response biases are systematically influenced by these same factors.

Correspondence: Peter Brugger, Neuropsychologische Abteilung, Neurologische Klinik USZ, Frauenklinikstrasse 26, 8091 Zürich, Switzerland. *Email: peter.brugger@usz.ch*
Kirsten I. Taylor, Dept. of Experimental Psychology, Downing Site, Cambridge CB2 3EB, U.K.

Journal of Consciousness Studies, **10**, No. 6–7, 2003, pp. 221–46

In an integration of Parts I and II, we propose that parapsychology should abandon the traditional, causal view of ESP as extrasensory perception; it should be recognized that the object under study is individual differences in guessing behaviour. By adopting a non-causal approach, the basic critiques of the traditional conceptualization of ESP become superfluous (e.g. that ESP would be incompatible with the laws of nature) and the interpretation of secondary effects such as psi-missing and displacement can more parsimoniously be explained. By exploring the factors that systematically influence ESP as an Effect of Subjective Probability, a new parapsychology could ultimately advance to a respectable discipline within the behavioural sciences.

I: Meaning, Randomness and Belief in a Paranormal Causation of Coincidences

> In crossing a heath, suppose I pitched my foot against a stone, and were asked how the stone came to be there; I might possibly answer, that, for anything I knew to the contrary, it had lain there forever: nor would it perhaps be very easy to show the absurdity of this answer. But suppose I had found a watch upon the ground, and it should be inquired how the watch happened to be in that place; I should hardly think of the answer I had before given, that for anything I knew, the watch might always have been there.   (Paley, 1809, p. 1)

William Paley employed this metaphor in *Natural Theology* (1809) to argue for the existence of God, the watchmaker: only a divine entity could have produced a mechanism as exquisitely ordered as a watch. Although this reasoning has since been judged to be 'wrong, gloriously and utterly wrong' (Dawkins, 1987, p. 5),[1] it nevertheless highlights a distinctively human characteristic: the tendency to invoke a supernatural agency to explain the existence of meaningful events whose origins are unknown.

William Paley was what we would today call a 'believer'. He perceived a harmonious orderliness in the watch, one which contrasted starkly with the barren background, and lacking an obvious reason for its existence there, invoked a supernatural causation instead of leaving it to chance or obscurity. Instead of a watch, an obviously highly organized object, Paley could just as well have employed the arrangement of stones in the shape of Moses. Other metaphoric travellers, however, might not have spontaneously recognized the same figure amidst the stones; people differ with respect to their propensity to perceive patterns (meaning) and, conversely, to appreciate randomness (the absence of meaning). In the following text, we will attempt to demonstrate that believers in ESP and other paranormal phenomena tend to see more patterns in random configurations and more meaning in coincidental events compared to disbelievers. We will argue that this lowered 'threshold of meaning attribution' compels them to seek a paranormal causation for events considered a mere coincidence by others.

---

[1] One main weakness of this metaphor is its presumed point of reference; is not the magnificent complexity of nature awe-inspiring compared to the banality of a watch (Robertson, 1902)? In other words, 'randomness is relative' (Kendall, 1941, p. 14) or, as Becknell (1940, p. 609) stated when specifically referring to the role of randomness in ESP research, 'without ideology, probability is meaningless'.

Meaning in randomness

The propensity for pattern perception can be investigated by presenting subjects with degraded visual stimuli and asking them what they see. Blackmore and Moore (1994) employed this methodology with a group of healthy subjects who had also completed the Paranormal Belief Scale (Tobacyk, 1988). The stimuli were photographs of common objects with varying degrees of computer-generated noise (noise levels 0%, 20%, 50% and 70%). Following each tachisto-scopic presentation of the pseudorandomized stimuli, participants were asked whether they could recognize and identify it. Believers made more positive responses than the disbelievers, especially with the most noisy stimuli, and made fewer correct identifications overall than the disbelievers (see also Blackmore *et al.*, 1994; Brugger *et al.*, 1993b; Lange and Houran, 2001). Thus, believers in the paranormal more readily constructed order from an ambiguous input.

A widespread symbol of randomness in our culture is the die. Despite its familiarity, healthy subjects fail miserably at judging the probabilities of sequences of consecutive die rolls. One robust attribute of their faulty judgments is 'repetition avoidance': although equally probable, healthy participants consis-tently judge the sequence 2–2–2 as less probable than 5–1–3. Direct repetitions are considered less probable — more meaningful — because a pattern can be detected (i.e. the numbers are consecutively repeated). When believers and dis-believers in ESP were confronted with sequences of consecutive die rolls, believ-ers rated sequences with *few* consecutive repetitions as significantly *more* probable than disbelievers (Brugger *et al.*, 1990; Musch and Ehrenberg, 2002).

Heightened repetition avoidance in believers is not only evidenced in percep-tual, but also in production tasks. When required to mentally produce random numbers by attempting to mimic the falls of a die, believers repeated numbers less frequently (i.e. heightened repetition avoidance) than disbelievers (Brugger *et al.*, 1990; see Bressan, 2002 and Brugger, 1997, for later replications).[2] A reanalysis of data collected in a telepathy experiment also revealed a more pro-nounced repetition avoidance in the guessing patterns of ESP-believers (Brugger *et al.*, 1990, Exp. 1). These findings have been replicated within the linguistic realm of meaning — semantics — with pairs of commonly associated objects (Brugger *et al.*, 1995). Participants were shown a die with three distinct pictures (each replicated on the die's opposite face): the ambiguous drawing of a duck/rabbit, a reed scene or a carrot (see Figure 1). In this implicit randomization experiment, the blindfolded participants were required to throw the die and, after each throw, to guess which picture they thought had appeared on the die's top face. All subjects displayed repetition avoidance at this high level of processing: subjects who had identified the ambiguous animal as a 'duck' avoided pairing

[2] An inverse 'sheep–goat effect' in repetition avoidance (i.e. less repetitions by *dis*believers in the para-normal) was reported by Lawrence (1990/1991) whose instructions differed significantly from those employed in the studies noted above, i.e., explicitly mentioned 'that 3, 4, 5, or more of the same sym-bol may appear consecutively' (p. 136). See Kirby (1976) for the effects of instructions on response alternation and repetition performances. Houtkooper and Haraldsson (1997) failed to replicate any association between repetition avoidance and belief in the paranormal.

this response with 'reed' and those who had identified the animal as a 'rabbit' avoided pairing this response with 'carrot'. However, this 'semantic repetition avoidance' was statistically more pronounced in believers compared to disbelievers in ESP.

These findings indicate that believers in ESP and other paranormal phenomena more readily perceive meaningful associations in noisy and random stimuli than disbelievers. Moreover, when the task is to produce randomness, believers' productions are more patterned (i.e. less random) than those of the disbelievers. In the next section, we will outline the neuropsychological studies which have begun to identify the neuroanatomical bases of these behaviours.

Figure 1.

The die used in the experiment on 'semantic repetition avoidance'. Note that the duck in the ambiguous duck/rabbit drawing is associatively related to the reeds (but not to the carrot) and the rabbit to the carrot (figure reprinted with permission from *Salud (i) Ciencia*, 1998: Vol. 9, No. 5, p. 5. © Sociedad Iberoamericana de Información Científica (SIIC); www.siicsalud.com).

The right hemisphere

> There is no doubt that right-hemisphere intuitive thinking may perceive patterns
> and connections too difficult for the left hemisphere; but it may also detect patterns
> where none exist. Skeptical and critical thinking is not a hallmark of the right hemi-
> sphere.   (Carl Sagan, 1977, p. 180)

The following result should by now come as no surprise: in an extension of
Blackmore and Moore (1994) we found that believers in ESP perceived significantly more meaningful patterns in random dot patterns than disbelievers
(Brugger et al., 1993b). What was different in this study was that the stimuli were
presented in a divided visual field paradigm,[3] i.e. either to the left visual
field/right hemisphere or right visual field/left hemisphere (LVF/RH and
RVF/LH, respectively). Thus, this study revealed a second significant finding,
i.e. that significantly more meaningful patterns were perceived in the LVF/RH
than in the RVF/LH irrespective of belief group. Was this latter finding due to the
special role of the RH in the identification of subjectively meaningful information (see van Lancker, 1991) or merely a result of the general dominance of the
RH for visuospatial processing?

Studies of hemispatial attention have helped to clarify this question. Each
hemisphere is responsible for the deployment of attention and initial processing
of visual information from the contralateral hemifield: the LH is responsible for
the right side of space and vice versa. With a common variant of the line bisection
task employed to assess hemispatial attention, Brugger and Graves (1997b)
instructed healthy, blindfolded participants to tactually bisect a rod. The participants also completed Eckblad and Chapman's (1983) Magical Ideation (MI)
scale measuring paranormal beliefs and experiences.[4] MI scale scores were significantly correlated with the amount of *leftward* deviation in a tactile rod bisection task (see also Kalaycioglu et al., 2000; and Luh and Gooding, 1999). Thus,
believers attended more to the left and less to the right side of space, even when
hemispatial attention was implicitly measured (Taylor et al., 2002).[5] It is unclear,
however, whether these findings reflect a relative LH underactivation (with consequent inattention to the right side of space) or a relative RH overactivation
(with consequent increased attention to the left side of space). To answer this
question, visual field/hemisphere performances must be directly compared.

The LH is dominant for linguistic processing in the majority of healthy,
right-handed individuals. Clinically speaking, this means that a disturbance of

[3] Divided visual field paradigms require subjects to fixate on the centre of a screen. Visual information
is then very briefly exposed (i.e. typically no longer than 150 msec) in the left and/or right visual field.
Since visual information falling in the right visual field is first processed in the left hemisphere and
vice versa, subjects' responses are assumed to primarily emanate from the hemisphere first receiving
the visual information.

[4] While some MI scale items directly refer to beliefs in ESP, others are less related to parapsychological
subject matters. We reanalysed our data with the subset of MI scale items on paranormal beliefs
(Thalbourne, 1985) and found the same pattern of results as with the entire scale.

[5] Incidentally, when instructed to fill in one of a pair of squares on an answer sheet, believers in ESP
showed a greater implicit inattention to the right side of space compared to disbelievers (Smith and
Canon, 1954).

language (aphasia) will result in this group following lesions to the LH, but not to the RH. LVF/RH performances on experimental divided visual field language tasks, however, are not at chance level, but simply inferior to those in the RVF/LH: hemispheric dominance for a given cognitive function is relative. We administered healthy, right-handed subjects a common task of hemispheric language functioning. Strings of letters forming either a word or a 'nonword' (i.e. nonsense) were presented to the LVF and RVF, and subjects were instructed to respond when they recognized a word (lexical decision task). Functional hemispheric dominance for this task was measured with laterality indices, i.e. ((LVF/RH − RVF/LH) performances / (LVF/RH + RVF/LH) performances), where negative values indicated a relative LH and positive values a relative RH dominance. All participants also rated their belief in ESP on a 6-point scale. A comparison of laterality indices revealed a greater LH functional dominance in disbelievers compared to believers in ESP (see Figure 2a). Critically, RVF/LH performances in both groups were comparable; the significant difference in laterality indices originated from believers' superior LVF/RH performances compared to the disbelievers (see Figure 2b; Brugger *et al.*, 1993a; see also Leonhard and Brugger, 1998). Consistently, the resting EEG patterns of believers showed less interhemispheric differences and more RH excitatory activity than those of disbelievers (Pizzagalli *et al.*, 2000). These findings indicate that a

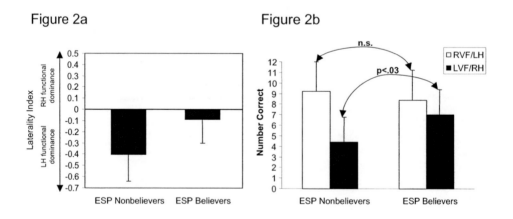

Figure 2.

a: Disbelievers and believers in ESP (as measured by a 6-point scale) performed a divided visual field lexical decision task. Laterality indices (see text) were computed to quantify relative functional hemispheric dominance on this task. Relative left hemisphere (LH) functional dominance was higher in the disbelievers than in the believers.

b: Additional analyses revealed comparable right visual field / left hemisphere (RVF/LH) performances in both groups but superior left visual field / right hemisphere (LVF/RH) performances in the believers compared to the disbelievers. These findings support the hemispheric imbalance model of paranormal belief (Taylor *et al.*, 2002) that may also account for delusion formation in psychiatric patients (Leonhard and Brugger, 1998).

relative RH overactivation, rather than LH underactivation, underlies believers' cognitive performance patterns.[6]

Can a relative RH overactivation account for the tendency of believers to perceive and produce meaningful patterns where disbelievers do not? Yes. Several lines of research converge to indicate that the RH plays a unique role in processing distantly, remotely, or indirectly related information. For example, it has long been recognized that RH brain-damaged patients exhibit specific deficits in the appreciation of metaphors, which require a nonliteral reading of literally unrelated material (Winner and Gardner, 1977; see also Brownell et al., 1990). These clinical findings have been confirmed in divided visual field (Anaki et al., 1998) and functional neuroimaging (Bottini et al., 1994) studies with healthy participants. Moreover, evidence from divided visual field studies have demonstrated that while the LH appreciates directly related words or concepts, the RH plays a dominant role in the appreciation of more remotely related words or concepts (e.g. Beeman et al., 1994; Chiarello and Richards, 1992).

These hemispheric differences in semantic-associative processing can be understood in terms of a semantic network model of our stored conceptual knowledge (Collins and Loftus, 1975). This semantic network consists of concepts connected by relational links. Thus, the more related two concepts are, the more links will connect them. Processing in the semantic network is hypothesized to begin when a concept is activated (e.g. by reading the word *apple*). This activation spreads equi-centrally and in a decreasing gradient through links to other related concepts in the network. Closely related concepts will thus require focal or less activation and distantly related concepts widespread or more activation for their coactivation. Critically, findings from divided visual field paradigms have revealed that the characteristic pattern of semantic network activation in the LH is focal and that in the RH diffuse (see, e.g., Beeman et al., 1994). Thus, the unique RH overactivation of believers would produce a more widespread activation of the semantic network and coactivate more distantly related concepts, resulting, as indeed has been demonstrated, in the appreciation of meaningful connections between e.g. randomly paired line drawings (Brugger 1992; Brugger et al., 1994b) or randomly paired nouns (Mohr et al., 2001a) and the generation of more 'remote' and uncommon associations in spontaneous word generation tasks (Duchêne et al., 1998). A recent divided visual field experiment confirmed that the enhanced capacity of believers to appreciate indirectly related information was specifically related to LVF/RH presentations (Pizzagalli et al., 2001).

It is at this point that the study of paranormal belief becomes relevant to domains extending far beyond the boundaries of 'anomalistic' psychology. The crucial role of associative processing in the emergence of pathological ideas of reference has long been recognized in cognitive neuropsychiatry. Specifically, a disinhibition of spreading semantic network activation was suggested as the

---

[6] Analogous breakdowns in normal laterality patterns associated with paranormal belief have been demonstrated in the olfactory modality (Mohr et al., 2001b) and motor system (Barnett and Corballis, 2002; Mohr et al., 2003).

basis of schizophrenic thought disorder (Spitzer, 1997, for an overview), and the RH was shown to be essential in establishing the remote associations inherent to delusional thought (Weisbrod *et al.*, 1998). In fact, a breakdown in the regular hemispheric pattern of language dominance is currently regarded as a key aspect in the genesis of psychotic disorders (e.g. Crow, 1997). The conceptual similarities between paranormal belief and schizophrenic thought disorder are clearly uncomfortable for parapsychologists and have accordingly been downplayed in the parapsychological literature.[7] The recognition of these commonalities, however, does not pathologize paranormal belief: the psychopathological distinction between (healthy) beliefs in the paranormal and (pathological) delusional thinking is obvious. Moreover, the propensity to perceive meaningful connections has been considered a prerequisite for some highly valued forms of thinking.

Implications for the understanding of creativity

One dimension of creative thinking can be conceptualized as the ability to bridge associative gaps, a task uniquely suited to the diffuse RH semantic processing style. While early speculations of an involvement of the RH in creative reasoning were harshly criticized on the grounds that testable hypotheses are lacking (e.g. Hines, 1991), recent empirical studies have significantly changed this picture. Weinstein and Graves (2001, 2002), for example, reported significant relationships between creativity, schizotypy and RH language processing as measured in divided visual field (2001, 2002) and dichotic listening (2002) tasks, and Gianotti *et al.* (2001) found that believers in paranormal phenomena generated more original solutions in verbal creativity tasks. Numerous other, exciting and easily testable research questions employing the neuropsychological methodologies described above remain to be further investigated: do highly creative people evidence a RH processing bias? Indeed, what are the similarities and *dis*similarities between creativity and paranormal belief?

The behavioural relationships reported above, including the association between belief in the paranormal and creativity, can be summarized in terms of signal detection theory (Tanner and Swets, 1954; see Blackmore *et al.*, 1994, and Kreweras, 1983, for the relevance to paranormal belief). According to this theory, specific kinds of error behaviour arise from the adoption of either loose or strict response criteria. An individual with a loose response criterion requires little signal strength before a pattern is detected. An individual whose response criterion is strict, on the other hand, will need a large signal strength before perceiving a pattern. Significantly, the overall accuracies of both groups of individuals are comparable, it is the *type of error* they commit which distinguishes them. The former group will tend to perceive patterns where none exist, resulting in 'false alarms', whereas the latter group will more often fail to detect existing patterns ('misses'; see Table 1). We suggest that differences in hemispheric

---

[7] A particularly distorted picture was presented by Irwin and Green (1998/1999), whose 'review' of the relationships between the concepts of schizotypy and paranormal belief neglected the relevant literature.

activation levels underlie an individual's proneness to one of these two error types. In particular, a heightened RH activation (corresponding to a widespread activation of the semantic network and coactivation of distantly related concepts) leads to more false alarms ('everything is related'), whereas an increased LH activation (corresponding to focal network activation and coactivation of closely related concepts) results in more misses ('objects are unrelated').

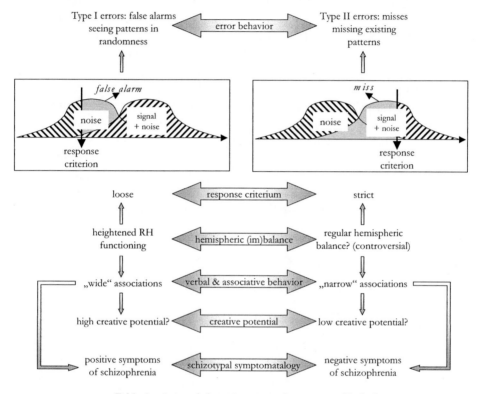

Table 1: A signal-detection view of paranormal belief

The identification of a meaningful pattern in noisy stimuli or a meaningful association between distantly related events does not inevitably lead to the belief that a paranormal phenomenon caused it. Indeed, some artists employ their pattern recognition capacities to inspire their creations, and not to argue for the existence of e.g. ESP. What underlies the tendency of some to attribute a paranormal causation to events others consider coincidental — how does this paranormal jump occur?

The paranormal jump

How do believers account for their subjective impressions of meaning in random displays or relationships between events with no obvious connection? To paraphrase Paley (1809), how did they come to be? To investigate this question, we adopted a problem-solving task from the behaviouristic literature on 'superstitious' behaviour (see Figure 3 and, for a comprehensive review, Brugger *et al.*, 1994a). Participants played a computer game which entailed moving a mouse from the lower left corner of the monitor onto a field containing a trap, after which they were either rewarded with a cheese or punished by the closing of the trap. They were instructed to find out during 100 trials how the game worked and report their hypotheses following the experiment. Unbeknownst to the subjects, the time interval between start and finish was the only factor determining the delivery of a reward or punishment. Believers (as measured by the MI scale; Eckblad and Chapman, 1983)[8] tested fewer hypotheses during the game and were more inclined to believe that their (at times elaborate; see Figure 3) motor patterns controlled the computer's feedback than disbelievers (Brugger and Graves, 1997a). In a similar vein, the belief that one is able to influence chance is positively associated with belief in the paranormal (the 'illusion of control'; Strickland *et al.*, 1966) in a variety of experimental settings (Blackmore and Troscianko, 1985; Brugger *et al.*, 1991; Musch and Ehrenberg, 2002).

Armed with these findings, the paranormal jump could be explained as follows: Believers tend to perceive more meaningful patterns in random and disordered stimuli and perceive more meaningful relationships between distantly associated objects or events than disbelievers. These oblique connections are

A   **B**

trial:	response sequence:	feedback:
1	RRUU	−
2	RURU	−
3	RRULLURR	+
4	RUUR	−
5	UURR	−
90 intervening trials		
96	URDLURDLURUR	+
97	URDLURDLURDLURUR	+
98	URDLURDLURDLURUR	+
99	URDLURDLURRU	+
100	URDLURDLURRU	−

Figure 3

A: The screen as it was presented to the subjects in the computer game designed by Brugger and Graves (1997a). Subjects were instructed to move the mouse from the lower left corner onto the field containing the trap. The final move was either 'rewarded' with the cheese or 'punished' by the closing of the trap. The type of feedback depended on the amount of time the participant took to reach the target field; times faster than 4 sec were punished and slower times were rewarded with the cheese. Subjects were unaware of these contingencies and were instructed to find out, during 100 trials, 'how the game worked'.

B: Sequence of key presses (D=down, L=left, R=right, U=up; '+' and '−' indicate negative and positive feedback, respectively) for the first and last five trials of one subject who claimed that 'in order to get the cheese, I had to jump on the central field at least 3 times, repetitious jumps separated by at least three jumps elsewhere'.

[8] See footnote 4.

characteristic of the cause–effect relationships postulated to underlie many paranormal phenomena, which are thus analogously perceived as being meaningful (i.e. real). Some paranormal phenomena, such as ESP or psychokinesis, implicate the active involvement of the subject. If one considers the believer as one element in the meaningful association, then events transpiring in the environment would be perceived as being meaningfully related to the believer, even when no obvious relationship exists. Moreover, believers perceive a causal relationship between their actions and these environmental events — they have the 'illusion of control'. Finally, believers tend not to test alternative hypotheses. The result is a highly resistant belief in a paranormal causation of the event.

II: From Causality to Correlation.
Extrasensory Perception as an Effect of Subjective Probability

> Random number generation is too important to be left to chance.
> (Robert R. Coveyou, 1969, p. 70)

Phantom hunt in para-parapsychology

Rupert Sheldrake's (1994) popular book *Seven Experiments that could Change the World* is intended to be a 'do-it-yourself guide to revolutionary science' (subtitle). In actuality, it is more of a collection of the seven deadly sins of science and, from a philosophy of science standpoint, a documentation of the reasons why parapsychology is regarded as a pseudoscience. Here we are concerned with only one of its fallacies, i.e. the misinterpretation of learning effects in guessing studies involving immediate feedback on response accuracy. For example, Sheldrake performed an experiment allegedly demonstrating that a phantom limb is more than a subjective phenomenon. The experimental setup was simple: in a long series of trials, an amputee either raised or lowered his phantom leg into a predetermined space. A sensitive person touched the space which would have 'contained' the amputee's raised phantom and decided after each trial whether or not he had the impression of touching the phantom. Sheldrake illustrated the results of some 200 consecutive trials in a figure that, as trivial as it may look, conveyed such fundamental information about 'implicit sequence learning' that we reproduce it here (Figure 4).

Sheldrake interpreted the statistically significant learning effect shown in Figure 4 as the improvement, over nearly 200 trials, of the sensitive person's ability to feel an amputee's phantom limb. However, two properties of the experimental situation (noted parenthetically among a list of precautions to guarantee 'sensory shielding') should prompt us to question this interpretation: (1) 'Rather than using a random generator to determine whether in any given trial the phantom was to be raised or lowered, the experimenter made up a random-type sequence as they went along' (Sheldrake, 1994, pp. 137–8); and (2) trial-by-trial feedback was provided. Given that healthy individuals' spontaneously generated 'random-type' sequences are far from being random (see Part I, for references) and that they are adept at identifying sequential biases in pseudorandom

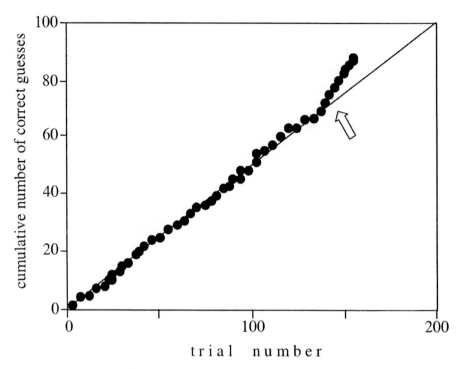

Figure 4. A sensitive's sudden increase in the accuracy of presence/absence decisions of another person's phantom limb after the subject 'had learned how the phantom felt'. The statistically significant deviation of guessing accuracy from about trial 140 onward (arrow) is arguably due to the implicit learning of the amputee's sequential bias in the binary sequence of phantom limb movements. This bias was transmitted to the sensitive by trial-by-trial feedback via normal sensory channels (redrawn from Sheldrake, 1994, Figure 11, p. 139).

sequences (Hake and Hyman, 1953), the learning effect illustrated in Figure 4 must be interpreted as a consequence of the feedback that enabled the 'sensitive' to adjust his guesses to the targets on a probabilistic basis. For example, after having learned (from feedback) that the amputee consistently raised his phantom leg on three, but not four consecutive trials, an effective guessing strategy would be to guess 'no phantom' following three consecutive raised phantoms. Classically, this type of information acquisition is referred to as 'statistical learning', 'probability learning' (Hunt and Aslin, 2001; Jones, 1971) or 'implicit sequence learning' (Destrebecqz and Cleeremans, 2001). As long as the feedback is provided via normal sensory channels, it cannot be disrupted by constructing Faraday cages, by covering the guesser's head with a hood (Sheldrake, 1994, p. 137) or by erecting a wall between the guesser and the amputee (p. 143). Since the source of the 'receiver's' learning is the feedback about the 'sender's' pattern sequence and not about the sender himself, this paradigm is one of common information transfer, far from involving anything paranormal and, in the present case, devoid of any 'objective reality' of phantom limbs.[9]

---

[9] The learning of sequential constraints could also be labelled 'phantom learning' in analogy to the phantom limb percept, as phenomenal awareness about the stimulus is absent in both cases. After deafferentation, an amputee's sensorimotor system 'fills in' the sudden gap in perception

Parapsychologists may argue that Sheldrake's (1994) phantom hunt is not representative of parapsychological research. Rupert Sheldrake is known as a successful author of best-selling books that foster folklore and may not be seriously intended to promote scientific progress. Although this do-it-yourself experiment on phantom limb perception may appear naïve, identical methodologies have been employed by some well-known research parapsychologists.

Phantom hunt in 'academic' parapsychology:
Implicit sequence learning in ESP research

A prominent example of implicit sequence learning is presented in an early book by Charles T. Tart (1976) entitled *Learning to use ESP*. Tart promoted the use of trial-by-trial feedback to efficiently activate subjects' latent ESP faculties in guessing situations. Unlike Sheldrake (1994), target sequences were not haphazardly constructed by humans, but methodologically by machines. Unfortunately, randomization is a process technically as difficult to achieve (Kosambi and Rao, 1958; Modianos *et al.*, 1984) as its product is difficult to unambiguously evaluate (Chaitin, 1975; Lopes, 1982). 'Pseudo-random generators' always employ some algorithm (i.e. a computer program) to generate sequences that are more or less patterned. This state is not improved by using 'true' random generators based on electronic noise or some other natural random process, as these likewise require an algorithm to translate the sampled bits into a string of discrete symbols, a procedure which may introduce bias (e.g. von Hoerner, 1957; see also the classified bibliographies on philosophy and techniques of random number generation by Sowey, 1972, 1978; and Sahai, 1979). The central factor in the present discussion, however, is the *predictability* of the employed sequence, irrespective of how it was generated. It is exactly here that opinions diverge: parapsychologists believe their target sequences to be unpredictable and thus interpret any above-chance guessing as indicative of ESP. Sceptics, on the other hand, interpret the same finding of above-chance guessing as an indication that the sequences employed were significantly predictable (and, thus, non-random).

This fundamental disagreement regarding predictability and randomness is reflected in conflicting interpretations of Tart's (1976) data. Gatlin (1979), Kennedy (1980) and Stanford (1977) showed that the target sequences used in Tart's data were significantly patterned, a fact that led to the conceptualization of ESP as a non-parapsychological pattern matching process mediated by feedback and therefore of general relevance to experimental psychology (Gatlin, 1977a; 1978; 1979). In brief, Gatlin (1979) reanalysed Tart's (1976) data and showed that the degree of non-randomness of a target sequence (i.e. its 'patterning') was

---

(Ramachandran, 1993), yet the subject experiences the phantom as 'originating' in extracorporeal space. A similar filling in occurs when a person is deprived of direct sensory information about a sequence of alternatives. This probabilistic information processing, which occurs in the absence of conscious monitoring, is ascribed to extrasensory hunches in paranormal sequence learning experiments. The critical feature differentiating scientific and pseudoscientific research of limb or cognitive phantoms is that the former recognizes their subjective nature whereas the latter assumes that they originate 'out there' (see Brugger, 2001, for a comprehensive review).

significantly correlated with a subject's ESP scores for that particular sequence. This finding suggested that subjects adjusted the sequence of their guesses to match that of the targets, just as the psychological literature on implicit learning of a statistical structure (e.g. Hake and Hyman, 1953) would have predicted. Tart defended his original ESP hypothesis by stating that the patterns in the target series he used (1) were too weak a signal to be detected by human subjects, and that (2) 'such patterns can be found, to varying degrees, in the data of any and every psychological and parapsychological experiment' (Tart, 1976, p. 82). We agree with the second statement, but unlike Tart, we see a serious problem for parapsychological research if the presence of such patterns is met with euphemism. If, however, the 'pararandom' nature (Gilmore, 1989, p. 333) of a target series, i.e. its deviation from randomness in an ideal sense, were taken seriously by parapsychologists, an entirely new view of 'learning to use ESP' would materialize.

Based on the reactions of the parapsychological community to the Gatlin–Tart controversy, the time did not appear ripe for such a paradigm shift. With the exception of Stanford (1977), numerous commentators rigidly defended their *a priori* belief in an extrasensory causation of above-chance matching, and the essence of Gatlin's message was clearly not understood. Braude (1979, p. 179), for instance, noted that ' her [Gatlin's] suggestions are, on the whole, either unintelligible or otherwise unacceptable' and Beloff (1978, p. 70) admitted: 'I cannot pretend that I understood Dr. Lila Gatlin's paper . . .'. As a consequence, parapsychologists have largely missed the opportunity to turn the artifacts they either downplayed or frankly denied into proper objects of investigation. Had they continued research along the lines proposed by Tart (1976), albeit concentrating on the known source of information (i.e. patterning in the target sequences) and the known way it was transmitted to the subject (i.e. the feedback), parapsychology could have contributed to basic questions of probabilistic information processing. Such an approach was adopted by Tart and Dronek (1982) who set out to empirically determine the extent to which the information in pseudorandom sequences could be exploited by a computer program. Their 'probabilitistic predictor program' (PPP) was designed to predict a target symbol on the basis of information about the preceding 5 symbols. They found that the PPP was less successful at predicting the original target sequences than human subjects. While we would interpret this finding as the superiority of feedback learning in human beings compared to the particular computer program used by Tart and Dronek (1982), the authors themselves arrived at quite a different conclusion, i.e. since the PPP's matching ability was assumed unassailable, the subjects' performances were interpreted as supporting the existence of ESP.[10] More recently, Colwell *et al.* (2000) demonstrated implicit feedback learning of sequential bias to occur in much less trials than Tart (1976) had administered. Palmer (1996; 1997) set out to quantitatively assess the contribution of implicit feedback learning to guessing scores in previously published ESP experiments. He found that

---

[10] '. . . we do claim that our procedure [the PPP] looks to be far more powerful than anything we could reasonably expect to find in a typical human being' (Tart and Dronek, 1982, p. 334).

while such learning took place, it could not fully account for the observed effect sizes.

As if intuitively feeling that Gatlin's (1977a) alternative account of ESP would constitute a deadly blow to what had always been regarded as the object of parapsychological research,[11] parapsychologists began to concentrate their efforts on non-feedback experiments. It was generally argued that, in the absence of feedback, nothing about the sequential structure of the targets could be learned and, therefore, any above-chance matching scores would necessarily be the consequence of an extrasensory information transfer.

Above-chance guessing in the absence of feedback[12]

Above-chance guesses of long sequences of target alternatives depends not only on trial-by-trial feedback. Goodfellow (1938/1992) comprehensively analysed over one million responses to a series of ESP tests broadcast by a radio company. Over the whole series, the guesses of the responding listeners significantly matched the target sequences selected by the radio company. Facing odds of 1 to 10,000,000,000,000,000,000,000, these findings seemed to indicate ESP on the part of the responders. However, by analysing the unequal distributions of single guesses and target symbol occurrences, Goodfellow convincingly demonstrated that response preferences could coincide with the target symbol patterning in the absence of any transfer of information (Goodfellow, 1938/1992). Contemporary leading parapsychologists regarded Goodfellow's report as only tangentially related to the subject matter of ESP. Pratt *et al.* (1940/1966), for example, pointed out that the broadcast tests were not representative of the techniques used in academic parapsychology as they only employed a very small number of trials per run and the possible choices were mostly binary.

Later critics of parapsychological matching procedures were more concerned with the common sequential dependencies within guess and target sequences. Specifically, any finite sequence of alternatives necessarily contains some bias (Brown, 1953a,b; 1957; Gatlin, 1977a) which, if *it happens* to match the pattern inherent in a human random generator, will inflate matching scores. If, on the other hand, a physical random generation device *happens* to produce a patterning that runs counter to human sequential response biases, matching scores will be lower than mathematical chance ('psi missing' in traditional parapsychological terminology). There are several ways in which a subject's guesses can be brought 'in phase' with target sequences. One method is to use instructions to bias the

---

[11] Beloff's (1978, pp. 70–1) emotional summary of Gatlin's (1977a) model reflects the general puzzle parapsychologists saw themselves confronted with: 'What a devastating conclusion to arrive at after a century of psychical research!'

[12] Here we are concerned only with the standard ESP paradigm, i.e. the forced-choice guessing of event sequences where each event has a limited number of alternatives. Some authors have claimed (e.g. Bem and Honorton, 1994) that alternative paradigms (especially those employed in ganzfeld and autoganzfeld studies; see Palmer's contribution to this issue of the *Journal of Consciousness Studies*) are undeserving of the critique outlined in this section. The inverse correlation between matching performance and the quality of target randomization in these paradigms (Hyman, 1985; 1994; but see Bem, 1994) questions this assumption.

Figure 5: A test person in an 'imaginary questionnaire' paradigm (Katz *et al.*, 1990; Whitfield, 1950) which requires subjects to make multiple-choice decisions irrespective of the content of the question (i.e. implicit randomization). Panel one illustrates how inferences about a single item could bring a response sequence in phase with the sequence of questions (cf. Goodfellow, 1938/1992). The statistical structure of imaginary questionnaire responses differentiates believers and disbelievers in ESP (Brugger and Baumann, 1994).

Adapted, with permission, from de Zeeuw and Wagenaar (1974) by Hazel Brugger.

very first guess (Goodfellow, 1938/1992). However, even in the absence of such instructions, 'population stereotypes' prevent the first of a sequence of guesses (or a single isolated guess) from being uncontaminated by bias (e.g. Hill, 1988; Kubovy and Psotka, 1976; see Figure 5).

This potential confound has been recognized since the beginning of the history of parapsychology. For instance, Willoughby (1935) suggested that the chance baseline for a match between guess and target sequences should not be the theoretical value of 1/n (where n is the number of alternatives to be guessed), but rather a value empirically determined by matching two sets of randomized target sequences. With respect to the special case of the target sequence of a deck of cards, he showed that matching one (well-shuffled) deck of cards with another could lead to an effect of pseudo-ESP, i.e. an above-chance matching even higher than that observed from matching human subjects' guesses to a deck of cards! Similar results were reported by Feller (1940, footnote 19). An especially ardent controversy within parapsychology was initiated by Brown (1953a,b; 1957), who obtained 'extra-chance' results when he matched the number sequences from published random number tables. He also demonstrated highly significant 'decline effects' (i.e. lower matching scores in the last compared to the first quartile of the data) in the same matching data originally used to refute his views (Oram, 1954; see also Mulholland, 1938, for similar observations). Brown's (1957) lengthy treatise on 'Probability and Scientific Inference' ultimately attempted to demonstrate that since finite sequences are never ideally random, traditional statistics based on probability models which assume ideal randomness are wrong. His philosophy aimed to counteract the common opinion that 'randomness' could easily be produced — an opinion popular at this time.[13] Brown did not set out to critique parapsychology; his critique was directed at all fields of science which based their conclusions on a statistical treatment of data. However, the issue of randomization is less prominent in most behavioural sciences than in parapsychology where performances notoriously scatter around 'chance': if a normally sighted person in a normally illuminated room is instructed to name the colour of a playing card (red vs. black) individually presented from the deck, naming accuracy will hardly depend on how well the deck was shuffled. If, on the other hand, card colour has to be telepathically 'perceived', the quality of randomization becomes a crucial issue.

It is surprising that a topic as hotly debated as the 'Spencer Brown intervention in psychical research' (Scott, 1958), especially in the correspondence sections of major parapsychological periodicals, stimulated so little prospective research.[14] One exception was a study by Pöppel (1967), which focused on the periodic components in subjects' guesses of card sequences in shuffled decks (each with twenty-five cards, five cards in each deck contained one of the five Zener symbols; classical chance expectation for a hit = 50.0). Subjects were administered ten 'down through' runs each according to the standard method proposed by Rhine and Pratt (1957), and their target sequences were subjected to periodicity analyses. Pöppel (1967) found (1) that matching performances of the entire group of twenty-one subjects significantly exceeded the classical chance expectation, and (2) a strong positive correlation across individual subjects between the number of hits and the phasic synchrony of the guess and target sequences' periodic components. In other words, since long, consecutive runs of the same symbol were underrepresented in the decks (because each symbol appeared only five times) as well as in the guesses (because of subjects' repetition avoidance), above-chance matching simply reflected the presence of similar sequential biases in both sequences, and not transfer of information. Instead of adopting Pöppel's (1967) analytical method in future empirical work, it was deemed inadequate. Timm (1967) criticized that Pöppel's experimental design did not allow

---

[13] Bork (1967) conceived of the popularity of random generation as one of the prominent characteristics of the twentieth century.

[14] A 'pseudo' effect of psi *missing* was later described in Harvie's (1973) study which matched computer generated random numbers to a table of published random digits. However, the absurdity of drawing causal inferences from local regularities in random sequences was most beautifully demonstrated by Cole (1957) in his analysis of the periodicities in the metabolic activity of unicorns.

for the refutation of genuine ESP and designated it a 'boomerang that comes close to prove the ESP that it set out to disprove' (p. 85). He suggested that the periodicities common to guess and target sequences were not increasing an individual's guessing accuracy, but were *due to* the subjects' ESP.[15]

The interpretation that above-chance matching performance results from common sequential information in guess and target sequences has been attacked on more rational grounds. One such counterargument was based on individual differences in ESP performance as a function of personality factors. For instance, Wassermann (1956, p. 139) noted in his critique of Brown (1953a,b) that 'the correlations between personality structure and scoring habits and between the subject's attitude and his scoring habits [. . .] could in no way be explained as being due to a lack of randomization'. At first, this point seems well-taken; performances in games of pure chance cannot be influenced by attitudinal factors. However, guessing performances with pseudorandom sequences may depend on guessing habits in the form of sequential response biases. Thus, subjects with differing personality structures and attitudes may very well score differently on ESP tests *if these same personality variables also systematically influence sequential guessing behaviour*. Indeed, some subject variables that modify ESP guessing performances are also known to systematically influence sequential response bias. For instance, subjects' age, extraversion scores and measures of psychoticism have all been identified as important factors in ESP research (see Blackmore, 1980; Palmer, 1978; Sargent, 1981, for respective overviews) and are at the same time among the variables which systematically influence the amount of information in subject-generated random sequences (Brugger, 1997, for overview). Similarly, the experimental manipulations which reportedly influence subjects' performances on ESP tasks (e.g. task duration, the mode and spontaneity of responding) are known to reliably affect the generation of subjective random sequences (see Brugger *et al.*, 1990 for a tabular overview). Of particular relevance are dimensional variables for which opposite ESP scores relative to 'chance expectation' are predicted (i.e. 'psi hitting' vs. 'psi missing'). One such variable is the class of centrally active drugs. While the administration of sedating and activating drugs was associated with above- and below-chance ESP performance, respectively (Sargent, 1977), these neuropharmacological

---

[15] In a rather polemic editorial in the same issue of the *Zeitschrift für Parapsychologie und Grenzgebiete der Psychologie*, which contained the contributions from Pöppel and Timm, late Professor Hans Bender (1967) proclaimed 'young author' Pöppel's contribution as fallacious, suggesting that it was biased by the social perception of a 'sceptical outsider' and that only the use of an established terminology made it appear reliable. As with Timm (1967), a similarly uncanny 'inertia of belief systems' (Fleck, 1935/1979) was exemplified by one commentator of Brown's (1953a) mock ESP experiments which had pairwise matched columns of random number tables: '. . . if the columns were selected by cutting a book, the result may have been influenced by extrasensory perception; if they were selected by rolling a die, the result may have been influenced by psychokinesis; and if they were selected by the next day's temperature, the result may have been influenced by precognition' (Nash, 1954, p. 582). Alcock (1981) provided more examples of how critique of ESP turns into evidence for ESP. Clearly, a similar will to believe can bias data interpretation within the established sciences; see e.g. the replies to Cook's (1995) fundamental critique of the interpretation of neural network simulations of perceptual processes.

interventions were also found to have opposite effects on at least one major sequential response bias, i.e. repetition behaviour (Douglas and Isaacson, 1966; Egger *et al.*, 1973; Squire, 1969). It thus appears that, rather than modifying *sensitivity* to ESP, centrally active drugs influence *response behaviour* and, consequently, matching performance in guessing experiments with pseudorandom target sequences.[16]

The variable parapsychologists recognize as most consistently accounting for between-subject variance in ESP performance is belief in the paranormal. The so-called 'sheep–goat effect' (Schmeidler and McConnell, 1958) states that believers in ESP ('sheep') commonly score better on ESP tests than disbelievers ('goats'). In view of the evidence presented in Part I above, the sheep–goat effect does not undermine the response bias account of ESP (e.g. Mischo, 1979, p. 14). On the contrary, the systematic differences between believers and disbelievers in paranormal phenomena in the appreciation and especially in the generation of randomness are consistent with (and even predict) differential matching performances of pseudorandomly arranged targets. The non-sensory view of ESP is more than a fundamental critique of traditional parapsychological concepts, it also offers a theoretical springboard for the constructive reformulation of the parapsychological subject matter.

Slaying the phantom:
The transition from a causal to a correlational study of paranormal phenomena

> Not the neglect of randomness, but its effective and purposeful use will promote research.   (Ernst Mach, 1896, p. 295)

In their analysis of the concept of subjective probability, Wagenaar and Keren (1988; p. 65) noted that 'few ideas are so deeply engraved in our minds as the notion that events have their causes'. In Part I, we attempted to describe the factors which lead people to believe in an extrasensory causation of everyday coincidences. Part II outlined an alternative view of ESP as an Effect of Subjective Probability. This new meaning of the acronym 'ESP' represents an extension of a previous suggestion to simply translate ESP as 'Error Some Place' (Wolfle, 1956) as the location of the error is now specified: matching performances reflect the degree of overlap between a sequence of guesses necessarily governed by the laws of subjective probability and a finite sequence of targets necessarily containing sequential bias. Thus, the proper study of ESP requires a correlational, rather than causal, approach. Table 2 summarizes several of the problems

---

[16] A particularly interesting secondary effect in ESP research was described by Haraldsson (1980) and labelled 'percipient-order effect'. Briefly, if the 'sender'–'percipient' pair in an ESP experiment switch roles, higher matching score will be achieved by the individual who first acted as the percipient than by the subject who was first the sender. This effect reflects a 'global feedback' of the constraints in target sequences (cf. Colwell *et al.*, 2000) which later boost matching performances. The fact that percipient-order effects are *not* observed in free-choice paradigms (with no feedback about the sequential structure of target sequences; Haraldsson and Gissurarson, 1986/1987; Houtkooper *et al.*, 1988/1989) further supports an implicit sequence learning view of matching performances. Unfortunately, to our knowledge, the effect of percipient-order on the sequential randomness of subjects' guesses has not yet been studied.

ESP as Extra-Sensory Perception

transfer of information, causal interpretation

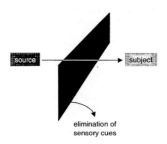

elimination of
sensory cues

ESP as an Effect of Subjective Probability

common sequential information, correlative interpretation

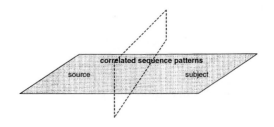

Inherent problems:	Resolutions offered:
The term 'extrasensory' is either paradoxical (if meant to stand for 'perception without sensory mediation') or apologetic (if referring to an as yet unknown sensory modality).	⇨ The term 'effect of subjective probability' unambiguously refers to a process that is extra-sensory in the radical sense of *non*-sensory. ESP is a phenomenon inherent to sequential response production.
Postulated information carrier is not known.	⇨ No carrier is implicated.
Postulated central nervous system circuits for the integration of ESP information is not delineated.	⇨ Role of frontal-subcortical circuits for sequential response production is outlined.
Independence of distance between source and subject (telepathy, clairvoyance) and reverse-causation (precognition) contradicts basic axioms of science.	⇨ Common sequential information is independent of the separation of source and subject in space and time.
Psychokinesis: in addition to a hypothetical extra*sensory* function, an extra*motor* function must be postulated.	⇨ Psychokinesis does not involve motor processing but is an Effect of Subjective Probability as well.
PSI-missing (i.e., below-chance ESP performance) and displacement effects (i.e., above-chance matching of guesses to targets shifted by a certain lag) require secondary coding processes whose nature is obscure.	⇨ Guess and target sequences contain opposite biases (below-chance matching) or shifted phase information (peak in the autocorrelation function).
Experimental manipulations which produce both opposite scores on ESP tests (i.e., above- vs. below-chance matching) as well as opposite effects on perceptual functions have not swayed parapsychologists to abandon the transfer view of ESP.	⇨ Such opposite effects are predicted on the basis of known opposite effects on sequential response production (e.g., administration of activating vs. sedating drugs).
Personality differences in ESP performance have distracted parapsychologists from abandoning the transfer-view of ESP although the same differences are also known to modulate perceptual functions.	⇨ Personality differences in matching performance are predicted by personality differences in response bias (e.g., extraversion/introversion).
Concerns about ideal randomness of the target sequences are not only futile but distract from further testing of the presumed effect and thus inhibit the development of testable hypotheses.	⇨ Systematic variations of the information content of target series (with or without simultaneous manipulations of response bias) increase the possibility to conduct replication studies and thus promote the development of testable hypotheses.
Models relying on causality without describing the exact relationship between cause and effect prevent the acceptance of parapsychology by the established behavioral sciences.	⇨ Matching paradigms as traditionally used in parapsychology become of interest to various fields of experimental psychology and especially neuropsychology if matching performance is interpreted as a function of shared sequential information.

Table 2: Two opponent paradigms of experimental parapsychology

The left column represents the traditional, causal view of ESP that implies a transfer of information from a 'source' (i.e., a pseudorandom target sequence) to the subject. The major incompatibilities of this view with traditional scientific knowledge are listed. The right column represents the alternative, noncausal view of a correlation between the source and the subject (i.e., a sequence of guesses) due to shared sequential information. This view is fully compatible with basic axioms of science and, once adopted, would radically change parapsychology's object of investigation (modified from Brugger, 1991, Figure 9).

inherent in the causal view of ESP as traditionally upheld in parapsychology. These begin at the level of terminology: the term 'extrasensory' is paradoxical if used to refer to 'perception without sensory mediation'. On the other hand, if 'extrasensory' refers to a form of anomalous information transfer *by an as yet undiscovered sense*, it becomes clear that its investigation will cease to be a subject of *para*-psychology once such a sense is discovered. This terminological problem is resolved when ESP is considered an Effect of Subjective Probability, as are problems resulting from the assumption of a transfer of information (i.e. information carriers, receptors and higher-level central nervous system functions). Table 2 also addresses secondary 'paranormal' effects which have been notoriously difficult to interpret, such as psi missing and displacement, and considers psychokinesis (PK; i.e. purported interactions between mind and matter) as conceptually related to ESP. New approaches, correlational in nature, to the investigation of these effects are suggested.

On first consideration, the model depicted in Table 2 resembles previous conceptualizations of ESP and PK which also postulated that information is not transferred from a 'sender' to a 'receiver'. For example, twenty-five years ago, Stanford (1978) introduced a 'conformance behaviour model' of ESP and PK as phenomena devoid of any perceptual or communicative processes and independent of the temporal and spatial separation of an individual from a natural source of randomness. Instead, he suggested that psi effects were based on the needs or behavioural states of an organism which accordingly biased the informational content of a random generator. It is evident from this teleological component that Stanford's model is still goal-directed and thus essentially causal. In contrast, our own model suggests that psi can be observed when the inherent biases in two sequences are congruous. In an experimental environment where all other factors remain constant, individual differences in psi would exclusively be the result of individual differences in the direction and size of the guessing biases.

The transition from a causal to a correlational interpretation of ESP is not a deadly blow to parapsychology; on the contrary, it offers parapsychology the opportunity to become a worthy field of investigation within the behavioural sciences.[17] Guessing behaviour, the process of anticipation and the learning of sequential constraints are all topical issues in behavioural neuroscience (e.g. Bischoff-Grethe *et al.*, 2000; Critchley *et al.*, 2001; Elliott *et al.*, 1999; Huettel *et al.*, 2002; Seidenberg, 1997) which would profit from the new data offered by the matching paradigms from parapsychology. Of special relevance will be interindividual differences in the randomization of guesses: although a 'randomizing homunculus' (Alcock, 1981, p. 155) may not exist in the brain (and sequential nonrandomness may be incompatible with even the most primitive manifestations of life; Brugger *et al.*, 2002), current neuropsychology shows a strong interest in the variables that influence sequential response biases (Brugger, 1997 for overview; cf. also Carpenter, 1999). An ideal approach would involve the joint collaboration of traditional parapsychology and neuroscience: findings from prospective research conducted by representatives of two apparently conflicting views will most likely be

---

[17] In fact, current theoretical parapsychology attempts to account for purported anomalous information transfer in terms of quantum mechanics, nonlinear dynamics or psychodynamic processes which bring to mind the naïve 'mental radio' metaphor for ESP forwarded when the radio was still a relatively new invention. Less exotic proposals which recognize the inappropriateness of causal interpretations of ESP have not been met with comparable acceptance (e.g. Baldwin, 1976; Flew, 1987).

taken seriously by both sides. We thus anticipate that, although psi would vanish from the scene as a process of information transfer, it would live on as a phenomenon of subjective probability worthy of scientific investigation.[18]

Acknowledgments

We thank Chris French (London) and Michael A. Thalbourne (Adelaide, Australia) for their bibliographic assistance and Hazel Brugger for her help with Figure 5.

Some of the research described in this article was supported by the 'Institut für Grenzbebiete der Psychologie und Psychohygiene' (Freiburg i. Brsg., Germany) and the Betty and David Koetser Foundation for Brain Research.

References

Alcock, J.E. (1981), *Parapsychology — Science or Magic?* (Oxford: Pergamon Press).

Anaki, D., Faust, M. and Kravetz, S. (1998), 'Cerebral hemispheric asymmetries in processing lexical metaphors', *Neuropsychologia*, **36** (4), pp. 353–62.

Baldwin, H.W. (1976), 'Conceptualizations of experimental clairvoyance', *Journal of Parapsychology*, **40**, pp. 136–44.

Barnett, K.J., Corballis, M.C. (2002), 'Ambidexterity and magical ideation', *Laterality*, **7**, pp. 75–84.

Becknell, E.A. (1940), 'Probability: a function of ideology', *American Journal of Psychology*, **53**, pp. 604–9.

Beeman, M., Friedman, R.B., Grafman, J., Perez, E., Diamond, S. and Lindsay, M.B. (1994), 'Summation priming and coarse semantic coding in the right hemisphere', *Journal of Cognitive Neuroscience*, **6**, pp. 26–45.

Beloff, J. (1978), 'On "meaningful information creation" ' (letter), *Journal of the American Society for Psychical Research*, **72**, pp. 70–1.

Bem, D.J. (1994), 'Anomaly or artifact? — Response', *Psychological Bulletin*, **115**, pp. 25–7.

Bem, D.J. and Honorton, C. (1994), 'Does psi exist? Replicable evidence for an anomalous process of information transfer', *Psychological Bulletin*, **115**, pp. 4–18.

Bender, H. (1967), 'Zum Problem der "Scheinsignifikanzen" bei ASW-Experimenten. Eine Diskussion', *Zeitschrift für Parapsychologie und Grenzgebiete der Psychologie*, **10**, pp. 61–2.

Bischoff-Grethe, A., Proper, S.M., Mao, H., Daniels, K.A. and Berns, G.S. (2000), 'Conscious and unconscious processing of nonverbal predictability in Wernicke's area', *Journal of Neuroscience*, **20**, pp. 1975–81.

Blackmore, S. (1980), 'A study of memory and ESP in young children', *Journal of the Society for Psychical Research*, **50**, pp. 501–20.

Blackmore, S.J., Galaud, K. and Walker, C. (1994), 'Psychic experiences as illusions of causality', in *Research in Parapsychology 1991*, ed. E. Cook and D. Delanoy (Metuchen, NJ: Scarecrow Press), pp. 89–93.

Blackmore, S. and Moore, R. (1994), 'Seeing things: visual recognition and belief in the paranormal', *European Journal of Parapsychology*, **10**, pp. 91–103.

Blackmore, S. and Troscianko, T. (1985), 'Belief in the paranormal: probability judgments, illusory control, and the "chance baseline shift" ', *British Journal of Psychology*, **76**, pp. 459–68.

Bork, A.M. (1967), 'Randomness and the twentieth century', *Antioch Review*, **27**, pp. 40–61.

Bottini, G., Corcoran, R., Sterzi, R., Paulesu, E., Schenone, P., Scarpa, P., Frackowiak, R.S.J. and Frith, C.D. (1994), 'The role of the right hemisphere in the interpretation of figurative aspects of language. A positron emission tomography activation study', *Brain*, **117**, pp. 1241–53.

Braude, S.E. (1979), 'Objections to an information-theoretic approach to synchronicity', *Journal of the American Society for Psychical Research*, **73**, pp. 179–93.

Bressan, P. (2002), 'The connection between random sequences, everyday coincidences, and belief in the paranormal', *Applied Cognitive Psychology*, **16**, pp. 17–34.

Brown, G.S. (1953a), 'Probability and psychical research', *Nature*, **172**, pp. 154–6.

Brown, G.S. (1953b), Letter, *Nature*, **172**, pp. 594–5.

Brown, G.S. (1957), *Probability and Scientific Inference* (London: Longmans, Green & Co.).

Brownell, H.H., Simpson, T.L., Bihrle, A.M., Potter, H.H. and Gardner, H. (1990), 'Appreciation of metaphoric alternative word meanings by left and right brain-damaged patients', *Neuropsychologia*, **28**, pp. 375–83.

---

[18] In the same vein, Gatlin (1977b, p. 152) enthusiastically commented: 'To me these findings [matching patterns in target and guess sequences] make the psi phenomenon more interesting than ever.'

Brugger, P. (1991), 'ASW: Aussersinnliche Wahrnehmung oder Ausdruck subjektiver Wahrschein-lichkeit?', *Zeitschrift für Parapsychologie und Grenzgebiete der Psychologie*, **33**, pp. 76–102.

Brugger, P. (1992), *Subjektiver Zufall: Implikationen für Neuropsychologie und Parapsychologie* (unpublished Doctoral Dissertation, Institute for Zoology, University of Zurich).

Brugger, P. (1997), 'Variables that influence the generation of random sequences', *Perceptual and Motor Skills*, **84**, pp. 627–61.

Brugger, P. (2001), 'From haunted brain to haunted science. A cognitive neuroscience view of paranor-mal and pseudoscientific thought', in *Hauntings and Poltergeists: Multidisciplinary Perspectives*, ed. J. Houran and R. Lange (Jefferson: McFarland & Company, Inc. Publishers), pp. 195–213.

Brugger, P. and Baumann, A.T. (1994), 'Repetition avoidance in responses to imaginary questions: the effect of respondents' belief in ESP', *Perceptual and Motor Skills*, **75**, pp. 883–93.

Brugger, P., Dowdy, M.A. and Graves, R.E. (1994a), 'From superstitious behavior to delusional thinking: the role of the hippocampus in misattributions of causality', *Medical Hypotheses*, **43**, pp. 397–402.

Brugger, P., Gamma, A., Müri, R., Schäfer, M. and Taylor, K.I. (1993a), 'Functional hemispheric asym-metry and belief in ESP: towards a "neuropsychology of belief" ', *Perceptual and Motor Skills*, **77**, pp. 1299–308.

Brugger, P. and Graves, R.E. (1997a), 'Testing vs. believing hypotheses: magical ideation in the judg-ment of contingencies', *Cognitive Neuropsychiatry*, **2**, pp. 251–72.

Brugger, P. and Graves, R.E. (1997b), 'Right hemispatial inattention and magical ideation', *European Archives of Psychiatry and Clinical Neuroscience*, **247**, pp. 55–7.

Brugger, P., Landis, T. and Regard, M. (1990), 'A "sheep–goat effect" in repetition avoidance: extra-sensory perception as an effect of subjective probability?', *British Journal of Psychology*, **81**, pp. 455–68.

Brugger, P., Macas, E. and Ihlemann, J. (2002), 'Do sperm cells remember ?', *Behavioural Brain Research*, **136**, pp. 325–28.

Brugger, P., Regard, M. and Landis, T. (1991), 'Belief in extrasensory perception and illusory control: a replication', *Journal of Psychology*, **125**, pp. 501–2.

Brugger, P., Regard, M., Landis, T., Cook, N., Krebs, D. and Niederberger, J. (1993b), ' "Meaningful" patterns in visual noise: effects of lateral stimulation and the observer's belief in ESP', *Psychopathology*, **26**, pp. 261–5.

Brugger, P., Regard, M., Landis, T. and Graves, R.E. (1995), 'The roots of meaningful coincidence', *Lan-cet*, **345**, pp. 1306–7.

Brugger, P., Regard, M., Landis, T., Krebs, D. and Niederberger, J. (1994b), 'Coincidences: who can say how "meaningful" they are?', in *Research in Parapsychology 1991*, ed. E.W. Cook and D.L. Delanoy (Metuchen, NJ: Scarecrow Press), pp. 94–8.

Carpenter, R.H.S. (1999), 'A neural mechanism that randomises behaviour', *Journal of Consciousness Studies*, **6**, pp. 13–22.

Chaitin, G.J. (1975), 'Randomness and mathematical proof', *Scientific American*, **232**, pp. 47–52.

Chiarello, C. and Richards, L. (1992), 'Another look at categorical priming in the cerebral hemispheres', *Neuropsychologia*, **30**, pp. 381–92.

Cole, L.C. (1957), 'Biological clock in the unicorn', *Science*, **125**, pp. 874–6.

Collins, A.M. and Loftus, E.F. (1975), 'A spreading-activation theory of semantic processing', *Psycho-logical Review*, **82**, pp. 407–28.

Colwell, J., Schröder, S. and Sladen, D. (2000), 'The ability to detect unseen staring: a literature review and empiral tests', *British Journal of Psychology*, **91**, pp. 71–85.

Cook, N.D. (1995), 'Artefact or network evolution?', *Nature*, **374**, p. 313.

Coveyou, R.R. (1969), 'Random generation is too important to be left to chance', *Applied Mathematics*, **3**, pp. 70–111.

Critchley, H.D., Mathias, C.J. and Dolan, R.J. (2001), 'Neural activity in the human brain relating to uncertainty and arousal during anticipation', *Neuron*, **29**, pp. 537–45.

Crow, T.J. (1997), 'Schizophrenia as failure of hemispheric dominance of language', *Trends in Neurosciences*, **20**, pp. 339–43.

Dawkins, R. (1987), *The Blind Watchmaker* (New York, NY: W.W. Norton & Company, Inc.).

Destrebecqz, A. and Cleeremans, A. (2001), 'Can sequence learning be implicit? New evidence with the process dissociation procedure', *Psychonomic Bulletin and Reviews*, **8**, pp. 343–50.

Douglas, R.J. and Isaacson, R.L. (1966), 'Spontaneous alternation and scopolamine', *Psychonomic Sci-ence*, **4**, pp. 238–44.

Duchêne, A., Graves, R.E. and Brugger, P. (1998), 'Schizotypal thinking and associative processing: a response commonality analysis of verbal fluency', *Journal of Psychiatry and Neuroscience*, **23**, pp. 56–60.

Eckblad, M. and Chapman, L. (1983), 'Magical ideation as an indicator of schizotypy', *Journal of Con-sulting and Clinical Psychology*, **51**, pp. 215–25.

Egger, G.J., Livesey, P.J. and Dawson, R.G. (1973), 'Ontogenetic aspect of central cholinergic involve-ment in spontaneous alternation behavior', *Developmental Psychobiology*, **6**, pp. 289–99.

Elliott, R., Rees, G. and Dolan, R.J. (1999), 'Ventromedial prefrontal cortex mediates guessing', *Neuropsychologia*, **37**, pp. 403–11.

Feller, W.K. (1940), 'Statistical aspects of ESP', *Journal of Parapsychology*, **4**, pp. 271–98.

Fleck, L. (1935/1979), *Genesis and Development of a Scientific Fact* (Chicago, IL: University of Chicago Press).

Flew, A. (1987), 'Factual impossibility and concomitant variations', *Behavioral and Brain Sciences*, **10**, pp. 586–7.

Gatlin, L.L. (1977a), 'Meaningful information creation: an alternative interpretation of the PSI phenomenon', *Journal of the American Society for Psychical Research*, **71**, pp. 1–18.

Gatlin, L.L. (1977b), Letter, *Journal of Parapsychology*, **41**, pp. 150–2.

Gatlin, L.L. (1978), 'Comments on the critical exchange between Drs. Stanford and Tart', *Journal of the American Society for Psychical Research*, **72**, pp. 77–81.

Gatlin, L.L. (1979), 'A new measure of bias in finite sequences with application to ESP data', *Journal of the American Society for Psychical Research*, **73**, pp. 29–43.

Gianotti, L.R., Mohr, C., Pizzagalli, D., Lehmann, D. and Brugger, P. (2001), 'Associative processing and paranormal belief', *Psychiatry and Clinical Neurosciences*, **55**, pp. 595–603.

Gilmore, J.B. (1989), 'Randomness and the search for PSI', *Journal of Parapsychology*, **53**, pp. 309–51.

Goodfellow, L.D. (1938), 'A psychological interpretation of the results of the Zenith radio experiments in telepathy', *Journal of Experimental Psychology*, **23**, pp. 601–32 (reprinted in *Journal of Experimental Psychology: General*, **121** (1992), pp. 130–44.).

Hake, H.W. and Hyman, R. (1953), 'Perception of the statistical structure of a random series of binary symbols', *Journal of Experimental Psychology*, **45**, pp. 64–74.

Haraldsson, E. (1980), 'Confirmation of the percipient-order effect in a plethysmographic study of ESP', *Journal of Parapsychology*, **44**, pp. 105–24.

Haraldsson, E. and Gissurarson, L.R. (1986/1987), 'Perceptual defensiveness, ganzfeld and the percipient-order effect', *European Journal of Parapsychology*, **6**, pp. 191–217.

Harvie, R. (1973), 'Probability and serendipity', in *The Challenge of Chance. Experiments and Speculations*, ed. A. Hardy, R. Harvie and A. Koestler (London: Hutchinson), pp. 119–56.

Hill, T.P. (1988), 'Random-number guessing and the first digit phenomenon', *Psychological Reports*, **62**, pp. 967–71.

Hines, T. (1991), 'The myth of right hemisphere creativity', *Journal of Creative Behavior*, **25**, pp. 223–7.

Houtkooper, J.M. and Haraldsson, E. (1997), 'Reliabilities and psychological correlates of guessing and scoring behavior in a forced-choice ESP task', *Journal of Parapsychology*, **61**, pp. 119–34.

Houtkooper, J.M., Gissurarson, L.R. and Haraldsson, E. (1988/1989), 'Why the ganzfeld is conductive to ESP. A study of observational theory and the percipient-order effect', *European Journal of Parapsychology*, **7**, pp. 169–92.

Huettel, S.A., Mack, P.B. and McCarthy, G. (2002), 'Perceiving patterns in random series: dynamic processing of sequence in prefrontal cortex', *Nature Neuroscience*, **5**, pp. 485–90.

Hunt, R.H. and Aslin, R.N. (2001), 'Statistical learning in a serial reaction time task: access to separable statistical cues by individual learners', *Journal of Experimental Psychology: General*, **130**, pp. 658–80.

Hyman, R. (1985), 'The ganzfeld psi experiment: a critical appraisal', *Journal of Parapsychology*, **49**, pp. 3–49.

Hyman, R. (1994), 'Anomaly or artifact? Comments on Bem and Honorton', *Psychological Bulletin*, **115**, pp. 19–24.

Irwin, H.J. and Green, M.J. (1998/1999), 'Schizotypal processes and belief in the paranormal: a multidimensional study', *European Journal of Parapsychology*, **14**, pp. 1–15.

Jones, M.R. (1971), 'From probability learning to sequential processing: a critical review', *Psychological Bulletin*, **76**, pp. 153–85.

Kalaycioglu, C., Nalcaci, E., Budanur, Ö.E., Genc, Y. and Cicek, M. (2000), 'The effect of familial sinistrality on the relation between schizophrenialike thinking and pseudoneglect', *Brain and Cognition*, **44**, pp. 564–76.

Katz, S., Lautenschlager, G.J., Blackburn, A.B. and Harris, F.H. (1990), 'Answering reading comprehension items without passages on the SAT', *Psychological Science*, **1**, pp. 122–7.

Kendall, M.G. (1941), 'A theory of randomness', *Biometrika*, **32**, pp. 1–15.

Kennedy, J.E. (1980), 'Learning to use ESP: do the calls match the targets or do the targets match the calls?', *Journal of the American Society for Psychical Research*, **74**, pp. 191–209.

Kirby, N.H. (1976), 'Sequential effects in two-choice reaction time: automatic facilitation or subjective expectancy?', *Journal of Experimental Psychology: Human Perception and Performance*, **2**, pp. 567–77.

Kosambi, D.D. and Rao, U.V. (1958), 'The efficiency of randomization by card shuffling', *Journal of the Royal Statistical Society*, **121**, pp. 223–33.

Kreweras, G. (1983), 'Approche bayesienne des phénomènes «paranormaux»', *Mathématiques et Sciences Humaines*, **21**, pp. 59–66.

Kubovy, M. and Psotka, J. (1976), 'The predominance of seven and the apparent sponaneity of numerical choices', *Journal of Experimental Psychology: Human Perception and Performance*, **2**, pp. 291–4.

Lange, R. and Houran, J. (2001), 'Ambiguous stimuli brought to light: the psychological dynamics of hauntings and poltergeists', in *Hauntings and Poltergeists: Multidisciplinary Perspectives*, ed. J. Houran and R. Lange (Jefferson: McFarland & Company, Inc. Publishers), pp. 280–306.

Lawrence, T.R. (1990/1991), 'Subjective random generations and the reversed sheep–goat effect: a failure to replicate', *European Journal of Parapsychology*, **8**, pp. 131–44.

Leonhard, D. and Brugger, P. (1998), 'Creative, paranormal, and delusional thought: a consequence of right hemisphere semantic activation?', *Neuropsychiatry, Neuropsychology, and Behavioral Neurology*, **11**, pp. 177–83.

Lopes, L.L. (1982), 'Doing the impossible: a note on induction and the experience of randomness', *Journal of Experimental Psychology: Learning, Memory, and Cognition*, **13**, pp. 392–400.

Luh, K.E. and Gooding, D.C. (1999), 'Perceptual biases in psychosis-prone individuals', *Journal of Abnormal Psychology*, **108**, pp. 283–9.

Mach, E. (1896), 'Über den Einfluss zufälliger Umstände auf die Entwickelung von Erfindungen und Entdeckungen', in *Populärwissenschaftliche Vorlesungen* (Leipzig: Barth).

Mischo, J. (1979), 'Zum Stand der sheep–goat Forschung', *Zeitschrift für Parapsychologie und Grenzgebiete der Psychologie*, **21**, pp. 1–22.

Modianos, D.T., Scott, R.S. and Cornwell, L.W. (1984), 'Random number generation on microcomputers', *Interfaces*, **14**, pp. 81–7.

Mohr, C., Bracha, H.S. and Brugger, P. (2003), 'Magical ideation modulates spatial behavior', *Journal of Neuropsychiatry and Clinical Neurosciences*, **15**, pp. 168–74.

Mohr, C., Graves, R.E., Gainotti, L.R.R., Pizzagalli, D. and Brugger, P. (2001a), 'Loose but normal: a semantic association study', *Journal of Psycholinguistic Research*, **30**, pp. 475–83.

Mohr, C., Röhrenbach, C., Laska, M. and Brugger, P. (2001b), 'Unilateral olfactory perception and magical ideation', *Schizophrenia Research*, **47**, pp. 255–64.

Mohr, C., Thut, G., Landis, T. and Brugger, P. (in press), 'Hands, arms, and minds: interactions between posture and thought', *Journal of Clinical and Experimental Neuropsychology*.

Mulholland, J. (1938), *Beware Familiar Spirits* (New York, NY: Scribner's).

Musch, J. and Ehrenberg, K. (2002), 'Probability misjudgment, cognitive ability, and belief in the paranormal', *British Journal of Psychology*, **93**, pp. 169–77.

Nash, C.B. (1954), 'Psi and probability theory', *Science*, **120**, pp. 581–2.

Oram, A.T. (1954), 'An experiment with random numbers', *Journal of the Society for Psychical Research*, **37**, pp. 369–77.

Paley, W. (1809), *Natural Theology: or, Evidences of the Existence and Attributes of the Deity*, 12th edn. (London: printed for J. Faulder).

Palmer, J. (1978), 'Extrasensory perception: research findings', in *Advances in Parapsychological Research*, Vol. 3, ed. S. Krippner (New York, NY: Plenum), pp. 41–82.

Palmer, J. (1996), 'Evaluation of a conventional interpretation of Helmut Schmidt's automated precognition experiments', *Journal of Parapsychology*, **60**, pp. 149–70.

Palmer, J. (1997), 'Hit-contingent response bias in Helmut Schmidt's automated precognition experiments', *Journal of Parapsychology*, **61**, pp. 135–41.

Pizzagalli, D., Lehmann, D. and Brugger, P. (2001), 'Lateralized direct and indirect semantic priming effects in subjects with paranormal experiences and beliefs', *Psychopathology*, **34**, pp. 75–80.

Pizzagalli, D., Lehmann, D., Gianotti, L., Koenig, T., Tanaka, H., Wackermann, J. and Brugger, P. (2000), 'Brain electric correlates of strong belief in paranormal phenomena: intracerebral EEG source and regional Omega complexity analyses', *Psychiatry Research: Neuroimaging*, **100**, pp. 139–54.

Pöppel, E. (1967), 'Signifikanz-Artefakte in der experimentellen Parapsychologie', *Zeitschrift für Parapsychologie und Grenzgebiete der Psychologie*, **10**, pp. 63–72.

Pratt, J.G., Rhine J.B., Smith, B.M., Stuart, C.E. and Greenwood, J.A. (1940/1966), *Extra-sensory perception after sixty years* (Boston: Bruce Humphries).

Ramachandran, V.S. (1993), 'Filling in gaps in perception: Part II: Scotomas and phantom limbs', *Current Directions in Psychological Science*, **2**, pp. 56–65.

Rhine, J.B. and Pratt, J.G. (1957), *Parapsychology — Frontier Science of the Mind* (Springfield, IL: Charles C. Thomas).

Robertson, J.M. (1902), *Letters on Reasoning* (London).

Sagan, C. (1977), *The Dragons of Eden. Speculations on the Evolution of Human Intelligence* (London: Hodder and Stoughton).

Sahai, H. (1979), 'A supplement to Sowey's bibliography and random number generation and related topics', *Journal of Statistics and Computer Simulation*, **10**, pp. 31–52.

Sargent, C.L. (1977), 'Cortical arousal and psi: a pharmacological study', *European Journal of Parapsychology*, **1**, pp. 72–9.

Sargent, C.L. (1981), 'Extraversion and performance in extrasensory perception tasks', *Personality and Individual Differences*, **2**, pp. 137–43.

Schmeidler, G.R. and McConnell, R.A. (1958), *ESP and Personality Patterns* (Westport, CT: Greenwood).

Scott, C. (1958), 'G. Spencer Brown and probability', *Journal of the Society for Psychical Research*, **39**, pp. 217–34.

Seidenberg, M.S. (1997), 'Language acquisition and use: learning and applying probabilistic constraints', *Science*, **275**, pp. 1599–603.

Sheldrake, R. (1994), *Seven Experiments that could Change the World* (North Pomfret: Trafalgar Square Publishing).

Smith, K. and Canon, H.J. (1954), 'A methodological refinement in the study of "ESP," and negative findings', *Science*, **120**, pp. 148–9.

Sowey, E.R. (1972), 'A chronological and classified bibliography on random number generation and testing', *International Statistical Review*, **3**, pp. 355–71.

Sowey, E.R. (1978), 'A second classified bibliography on random number generation and testing', *International Statistical Review*, **46**, pp. 89–102.

Spitzer, M. (1997), 'A cognitive neuroscience view of schizophrenic thought disorder', *Schizophrenia Bulletin*, **23**, pp. 29–50.

Squire, L.R. (1969), 'Effects of pretrial and posttrial administration of cholinergic and anticholinergic drugs on spontaneous alternation', *Journal of Comparative and Physiological Psychology*, **69**, pp. 69–75.

Stanford, R.G. (1977), 'The application of learning theory to ESP performance', *Journal of the American Society for Psychical Research*, **71**, pp. 55–80.

Stanford, R.G. (1978), 'Toward reinterpreting psi events', *Journal of the American Society for Psychical Research*, **72**, pp. 197–214.

Strickland, L.H., Lewicki, R.J. and Katz, A.M. (1966), 'Temporal orientation and perceived control as determinants of risk-taking', *Journal of Experimental and Social Psychology*, **2**, pp. 143–51.

Tanner, W.P. and Swets, J.A. (1954), 'A decision making theory of visual detection', *Psychological Review*, **61**, pp. 401–9.

Tart, C.T. (1976), *Learning to use ESP* (Chicago, IL: University of Chicago Press).

Tart, C.T. and Dronek, E. (1982), 'Mathematical inference strategies versus psi: initial explorations with the probabilistic predictor program', *European Journal of Parapsychology*, **4**, pp. 325–55.

Taylor, K.I., Zäch, P. and Brugger, P. (2002), 'Why is magical thinking related to leftward deviation on an implicit line bisection task?', *Cortex*, **38**, pp. 247–52.

Thalbourne, M.A. (1985), 'Are believers in psi more prone to schizophrenia?', in *Research in Parapsychology 1984*, ed. R.A. White and J. Solfvin (Metuchen, NJ: Scarecrow Press), pp. 85–8.

Timm, U. (1967), 'Der Einfluss sequentieller Abhängigkeiten auf die Signifikanz von ASW-Experimenten', *Zeitschrift für Parapsychologie und Grenzgebiete der Psychologie*, **10**, pp. 73–97.

Tobacyk, J. (1988), *A Revised Paranormal Belief Scale* (unpublished manuscript, Ruston, LA: Louisiana Technical University).

van Lancker, D. (1991), 'Personal relevance and the human right hemisphere', *Brain and Cognition*, **17**, pp. 64–92.

von Hoerner, S. (1957), 'Herstellung von Zufallszahlen auf Rechenautomaten', *Zeitschrift für angewandte Mathematik und Physik*, **8**, pp. 26–52.

Wagenaar, W.A. and Keren, G.B. (1988), 'Chance and luck are not the same', *Journal of Behavioral Decision Making*, **1**, pp. 65–75.

Wassermann, G.D. (1956), 'Some comments on methods and statements in parapsychology and other sciences', *British Journal for the Philosophy of Science*, **6**, pp. 122–40.

Weinstein, S. and Graves, R.E. (2001), 'Creativity, schizotypy, and laterality', *Cognitive Neuropsychiatry*, **6**, pp. 131–46.

Weinstein, S. and Graves, R.E. (2002), 'Are creativity and schizotypy products of a right hemisphere bias?', *Brain and Cognition*, **49**, pp. 138–51.

Weisbrod, M., Maier, S., Harig, S., Himmelsbach, U. and Spitzer, M. (1998), 'Lateralized direct and indirect semantic priming effects in people with schizophrenia', *British Journal of Psychiatry*, **172**, pp. 142–6.

Whitfield, J.W. (1950), 'The imaginary questionnaire', *Quarterly Journal of Experimental Psychology*, **2**, pp. 76–87.

Willoughby, R.R. (1935), 'Prerequisites for a clairvoyance hypothesis', *Journal of Applied Psychology*, **19**, pp. 543–50.

Winner, E. and Gardner, H. (1977), 'The comprehension of metaphor in brain-damaged patients', *Brain*, **100**, pp. 717–29.

Wolfle, D. (1956), 'Extrasensory Perception', *Science*, **123**, p. 7.

de Zeeuw, G.D. and Wagenaar, W.A. (1974), 'Are subjective probabilities probabilities?', in *The Concept of Probability in Psychological Experiments*, ed. C.A. Stael von Holstein (Dordrecht: Kluwer Academic Publishers), pp. 73–101.

SUBSCRIPTION ORDER FORM — *Journal of Consciousness Studies* (ISSN 1355 8250)

Name. . . . .

Address. . . . .

. . . .
Credit card subscribers must give cardholder registered address

Home telephone . . . . Email . . . .

ANNUAL SUBSCRIPTION RATES: Volume 10 (2003)

Twelve monthly issues. Libraries: $273/£176.50, Individuals: $96/£62
Full-time students: $72/£46.50 (status evidence & course completion date required)
Prices inc. accelerated delivery (UK & USA), rest of world surface.

☐Please enter my Library/Individual/Student subscription for Volume 10   ☐Airmail extra: $45/£26

Free with new subscription. Choose one of the following special back issues:

☐ *The View from Within* (6, No.2/3), ed. Francisco Varela & Jonathan Shear
☐ *The Varieties of Religious Experience: Centenary Essays* (9, No.9/10), ed. Michel Ferrari
☐ *Is the Visual World a Grand Illusion?* (9, No.5/6), ed. Alva Noë
☐ *Evolutionary Origins of Morality* (7, No.1/2), ed. Leonard Katz
☐ *Cognitive Models and Spiritual Maps* (7, No.11/12), ed. Jensine Andresen and Robert Forman
☐ *Between Ourselves: Second Person approaches* (8, No.5–7), ed. Evan Thompson
☐ *The Emergence of Consciousness* (8, No.9/10), ed. Anthony Freeman
☐ *The Volitional Brain: towards a neuroscience of free will* (6, No.8/9), ed. Benjamin Libet *et al.*
☐ *Reclaiming Cognition: action/intention/emotion* (6, No.11/12), ed. Walter Freeman & Rafael Núñez

Back Volumes: Special Offer

Order the full set of back volumes 1–9 (1994–2002) at *70% discount*.
Individuals: $260/£167; Students: $195/£125; Institutions: $737/£476.

☐Please enter my Individual/Student/Institutional discount back volume order.

Payment Details

☐Check enclosed (pay 'Imprint Academic' — $ [drawn on US], or £ Sterling [drawn on UK])
☐Please charge: ☐VISA ☐MASTERCARD ☐AMEX ☐SWITCH ☐DELTA ☐JCB

Card No. . . . . Expiry date . . . . . Signed . . . .

N.B. US Amex cards charged in $. All other cards charged in £UK and converted to local currency by card issuer

---

☐ **10% introductory discount on Vol.10 subscription for CCDD (credit card direct debit)**
We have been vetted and authorized by our card processor (Barclays Merchant Services) to operate their direct
debit system, whereby we automatically charge your card at annual subscription renewal time. We will notify you
by post well in advance to give you plenty of time to cancel the transaction, and your rights as a consumer are
fully protected by your card issuer. *I authorise Imprint Academic to charge my subscription and to recharge my
card on the annual renewal date. Signed.* . . . .

North American order office:
Consciousness Studies, Department of Psychology, University of Arizona, Tucson AZ 85721, USA

Rest of world
Imprint Academic, PO Box 200, Exeter EX5 5YX, UK.
Tel & Fax: +44 1392 841600; Fax: 841478; Email: sandra@imprint.co.uk   **www.imprint.co.uk/jcs**

- -

To: The Head Librarian/The Library Committee

From . . . .

Department. . . . .

I/we have studied the *Journal of Consciousness Studies* (ISSN 1355 8250), and recommend
that the journal be purchased for the Main/Department Library.

INSTITUTIONAL SUBSCRIPTION RATES: Vol. 10 (2003), $273/£176.50, 12 issues p.a.
Prices include airlift delivery (UK & USA), surface delivery rest of world.

BACK VOLUMES 1–9 (1994–2002). Rates as above. All issues currently available.
SPECIAL OFFER: Place an order for Volume 9 (2002) and buy all the back volumes at *70% discount*

North American enquiries:
Consciousness Studies, Department of Psychology, University of Arizona, Tucson AZ 85721, USA

Rest of world
Imprint Academic, PO Box 200, Exeter EX5 5YX, UK.
Tel & Fax: +44 1392 841600; Fax: 841478; Email: sandra@imprint.co.uk   **www.imprint.co.uk/jcs**

Executive Editors

Joseph A. Goguen (Editor in Chief). Department of Computer Science
University of California at San Diego, La Jolla, CA 92093-0114, USA.
Phone: (858) 534-4197. Fax: (858) 534-7029. Email: goguen@cs.ucsd.edu
Robert K.C. Forman, Program in Religion, Hunter College, CUNY, 695 Park
Avenue, New York, NY 10021, USA.
Tel/Fax: (914) 478 7802. Email: Forman@TheForge.org
Keith Sutherland (Publisher). Imprint Academic, PO Box 200, Exeter EX5
5YX, UK. Tel/Fax: +44 1392 841600 Email: keith@imprint.co.uk

Managing Editor (address for manuscript submissions and books for review)
Anthony Freeman, Imprint Academic, PO Box 200, Exeter EX5 5YX, UK.
Tel/Fax: +44 1392 841600. Email: anthony@imprint.co.uk

Associate Editors

Jean *Burns*, 1525 – 153rd Avenue, San Leandro, CA 94578, USA. Tel: (510)
481 7507. Email: jeanbur@earthlink.net
Ivo Mosley, Imprint Academic, PO Box 200, Exeter EX5 5YX, UK. Tel/Fax:
+44 1392 841600. Email: ivomosley@aol.com
Chris Nunn, Imprint Academic, PO Box 200,Exeter EX5 5YX, UK. Tel/Fax:
+44 1392 841600. Email: chrisnunn@compuserve.com
Mark Rowlands, Department of Sociology, Amory Building, Rennes Drive,
Exeter EX4 4RJ, UK. Email: M.N.J.Rowlands@exeter.ac.uk
Jonathan Shear, Department of Philosophy, Virginia Commonwealth
University, Richmond, VA 23284-2025, USA.
Tel/Fax: (804) 282 2119. Email: jcs@infionline.net

Annual Subscription Rates (for 12 monthly issues)
Individuals: \$96/£62
Institutions: \$248.50/£160.50
Includes accelerated delivery (UK & USA), surface mail rest of world.
Orders to : Imprint Academic, PO Box 200, Exeter EX5 5YX, UK.
Tel: +44 1392 841600; Fax: 841478; Email: sandra@imprint.co.uk.
Cheques (£ or \$US 'Imprint Academic'); VISA/AMEX/MASTERCARD

STYLE SHEET AND GUIDE TO AUTHORS

JCS is aimed at an educated multi-disciplinary readership. Authors should not assume prior knowledge in a subject speciality and should provide background information for their research. The use of technical terms should be avoided or made explicit. Where technical details are essential (for example in laboratory experiments), include them in footnotes or appendices, leaving the text accessible to the non-specialist reader. The same principle should also apply to non-essential mathematics.

Articles should not normally exceed 9,000 words (including footnotes). A short 150 word summary should accompany each submission. In general authors should adhere to the usages and conventions in Fowler's *Modern English Usage* which should be consulted for all questions not covered in these notes.

Footnote numbering should be consecutive superscript throughout the article. References to books and articles should be by way of author (date) or (author, date). Multiple publications from the same year should be labelled (Skinner, 1966a, b, c . . .). A single bibliography at the end should be compiled alphabetically observing the following conventions:

1 **References to complete books** should take the following form:
   Dennett, D.C. (1998), *Brainchildren* (Cambridge, MA: MIT Press).

2 **References to chapters in books** should take the following form:
   Wilkes, K. (1995), 'Losing consciousness', in *Conscious Experience*, ed. T. Metzinger (Paderborn: Schöningh).

3 **References to articles** should take the following form:
   Humphrey, N. (2000), 'How to solve the mind–body problem', *Journal of Consciousness Studies*, **7** (4), pp. 5–20.

SUBMISSION OF MANUSCRIPTS BY EMAIL

Authors are encouraged to email their wordprocessor files (retaining italics, accents, superscripts, footnotes etc.) or PDF files. We cannot currently review LaTex files. Send all submissions to **anthony@imprint.co.uk**.

Where it is necessary to send contributions by normal mail, they should be clearly typed in double spacing. One hard copy should be submitted, plus a copy of the article on disk. This will enable us to email it to editors and reviewers and speed up the review process. Please state what machine and wordprocessing program was used to prepare the text.